DESCRIPTIVE STATISTICS
FOR SOCIOLOGISTS

DESCRIPTIVE STATISTICS FOR SOCIOLOGISTS

AN INTRODUCTION

HERMAN J. LOETHER
*California State College,
Dominguez Hills*

DONALD G. McTAVISH
University of Minnesota

Allyn and Bacon, Inc.
Boston, London, Sydney, Toronto

Library of Congress Catalog Card Number: 73-80548

Printed in the United States of America

ISBN: 0-205-03736-4

Third printing . . . March, 1976

To our wives, Louise Loether and Janet McTavish, and our children, Chris Loether, Kathleen, Karen and Steve McTavish, with love and appreciation.

CONTENTS

Preface   xi

I.   SOME BASIC CONSIDERATIONS

1. **An Introduction to Statistics in Sociology**   3
   1.1   Some Basic Concepts in Statistics
   1.2   The Field of Statistics
   1.3   The Relationship Between Statistics and Sociology
   1.4   What You Can Expect in Studying Statistics
   1.5   Purposes and Objectives of This Book's Approach

2. **Measuring Variables**   14
   2.1   Meanings and Measurement
     2.1.1 Level of measurement; 2.1.2 Scale continuity; 2.1.3 Grouping scores into classes; 2.1.4 Roles variables play in research
   2.2   Measurement in Sociology
   2.3   Summary

II.   DESCRIPTIVE STATISTICS: ONE VARIABLE

3. **The Basic Logic of Valid Comparison**   37
   3.1   Kinds of Comparisons
     3.1.1 Group-group comparisons; 3.1.2 Group-individual comparisons; 3.1.3 Study outcome versus standard comparisons; 3.1.4 An example of comparison operations
   3.2   Basic Comparison Operations
     3.2.1 Organization of sources; 3.2.2 Grouping scores into classes; 3.2.3 Distributions; 3.2.4 Other uses of ratios for comparison; 3.2.5 Time-based ratios
   3.3   Summary

4. Graphic Presentation and Analysis 69

    4.1   Ratios—A Graphic Example

    4.2   Basic Techniques for Graphing Distributions

        4.2.1 Histogram; 4.2.2 Polygons; 4.2.3 Ogives; 4.2.4 Line graph; 4.2.5 Distortions in graphing

    4.3   Variations on Basic Graphic Techniques

        4.3.1 The bar-chart; 4.3.2 The population pyramid; 4.3.3 The pie chart

    4.4   Other Approaches to Graphic Analysis in Sociology

        4.4.1 Statistical maps; 4.4.2 The scatter diagram; 4.4.3 Triangular plot; 4.4.4 The semi-logarithmic chart

    4.5   Summary

5. Summary Measures of the Location, Variation, and Form of Univariate Distributions 119

    5.1   Univariate Distributions—An Example and Overview

    5.2   The Form of a Distribution—I

        5.2.1 Number of modes; 5.2.2 Symmetry; 5.2.3 Kurtosis

    5.3   Location of a Distribution

        5.3.1 Mode (mo); 5.3.2 Median (mdn); 5.3.3 Arithmetic mean ($\bar{X}$); 5.3.4 Special kinds of means; 5.3.5 Selecting the most appropriate measure of central tendency; 5.3.6 Smoothing trend lines: The moving average

    5.4   Variation

        5.4.1 Range; 5.4.2 Interquartile range (Q); 5.4.3 Average absolute deviation (AD); 5.4.4 Variance and standard deviation (s^2 and s, respectively); 5.4.5 Index of dispersion (D); 5.4.6 Selecting the most appropriate measure of variability; 5.4.7 Standard scores

    5.5   Form of a Distribution—II

        5.5.1 The moment system; 5.5.2 The standard normal distribution; 5.5.3 Other mathematical descriptions of form

    5.6   Summary

III. DESCRIPTIVE STATISTICS: TWO VARIABLES

6. Cross Classification of Variables 171

    6.1   Bivariate Distributions: An Example

    6.2   Conditional Distributions

    6.3   How To Set Up and Examine Tables

        6.3.1 Creating a bivariate frequency distribution; 6.3.2 Traditions of table layout; 6.3.3 Percentaged tables; 6.3.4 More complex conditional distributions

    6.4   Four Characteristics of an Association

        6.4.1 The existence of an association; 6.4.2 Degree (strength) of association; 6.4.3 Direction of association; 6.4.4 The nature of association

    6.5   Creating Measures of Association

        6.5.1 In pursuit of a normed measure of association; 6.5.2 Meanings of perfect association

6.6   Grouping Error

6.7   Symmetric and Asymmetric Measures of Association

6.8   Summary

7.   Measures of Association for Nominal, Ordinal, and Interval Variables   209

7.1   Proportionate Reduction in Error Measures ("PRE")

7.2   Measures of Association for Nominal Variables

7.2.1 Lambda; 7.2.2 Goodman and Kruskal's tau-*y*

7.3   Measures of Association for Ordinal Variables

7.3.1 Types of pairs; 7.3.2 Measures of association

7.4   Measures of Association for Interval Variables

7.4.1 Regression equations; 7.4.2 Product-moment correlation coefficient (r); 7.4.3 Another way to express correlation and regression; 7.4.4 The correlation ratio, Eta (E_{yx}), a measure of association for non-linear relationships

7.5   The Correlation Matrix

7.6   Selecting a Useful Measure of Association

7.6.1 Symmetry and asymmetry; 7.6.2 Level of measurement; 7.6.3 Nature versus strength of association; 7.6.4 Interpretation

7.7   Some Cautions about the Interpretation of Association Measures

7.71 Causation and association; 7.7.2 Ecological fallacy; 7.7.3 Built-in correlations

7.8   Summary

IV.   DESCRIPTIVE STATISTICS: THREE OR MORE VARIABLES

8.   Elaborating the Relationship Between Two Variables   264

8.1   Examining Relationships Between Variables

8.1.1 Morale and interaction—An illustration of elaboration; 8.1.2 Total tables and conditional tables; 8.1.3 The role of theory; 8.1.4 Analysis of conditional and total associations

8.2   Patterns of Elaboration

8.2.1 Specification; 8.2.2 The causal hypothesis; 8.2.3 A causal sequence of influence; 8.2.4 Suppressor variables; 8.2.5 Social system analysis

8.3   The Average Partial Table

8.3.1 Standardization; 8.3.2 Partial correlation coefficients

8.4   Statistical Considerations in Research Design

8.5   Summary

9.   Path Analysis and Multiple Regression   306

9.1   Multiple Regression and Multiple Correlation

9.1.1 Some assumptions of multiple regression; 9.1.2 One independent variable: A review; 9.1.3 Two or more independent variables; 9.1.4 Regression weights and partial correlation coefficients; 9.1.5 Multiple correlation; 9.1.6 An illustration

9.2   Path Analysis: An Application of Multiple Regression to Problems of Theory

9.2.1 Path analysis; 9.2.2 An example of path analysis in sociology; 9.2.3 Testing an alternative model

9.3   Multiple Regression Using Unstandardized Scores

9.3.1 An example of multiple regression using raw scores

9.4   Dummy Variable Multiple Regression

9.5   Stepwise Regression Procedures

9.5.1 An example of stepwise multiple regression

9.6   Curvilinear Association in Multivariate Analysis

9.7   Summary

10.   **Space Analysis in Sociology**   341

10.1   Multidimensional Sociological Space

10.2   Cluster Analysis

10.2.1 "Belongingness coefficients" (*B*-coefficients); 10.2.2 Hierarchical cluster analysis

10.3   The Similarity/Dissimilarity Matrix

10.3.1 Measures of similarity or dissimilarity; 10.3.2 The *R*-matrix and the *Q*-matrix

10.4   Smallest Space Analysis

10.5   Factor Analysis

10.6   Summary

V.   SUMMARY AND CONCLUSIONS

11.   **The Place of Descriptive Analysis in Sociology**   358

11.1   Themes in Descriptive Statistics

11.1.1 Quality of data; 11.1.2 The defined meaning of scores; 11.1.3 Identifying relevant data; 11.1.4 The importance of comparison; 11.1.5 The usefulness of ratios; 11.1.6 Working with variation; 11.1.7 The active role of the investigator

11.2   Descriptive and Inferential Statistics

Appendix: Statistical Tables   363

Indexes   371

PREFACE

Sociology is coming of age. Armchair philosophizing in this field has given way to theory building and theory-testing research. Increasing use is being made of a range of scientific methods and techniques. Anyone with a serious interest in doing sociology or in understanding what sociologists do must become familiar with these tools of the sociologist's trade. An important ingredient of the sociologist's tool box is that set of techniques collectively known as statistics. Our purpose in writing this book and its companion volume, *Inferential Statistics for Sociologists,* is to acquaint the reader with the statistical techniques that sociologists commonly use and, more especially, to illustrate *how* sociologists make use of them.

Rather than present applied statistics as a field that stands by itself, divorced from any particular subject matter, we have focused our attention upon sociology and have portrayed statistics as a set of tools that sociologists use in the process of making decisions about their data. We have tapped the literature of sociology, government sources, and our own research for studies and data to serve as points of departure for the discussion of particular statistical techniques.

We believe that the common practice of teaching statistics in isolation from any particular discipline has the effect of making it seem unnecessarily abstract, complex, and purely mathematical. Too often students are turned off by the subject because they cannot see its relevance for their major field of interest or they come to see statistics in a ritualistic fashion, as if use of these techniques by themselves would certify the truth of research conclusions. Sociology students are generally interested in inquiry in sociology, but not in statistics per se. We have found in our years of teaching statistics that the subject can be made relevant and even exciting by presenting it as one among a number of sets of tools that sociologists use. When the subject matter of statistics is integrated into inquiry in the subject matter of sociology, students realize its value for sociology and for them.

For the most part, statistical theory and the techniques of statistics have been developed by mathematical statisticians who were not unduly concerned with applications. Consequently, the derivations of formulae tend to be based upon sets of ideal conditions such as scores free of measurement problems and error or "a normally distributed random variable." The sociologist whose primary concern is with the real world usually must work with data that do not satisfy these ideal conditions. When statistics is taught in isolation from subject matter there is a real danger students will get the impression that the ideal conditions are usually realized when research is done. By focusing on the uses of statistics in sociology it is possible to show how statistical techniques are actually applied, how these applications relate the ideal forms of many techniques to the actual data available, and what the consequences of this adjustment may be. In this and in our companion volume we have made a point of calling to the reader's attention the meanings and quality of data to be analyzed. Hopefully, this will lead the reader to become a more informed user of statistics and to be more cautious about the unqualified acceptance of findings of others.

Whenever the occasion has arisen we have raised methodological and research design issues of concern to sociologists. We do not believe that students of elementary statistics need to be shielded from the problems of doing sociology. Rather, we believe that a preliminary consideration of methodological issues at an early stage gives the student a better appreciation of the interrelationship of theory, methods, and statistics. These issues are not considered in great detail here, but their introduction at this point should highlight the broader range of analytic problems facing the sociologist and raise the student's level of interest in pursuing them further.

Although statistics is based upon mathematical considerations we do not feel that it is necessary at this level to present rigorous, mathematical definitions of concepts or formal mathematical proofs of theorems. The underlying logic of the field of statistics is relatively simple and can be understood, to a large extent, from a verbal presentation. It is true, of course, that mathematical sophistication is both desirable and necessary for more extended treatments. Students who are curious about mathematical proofs and derivations of formulae should consult more mathematically oriented texts (some of these are included in the references at the end of chapters).

This volume explains the use of statistics to describe and contrast the data at hand. Often these data are sampled from a broader population and the sociologist is interested in generalizing conclusions based on descriptions of the sample at hand to conclusions about descriptive features of the population from which the sample was drawn. In the companion volume, *Inferential Statistics for Sociologists*, we focus our attention on those statistical techniques which help make such inferences possible.

A discussion of inferential techniques is a logical outgrowth of a discussion of descriptive techniques; consequently, the inferential statistics volume could be used for a second quarter or second semester of a two-quarter or two-semester sequence of elementary statistics courses for sociology students, following the use of our volume on descriptive statistics. Alternatively, materials from both the descriptive and the inferential volume can be used selectively for a one-quarter or one-semester course. It is also possible to use the descriptive volume without the inferential volume, or the inferential volume without the descriptive volume for those courses that deal exclusively either with descriptive or with inferential techniques.

A number of features have been included in this book which are designed to assist the reader in mastering the subject matter covered. Immediately following the discussion of each technique is a "diagram" which summarizes the essential steps in its use. These diagrams may serve as reviews of the techniques and may also be useful as "recipes" for their use.

At strategic points throughout the text we have inserted "loop-back" boxes that flag important points in preceding discussions and refer the reader to other sections of the text that may help clarify the subjects covered.

Lists of key concepts have been included at the end of each chapter and are well worth reviewing. Any concept with which the reader is unfamiliar should be looked up and the explanation of it should be reviewed until the concept is understood.

At the end of each chapter is included a number of discussion questions which require the reader to integrate materials from the chapter or to apply what has been learned.

For those readers who wish to explore some of the topics covered in more depth, at the end of each chapter is an annotated list of references which supplement the discussion of the chapter.

The conscientious student who takes advantage of these learning aids will undoubtedly benefit from the effort he devotes and gain a more thorough understanding of the subject matter of the book.

All cross-reference citations within the text are made with reference to the various numbered sections within each chapter. To spot a section number location in cross-reference, use the first digit of the numbered section to identify the chapter; two-digit numbers indicate major section divisions; three-digit numbers indicate minor section divisions; numbering sequence runs from major to minor divisions (if any) and back to the next major division (thus, in Chapter 3: Sections 3.1; 3.1.1; 3.1.2; 3.1.3; 3.2; 3.3; 3.3.1; etc.). In addition, major or minor numbered sections may have subsections designated by an added lower case letter (thus: Sections 3.1a; 3.1b; 3.1.1a; 3.1.1b; etc.), usually indicating a paragraph heading for a particular topic.

There is available through the publisher a student manual designed to accompany this book and its companion volume. Among other things, the student manual includes a wealth of sociological data which can be analyzed using the statistical techniques covered here and in the companion volume. We have found that the best way for the student to master statistical techniques is to use them to analyze data. Readers should try their hands at applying what they have learned to some of these data sets or other comparable sets of data at their disposal.

For material in the inferential volume we are indebted to the literary executor of the late Sir Ronald A. Fisher, F.R.S., and to Oliver and Boyd, Edinburgh, for permission to reprint Tables III, IV, and V from their book, *Statistical Tables for Biological, Agricultural, and Medical Research.*

We are indebted to Richard J. Hill of the University of Oregon and Edmund D. Meyers, Jr., of Dartmouth College, who read both manuscripts (descriptive and inferential) and to Marian Deininger of St. Cloud State College, who read the descriptive volume. Their numerous suggestions have added significantly to the quality of the finished products.

We are indebted, too, to our students at California State University, Los Angeles; California State College, Dominguez Hills; and the University of Minnesota who contributed so much over the years to the development of this book and its companion volume.

Finally, this book and its companion volume have been joint products of the authors. The order in which our names appear on the title page should not be taken to imply that one of us is the senior author. The names could easily have been reversed. They are merely listed in alphabetical order.

H.J.L. and D.G. McT.

SOME BASIC
CONSIDERATIONS

AN INTRODUCTION TO
STATISTICS IN SOCIOLOGY

The Civil Rights Act of 1964 included a section requiring the U.S. Commissioner of Education to conduct a study, ". . . concerning the lack of availability of equal educational opportunities for individuals by reason of race, color, religion or national origin in public educational institutions. . . ." Early in the following fall a team of social scientists headed by James Coleman, a sociologist at Johns Hopkins University, administered questionnaires to nearly 650,000 grade school and high school pupils, teachers, and administrators across the United States. People questioned in the study were carefully selected, using a "two-stage, stratified, probability sampling plan" (Coleman, 1966: I, 22).

Among the wealth of findings in the voluminous report is the conclusion that the achievement of minority pupils relates more to the schools they attend than does the achievement of majority-group pupils. For example, 20 percent of the variation in achievement of blacks in the south is associated with differences in the schools they attend, whereas only 10 percent of the variation in achievement of whites in the south is associated with differences in the schools they attend. If true, this finding has implications for improving educational opportunity of all the nation's youth. Majority pupils presumably would not be greatly harmed by attending poorer minority-area schools, and minority students would be aided by transfer to white schools. Perhaps busing is a possible solution to educational inequality?

This report is one of many available to any citizen, and it has been quoted several times in the mass media and in other specialized reports to legislators. The report includes sections on such topics as sample design, sampling variability, correlation, percentage distributions and many others. Conclusions of such studies often find their way into texts and technical reports, as well as to the mass media, and increasingly form the basis for policy decisions.

But is the conclusion true, and does it characterize the nation as a whole? Can we afford to reject out of hand such extensive research results or, for that matter, can we afford to accept them without question? Furthermore, if we question these findings, what information do we want or need to make a reasoned judgment of the study's worth? Are the revealed differences sufficiently large so that we should say they are meaningful and should compel action? What sorts of bias and error, if any, might creep in, and were these possibilities taken into account in the study? This study is an excellent example of full and careful research reporting, but how should a concerned citizen or legislator use this information? Is any of this helpful to the school superintendent planning his program for the next few years?

Clearly we would want the legislator to have sufficient understanding of statistics to make a responsible judgment.* Furthermore, we would want sufficient insight into these matters to assure ourselves both that good information is properly used by those in a position to influence important decisions, and also that unworthy information is recognized and set aside.

One of the most impressive developments in contemporary society has been the vast growth of research into all aspects of our physical environment, our society, and ourselves. Increasingly, statistically analyzed research results and statistical models are used as a basis for gaining insight and making decisions. To understand contemporary society, to understand the basis of many decisions, to follow intelligently and evaluate the output of others' study, or to handle important lines of thought and reasoning, the knowledge of elementary statistics is essential. The demand for research is growing, and research is being conducted by neighborhoods, political parties, and public and private agencies, as well as university investigators. The chances are rather high that you will become involved in the conduct and evaluation of some kind of research yourself. Certainly we cannot read critically and interpret most of the literature in sociology, much less make original contributions to knowledge in this area, without a relatively detailed knowledge of how to interpret statistical arguments and descriptions and apply them to our own ideas and research. For leader or legislator or citizen, for poet or social scientist, the need for statistical insight seems to be a fact of contemporary life and a powerful tool for understanding and decision-making.

1.1 SOME BASIC CONCEPTS IN STATISTICS

The Coleman study involved questioning a rather large number of students in grades 1, 3, 6, 9 and 12 across the nation at the end of September, 1965. Each student in the study was asked questions about such things as ethnic status, age, sex, background, and batteries of items to measure academic ability. Each of these questions was designed to measure a property or characteristic of the student. Properties such as age, ethnic status, or academic ability are called **variables,** ways individuals could differ from each other which are of interest to the investigators. Sometimes it is helpful to refer to the scores, or measured

---

*The Coleman study used a statistical technique called *multiple regression*. This technique is discussed in Chapter 9 in this book.

values, on variables (such as those Coleman collected) as **statistical observations** or simply **observations.** Typically, statistical observations are expressed as numbers (*e.g.* age in years, academic ability scores) although numbers are not essential to the use of statistics.

It is important to know what one's statistical observations are, of course. The number 11 hardly has any meaning until one learns that it is the age in years of a student who was in school in the United States in September, 1965. Notice that the statistical observation was described in terms of three things: (a) what the variable was that was measured (*e.g.* age in years), (b) what the variable was measured on (*e.g.* a person who was a student in one of the five target grades in the study), and (c) where and when this student was located. The second point deserves a further comment. Part of Coleman's study did not deal with individual students, but dealt with individual teachers, and other parts of the study dealt with entire schools. Any of these parts could involve measurements in terms of age, of course, but what one concludes from a study would be vastly different if "age-of-student" were measured rather than "age-of-school." The kind of "object" being measured is called the **unit of analysis,** and in the part of Coleman's study cited earlier, the unit of analysis was the individual student, not the individual school. Sociology often deals with different units of analysis, and this makes clarity on this point very important.

The scores on all of the variables included in Coleman's study,—for all of the students in grades 1, 3, 6, 9, and 12 in the United States in September, 1965,—describe a statistical population, the population that Coleman was ultimately interested in describing. A **statistical population,** sometimes called a **universe,** is composed of scores on all the variables the investigator wants to measure on all of the "objects" at the time and place indicated; in short, a statistical population is *all relevant statistical observations.* In this case, the statistical population was **finite,** since, in principle, the statistical observations in such a statistical population could be counted. Often this is not the case, particularly in scientific pursuits which hope to develop principles applying to certain kinds of phenomena wherever and whenever they may occur. An **infinite** statistical population, sometimes called a **conceptual** or **general universe,** would be one in which relevant statistical observations are not limited to any particular time and/or location. The size of cities (any time or place they may exist), the stratifica-

---

BOX 1.1 FOR THOSE WHO LIKE OVERVIEWS

There are certain basic *themes* and ideas which unite the various specific techniques in different chapters of this book. These themes are reviewed in Chapter 17, and it may be helpful to you to read through that chapter now. Chapter 17 should alert you to possible ways of organizing your thinking about statistics.*

---

*"Loop-back" Boxes such as this will be used here and there in the text to flag important ideas you should be sure to get at that point, or to suggest points where you should pull yourself back and reflect on your own grasp of the argument being made. We will refer and cross-refer you to points where necessary ideas can be found and reviewed.

tion systems of societies, the powerlessness feelings of people, or the patterns of coalition-formation in small groups would all be examples of infinite statistical populations or conceptual universes.

Whether the universe being studied is infinite or finite, investigators rarely enumerate an entire statistical population (*i.e.* they seldom examine *all* statistical observations), but rather, they select a subset of the scores called a **statistical sample.** Coleman's study was based on a sample from a defined statistical population. Although any subset of a statistical population would constitute a sample, in practice some kinds of samples may not represent very well the population from which they were drawn. Usually the investigator's interest is in selecting an appropriate sample which will give him accurate information about the population from which it was drawn. He wants to make inferences about the population, but he wants to do this in a way that is sound, practical and economical. Samples are, of course, always finite, although they may also be large as in Coleman's case. The field of inferential statistics is concerned with the ways in which reliable samples may be drawn and how inferences can be based on them.*

1.2 THE FIELD OF STATISTICS

Like most words, the word *statistics* is used in several ways in everyday speech. Some use it to refer to virtually any number which describes something, such as the height of Mont Blanc, the number of babies born in Vermont, or the turning radius of a Ford. *Statistics* is also used in two more technical ways: first, to refer to a certain subject matter or field of intellectual pursuit, and, secondly, in a specific and narrow sense (which will be defined later) related to the description of statistical samples.

The field of statistics, broadly viewed, encompasses a range of techniques and human activities that border on mathematics on one side, and on the other, on the problems that investigators and people in everyday life want solved. Basically, statistics involves logical thinking about statistical samples or populations, either for the purpose of arriving at a compact and meaningful description, or for the purpose of assessing some of the risks involved in extending conclusions based on samples to conclusions about populations. Logical thinking about such collections of scores involves knowing which comparisons to make as well as how to make the comparisons in an informative way. The field of statistics includes a growing "kit" of techniques particularly useful for making these descriptions and inferences.

The subject-matter of statistics may be divided up into two parts. One part, called **descriptive statistics,** consists of tools and issues involved in describing collections of statistical observations, whether they are samples or total populations. The other part, called **inferential** or **inductive statistics,** deals with the logic and procedures for evaluating risks of inference from descriptions of samples to descriptions of populations.

---

*See H. J. Loether and D. G. McTavish, *Inferential Statistics for Sociologists*, for a thorough survey of sampling procedures in sociology.

This book will focus primarily on descriptive statistics. A full analysis of how statisticians make inductive inferences through drawing reliable samples must be pursued in a separate volume.* One last terminological distinction may be worth making at this point. A second technical meaning of the word *statistics* refers to any description of a *sample* of statistical observations. If, however, the collection of statistical observations which is described is a statistical *population*, then a description of these observations would be called a **parameter.** For instance, the average achievement level of all twelfth graders in the United States in 1965 could be treated as a population *parameter*, and the average achievement level of twelfth graders obtained from Coleman's sample could be treated as a *statistic*. A statistic and a parameter may be the same kind of description (*i.e.* a percentage or average or ratio). It is *what* is described — population or sample — that makes the difference between these terms. The focal problem of inferential statistics is the relationship between a statistic and a parameter. The problem of descriptive statistics is the development of ways to describe samples *or* populations, that is, to develop different kinds of statistics and parameters which could be used on any given collection of scores.

The field of statistics has grown enormously in the past fifty years or so. Doctorates are offered in this specialty, and there are professional associations and professional journals which report new techniques and raise and resolve new issues. Student memberships are offered for these, and it would be worthwhile for you as a student to look at some of the ideas and publications in this field. Its history makes fascinating reading.†

---

*See Loether and McTavish, *Inferential Statistics for Sociologists.*
†The development of the field of statistics is one of the more interesting segments of our intellectual history. One theme in statistics (a word coined in a 1770 British publication) has been the interest of politicians in characteristics of their citizenry, usually for taxation purposes. Among early "political arithmetic" was the work of Englishman John Graunt (1620–1674) who was one of the first to describe gross population data in his book *Natural and Political Observations Made Upon the Bills of Mortality*, which described 1604–1661 London death records. This was shortly followed by an analysis by English astronomer Edmund Halley to "ascertain the prices of annuities upon lives," the first life insurance tables. Quetelet (1796–1874), Belgian supervisor of statistics and "father of the quantitative method in sociology," and Galton (1822–1911) extended work in statistical description, the latter developing percentiles, the median, correlation, and regression, — all ideas we will discuss later in this book. Karl Pearson (1857–1936), English biologist, extended statistics in the areas of regression, correlation, and chi-square. A second theme is that of probability. In China as early as 300 B.C. there is reported discussion of the probability of an unborn child being a boy or girl. Early pondering on outcomes of games of chance (*e.g.* dice rolling, card dealing) led to the development of formal rules of probability and their application to the fledgling field of astronomy by such men as Galileo (1564–1642), Pascal (1623–1662), and Fermat (1601–1665). The French astronomer Demoivre (1667–1754) was first to describe the *normal curve* as a description of errors in his observations. James Bernoulli (1654–1705) is credited with what was later called the "Law of Large Numbers," a principle central to statistical inference which states what the expected sample value of proportions will be, and how the probability of a given difference between sample and true proportions decreases as the size of a sample increases. Gauss (1777–1855) extended thinking on probability and worked with the concepts of standard deviation and standard error and, under a pseudonym, "Student," William S. Gossett extended further our knowledge of sampling distributions. In the early 20th century, Ronald A. Fisher developed the analysis of variance and other statistical tests, and contributed in important ways to knowledge about the design of experiments. You will encounter the names of other pioneers in statistics as you read through these books — names such as Cochran, Yule, Yates, Spearman, Markoff, Poisson, and others. An interesting presentation of the work of some of these pioneers appears in James R. Newman's *The World of Mathematics*, Simon and Schuster, New York, 1956. The development of statistics is far from finished, and one of the exciting current topics in sociology is the tailoring and creation of new and more useful statistical techniques.

BOX 1.2 TERMS TO CONSIDER FURTHER

Some of the terms defined here will be used in later chapters. To familiarize yourself with these, it might be helpful at this point to flip through a sociology book or journal to see if you know the meanings of these terms and can find examples of each of them. Especially important ideas are the following in Section 1.1:

Statistical observation
Variable
Unit of analysis
Statistical population

1.3 THE RELATIONSHIP BETWEEN STATISTICS AND SOCIOLOGY

Sociologists are interested in studying individual social actors, groups, or organizational processes, interaction patterns, norms, and social behavior of various types. Typically, a sociologist concerned with, say, the age structure of societies and its consequences for kinship structures might begin by simply gathering information on age structure from each of a series of societies with existing records. In order to highlight the age structure rather than simply the size of the society, he will use statistical procedures for creating, say, averages or proportions of those over 65, or perhaps "dependency ratios" (*i.e.* the ratio of the number of young and old people to the number of middle aged). Since the data are quite likely based on a careful sample of existing societies, he may well want to know how much confidence he should place in these figures, and again he will turn to statistics, especially inferential statistics, to help reason out the risks involved in using a sample. He may also examine the record-creating procedures in different societies for evidence of bias, and perhaps he might compute an index number of some sort to show the way two or more variables are related— a correlation coefficient, for example.

Simple statistical description frequently leads to more detailed theoretical work and, perhaps, the creation of some type of model or theory about the way age structure would be expected to influence kinship. Usually this process will lead the sociologist to take account of other variables, such as the level of technology in a society, or sex ratios, and generally he will then have to set out to measure these variables on a sample of societies. If he is fortunate, information may already exist in some archive, but usually he will have to organize records for his own purposes or gather new data. These processes pose issues of *validity* (*i.e.*, questions of whether you are measuring what you want to measure) and of *reliability* (*i.e.*, questions of whether the measurement process itself is stable), and these again may be examined with statistical tools. In fact, he will probably express his hypotheses or theories in terms of statistical descriptions and will compare his revised theories with new data in terms of statistical tools.

A brief look at some of the main journals in the field, the *American Sociological Review*, the *American Journal of Sociology*, or *Social Forces*, for example, should convince you of the centrality of statistical expression and analysis in our field. An increasingly interesting area of sociology, in fact, is in the development of more useful statistical tools for handling some interesting new questions about social behavior. One of the purposes of this book is to help you move to the forefront of sociology where interesting phenomena are described in new and different ways.

1.4 WHAT YOU CAN EXPECT IN STUDYING STATISTICS

You will do much better, we feel, if you have some knowledge of what to expect in general from your encounter with statistics. Most students seem to find the area somewhat different from others they know, requiring something of a new approach.

First and most basic, the field of statistics is oriented toward drawing logical conclusions. This implies that there is some type of *question* or *problem* which commands an interest in finding an answer. Coleman's study addressed several different questions. What is the extent of ethnic segregation? What differences are there between schools and in achievement? What is the relationship between students' achievements and the kinds of schools they attend? Procedures for supporting the claim that an answer has indeed been found are basically those of logic. Statisticians develop various measures, examine their logical implications, and then critique and develop statistical models which may be of use in finding answers in certain restricted situations. While this characterizes many of the interests scholars and citizens have about the world, it by no means exhausts the things they are interested in doing to discover or experience what their world is like. It is, nevertheless, a surprisingly useful approach.

Secondly, the field of statistics is quite similar to a language. There are several key concepts and technical terms, some of which we have already introduced, and there is a kind of grammar involved in using them. The language is relatively carefully worked out and consistent, although sometimes the same idea may be symbolized by somewhat different symbols in different contexts. Once you learn how to express yourself in the language, you will find that you have a very powerful way to make important distinctions and express logical relationships. In fact, it is often true that difficult problems disappear once the problem is expressed in a clear and consistent fashion. The early part of the book will emphasize the important "language of statistics."

Thirdly, while it is true that many of the summary measures and lines of reasoning are expressed in numerical form, there is a basic underlying logic of statistical reasoning which can be discussed and handled apart from much of mathematics. Mathematical-logical procedures, however, are such powerful and logically clear tools for handling statistical reasoning that they are nearly always of interest to the professional statistician. This means, for example, that it is often helpful to look for ways to express ideas and relationships in numeric form, although this is not always true nor formally necessary. It also means that one could neatly express the logical relationships between different ideas by mathematical notation and derivation. In this beginning treatment of statistics we will highlight the underlying logic without resorting to more than elementary algebra, but it is clear that we are imposing a limitation on expression which could not be conveniently imposed on general treatments of statistical reasoning. Other books use more mathematical expression to explain the reasoning involved, and you may want to consult one of these references from time to time.

Finally, the field of statistics focuses upon situations where there are repeated or repeatable operations—such as in taking a measurement of the organizational involvement of each of 137 people who are members of the local YMCA, or as in tossing an imaginary coin an infinite number of times and recording whether the outcome each time is "heads" or "tails," or as in drawing samples of organizations in order to measure the relationship between the height of their stratification system and productivity. In principle, these repeated or repeatable operations (*i.e.* samplings, tossings, measurings, etc.) must be such that there could possibly be a range of different outcomes. For example, in principle, people might be of different degrees of organizational involvement, coins might turn up "heads" or "tails," and an organization might have a "tall" or "flat" stratification hierarchy, or have high or low productivity.

If one's approach does not involve *logical* progress toward a solution of an interesting problem, if there is no interest in *supportable* findings, if *repeated or repeatable* operations and the possibility of *differences* in outcomes are not involved, then the language of statistics probably does not have much to offer. The surprising thing is that statistical reasoning *is* so useful in handling many of the truly important problems confronting scholars in sociology and many of the issues confronting those who govern and are governed. Basically we are interested in drawing logically supportable conclusions in situations where we have carried out some kind of measurement procedure on a number of subjects (often on samples of subjects). We need to summarize our findings clearly, assess risks of inference, and draw valid conclusions. Most of all we need to get to the point where we can use useful tools to promote important inquiry in our field without losing sight of the original purpose of our inquiry. Hopefully the organization of this volume will help.

1.5   PURPOSES AND OBJECTIVES OF THIS BOOK'S APPROACH

The aim of this beginning course in sociological statistics is to introduce you to those aspects of statistical description and inference which will be most useful to you as a consumer and potential creator of statistical information. The emphasis will be on applications of statistical reasoning, description, and inference and on some of the theory behind it, as well as on interpretation of these procedures in the context of sociological research. At the end of the course you should be able to read intelligently and evaluate statistical arguments made in the current sociological journals and monographs.

To accomplish this we are presenting an elementary text with a coverage of current techniques somewhat broader than usual; we incorporate in a subordinate role the methodological issues that you will encounter in more depth in other social science research methods courses; we attempt to emphasize a user's approach and understanding in the context of social science problems and current usage; and we minimize the more formal mathematical mode of expression as well as minimizing most aspects of clerical mathematics. We have assumed that the more clerical or computational aspect of statistics is less important at an elementary level, and in any event will most likely be handled by electronic calculator or computer when the need to compute arises. It is our view that it is much more important to gain a comprehension of statistical measures through several encounters with summary measures in real research contexts, rather than to emphasize computational routine or shortcuts on a few fictitious examples of "error-free" data.

Ideas are fun, particularly when one has the tools to rub them together in interesting ways. It is hoped that the pursuit of statistics in sociology will be interesting, challenging, and fun too. The next chapter introduces some of the ideas behind measurement in sociology.

CONCEPTS TO KNOW AND UNDERSTAND

statistical observation
statistical population
statistical sample
descriptive statistics
inferential statistics

unit of analysis
statistic
parameter
variable

QUESTIONS AND PROBLEMS

1. Some sociologists study the phenomenon of power balance in families by having a family (parents and children) play a game of some type in a laboratory setting. As the game progresses the investigators record verbal and non-verbal interaction (*e.g.* who asks questions of whom, who provides information or gives direction or commands). What might be the unit of analysis, the main variable of interest to the investigator, and an example of a statistical observation he might make? Define a statistical population such an investigator might become interested in studying.

2. Select any sociological journal or research monograph which reports the results of research and then select an interesting article. Identify the statistical observation, unit(s) of analysis, and variables the investigator uses. Then describe the sample and population he is dealing with. Point out situations where descriptive and inferential statistics are used, and give an example of a statistic and a parameter.

3. Usually, at this point, it is helpful to gather some actual statistical observations yourself. You might take some hints from a research article or from a workbook that includes some problems to suggest how you might proceed.*

GENERAL REFERENCES

Amos, Jimmy R., Foster Lloyd Brown, and Oscar G. Mink, *Statistical Concepts: A Basic Program*, (New York, Harper and Row), 1965.
   This is a brief programmed book covering the central argument of descriptive and inferential statistics. It is useful as a brief overview of statistics. You might read through it quickly, not worrying much about trouble in understanding the details, at this early stage.
McCollough, Celeste, and Loche Van Atta, *Introduction to Descriptive Statistics and Correlation*, (New York, McGraw-Hill), 1965.
   For those interested in a programmed approach to some of the earlier material in descriptive statistics.
Wallis, W. Allen, and Harry V. Roberts, *Statistics: A New Approach*, (New York, The Free Press of Glencoe), 1956.
   Chapters one and two present an interesting introduction to statistics and some of the uses to which it is put. A large number of brief illustrations are presented.
Hagood, Margaret Jarman, and Daniel O. Price, *Statistics for Sociologists*, revised edition, (New York, Holt), 1952.
   Part one describes quantitative methods in sociology and some of the kinds of sources and ways to handle data.
Tufte, Edward R., (ed.), *The Quantitative Analysis of Social Problems*, (Reading, Mass., Addison-Wesley), 1970.
   This book is a collection of articles on social problems and studies about them which use statistics or a quantitative approach. Although some of the issues are beyond the scope of this text, the articles are all interesting and help point out some of the difficulties and successes in studies for which statistical analysis may be relevant.
Blalock, Hubert M., Jr., *Social Statistics,* Second Edition, (New York, McGraw-Hill), 1972.
   Often it helps to read the discussion of some statistical procedure in more than one text, and the intermediate level text *Social Statistics* would be especially recommended for this purpose. It is detailed, relevant to our field and covers most of the topics included in this book.

OTHER REFERENCE

Coleman, James S., *et al., Equality of Educational Opportunity,* (Washington, D.C.), 1966.

*See Loether and McTavish, *Statistical Analysis for Sociologists: A Student Manual.*

2

MEASURING VARIABLES

A number of sociologists have argued that a change from a community-based society toward a mass society means that individuals become separated from binding social norms, and this then increases an individual's feeling of isolation and powerlessness. In a mass society, it is argued, membership in organizations which are intermediate between the family and mass society (*e.g.* unions, church groups, and various voluntary associations) are essential if a person's sense of mastery is to be maintained. Those who maintain membership of this sort will feel more in control of their lives, greater mastery, and less isolation than those who do not. This is the "mediation hypothesis" of organizations and powerlessness.

At this point, the ideas being discussed — about why individuals feel the degree of powerlessness they do — are very general and abstract. What is needed is some specific evidence and useful indicators showing that the real world behaves in this way. We could start by selecting a specific example of an intermediate organization, such as a union. If ideas about powerlessness are useful, then we might expect that workers who are members of a union will have a lower degree of powerlessness than workers who are not union members. This relationship was examined by Neal and Seeman (1964) in a study of adult males who were residents of Columbus, Ohio.

In addition to the research problems of locating and selecting research subjects, securing their cooperation, and recording their responses, there are two basic problems to be solved which lead directly to a consideration of what statistical reasoning is all about. These problems are (a) classifying subjects on their degree of powerlessness and group membership, and (b) comparing powerlessness scores for the group of subjects who are members of a task group and for those who are not members. The first problem will be discussed in the remainder of this chapter. The second problem will be dealt with in the next chapter where some of the difficulties and possibilities for making valid comparisons will be described.

2.1 MEANINGS AND MEASUREMENT

The first problem, noted above, is measuring powerlessness and group membership. **Measurement,** most simply stated, is a procedure for carefully classifying "cases" (called research subjects, respondents, or, more generally, "objects," such as a person, an interacting pair of people (a dyad), a company, a whole society, etc.) and putting them into previously defined categories of some variable. A **variable** is simply any characteristic or property of a case which has a series of two or more possible categories into which a "case" could potentially be classified. Group membership and powerlessness are two variable characteristics of individuals. Classifying a person as a "group member" or "not a group member" is an example of a simple measurement process. Alternatively, one might investigate the number of groups to which an individual belongs and use a series of categories such as 0, 1, 2, 3, or more, and "no response." The result of this process is a **statistical observation** or, simply, an **observation** which is usually labelled with an appropriate name or number.

There are two general types of problems that must be faced in deciding upon a measurement procedure. One problem concerns the *adequacy* of the actual measurement process to carry out a defined classification procedure required to classify cases on some variable characteristic. For example, it is probably useless to measure a person's blood type by asking him what it is. This procedure depends upon his knowing what it is, and he may not know. Other procedures, such as taking a blood sample for laboratory testing, are likely to lead to a better classification or measurement of blood type. Adequacy of a measurement procedure is usually discussed in terms of **validity** (does the procedure measure what it is intended to measure?) and **reliability** (would the same classification result if the same procedure were tried over again under the same conditions where there was no real change in the variable being measured?). These are difficult questions to answer, and some approaches to checking validity and reliability will be discussed in Section 2.2a of this chapter.

The second general problem posed by the measurement process concerns the *meanings* that are to be conveyed by measurement categories. We must ask, what does "group membership" or "powerlessness" refer to? What sorts of information can we glean from knowledge that a subject is classified into the "high powerlessness" category, for example, rather than another category? In our present example, this second problem will be solved as soon as we *define* what is meant by a variable like powerlessness.

2.1a Concepts and Indicators. The **concept,** or idea, of powerlessness refers to the degree that individuals expect not to have some control over events around them which affect their lives. It is usually considered a property of individual social actors, and in this sense it is used to describe an actor's own feelings about his control of events. Individuals may differ in the feelings of powerlessness; some feel a greater sense of mastery than others. The feeling of powerlessness is one of the ways by which individuals can be said to be alienated from their surrounding social structure. This formal definition of the concept of "powerlessness" could be stated more elaborately or with examples, of course, and some investigators devote considerable effort to careful definitions of this sort. Clarity here is essential if an investigator wants to examine the validity of some measurement procedure.*

When it comes to measuring the concept of "powerlessness," one might think of a number of **indicators,** or items that will serve to measure this concept. One might, for example, ask a person if he agrees with the following statement: "We are just so many cogs in the machinery of life." If a person agrees, he would be classified as having a feeling of "more" rather than "less" powerlessness than would someone who disagreed. Sociologists often use several similar questions to form an attitude scale where the answers to all of the questions are combined in some way into an overall "powerlessness" score. Techniques for creating these scales are discussed at some length in most research methods texts. Usually the result of measurements like this is a number, datum or **score** (*i.e.* a statistical observation). A collection or group of several of these scores is called **data.**† Descriptive statistics are aimed at describing data.

The meaning of a score resulting from a measurement process depends upon the way variables are defined (as discussed in Chapter 1) and the adequacy of the measurement process itself. The way these scores are statistically described depends on the information they contain, and it also depends upon the specific use of the variable in an overall research project.

Three differences between variables will be pointed out in the following discussion. These are (a) level of measurement (Section 2.1.1), (b) scale continuity (Section 2.1.2), and (c) the role the variable plays in a research project (Section 2.1.4).

2.1.1   Level of Measurement

To illustrate some of the different types of information a defined variable is intended to convey, it is convenient to distinguish among four **levels of measurement.** These four types of measurement are traditionally listed in statistics texts primarily as a way to reinforce the importance of knowing what information is contained in scores which are assigned.

This difference is one of several which have an important influence on the kinds of statistical summary one chooses, and it certainly influences the kinds of interpretations that are warranted. It is worth noting that some scholars distinguish more levels of measurement than these four, and they may include different mixtures of these which feature some of the properties of the levels mentioned below (Stevens, 1946).

---

*It is interesting to note that the problem of definition is sufficiently serious for whole books to be written about it. One interesting and useful book is by Robinson (1954).
†Note that the word *data* is plural. One way an investigator's data *are* described is by using the statistical descriptions discussed in this book.

2.1.1a Establishing Categories of Measurement. Any adequately specified measurement procedure must have a category into which each and every case can be classified; it must be **inclusive.** If only the categories 0, 1, and 2 were available to classify individuals on the number of groups to which they belong, there would be no category for those belonging to more than two groups. Such a situation could be corrected by making the last category "2 or more" or by providing a category labeled "other," if additional categories could not be defined in a more positive way. The "other" category is sometimes used simply to create a logically complete or inclusive classification system. In most actual research it turns out that categories for "don't know" (often symbolized in printed tables as *D/K*) and "no answer" (often symbolized as *NA*) are often needed as well. These categories pose problems for the thinking statistician.

Another property of a good classification system is that its categories are **mutually exclusive** as well as exhaustive; that is, it is possible to classify an individual case into one and *only one* category of the classification system. If a variable has two categories "married" and "has children," for example, it would not be adequately defined in this sense, because married people with children could be classified into both categories. The categories are not mutually exclusive. "Ever married" and "never married," on the other hand, are mutually exclusive categories. It is true, of course, that individuals change over time, but at any given point when the measurement is made it should be possible for a case to fall in only one category.

It is preferable, generally, to have a measurement procedure which is as **precise** as possible; that is, one which makes more rather than fewer distinctions. The measurement scheme: "never married," "currently married," and "other" would be less adequate in this regard than "never married," "currently married," "divorced," "widowed," and "separated," simply because there are more categories in the second scheme. Knowledge that a subject is "divorced" is less ambiguous and conveys more information than knowledge that he is an "other." Adequately defined variables are generally classified into the following four levels of measurement.

2.1.1b Nominal Variables. Nominal variables are those which are properly defined with logically exhaustive and mutually exclusive categories, so that equivalences or differences are clearly established. Good nominal-variable measures are *precise* and have *positively defined* categories. There is no implication thus far of any ordering of categories; there is no implication that distance exists between one category and the next; the categories are simply logically *different* or distinct from each other. Many scientific variables are of this kind. In sociology, nominal variables include marital status, sex-role, group membership, type of community, kind of role relationship, etc.*

---

*The idea of level of measurement refers to the relationship between *categories* of a variable. For nominal variables the categories are simply different, whether or not they are labeled with numbers. It would not be appropriate to add together, for example, the category labels of a nominal variable. Sometimes students wonder why formulas are used to compute statistics on nominal variables if this is so. The reason is that the formulas make use of category frequencies, the number of cases in each category, and not the numeric label that may be used to identify any particular category of the variable. It *does* make logical sense to say that there are twice as many "ever-married" people as "never-married" people, but it would not make sense to add up numbers which may be used to label marital status categories (although it would make logical sense to do this for a variable such as age).

2.1.1c Ordinal Variables. Ordinal variables are those which are defined to include the features of nominal variables, plus the feature that categories are *ordered* or *ranked* in a described way. For example, "friendliness," as we usually think of it, is defined as an ordinal variable. Categories generally distinguished (low, medium, and high, for example) not only imply categorical differences but also imply an order from low to high on that variable. We are not able to define *amount* of difference between these categories however; it is only sequence that we can define in an ordinal variable. Traditional class grading schemes are often thought of as ordinal properties of students. Social class is ordinal (*e.g.* lower-lower, upper-lower, lower-middle, upper-middle, lower-upper, upper-upper class), no matter how precisely it may be measured. In principle, it is not defined in such a way that a "degree" or "unit" of social class is meaningful or distinguishable, although we feel we can distinguish rankings by social class. Rank order is defined in variables such as powerlessness, desirability, segregation, and many other attitudinal variables used in sociology.

2.1.1d Interval Variables. Interval-level variables, a third level of measurement which is usually distinguished, includes the logical and ranking features of ordinal and nominal variables, but in addition, its categories are defined in terms of a standard *unit of measurement*, such as the individual "social actor," the year of age, or the inch, ounce, liter, or degree. Definition of a unit which can be unambiguously detected and counted is a difficult undertaking. You may recall accounts of the very elaborate definitional procedures to establish the foot or meter, the degree Fahrenheit, the ton, or the U.S. Dollar. The U.S. Bureau of Standards, a special governmental agency, is concerned with the definition of certain standard measurement units such as these. Given a recognizable unit such as "one social actor," however, one is able to compare the difference between families with one or two members and those with three or four members. The *differences* are the *same*. We can distinguish this sameness by virtue of having defined "one social actor." The scale of measurement of an interval variable is defined in terms of a standard unit size.

Determining the interval for a variable is an unusually important step up from nominal and ordinal variables, in that it greatly increases the amount of information which is contained in numeric scores. Given interval-level variables, a large amount of mathematical manipulation is possible, and conclusions can be drawn that are often not at all obvious from the raw scores themselves. Much of statistics implies the use of interval-level scores, and because of the added power of these procedures, there is a strong motivation to use these techniques whenever they can be justified.

2.1.1e Ratio Variables. Finally *ratio* variables include the foregoing characteristics and, in addition, the scale of measurement has a defined origin, or zero point. A zero point is a theoretically defined point on a scale representing the absence of any of the property being measured. Not all properties can easily be measured from zero. Zero social class, for example, is not a meaningful concept thus far in sociology. On the other hand zero inches of length, or families of size zero is meaningful in this sense. Prior to the development of theoretical ideas of an absolute zero point in measurement of temperature, other temperature scales used the concept of zero degrees (as in Centigrade or Fahrenheit) as a relative measurement that did not correspond to a theoretical absence of any positive features of the property "temperature." In the Fahrenheit and Centi-grade scales, since degree-units were defined, but zero did not represent any absolute in temperature, their degree-unit would be classified as an interval, not a ratio variable. With the development of the Kelvin scale, temperature became a ratio variable.

If it is possible to define a variable as a ratio variable, then it is also pos-sible to talk about ratios, (*e.g.* two years of education is half of four years and this ratio is the same as the ratio of 12 years to 24 years). These statements would not be possible if one could not count units (*e.g.* year-units) from a meaningful zero starting point. However, if one is interested in the variable "amount of learned knowledge," the number of years of education might be used as an indi-cator of this concept. In this case, however, because of the way "amount of learned knowledge" is usually defined, we may not have available a specified unit of "learned knowledge" nor a meaningful zero point on the "learned knowl-edge" scale. Notice that the way a variable is defined governs its level of mea-surement. We probably would not want to say, for example, that a person with four years of education has exactly twice the amount of learned knowledge that a person with only two years of education has.

In most cases, once one has defined a standard unit of measurement in an interval scale, a zero point is also established. Examples of interval variables are rare. In our work we will not make this possible distinction between interval and ratio levels of measurement, but will refer to either type as "interval/ratio" or simply "interval" variables. Sociological examples of such variables include counts like "family size," "number of levels in an organizational hierarchy," "group size," "number of years of formal education," and perhaps "social sta-tus.*

Figure 2.1 illustrates the cumulative character of levels of measurement. The important point is that the way one defines a variable has consequences for the categories developed, the relationships between them, and the meaning of an assigned score.†

2.1.1f   Using Level of Measurement Information.   Labels for catego-ries can be of a wide variety of different types. Names ("married," "high-power-lessness," etc.) are often convenient to use, although sometimes letters or, more frequently, numbers are used. The utility of numbers lies in the possibility of an unlimited set of symbols and in the fact that there is a set of powerful logical rules (mathematics) for handling numbers. The symbols one uses and the avail-able means for operating on the symbols has far greater consequences than is immediately apparent. It leads most scientists to the use of numbers and to vari-ous branches of mathematics for handling these number codes, although in prin-ciple the logical distinctions could be handled (usually inefficiently and with great effort and risk of confusion) by other code schemes such as words.

A word of caution is necessary at this point. It is clear that number-sym-bols could be used to label the categories of a variable like marital status, as well as the categories of the variable age. Marital status, however, is a nominal

---

*An example of work toward establishing a ratio scale of measurement for social status is Jones and Shorter, (1972). See also Hamblin (1971).

†A very helpful chapter on measurement in sociology, and on some of the meanings which may be avail-able in scores, is Clyde Coombs' Chapter 11 in Festinger and Katz (1953).

Defined Characteristics
of Category Systems

Level of Measurement	Exhaustive, Mutually Exclusive Categories	Categories Defined to Have an Ordering	Defined, Standard Unit of Measurement	Meaningful Zero Point on Scale
Nominal	X			
Ordinal	X	X		
Interval	X	X	X	
Ratio	X	X	X	X

FIGURE 2.1 PROPERTIES OF DIFFERENT LEVELS OF MEASUREMENT

variable, since its categories have no defined ordering and age is usually defined as an interval/ratio variable. For marital status of a group of individuals, one could not use the mathematical operation of adding up the number-labels, for example, because such a manipulation of the scores would rely upon information about ordering and relative spacing of categories, and these are not part of the (usual) definition of marital status. The adding operation is, of course, appropriate when the variable is years of age, an interval/ratio variable. To take another example, if one were to score ten individuals on sex, assigning the number code 0 for males and 1 for females, a collection of ten scores such as the following might be available.

$$0 \quad 0 \quad 1 \quad 0 \quad 0 \quad 1 \quad 1 \quad 1 \quad 0 \quad 1$$

If these ten numbers were added and then divided by ten to create a simple average score for the group, the average-sex would be 0.5. Adding and dividing scores in this manner clearly involves the assumption that females are higher — one unit higher — than males. A statement that the average sex of this group of scores is 0.5 is nonsense, but on the other hand if this were reinterpreted as a proportion or percentage (e.g. 50 percent of the group are female) the results can be meaningfully interpreted.

There are statistical procedures which are created in such a way that only nominal or only ordinal or only interval/ratio meanings in scores are relied upon. It is most appropriate logically to use the statistical procedure which features the kind of information contained in the scores. As indicated in Figure 2.2, if statistics appropriate for lower levels of measurement were to be used on scores defined at a higher level of measurement, no *technical* error would be made, since the properties of levels of measurement are cumulative. An interval-level measure contains all of the properties of a nominal variable plus added properties — added information. However, though no technical error was made, a serious research problem would arise in that this procedure did not use all of the information that was readily available in the higher-level score.

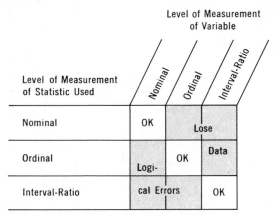

FIGURE 2.2   CORRESPONDENCE OF STATISTICAL PROCEDURES AND LEVEL OF MEASUREMENT

A technical "error" *is* made, however, if we use statistical procedures appropriate to higher levels of measurement when the data are defined at a lower level of measurement. In this case, we would be acting by our statistical operations as if the scores contained more information than they were defined to have — *i.e.* we would have assumed a property of order where there was none, or of defined distances where there were none. Consequences for the interpretation of research findings when this technical error is made have been the subject of detailed discussion in sociology; (see Burke, 1971; Labovitz, 1970; replies by Vargo *et al.*, 1971). Thus the strong preference of most careful investigators is to select appropriate statistics for the data at hand.

Statistical procedures appropriate to higher levels of measurement generally have the advantage of permitting more compact descriptions of data, as we shall see. In the case of our dichotomous (two-category) nominal variable of sex in the example above, the "average-sex" could be readily re-interpreted as a percentage: a meaningful interpretation. On the other hand, if we discovered that the average "marital status" scores were 2.563, we would be essentially at a loss to provide a meaningful interpretation of this figure. Some research on the issue indicates that for many purposes, a procedure that moves from ordinal to interval-level statistics while using ordinal data does not result in great errors in interpretation of the statistical results. The important point is to know what differences between scores constitute meaningful variation, and then to use statistical procedures which highlight meaningful variation in scores, ignoring undefined or meaningless differences.

An associated problem is that of not collecting sufficient information in the process of measurement to classify a case adequately. For example, if one

> **BOX 2.1**   LEVELS OF MEASUREMENT—SOME REVIEW EXAMPLES
>
> It would be well to pause at this point and think of some examples of variables which fit each *level of measurement* we have been discussing. If you are clear about this first classification of variables, then you are ready to go on to the other two ways to classify variables—by scale continuity, and by role in a research project.
>
> As a review-starter, try defining "age" first as a nominal variable, then as an ordinal variable, and finally as an interval or ratio variable.

wanted to measure age (an interval/ratio characteristic) but found that employment forms only listed the person as "old," "middle-aged" or "young," one would have to treat the variable as if it were ordinal because information on number of units (years) is not available in this classification for use in computation of interval/ratio-level statistics. If the information is not contained in the data one gathers, no amount of statistical manipulation will create it.

2.1.2   Scale Continuity

Another distinction between variables in addition to level of measurement involves whether or not variables are defined to have a continuous or discrete scale of measurement. A **continuous** variable, as Figure 2.3 suggests, is defined in such a way that in principle individuals could have infinitely varied fractional scores—*i.e.*, scores located at any point on an unbroken scale. The same concept can be stated in at least three other ways. First, given any two scores, however close together, in principle a third score could always fall between them; or second, the probability that any two scores will be identical is zero; or third, an infinite number of different scores are possible between any two points on the scale. In any case, this concept implies an unbroken scale of possible score values. In sociology such variables as age, alienation, segregation and social class are defined (usually) as continuous variables. There is a well-known debate in the social stratification field over whether the phenomenon of social class is most usefully defined as discrete or continuous (Duncan and Artis, 1951).

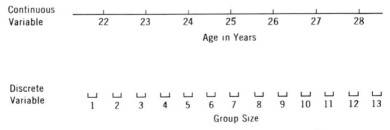

FIGURE 2.3   CLASSIFICATION OF VARIABLES BY SCALE CONTINUITY

A contrasting type of variable is a **discrete variable.** This type is defined in such a manner that, again in principle, only a *limited set* of distinct scores can be achieved. Stated differently: (a) the scale of measurement is broken by "gaps" in the numbering scale which, in principle, can not contain measured cases; only integers are needed to label scale categories appropriately, not decimal fractions; or, (b) within a finite range there are only a finite number of possible score categories. Thus a variable such as family size (as usually defined), in principle, is a discrete variable, because families can only be of size one or two or three . . . etc.; there can be no example of a fractional size such as 2.5. This is true of most "count" type variables; nominal variables are always discrete. It should be noted that "average family size" is a different variable. It is measured on "cases" which are *groups*, such as states or nations or cities; it is possible for that kind of variable to take on fractional values, since it is usually defined as a continuous variable characteristic of *groups* of observations.

2.1.3 Grouping Scores Into Classes

From the start, most measurement processes in sociology have tended to group scores into defined classes. In the case of nominal and ordinal variables, it is usually quite clear that categories of social class, anomie, marital status, or productivity have to be defined before one can begin to measure or ask which of these categories the individual falls in. Actually this is the case with interval- and ratio-level variables as well.

2.1.3a Units of Measurement and Nearest Whole Units. Typically an investigator, confronted with the problem of measuring an interval variable, decides upon a **unit of measurement** such as the inch, foot, year, or 1000's of people. He then counts up the number of these "units" which can be said to characterize the object being measured rather than attempt to continuously measure the exact amount of these variables.* The interpretation of continuous variable scores is different from the interpretation of discrete scores, and this difference is shown in the way continuous variables are measured.

For continuous variables, the problem is one of deciding where any given case should fall in a classification scheme, and then, secondly, characterizing the category so that its meaning can be interpreted. Take the age category, for example, that we usually refer to as "65." Assuming that age has been measured by asking individuals what age they were, at their *nearest* birthday, the category could be said to include those who are past their 64th birthday by just over a half a year (half a unit of measurement) and that category would still include a person who is almost half a year over his 65th birthday. To be precise, the category would extend from 64.5 to 65.5 years as illustrated in the following diagram.

---

*A thermometer measures temperature in a continuous fashion, since the physical height of a column of fluid varies with temperature. We usually record temperature, however, as if the variable were discrete, in terms of degrees or tenths of degrees. An analog computer works on the principle of continuous measurement by varying electrical current. A digital computer, on the other hand, operates in terms of discrete states where a switch is either on or off, or a magnet is polarized in one direction or not, etc. Most measurement of continuous variables involves counting units of measurement to yield discrete-looking scores. However, the differences, built in by definition, between discrete and continuous variables mean that scores can be manipulated and interpreted differently.

Measuring Age To The Nearest Whole Year:

62.5   63.5   64.5   65.5   66.5   "real limits" or class boundaries

        63.0   64.0   65.0   66.0   class midpoints

A category of an interval variable is generally referred to by its **midpoint**. In this case, using one year as a *unit* of measurement, the category midpoints would be 63.0, 64.0, 65.0, 66.0, etc. Scores, or measured values, would be classified into the nearest category, which means that scores in the category 65.0 may be as small as 64.5 and as large as 65.5. These limits, extending one half unit on either side of the midpoint, are called **real limits** or **class boundaries.***

    2.1.3b Significant Digits and Rounding. How far one should round off an answer, to how many digit places, is determined basically by the degree of precision in the original measurement process. If a measurement is exact (*e.g.* counting the number of people in a group, a discrete variable), then it is appropriate to retain all significant digits in a score and to carry out computations involving these scores to as many decimal places as desired, treating the results as meaningful and significant (although this could easily be carried to the point of absurdity, *e.g.* average family size = 2.5632567). If, however, measurement is inexact, as it is in the case of continuous variables, then the answer should not be expressed to more digits than are significant in the original scores; (sometimes the rule is to admit one more digit than this). Thus, if one were measuring age in years, then answers should be rounded to

---

If a number, such as 34.6 were to be rounded to a whole number, the digit to the right of the place to which it is to be rounded should be examined. In this case, that digit is "6." Then:

    (a) If that digit is greater than 5, round up by increasing the digit to the left by one. In the example above, this would result in a rounded number of 35.

    (b) If that digit is less than 5, round down by simply dropping digits to the right of the last place in the desired answer.

    (c) If the digit is exactly 5 (followed by zeros), then the rule is to round up if the last digit in the desired answer is odd, and round down if the last digit in the desired answer is even. This is the so-called "engineers rule" and its logic is simply that odd and even numbers are likely to occur equally frequently so that no bias in rounding up or down will occur if this is always followed.

Some examples should help.

        65.60   could be rounded to   66
        64.50   could be rounded to   64
        65.50   could be rounded to   66
        64.51   could be rounded to   65
        65.49   could be rounded to   65

FIGURE 2.4 RULES FOR 'ROUNDING OFF'

---

*Students are usually concerned about classification of scores near class boundaries—a relatively rare and minor problem in most research. What if a "super-precise" subject reported his age as 65.51 years or 65.49 or 65.50; how shall one classify these age figures? The rules of *rounding* solve the problem. These rules are given in Figure 2.4, and they would result in classifying the first age above as 66, the next as 65, and the third as 66.

whole years (or, perhaps, tenths of years) even though the computational process (as in computing an average) may result in a fractional number which could be carried out to many decimal places. If births are recorded to the nearest 100, then the answers from computations using these scores should be expressed to the nearest 100 births. To express the result to more digits gives readers a distorted impression of accuracy. It is an appropriate practice, however, to retain as many digits as possible throughout a computational procedure rather than rounding at each step, since this practice avoids the accumulation of small rounding errors at each computational step. Only the final answer should be rounded. On the other hand, at any point where digits are to be dropped (*i.e.,* the number is too big for your calculator) they should be rounded off rather than simply dropped so that systematic distortions are not built into the result.

These principles can be quickly illustrated if we think of an example where two ages are to be added together, say, age 65 and the age 69. A score called 65 (the midpoint of its category) could actually be anything between 64.5 and 65.5 in actual value. Likewise a score called 69 could be between 68.5 and 69.5. Adding the class midpoints of these two scores gives a total of 134 (65 + 69 = 134), but the actual sum of the two scores could be as small as 133 or as large as 135; (64.5 + 68.5 = 133.0 and 65.5 + 69.5 = 135). Perhaps the sum should be expressed with only two significant digits as about 130. or as 134. but certainly not 134.0 which gives the impression that measurement was to the nearest tenth of a year. With more scores, of course, the problem becomes potentially more serious.

When a classification scheme is published in a table or chart, it is common practice to express the category boundaries in a fashion which clearly indicates that the categories do not, in fact, overlap, but are mutually exclusive. Thus the series of age categories,

Years Age
31 – 35
36 – 40
41 – 45

would be preferred over an expressed system such as:

Years Age
30 – 35
35 – 40
40 – 45

However expressed, the meaning of a score on a continuous variable extends from real limit to real limit.

2.1.3c Measurement to the Last Whole Unit.   Measurement to the **last whole unit** is sometimes used rather than measurement to the *nearest* whole unit. This introduces a complication which is worth a word of caution. A common example of this is in the measurement of age where an individual typically is asked for or gives information on his age at his *last* birthday even though his next birthday may be nearer. The meaning, then, of the age expressed as "65" would change, and the data would have to be treated slightly differently as a result. The real limits of the age 65 measured to the *last full year* would be 65.0 and 66.0, as shown in the diagram below.

Age Measurement To The Last Whole Year:

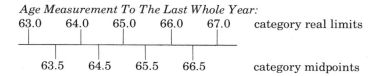

Although the difference between measurement to the "nearest" or "last" whole unit may seem to be slight and may not lead to gross errors in interpretation if caution and consistency are adhered to, failure to use the appropriate midpoint will have the effect of adding (or subtracting) a constant from each score. It is important that information measured by a measurement procedure be correctly represented.

The relationship between scale continuity and levels of measurement is shown in Figure 2.5 below and it is usually helpful at this point if you read a sociology text or journal article and attempt to classify the variables used in terms of *both* scale continuity and level of measurement. An abstract from an article by Marsh is reproduced in Figure 2.5B. Can you identify the different variables, units of analysis, and types of information probably contained in scores on the different variables?

For most statistical purposes, the distinction between continuous and discrete variables, where ordinal and interval/ratio variables are concerned, is of less importance.* In some treatments of statistics and in other parts of statistics than the descriptive, the distinction would be more consistently carried through. Here we will make the distinction at points (such as in graphic presenta-

	Scale Continuity	
Level of Measurement	Discrete	Continuous
Nominal	sex a	~~Logically Impossible~~
Ordinal	b	d
Interval-Ratio	family size c	e

To illustrate the use of the figure above, sex (a nominal, discrete variable the way it is usually defined) is an example in cell *a*. Meanwhile, family size (a ratio variable, and a discrete variable, if it is defined in terms of number of related people) is an example of a variable appropriately classified in cell *c* above.

FIGURE 2.5A   CLASSIFICATION OF VARIABLES

*Note that we have used the term "variable" in a broad sense in this chapter to refer to properties we may be interested in measuring, regardless of their level of measurement or scale continuity. In many statistics texts the term "variable" is reserved for only those characteristics which are defined as interval or ratio in level of measurement and, perhaps, are also continuous. Other characteristics, in this usage, are then referred to as "attributes" or "categorical" data. Whichever usage you and your instructor prefer, the important point is that you should carefully inquire into the meaning of the scores that are assigned.

The following is an abstract from an article by Robert M. Marsh (of Brown University) *Social Forces*, 50, (December, 1971) p 214–222. Most journals include these brief abstracts or "road-maps" to a research report, and in most cases they indicate the main variables, the ideas to be examined, and some of the main conclusions. Can you classify the variables Marsh talks about in terms of Figure 2.5A above?

THE EXPLANATION OF OCCUPATIONAL
PRESTIGE HIERARCHIES

Abstract
The ranking of occupational prestige in Taiwan is highly similar to that in the United States and the numerous other societies—both modernized and relatively non-modernized—in which such studies have been conducted. Previous explanations of this important cross-societal invariant, occupational prestige evaluation, have emphasized *common structural features* of any complex society, whether industrialized or not. It is not clear how this proposition can be empirically falsified. A more satisfactory explanation is sought in terms of *specific properties of occupational roles* in any society, viz., education, responsibility (or authority), and income. The relationship of each of these variables to prestige is analyzed with data from Taiwan, Denmark, and the United States.

Reprinted by permission of the publisher.

FIGURE 2.5B CLASSIFICATION OF VARIABLES IN RESEARCH

tion of data) where it is necessary to describe data accurately. Our main point here is that the scores one chooses to summarize contain certain kinds of information, and the manipulations and conclusions one is able to draw from them depend upon a clear understanding of their meaning. The results of statistical description do not contain any more information or meaning than the scores which were originally produced by measurement.

2.1.4 Roles Variables Play in Research

A third and crucial way in which variables differ from each other is in the use made of them in research. Usually two main categories of variables are distinguished: **independent** and **dependent** variables.

Frequently an investigator begins his research with a curiosity about the ways in which a certain variable fluctuates from case to case in a population. It is noted, for example, that some marriages last a long time and others last but a brief time; some persons have more power than others; some have more income than others; some are more respected; some organizations are more effective than others, and so on. The next question is usually: Why? Why does the variable vary as it seems to do? This then leads to explanations and predictions of the variation in one variable based on variations in other variables, and this eventually becomes the general substance of theory or scientific knowledge.

2.1.4a Dependent Variables. The variable of prime interest, the one whose variation is to be explained in the research, is called a **dependent** variable. Differences between scores on this variable are thought to depend upon certain other variables. Dependent variables are usually defined as those which are influenced by some other variable, but sometimes they are defined merely as the crucial variable whose variation an investigator is interested in examining.

2.1.4b Independent Variables. Independent variables are those which are thought to influence dependent variables; that is, they are explanatory variables which may help account for why a dependent variable fluctuates as it does in some population. If one thinks in cause/effect or influencer/influenced terms, as most people do who are interested in theory development, the relationships between independent and dependent variables are frequently expressed in terms of a directional arrow or path pointing from the independent variable at the left to the dependent variable at the right, as shown below.

An investigation of how to look at data to see whether this type of argument is reasonable will be one of the central purposes of this book. Some statistical procedures are meaningful only if we can clearly settle the role the variable plays in the research.

2.1.4c Intervening Variables. Referring back to the example of membership in organizations and powerlessness, cited at the beginning of this chapter, since powerlessness was the variable of central concern, and was thought to be influenced by other variables, it would clearly be the dependent variable. Whether or not an individual is a member of organized groups is then the independent variable, because it is seen as having an influence on the dependent variable. In fact, we could introduce a third variable from that study, namely, whether or not a society is a mass society. It is thought to have an effect on powerlessness which may be controlled or modified in important ways by organizational membership. This three-variable relationship could be shown as follows with organizational membership **intervening** between the other two variables:

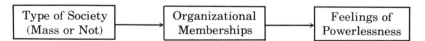

The role a variable plays in one piece of research may not be the same as the role it plays in another. For example, it may be reasonable to think about the influence of an individual's level of powerlessness at one point in time on the likelihood that he would join any group at a later point in time. In that research, the role of the variables would be just the opposite from the role they played in the Neal and Seeman study.

Research can be more complex in the sense of involving relationships between more than two or three variables. Often there are several independent (or dependent) variables, and not infrequently some variables intervene (and are called intervening variables for that reason) as illustrated in the three-variable example above and the five-variable example below.

Elder, in a study of marriage mobility of women from middle and working class families, hypothesized that the five variables shown below would all be related (Elder, 1969). Women in his sample were first rated on "attractiveness" and some other personal variables; "husband's occupational status" was measured in a re-interview several years later. In this study, "husband's occupational status" is the primary dependent variable, and the other four variables are inde-

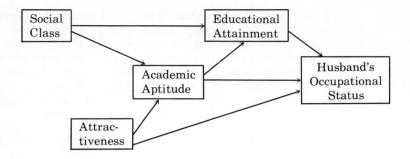

pendent variables which are thought to help explain or account for score differences on the dependent variable. One could focus on other pairs of variables, however. For example, "social class" is an independent variable with respect to the dependent variable, "educational attainment"; one could go further and speak of "educational attainment" as intervening between "social class" and "husband's occupational status." The diagram shown here in effect shows the theoretical relationships between variables which Elder believes exist, and his statistical analysis will be focused on the question of whether the data he examines behave as his model would predict they would.

Usually a great deal of clarity can be gained in reading a research report if one first draws out the relatonships hypothesized in the article in a fashion similar to that shown by Elder. The abstract presented at the beginning of most journal articles usually presents the model the investigator is considering. The important point here is that variables do play different roles in research; their role will generally determine the kinds of questions which are raised and, in turn, the kinds of statistical operations which are most appropriate in answering the questions.

2.2 MEASUREMENT IN SOCIOLOGY

The crucial role of measurement in sociology is becoming recognized, and there are a number of sociologists working on problems of how to measure significant variables adequately, how to move toward interval and ratio scales without leaving all sense behind, and how to actually carry out measurement of rapid-paced interaction on subjects who often are influenced by the measurement process itself. Bonjean, Hill, and McLemore in a recent assessment of measurement used in articles in main sociological journals between 1959 and 1963, found over 2,000 different scales were used in addition to the simple background information such as sex and age (Bonjean *et al.*, 1965). Most of the measures were defined as ordinal, and most also as continuous variables. No defined, standard unit of measurement was used, no zero points were defined for scales in most cases, and most of the measures were not extensively examined for validity and reliability. Measurement is clearly a first priority problem.

Statistical procedures, as we will show later on, aid a great deal both in focusing attention on the need for better measurement and in providing ways to assess the quality of measurement scales. With increased sophistication in statistics and with more investigators aware and concerned about the problem, it appears to us that some exciting and significant strides will be made in sociological measurement. We already have a number of measurement devices of impressive and demonstrated quality, and many, such as social class measures, have received repeated examination and improvement.* In a few sentences we would like to point out some of the issues and developments.

Because much of what sociology is interested in predicting and explaining turns out to be variable characteristics of people, interacting pairs, and the various groups people create and engage in, it is natural that individual people are among the most helpful sources of information. Much measurement in the past and present has involved **questioning** people. Particularly in the area of attitude research, this questioning has taken the form of batteries of questions which are then examined for consistency and combined into attitude scales. One of the problems with this approach is that people sometimes become aware of the purpose of the questions and specifically are influenced by this knowledge. In other cases, respondents are not particularly knowledgeable and simply do not know the answer to the questions that are asked. Where this is the case, alternative measurement procedures are pursued.

With the advent of the field of electronics, a number of devices have been invented which greatly aid the measurement process. One device, for example, involves a simple ten-key keyboard much like that on an adding machine. This is connected to a portable tape recorder and, by setting up numeric codes for categories of interaction, an investigator can make records of the type of interaction in group settings. The tape, of course, moves at a certain rate, and so the record permits an examination of the shuttle of interaction through time, in terms of meaningful variables. This permits a kind of observation of interaction that pencil and paper methods cannot achieve, of course, and with the improvement in equipment comes improvement in the quality of measurements.† A very interesting book about possible ways to solve the problem of "reactive" measurements, those which also influence the measurements taken, is *Unobtrusive Measures: Nonreactive Research In The Social Sciences*, by Webb and others (1966). Such measurement problems, of course, are evident in every area of inquiry.

Personal **observation** by a trained social scientist is another approach to measurement of sociological variables. In laboratory settings, of course, more control and more options for measurement are available, but many situations of interest either cannot be readily captured in a laboratory or cannot be artifically created. War might be an extreme example. On the other hand, some aspects of competition and conflict can be simulated, and sometimes this takes the form of

*For an inventory of sociological measures, see Bonjean *et al.*, (1967); for more specialized collections of measurement scales, see Shaw and Wright, (1967), and Price, (1972).

†Early instruments to do this in laboratory settings were developed by Bales at Harvard. The device described here is called "MIDCARS," and it was developed and refined by Richard Sykes and other sociologists at the University of Minnesota. The cassette tapes are converted to computer tape, and the computer is able to carry out the needed statistical analysis using programs written by the researchers. This is only one example of a number of technological developments which have impressive consequences for the quality of sociological measurement.

a respondent playing a carefully devised game where measurements have been built into the process of playing or scoring outcomes.

Records created in the normal process of agency operation, or especially created records from the U.S. Census or from vital statistics, for example, form the basis for much other measurement and research work. Unfortunately, many people think only of questionnaire research as the basic source of information for sociology, and one of the reasons this brief section is included now is to get you to think seriously about measurement possibilities and be sensitive to the issues and possibilities implied by different types of data.

2.2a Validity and Reliability. Regardless of the procedure by which a measurement is taken, the issue of quality of the procedure has to be resolved before statistical manipulation is useful or interpretable. The quality of measures is usually phrased in terms of two questions: (a) Is the procedure valid? and (b) Is the procedure reliable? **Validity** is usually taken to mean the extent to which a measurement process is able to make distinctions based (only) on the variable one intends to measure. Measurement procedures, for example, which measured family size by recording the number of people in a dwelling unit would be less valid to the extent that boarders, visitors, and domestic help are not identified and eliminated from the count.

There are several ways by which validity of a procedure can be checked. Generally these involve the use of some criterion measure and comparison of scores on this and the new measurement procedure. Statistical tools help in making these contrasts and comparisons.

The problem of **reliability** refers to the stability of the measurement process itself when applied under standard conditions. If there is a good deal of sloppiness in the measurement, then to that extent the measurement is unreliable. A classic example of an unreliable measurement instrument would be an elastic measuring tape which would be likely not to give the same reading upon repeated measurement of the same object (where the object itself is known not to have changed). One would have to separate simple change in the phenomenon under study from unreliability of a measurement instrument, of course, and again statistical procedures (often correlation coefficients, discussed in Chapter 7, or path coefficients, discussed in Chapter 9) are available to help in the evaluation of reliability.

Validity and reliability are linked. To the extent that a measurement is unreliable, it can not be said to be a valid measure of an intended variable. Again this relationship can be expressed in terms of statistical descriptions that will be developed in this volume. We will not develop the topic of validity and reliability at any great length here (that will be a main topic in a research methods course), but we will develop some of the elementary tools of thought which are helpful in handling these and other questions of inquiry.

2.3 SUMMARY

This chapter has dealt with the central problem of measurement. It is central because the scores we will be describing statistically are the result of a measurement process, and their meaning and quality depend upon what happens there. It is central too, because the information contained in scores helps determine what sorts of statistical summary are appropriate and how they can be interpreted. Finally, as sociologists, we are interested in making significant statements about the phenomena we find interesting, and that means we have a central concern for the ability of scores to capture the variations we intend to examine and feel are important.

The next chapter begins the more organized pursuit of statistics itself by showing the importance of comparison and the various ways comparisons may be made statistically. The next chapter will also establish some of the basic themes which serve to organize the whole field of sociological statistics.

CONCEPTS TO KNOW AND UNDERSTAND

measurement
level of measurement
   nominal
   ordinal
   interval
   ratio
scale continuity
   continuous variables
   discrete variables
role of variables in research
   dependent
   independent
   intervening
reliability

validity
inclusive
mutually exclusive
precision
grouping into classes
   class midpoint
   real limits
measurement
   to nearest whole unit
   to last whole unit
significant digits
rounding
concept
indicator

QUESTIONS AND PROBLEMS

1. Pick an interesting variable and define it (you may want to look up other definitions and critique them). Is it adequately defined and, if not, what difference does poor definition make, specifically? How can it actually be measured? What other variables might be used as independent or intervening variables with this variable? (Examples of variables might be alienation, urban segregation, age, social class, marital status, deviance, level of industrialization, social integration, or morale.)

2. By reviewing research articles, either in journals or as reprinted in workbook exercises for sociological statistics, you can find challenging ways to examine problems with variables.* First, you might pick out and classify variables in

*See H. J. Loether and D. G. McTavish, *Statistical Analysis For Sociologists: A Student Manual,* for useful exercises involving research variables.

abstracts of research reports in the sociological literature. It usually helps to read the entire article, too. Secondly, you might at this point pick out variables and begin to specify how you would prefer to measure and relate them to hypotheses in a study of your own.

GENERAL REFERENCES

Mueller, John H., Karl F. Schuessler, Herbert L. Costner, *Statistical Reasoning in Sociology,* Second Edition, (Boston, Houghton Mifflin), 1970.
Chapter 2 discusses social variables and their measurement.

Miller, Delbert C., *Handbook of Research Design and Social Measurement*, (New York, David McKay), 1970.
This book provides compact summaries of various facets of research and statistics. Part I includes an outline of steps in typical research projects and Part III includes comments on statistical analysis. The book also includes a sampling of scales used to measure sociological variables.

Lieberman, Bernhardt, *Contemporary Problems in Statistics: A Book of Readings for the Behavioral Sciences*, (New York, Oxford University Press), 1971.
A reader, this book includes in Section 1 a number of articles on measurement. The article by S. S. Stevens is included, as well as more detailed treatments of problems and possibilities in measuring.

OTHER REFERENCES

Bonjean, Charles M., Richard J. Hill, and S. Dale McLemore, "Continuities in Measurement, 1959–1963," *Social Forces,* 43 (March, 1965), p 532–536.

Bonjean, Charles M., Richard J. Hill, and S. Dale McLemore, *Sociological Measurement: An Inventory of Scales and Indices*, (San Francisco, Chandler Publishing Company), 1967.

Burke, Cletus J., "Measurement Scales and Statistical Models," Chapter 7 in Bernhardt Lieberman, *Contemporary Problems in Statistics: A Book of Readings for the Behavioral Sciences*, (New York, Oxford University Press), 1971.

Duncan, Otis Dudley, and Jay W. Artis, "Some Problems of Stratification Research," *Rural Sociology*, 16 (March, 1951), p 17–29.

Elder, Glen H., Jr., "Appearance and Education In Marriage Mobility," *American Sociological Review*, 34 (August, 1969), p 519–533.

Festinger, Leon, and Daniel Katz, *Research Methods in the Behavioral Sciences*, (New York, Holt, Rinehart and Winston), 1953. Chapter 11 by Clyde H. Coombs, is entitled, "Theory and Methods of Social Measurement."

Hamblin, Robert L., "Ratio Measurement for the Social Sciences," *Social Forces*, 50 (December, 1971), p 191–206.

Jones, Bryan D., and Richard Shorter, "The Ratio Measurement of Social Status: Some Cross-Cultural Comparisons," *Social Forces* 50 (June, 1972), p 499–511.

Labovitz, Sanford, "The Assignment of Numbers to Rank Order Categories," *American Sociological Review*, 35 (June, 1970), p 515–524.

Neal, Arthur G., and Melvin Seeman, "Organizations and Powerlessness: A Test of the Mediation Hypothesis," *American Sociological Review*, 29 (April, 1964), p 216–226.

Price, James L., *Handbook of Organizational Measurement,* (Lexington, Mass., D. C. Heath and Company), 1972.

Robinson, Richard, *Definition*, (London, Oxford University Press), 1954.

Shaw, Marvin E., and Jack M. Wright, *Scales for the Measurement of Attitudes*, (New York, McGraw-Hill Book Company), 1967.

Stevens, S. S., "On the Theory of Scales of Measurement," *Science*, 103 (1946), p 677–680.

Vargo, Louis G., Donald G. Schweitzer, Lawrence S. Mayer, and Sanford Labovitz, "Replies and Comments," *American Sociological Review*, 36 (June, 1971), p 517–522.

Webb, Eugene J., Donald T. Campbell, Richard D. Schwartz, and Lee Sechrest, *Unobtrusive Measures: Nonreactive Research In The Social Sciences*, (Chicago, Rand McNally), 1966.

DESCRIPTIVE STATISTICS:
ONE VARIABLE

3

THE BASIC LOGIC
OF VALID COMPARISON

Not long ago, an advertisment proclaimed that a major brand of cigarettes had 16 percent less tar and nicotine. While we probably could agree that less is better than more, the ad clearly goes on to suggest that because of this, the specific brand advertised is better than other cigarettes in this respect. Such an extension of the argument is, of course, inappropriate given only this evidence. The reason? Comparison information is not given. The 16 percent figure can not be interpreted. Does this brand have less tar and nicotine than it did formerly? Is this 16 percent less than the cigarette with the next least tar? Is it merely 16 percent less than the average of all tobacco products, or 16 percent less than the cigarette with the most tar? Even with the 16 percent drop, we do not know whether the levels of tar and nicotine are at a dangerous level or not, and there is no information which would permit one to judge the accuracy of the figure itself.

The problem is that a comparison is implied, but only half of the comparative information is given. Without some standard or something specified with which to compare the 16 percent, little can be concluded from this information.

This kind of problem confronts nearly everyone, whether sociologist or lawyer or layman. We are nearly always faced with comparative problems which call for some way to make a clear and valid contrast between things we want to compare. Is a figure of 9.9 percent of the population in the 65-and-older age bracket (as it was in the U.S. in 1970) a high or a low figure? A major university has a staff with 6.6 percent who are from minority groups. Does this indicate discrimination or not? In each case, comparative information is needed to reach a conclusion.

Appropriate comparisons are central to any inquiry, as the following illustrations suggest.

Do radio and television reports of National election results from the east coast influence voting behavior on the west coast where the polls close later? A sample of California voters was interviewed the day before and immediately after the 1964 Presidential elections. Among those voting after the eastern polls closed, [and] who were exposed to election broadcasts of eastern poll outcomes, 97 percent reported voting for Johnson, the eventual landslide winner. Among late voters who did not hear the broadcasts, 96 percent reported voting for Johnson; [this is] a comparison suggesting that eastern election victory reports had little overall effect on the later vote outcome. (Mendelsohn, 1966.)

Where does the after-tax, personal income go? In 1955, 27 percent of the total went to the tenth of the populaton with the highest incomes and 1 percent of the total went to the tenth of the population with the lowest incomes, an outcome generally predictable from social stratification theory. (Kolko, 1962.)

Presently, the birth rate in Africa is approximately 47 births per 1,000 population, compared to 38 for Asia and 18 for Europe. (Population Ref. Bur., 1971:6.)

"Do you think everyone should have the right to criticize the government, even if the criticism is damaging to our national interests?" In a 1970 national survey, 61 percent of the college graduates said "yes," 44 percent with a highschool degree said "yes" and 28 percent with a grade school education said "yes." The higher the education, overall, the higher the percentage of "yes" responses. (Erskine, 1970:491.)

Among those 16 to 24 years old who were enrolled in high school or college in 1969, 6.5 percent were married. In this age bracket, 51 percent of those not enrolled in school were married. (U.S. Bur. Census, 1971: Series P-23.)

The percent illiterate in the U.S. dropped from 20 percent in 1870 to 11 percent in 1900 to 4 percent in 1930 and to 1 percent in 1969. (U.S. Bur. Census, 1971: Series P-20.)

A midwestern congressman who regularly polls some 150,000 households in his district revealed that the top-rank public concern was inflation and the cost of living, followed by concern for the Vietnam war and unemployment. The year before (1970) pollution was the number-one concern. (*Contact*, 1971.)

Does ordinal position in the family have an influence on potential scientific creativity? No, according to Lois-Ellin Datta, who studied a group of male high school seniors who competed in the 1963 Westinghouse Science Talent Search. Average creativity ratings for oldest boys was 6.1 on her scale and it was 6.0 for youngest boys. Other factors, however, influenced average rankings of both oldest and youngest boys. (Datta, 1968.)

Throughout these examples you will notice that there is a heavy emphasis upon comparison as the basis on which questions are posed and answered. These examples also indicate several ways in which comparisons can be made. At this point, two questions arise. First, for a camparison to be valid, *what* should be compared, and secondly, *how* should a comparison be made?

3.1 KINDS OF COMPARISONS

The answer to the question, "What should be compared?" depends largely on what one is interested in studying. A clearly stated question or research problem is basic to all comparisons. Without a clearly formulated problem, it is difficult to decide which of the myriad possible comparisons one should make and how it should be interpreted. Comparisons are aided if variables are carefully formulated and measured, and if objects to be measured are clearly and consistently identified so that comparable groups can be contrasted. Problems of theory, conceptualization, measurement, and research design cannot be over emphasized in statistics, although they are usually reserved as topics for a course in research methods. Here we will repeatedly call attention to these issues; you may want to read about some of them in a more systematic research methods text as well.*

In general, comparisons are made (a) *between groups* (group-group comparisons), either within the same study or in different studies, (b) *between a group and an individual* from that group (group-individual comparisons), or (c) *between study outcomes and standards* which have been established by previous research or are predictions derived from a formal model or theory the investigator is interested in testing.

3.1.1 Group-Group Comparisons

Group-group comparisons might be made between an experimental group that has been given some type of special treatment, such as a new instructional program, and a control group which has not had special treatment.† Comparisons could also be made between groups which have different characteristics but are from the same population, such as old versus young people or males versus females. Different contrasted groups might also represent different populations, such as a cross-cultural study where different societies are compared or an urban study where regions of a city (central city and suburbs) are contrasted. Which groups one compares depends to some degree, of course, on what problem one is studying. If the problem at hand is whether there is a difference in reactions to stress by men and women, then comparisons of stress-scores between sex groupings would clearly be the relevant contrast. The problem then becomes the statistical one of summarizing the stress-scores for each sex group so that the two summaries can be compared. In each instance, the groups that are compared are themselves composed of a number of scores measured on a series of definable cases or objects. Groupings could consist of measurements made on cases other than individual people, of course, such as groups of different kinds of organizations, or different kinds of dyads, or different types of encounters between people and organizations.

*An excellent research methods text which examines the design logic of several of the classic sociological studies is by Riley (1963).
†Contrasts which are set up so that some subjects are assigned to an experimental group and some to control groups are usually discussed under the topic "experimental design." See Stouffer (1950) for a good reference to study design which introduces some alternatives.

3.1.2 Group-Individual Comparisons

Another kind of comparison is between a group and an individual who is a part of the group itself. Examples of individual-group comparisons would be a contrast of one person's grade in a course with the average grade for his class, or the increase in cost of living in one city compared to an overall, national average cost-of-living rise. Ranking states by the percentage of their population in institutions provides a somewhat different way to express where an individual unit (a state) falls in comparison to others in a group. The Coleman report cited in the first chapter compares test scores for specific minority groups with overall test outcomes, and in almost every grade studied, and for almost every minority group, average test scores were lower than overall, national test outcomes.

3.1.3 Study Outcome versus Standard Comparisons

Finally, there are comparisons in which data one has collected in a study are contrasted with some outside standard. Outside standards come from a number of sources. For example, one might have past data with which to compare some new information, such as comparisons between the percentage of males in a sample one has just drawn as against the percentage of males found in the latest census figures for that sampled area. Comparisons may be made between a study in a new setting as against a previous study in a similar group. Theory provides a powerful source of expectations or standards for comparison. Social stratification theory suggests that lower-class individuals will be relatively deprived (have poorer "life-chances") on many of the characteristics the society values, as compared to upper-class individuals. Population models of the transition of societies from non-industrial to industrial predict a change from high birth and death rates to low birth and death rates, and a resulting change in the age distribution and rate of growth of the society. One could compare changes in a society over time, with such model expectations to see if the theory of population transition works out as expected, or whether some modification or qualification in the theory needs to be made. Clearly, the more carefully thought out the standard and the more precisely it permits predictions to be made, the more interesting and useful it is to compare study data with the standard. This, in fact, is one of the main reasons why sociological theory is so important as a context for learning statistical reasoning.

Some time ago, Samuel Stouffer suggested the theory of "intervening opportunity," according to which the number of persons who make a move of a given distance is directly proportional to the number of opportunities at that distance, and inversely proportional to the number of intervening opportunities. Does this theory apply to the number of people who travel a given distance in the selection of marriage mates? A study could be designed in which the premarital residence of married partners is plotted on a map, and then the number of available partners of equivalent social class, ethnicity, education, and religion at that point and in intervening regions between the two partner's premarital residences is calculated. If the theory holds, the number of partners whose eventual spouses lived greater distances apart should decrease as intervening oppor-

TABLE 3.1 Number of Inmates of Care and Custodial Institutions for States Classified as Rural or Urban, U.S. Census, 1970 (In Thousands)*

Rural States	Urban States	
10	78	
8	~~1100~~ 11	
5	34	
124	219	
51	59	
60	106	
51	111	
37	86	
48	40	
9	9	
10	60	
22	113	
31	23	
5	12	
46	7	
14	3	
48	210	
22	4	
48		
26		
34		
31		
16	*Total Inmates*	
20	Rural States	933
33	Urban States	1185
37	All States	2118
8		
6		
3		
6		
38		
24		
2		

Source: U.S. Bur. Census, 1971: PC(V1)-1 and PC(V2)-1.
*An "urban" state is defined as one with 73.5 percent or more of its population residing in urban areas. This figure is the percent of the people in the U.S. who reside in urban areas. Other states are classified as "rural" in this example.

tunities for marital partners are increased, and there should be an increase in longer moves as the number of potential partners at a given distance increases relative to intervening marital opportunities. This is an example of comparison between a study outcome and outcomes which would be predicted from a theoretical statement.

3.1.4 An Example of Comparison Operations

Suppose we start with a small study in which we are interested in the institutionalized **population** of certain states. The institutional solution to problems of care and custody might be expected to be related to a more urbanized style of life with greater density of population, greater mobility of families, more specialization of jobs, and bureaucratization. Rural states might be expected to make less use of institutions as a solution to care and custody problems of the handicapped, homeless children, old people, and the various categories of deviants, because families and neighbors are more readily available alternatives to institutional custodial care. Given this formulation it is clear that rural-urban groups are to be *compared* on number of inmates in institutions.

Table 3.1 provides a list of 1970 data on the number of inmates of custodial and care institutions for all 50 states and the District of Columbia. Rural states are defined here as those states with less than 73.5 percent (the overall national percentage) of their people living in urban areas. The variable, "number of *inmates of institutions*" is defined as a discrete, ratio variable measured to the nearest one-thousand persons for each state on a scale that begins with zero.

First of all, before we proceed with our comparison example, we have to be alert to the possibility of error in the data. The number of inmates in the second score in the urban column is for Rhode Island, which has a total population of 946,725 so clearly it could not have over a million inmates of institutions! Upon checking, we would find the last two zeros were a clerical error. The number should have been 11 (thousands) rather than 1100 (thousands). We do not know if there was bias in the original data gathering operation. The data came from a source which is usually reliable and careful. One should keep in mind that the data are for 1970 and that this may have been an unusual year. Since the results of a comparison depend upon the quality of the original data, it is always worthwhile to check carefully for accuracy.

Although differences between rural and urban states are probably more accurately known when the actual figure for number of inmates is known than when one bases a comparison only on the impressions of an investigator who traveled around visiting institutions, the cause of comparison is still not greatly served by a list of scores such as those in Table 3.1. It is clear that without some type of ordering of even this small amount of data one could not say, in general, how much difference there is between rural and urban states. Certainly if more variables were measured or if there were more cases (*i.e.* if we measured counties rather than states), as there usually are in sociological studies, the problem of drawing a conclusion would be greatly compounded. Our first task, then, is to develop some of the basic ways to go about the task of making valid comparisons.

3.2 BASIC COMPARISON OPERATIONS

There are many procedures available for making comparisons. The field of descriptive statistics takes as one of its central problems that of the development of techniques for making valid comparisons among collections of quantitative data. In this chapter we will develop some of the basic ways data can be organized, and we will explore some of the summary indices which can be used in making comparisons. Chapter 4 will deal with graphic means for analyzing contrasts of interest to us, and later chapters will move toward more general and searching procedures for describing quantitative information in ways which facilitate valid comparisons the researcher or citizen wants to make.

There are two general operations which are usually involved in comparisons: One is the organization of scores into some convenient form or distribution, and the other is the arithmetic manipulation of scores, usually by means of subtraction and/or division. You will find that the division idea, the creation of a ratio of one number (numerator) to another (denominator), is one of the basic organizing themes of descriptive and inferential statistics. The problem is, of course, what to divide into what! The remaining part of this chapter is a discus-

TABLE 3.2 SCORES FROM TABLE ONE IN AN ARRAY, SEPARATELY FOR RURAL AND URBAN STATES

Rural States (N=33)		Urban States (N=18)
2	Lowest Score	3
3		4
5		7
5		9
6		11
6		12
8		23
8		34
9		40
10		59
10		60
14		78
16		86
20		106
22		111
22		113
24		210
26		219
31		
31		
33		
34		
37		
37		
38		
46		
48		
48		
48		
51		
51		
60		
124	Highest Score	

Source: U.S. Bur. Census, 1971: PC(V1)-1 and PC(V2)-1.

sion of these basic comparison operations, and you will find that they underlie most of the concepts in this book.

3.2.1 Organization of Scores

An unordered listing or accumulation of scores, as in Table 3.1, is relatively useless in itself for comparison purposes simply because it does not communicate the information that is there in a way that permits a focused contrast. Somewhat more helpful is an ordered list of scores, called an **array,** shown in Table 3.2. If scores are punched in hollerith cards,* an array would be created by sorting the cards into order from lowest number of inmates to the highest number of inmates. This ordering makes evident where one group starts and stops as compared to

---

BOX 3.1 MAIN POINTS IN THE ARGUMENT

The first chapter introduced some of the important concepts of the language of statistics such as "variable," "statistical observation," and "sample." Chapter 2 emphasized the importance of knowing something about the scores one has generated from a measurement process; also, the distinctions between "level of measurement," "scale continuity," and "independent" and "dependent" variables were discussed. At that point we were ready to make use of these ideas in sociological research.

The first part of this chapter emphasizes the point that almost all research involves some kind of comparison (three general kinds of comparison were noted). Now, the problem is how to set up a valid comparison. We have just introduced the first (relatively simple-minded) approach to comparison—make a list of scores. Next, we will talk about the very *important idea of creating distributions* of scores (three general kinds of distributions will be discussed plus some of the problems associated with their creation and meaning). Finally, in this chapter, we will discuss several kinds of ratios which are very valuable statistical tools for summarizing data and making valid comparisons.

The next two chapters will carry the theme started here. Chapter 4 will discuss graphic means for making comparisons, an all-too-frequently underrated approach, and Chapter 5 will discuss ways to summarize whole distributions of scores by using some selected index numbers. Chapter 5 depends rather heavily upon your understanding of the notion of "distributions," which we are about to begin here.

---

*A hollerith card is the standard punched card used in computer analysis. It has 80 columns, numbered from left to right, and each column has 12 possible punch positions. These are used for indicating the numbers 0 through 9, and letters are coded by punching two places in a single column. Some special characters are coded with three punches in a single column. The "hollerith" card got its name from Herman Hollerith (1860–1929) who developed a punch-card system used for vital statistics in Baltimore in 1887 and in the 1890 U.S. Census. Work in punch card processing can be pursued further in a statistics workbook, (such as Loether and McTavish, *Statistical Analysis for Sociologists: A Student Manual*).

BOX 3.2 SYMBOL NOTATION IN THIS BOOK

At this point a number of useful symbols are being introduced to simplify some often-used statistical expressions. Your attention is called to the following frequently used symbols.

N refers to sample size (the number of cases). An example of its use is in Table 3.3c.

X_i refers to a single score, the ith score. In grouped distributions it refers to the midpoint of a class, and these two uses will be clear from the context in which they are used. Sometimes, for simplicity, the subscript is dropped and only X is used.

f_i refers to the frequency in the ith category of a frequency distribution.

$\sum_{i=1}^{N}$ this is the *summation* operator. It instructs one to add up whatever is listed after the symbol. *Limits* of the summation operator are given below and above Σ (the capital Greek letter Sigma). In the instance shown above, the limits are where i equals one and where i equals N.

A comparable summation operation, expressed as $\Sigma_{i=1}^{k} f_i = N$ merely instructs one to add up frequency of cases in each of the k categories of a distribution, starting with the first category ($i = 1$) and stopping after all k category frequencies have been summed. This is a more elaborate way of symbolizing what is meant by N. $\Sigma_{i=1}^{N} X_i$ would symbolize the operation of adding up raw scores (X_i), starting at the first score in a list ($i = 1$) and ending when all N scores had been summed. Sometimes, in statistical notation, the limits of the summation operator are omitted because they almost always require addition over *all* the N scores. We will generally follow this practice, but we will include limits on the summation operator when they seem needed for clarity.

other groups, and by close examination one might be able to discern the general concentration of scores in the array. One could, for example, locate the score in the middle (later we will refer to this score as the 50th percentile or median) and gain some idea of the distance between the lowest and highest scores (later we will refer to this as the crude range). If the scores are on a nominal variable, simple clustering of like scores together would be analogous to an array of ordinal or interval/ratio scores.

At this point the process of organizing data for the purpose of comparison has to stop, *unless* we are prepared to lose or de-emphasize some detail in order to highlight or present some interesting characteristic. This is, in fact, usually a desirable step to take, since we usually want to make a comparison of scores in some particular respect rather than compare all of the raw scores with each other in various groups. In fact, one of the keys to valid comparison is to be selective in eliminating from the comparison those things which are distracting or contaminating as far as the comparison of interest is concerned. One of the important points beginning investigators sometimes forget is that irrelevant information, no matter how precise and accurate, is not only *not* positively worthwhile, but it is often a distinct handicap to making clear comparisons and drawing correct conclusions.

3.2.2 Grouping Scores into Classes

One of the procedures by which raw scores are further organized is that of creating a series of categories and then grouping the scores into these categories. Sometimes very little information is lost in the process. For example, if marital status were measured (Table 3.3(a) lists scores on marital status for 16 respondents) and a category system such as that in Table 3.3(b) were created, no information is lost by classifying the raw data in 3.3(a) into these categories. Clearly the "4" indicates that there were four subjects with the same "score"; that is, they

TABLE 3.3 Creating a Distribution of Data: An Example

(a) Raw Data on a marital status question asked of 16 adults.

Married	Single	No response
Single	Separated	Separated
Single	Divorced	Married
Divorced	Widowed	Married
Single	Single	Separated
Married		

(b) Frequency Distribution of the scores from 3.3(a) above.

Score Categories	Frequency of Cases in Each Score Category
Single	5
Married	4
Widowed	1
Separated	3
Divorced	2
No Response	1
Total Cases	16

(c) Grouped Frequency Distribution (Widowed, Separated and Divorced from Table 3.3(b) above have been grouped into a single category called "other").

X_i	f_i
Single	5
Married	4
Other	6
No Response	1
	$N = 16$

were each married. If we group the categories of marital status further, such as in Table 3.3(c), we have lost some information about whether some of the six respondents in the "other" category are widowed, divorced or separated. All we know from 3.3(c) is that there were six who were either divorced or widowed or separated. The organization of scores in (b) and (c) are called *frequency distributions*, a topic discussed in the next section. First, a note on "non-response."

The "non-response" category poses some problems. Clearly it is not a marital status, but just as clearly it is a type of result of the measurement process involved in measuring marital status. Usually, non-response is considered to reflect on the quality of the measurement procedures (and thus, most investigators take great pains to keep the rate of non-response very low and double-check possible biases which non-responses may create in the analysis of data), and non-responses would be reported in a footnote to a table rather than being included as a separate category of the variable being statistically summarized. On the other hand, one could be interested in studying non-responses, in which case this category would be included in statistical analysis. The fact that some groups (*e.g.* older people) are more likely than others to respond with "no response," is one of the factors a thoughtful investigator considers carefully in making statistical summaries.

3.2.3 Distributions

There are three types of distributions which are commonly used to organize data further. These are: (a) a frequency distribution, (b) a percentage distribution, and (c) cumulative frequency or percentage distributions.

3.2.3a Frequency Distributions In creating **frequency distributions,** we first list score categories and then tally up the number of cases which fall in each category.* Diagram 3.1 below lists some of the main rules for creating a frequency distribution. Any one of the frequencies in the "f" column is called a **cell frequency,** or category frequency, and is symbolized by the small letter f or f_i where the subscript i refers to the i-th class of the variable. The total number of cases is simply the sum of the frequency column and is symbolized by the letter N (or Σf_i).

While category labels for nominal variables are quite explicit (as in Table 3.3(b), for example) those for continuous variables need further explanation. Categories for the age distribution below, for example, are expressed in terms of a unit of measurement, in this case, "one-year" units. If age is measured to the

---

*A "tally" is created by putting a mark beside the category into which a score is to be classified for each score as one moves through a list of raw scores. It is usually a good idea to move systematically through a list of scores rather than jump around in an attempt to count all scores of a certain value, since this usually leads to fewer clerical errors. The following would be a tally of scores from which Table 3.3b was created.

   IHI Single
   IIII Married
     I Widowed
   III Separated
   II Divorced
    I No Response

AGE OF STUDENTS IN A CLASS

Age (Nearest Year)	Real Limits	f_i
11	10.5 – 11.5	3
12	11.5 – 12.5	6
13	12.5 – 13.5	9
14	13.5 – 14.5	4
		$N = 22$

nearest whole year, however, the three people in the 11-year-old class could have had ages between 10.5 and 11.5. We do not know what their exact age is but we know, if this has been accurately done, that they are nearer to 11 years old than they are to 12 or 10. The **real limits** (also called class boundaries and symbolized by L_i for lower real limit and U_i for upper real limit) of category 11 are 10.5 and 11.5, as discussed in Chapter 2. Eleven is, thus, the **midpoint** (symbolized by X_i) of a category which potentially covers a range of scores. For the purposes of further summary work, we use the value of the class midpoint to stand for the scores in that class. The **class width** (also called the **interval width** and symbolized by the small letter w_i) is one-year, the difference between the real limits of that class. Each category has real limits which extend half of one unit (here the unit is one-year) above and half a unit below the expressed limits of the class.

The problem of classification of age scores is handled for the investigator by rounding rules discussed in Chapter 2.

Sometimes a frequency distribution is *grouped* into fewer categories for ease of presentation. The distribution of age, above, might be grouped as follows:

Age in Years (Expressed Limits)	f_i	Class Midpoint X_i	Real Limits
11–12	9	11.5	10.5 – 12.5
13–14	13	13.5	12.5 – 14.5
	$N = 22$		

Here again, since the unit of measurement is one year of age, and measurement is to the *nearest* whole unit (year), the real limits extend one half of one unit (half a year in this case) on either side of the *expressed* category limits. The interval width is again the difference between real limits for a class, and in this example both classes have a width of 2 years.

(3.1)
$$w_i = U_i - L_i$$
$$2 = 12.5 - 10.5$$

Notice that the wider the categories become, the greater the loss of detailed information about specific scores. Again, the scores in each category are known by their midpoints, which can be found by adding half the interval width to the lower real limit of a class, as follows:

(3.2)
$$X_i = L_i + \frac{w_i}{2}$$

The midpoint of a class is referred to by the symbol X_i where i refers to the specific category being considered. This is the same symbol used for a raw score; but notice that, when data are grouped, the most reasonable single value to use for that raw score is the midpoint of the class into which it is classified. The X_i stands for "score" — raw scores where these are available; class midpoints where they are not. The usage is always clear in context. For the first class in the grouped frequency distribution above, the midpoint is $(10.5 + 2/2 = 10.5 + 1.0 = 11.5)$.

BOX 3.3   AN EXCEPTION IN CLASS LIMITS

The important exception to this class interval procedure is where measurement is to the *last* whole unit (rather than the *nearest* whole unit), a frequently used way of measuring age. The difference this makes in category midpoints and limits is discussed in Section 2.1.3c.

   While grouping is frequently helpful to summarize information, it also poses some problems, or may pose problems, depending upon how the scores are distributed within categories, and upon the number of categories that are distinguished. The frequency distribution in Table 3.4a includes a set of 17 scores classified in a six-category distribution, each category width being one unit. The third column in Table 3.4(a) (headed fX_i or f_i times X_i) shows the total of the scores within each class. In the "1" category, for example, there are ten scores, each with the value of 1 (the midpoint of that class). The total or sum of these scores would be 1 times 10, or 10. There are two scores with the value 2 in the distribution, so the total of these scores would be $2 \times 2 = 4$, and so forth. If we add up the third column we would get the total of all of the 17 scores, and this value is 40 (also symbolized as ΣfX or the sum of the f times X column). Notice that the interval width is 1 for each category in this distribution.

   Now, let us group these same scores into three categories instead of six. Each category will have a width of 2 rather than 1. The cell frequencies would be combined from cell frequencies in Table 3.4a, and they would still total to 17 cases, because we are not adding cases. The total value of the 17 scores (ΣfX) in Table 3.4b appears to differ from the same data classified into six categories in 3.4a.

   We are again using the class midpoint as the value which stands for each of the scores in a category. The product of the midpoint and the category frequency (fX) yields the total of the scores which fall in that class. Twelve scores with an assumed value of 1.5 is a total of 18.0, for example. The sum of the fX column is the total of all scores. Notice that this figure is not equal to 40, the sum of the fX column in the distribution in 3.4a. Finally, let us group the original six categories into only two, with a width of three years of age, shown in Table 3.4c. Here the total of the scores appears to be 46.0 rather than 43.5 or 40.0. The difference is called **grouping error,** and it occurs because the midpoints of classes in this example do not adequately represent the value of the cases which fall in each class. The midpoint 2, for the 1–3 class in Table 3.4c, includes 10 scores of 1, 2 scores of

TABLE 3.4 An Example of Grouping Error

(a)

X_i	f_i	fX_i	$w=1$
1	10	10	
2	2	4	
3	1	3	
4	0	0	
5	1	5	
6	3	18	
$N=17$		$40=\Sigma fX_i$	

(b)

Class	X_i	f_i	fX_i	$w=2$
1–2	1.5	12	18.0	
3–4	3.5	1	3.5	
5–6	5.5	4	22.0	
	$N=17$		$43.5=\Sigma fX_i$	

(c)

Class	X_i	f_i	fX_i	$w=3$
1–3	2	13	26	
4–6	5	4	20	
	$N=17$		$46=\Sigma fX_i$	

2, and 1 score of 3, and simply does not reflect the value of the scores in that class very well. Ideally, the cases in a class would be distributed rather uniformly across the interval. For this reason, especially where further computation is to occur, statisticians prefer a larger number of categories (such as 10, 15, or 20, depending on their purposes) or better yet, the raw scores themselves. Where grouping occurs, categories should be set up with some care and sensitivity to the way class midpoints reflect the value of cases in the class.* Other rules for creating frequency distributions are more a matter of convenience. Some useful guidelines are listed in Diagram 3.1.

The frequency distribution is exceedingly helpful in summarizing scores, partly because one can gain a sense of the way scores are spread over a scale, and partly because this distribution is often used as a basis for computing other summary measures. Later in this book we will avoid using grouped distributions as a basis for presenting other summary statistics, and instead will give only the raw-score form of these summary measures. It should be clear from the discussion above that we could readily convert raw-score formulas to formulas for grouped

---

*It probably goes without saying that statistical tools which have power to summarize data to facilitate comparison also are capable of summarizing errors and distorting comparisons if they are not appropriately used. The grouping error shown in Table 3.4, for example, comes about in spite of the fact that there are no technical errors in creating those frequency distributions. If one wanted to over-emphasize the total scores one could, of course, present only Table 3.4c, thereby misrepresenting the data and misleading the reader. Improper presentation of data can come out of inexperience as well as intention. A very nice presentation of some of the ways people inadvertently or intentionally give a distorted picture is in the book *How To Lie With Statistics* by Huff (1954).

data if we remember that class midpoints stand for each score in a class, and so instead of summing up the scores themselves we have to multiply class midpoints by class frequencies before summing. The reason we are going to drop grouped formulae for the most part is that the logic behind statistical reasoning can be presented quite nicely with raw scores, and most investigators and students have access to computers where programs typically accept raw-score rather than grouped data.

Table 3.5 presents frequency distributions of the data in our previous example in Table 3.1 on number of institutional inmates in various states. Notice that the frequency distributions for rural and urban states shown in Table 3.5

TABLE 3.5 DISTRIBUTIONS OF STATES ON NUMBER OF INMATES OF CARE AND CUSTODIAL INSTITUTIONS BY RURAL AND URBAN STATES, U.S. CENSUS, 1970, NUMBERS IN 1000's

(a) *Rural States*

Number of Inmates in Thousands	Frequency	Percent	Cumulative Frequency	Cumulative Percent
0–24	17	51.5	17	51.5
25–49	12	36.4	29	87.9
50–74	3	9.1	32	97.0
75–99	0	0.0	32	97.0
100–124	1	3.0	33	100.0
125–149	0	0	33	100.0
150–174	0	0	33	100.0
175–199	0	0	33	100.0
200–224	0	0	33	100.0
Totals	33	100.0 (33)		

(b) *Urban States*

Number of Inmates in Thousands	Frequency	Percent	Cumulative Frequency	Cumulative Percent
0–24	7	38.9	7	38.9
25–49	2	11.1	9	50.0
50–74	2	11.1	11	61.1
75–99	2	11.1	13	72.2
100–124	3	16.7	16	88.9
125–149	0	0	16	88.9
150–174	0	0	16	88.9
175–199	0	0	16	88.9
200–224	2	11.1	18	100.0
Totals	18	100.0 (18)		

Source: Data from Table 3.1.

DIAGRAM 3.1   Creating Distributions

THE PROBLEM

To organize raw data (separate scores) into a frequency distribution or percentage distribution which accurately reflects the data.

1. *Setting Up Classes.*

   If the data are to be used for *further statistical computation* it is best to either (a) use the raw data rather than create a distribution (computers are helpful in reducing the clerical problems in handling raw scores), or (b) preserve a relatively large number of classes (such as 10 to 15 or more). If the data are for *presentation* only, then fewer classes may be used and the problem is one of setting up classes which accurately portray main differences of importance in the data. Often this takes the form of an interest in grouping classes together so that minor differences are eliminated (the jaggedness of most distributions) and a more smoothed-looking distribution is shown.

   a.) *Select the number of categories* you want to use. Usually this should be more than two and probably no more than fifteen, depending on the purpose of the distribution (see point b, above). Five to ten is a useful range. Call this k.

   b.) *Find the interval size needed.* An approximation can be found by:

   $$w = \frac{(\text{highest score}) - (\text{lowest score})}{k}$$

   and take the nearest integer. This is the interval width, w. An odd number for w is preferred because then class midpoints can be arranged so that they are integers, but often this aid to hand computation is not necessary. Widths of multiples of 1, 2, 3, 5, or 10 are common.

   c.) *Set up categories.* Start with a lower limit for the lowest class which is (a) equal or less than the smallest score, and (b) preferably (traditionally) is some multiple of the selected class width, w. For example, if the class width was 5, one might begin the lowest class with some value such as zero, 5, 10, 15, etc. Thus the lower limit of each successive class is a multiple of the class width. It is generally preferred to have classes all of the same width although sometimes this rule is broken particularly where class frequencies are very small for large parts of the scale. It is also pru-

DIAGRAM 3.1 *(Continued)*

dent practice to create categories (especially if later statistical computation is to be carried out) so that there is a specified upper and lower limit for each class including the extreme ones. For presentation purposes sometimes the extreme classes are left "open" (*e.g.* 65 and over), but this practice makes it impossible to determine a class midpoint and thus makes the computation of some of the statistics discussed in Chapter 5 impossible.

d.) *Check the categories* to see if they accurately reflect the data they are to contain. That is, does the set of class midpoints fairly accurately reflect the balance of cases in the classes? Ideally, the sum of raw scores would equal the sum of class midpoints times class frequencies for interval-level variables, where this check is appropriate. If there is gross distortion, reset class limits, change (increase, usually) the number of classes, or change (decrease, usually) the class width.

2. *Group Cases Into Classes.*

If a computer or sorter is not available, the easiest and most accurate way to classify scores in categories is to create a "tally." Be sure to move systematically through the list of scores, tallying each score by making a tally-mark in the appropriate category rather than skipping around through the data to find identical scores.

3. *Creating The Desired Kind of Distribution.*

Most kinds of distributions are created from an initial frequency distribution, so the frequency distribution should be totaled and checked for accuracy.

a.) *Percentage distribution.* Divide each class frequency in a frequency distribution by the total number of scores, and multiply each result by 100. When this kind of distribution is presented, it is good practice to include N, the total number of scores upon which the percentage is based, in brackets or parentheses below the total of the percentages.

b.) *Cumulative distributions.* Beginning with the lowest-value score category (traditionally), create a cumulative column by entering the class frequency of the lowest class next to that class, the total of the frequencies for the lowest two classes next to the second-lowest class, etc. In the case of a cumulative percentage distribution, the percentage distribution entries are accumulated. The last class (highest score category) should have N or 100 percent entered next to it.

allow us to get a much better picture of the distribution of scores than did the raw data in Table 3.1 or the array in Table 3.2. Here it is apparent that the urban states are less concentrated in the low-number-of-inmates categories, for example.*

3.2.3b Percentage Distributions. In creating **percentage distributions,** we simply divide each cell frequency by the total number of cases and multiply by 100.† Thus, the 0–24 category in Table 3.5(a) with a frequency of 17 out of 33 corresponds to a percentage:

$$\text{Percent} = \frac{f_i}{N}(100)$$

(3.3)

$$= \frac{17}{33}(100) = 51.5\%$$

The total of the percentage distribution should equal 100.0 percent except for very minor differences due to rounding.‡

While the frequency distribution permitted a somewhat clearer summary and contrast between urban and rural states than the original raw scores or the arrays, the percentage distribution contributes a great deal more to the ease and validity of comparison because it removes an important source of possible error. Notice that the percentage is a simple ratio, one which, incidentally, is easily understood in our culture since we tend to think in terms of parts of 100. Significantly, it takes account of the comparison problem of different totals, converting each total to 100. While 17 and 7 in Table 3.5a and 3.5b were not directly comparable because there were, after all, different numbers of rural and urban states, 51.5% and 38.9% are comparable because these are expressed as parts of the same total, namely 100 percent. One could, then, compare percentage distributions even though there were differing total frequencies, because this distorting feature of a distribution has been eliminated by computing percentages. Many comparisons that you will be making will be in terms of percentages, and you will get the feeling that they convey a good deal of useful information for making valid comparisons.

Table 3.6 presents data on reasons given by men aged 18 to 64 for a recent

---

*While the number of inmates is, as defined, a discrete variable, we will not treat these data differently in this book from a continuous variable for two reasons. First, the difference in the kinds of descriptions we will be making is often of less importance than other distinctions we have to make, and, generally, the results are identical. For example, if we treated the real limits of the first class in the distributions in Table 3.5 as extending from −0.5 to +24.5, it would be apparent that the category width is indeed 25. This is the same result one would get if one counted the interval widths in thousands. The class midpoint is −0.5 + ½(25) = 12.0, and so forth. There are points in statistics where different computations would be implied by differences between discrete and continuous variables. Here it is important because it is one aspect of the meaning of a score and it will be sufficient to keep its meaning in mind in interpreting computations.

†A *proportion* is simply a cell frequency divided by the total number of cases in a distribution. It is sometimes used instead of a percentage (which is the same ratio multiplied by 100). The chief virtues of percentages are cultural. We are familiar with parts of 100 and, in fact, these are more often whole numbers rather than small decimal fractions. Both proportions and percentages convey the same information about a distribution, however.

‡Some investigators make slight adjustments in the distribution so that the total actually comes out to 100.0 percent, and others let the total equal what it will, with a footnote indicating that the small difference (if any) is due to rounding errors. Rounding errors should be very small, otherwise one would suspect some computational error has been made.

TABLE 3.6 Percentage Distribution of Reasons Given by 6,292,000 Men Aged 18–64 for a Recent Change in Residence within the Same County, 1963

Reasons	Percentage
To take a job	2.7
To look for work	1.0
Job transfer	0.4
Commuting or Armed Forces	7.5
Housing	60.4
Change in Marital Status	11.0
Join or move with family	8.1
Health	1.1
Other reasons	7.9
	100.1
	(6,839,000)

Source: U.S. Bur. Census, 1966.

change of residence which was within the same county. It would probably not be hard to find someone who would claim, on the basis of these data, that 2.7 percent of the 6,292,000 men whose responses are summarized in the table moved to take a job. This is, of course, an error. The base of the percentages in Table 3.6 is not individual *men* who moved, but the 6,839,000 *reasons* that these 6,292,000 men gave for making the move. Some people gave more than one reason. The correct interpretation of the percentage would be that 2.7 percent of the reasons that were given for moving within the same county were to take a job. A good caution in reading a percentage table is to find out what 100 percent (the base or denominator of the percent) refers to. This total is supplied in parentheses below the total of the percentage column.

3.2.3c Cumulative Distributions. Table 3.5 also presents two **cumulative distributions,** one for *frequencies* and one for *percentages*.* A cumulative distribution is formed by indicating for each category, the number (or percentage) of cases which fall below the upper real limit of that class.† It is the sum of the frequency (percentage) in a given class and the frequencies (percentages) in all of the classes below that class. Thus for rural states in Table 3.5(a), the cumulative frequency of 29 means that by the upper real limit of the "37" class (that is, by the time one reaches the score of 49.5), 29 states have been categorized out of a total of 33 states. By the time one reaches the top of the "112" class, (using the midpoint to identify the class), all 33 cases have been classified and all of the cases have also been classified below the upper real limit of the 212 class. The same

*Just as frequency distributions are symbolized by the small letter f, percent and cumulative distributions have traditional labels. Percent distributions are labelled "%" or "Pct," cumulative distributions are labeled "cum %" or "cum$f$." Some authors use capital F to stand for a cumulative frequency distribution, but the more explicit "cum$f$" will be used in this text.

†In this book, we will adopt the convention of creating cumulative distributions by starting to accumulate from the low scores and accumulating so that N or 100% is by the high-score category. Here the low-score category is 0–24 (the smallest number of inmates) and the high-score category is 200–224 (the largest number of inmates). It has nothing to do with the geography of the printed page. In some cases the small scores will be printed at the bottom of the table and in other cases (as in Table 3.5) the small scores are printed at the top. This convention merely saves presentation of alternative formulae where accumulation is from high to low scores.

type of expression applies to the cumulative percentage distribution. By the upper real limit of the "37" class, 87.9 percent of the cases have been classified, or, 87.9 percent of the cases fall below the upper real limit of that class.

Cumulative distributions are useful for comparison if one wants to compare the way cases are spread across a scale. For example, for rural states, 97 percent have numbers of inmates below 99.5 (thousand) while for urban states, only 72.2 percent have numbers of inmates below 99.5 (thousand).

3.2.3d Percentiles. The score below which a given percentage of cases fall is referred to as **percentile.** The score below which 100 percent of the cases fall, for example, is known as the 100th percentile. For urban states this value is 224.5 (thousands) of inmates. One could be interested in any percentile, of course: for rural states the 51.5 percentile is the score 24.5 (thousands) of inmates; the 50th percentile for urban states is 49.5 (thousands). That means that half of the urban states have number-of-inmate scores below 49.5 (thousands) and half above this score. The 50th percentile is a frequently used percentile in statistics (later to be called the *median*). Frequent reference is also made in research to the 10th, 25th, 33rd, 66th, 75th, 90th, 95th and 99th percentiles.* Results of tests, such as the College Board Exam or the Graduate Record Exam, are reported in terms of percentiles—the percentage of individuals in some defined test-norm group, which have scores equal to or less than a particular person's score. Diagram 3.2 illustrates and explains how any percentile can be computed from a frequency distribution.

3.2.4 Other Uses of Ratios for Comparison

The percentage is a good example of the use of a ratio to create numbers which can be compared more validly. It takes account of the total number of cases, converting it to 100 for each distribution, and because of that, percentages can be directly compared without the distortion created by differing numbers of cases in the different distributions. There are other situations where ratios can be used and where other sources of distortion are controlled to provide a basis for a comparison. A classic example is the sex ratio.

The *sex ratio* is usually computed as a ratio of the number of men in a group divided by the number of women in that same group. Because the resulting number is a decimal, it is traditionally multiplied by 100 so that it reflects the number of males in the population per 100 females (rather than the number of males per one female).† Table 3.7 shows the sex ratio for the U.S. over three census years for the whole population and for various age groups. Although slightly more males than females are born, this ratio reduces to nearly an even split under 45 years of age, and decreases dramatically in the older years as women outlive men. From other information we know that the life expectancy at birth for males

---

*It should be noted that any "fractile" could be computed using the general logic shown here. Percentiles (100ths), deciles (10ths), and quartiles (4ths) are only the most frequently used.

†William Petersen, in his book *Population* (1961), notes that the European tradition is to define the sex ratio as the number of females per 100 males. More recently, the U.S. and European tradition is to express the sex ratio per 1000 rather than per 100, thus eliminating a decimal position. A number of other ratios useful in the field of demography are defined and used in this book.

TABLE 3.7 SEX RATIOS BY AGE GROUP, U.S. 1950–1970

	Males Per 100 Females		
Age	1950	1960	1970
All ages	98.7	97.1	94.8
Under 65	99.6	98.6	97.7
At Birth	105.8	105.5	104.2
Under 45	99.4	99.5	99.5
45–64	100.2	95.7	91.7
65 and Over	89.7	82.8	72.2
65–74	93.0	87.0	77.6
75 and over	82.7	75.1	64.0

Source: Brotman (1970).

was 67.0 years in 1967 and 74.2 years for women. By the year 2000 one estimate by the U.S. Census is a life expectancy at birth of 69.1 years for men and 75.3 for women.

Another interesting ratio is the *dependency ratio,* which is designed to show the relationship between the population in the middle years (21–65) and that at the young and older years. It is computed by using a numerator which is an estimate of the number of dependents (*i.e.* those "culturally defined" as younger than "adult" or "probably retired," namely below either 18 or 21 and above 65) and a

TABLE 3.8 DEPENDENCY RATIOS FOR SELECTED COUNTRIES FOR CENSUS DATES IN THE EARLY 1960s

Columbia	98.6
Mexico	96.6
Venezuela	92.5
Taiwan	91.5
Peru	89.9
Thailand	85.1
Chile	78.6
Canada	68.8
United States	67.8
Poland	64.6
Germany	61.4
Australia	61.2
Netherlands	60.8
Portugal	59.8
Yugoslavia	59.7
France	59.1
Japan	51.1
Hungary	50.7
Sweden	50.7
Switzerland	49.6
Bulgaria	48.0

Source: Metropolitan Life, 1968. Reprinted by permission of the publisher.

DIAGRAM 3.2 Computing Percentiles

The 10th percentile is the *score* value below which 10 percent of the scores fall. The ith percentile is the *score* below which i percent of the scores fall. There are two typical kinds of percentile problems one might want to solve.

a.) *Find the percentile rank of a given score.*

$$\text{Percentile Rank of a Given Score} = (100) \frac{\text{cum}f \text{ up to and including that score}}{N}$$

The percentile rank of the score "7" in the example below is:

Raw
Scores

1
4
4
6
7
8
12
14

$\left\{ \begin{array}{l} \text{Percentile Rank} \\ \text{of the Score 7} \\ \text{Since } N = 8 \text{ and the score 7 is the 5th one} \\ \text{in an array of these scores.} \end{array} \right.$ $= (100)5/8 = 62.5$

b.) *Find the score at a given percentile rank.*

Score at a given percentile is found by:
(1.) First, multiplying the percentile by N, and
(2.) Secondly, counting up an array of scores until that numbered score is found. The score value of that score is the desired value.

If one wanted the 62nd percentile in the above example, he would multiply .62 by N which in this example is 8. The result is 4.96 or, rounded to an inte-

DIAGRAM 3.2 *(Continued)*

ger, 5. We would then begin at the first score in the array above and count up to the 5th place. That fifth score is 7 and that would be the score at the 62nd percentile.

Grouped scores pose a slight problem. Usually in finding the score at a given percentile the class containing this score is identified and then a score value in that class is found by interpolation. The following formula may be used for this purpose and it is discussed later in Chapter 5 and in Diagram 5.1 in connection with the median, which is the 50th percentile.

$$\text{Score at a given percentile} = L_p + \left[\frac{(N)\ (P) - \text{cum}f_p}{f_p} \right] w_p$$

where L_p is the lower real limit of the class containing the Pth percentile score. This is determined by inspection of the cumulative frequency or cumulative percentage distribution;

w_p is the class width of the class containing the Pth percentile;

N is the number of cases (scores);

P is the percentile of interest, expressed as a proportion;

$\text{cum}f_p$ is the cumulative frequency up to but *not* including the frequency in the class containing the Pth percentile;

f_p is the frequency in the Pth percentile class.

Percentile rank of a score or score at a given percentile may be found as well by inspection of a graph of a cumulative percentage distribution as discussed in the next chapter.

denominator which is the number of people in the middle years (*i.e.* culturally defined as in their "productive" or "self-supportive" years), and multiplied by 100. Dependency ratios are shown in Table 3.8 for several different countries for the early to middle 1960's, again permitting a comparison across societies. The next question, of course, is why. Why do the ratios differ from country to country as they do?

Turning to our earlier example of the number of inmates for different states, suppose we wanted to compare New Hampshire's 7,917 inmates and Massachusetts' 77,752 inmates. It seems likely that a direct comparison of these two figures may be misleading if for no other reason than because Massachusetts has 5.7 million people within its borders and New Hampshire has only slightly less

TABLE 3.9 PERCENTAGE OF THE POPULATION OF STATES WHICH ARE INMATES OF CARE OR CUSTODIAL INSTITUTIONS FOR RURAL AND URBAN STATES, U.S. CENSUS, 1970

Rural States	Urban States
1.05	1.37
1.07	1.15
1.19	1.13
1.05	1.20
.98	.82
1.35	.99
1.35	1.00
1.32	.97
1.03	1.01
1.43	1.19
1.58	.88
1.45	1.01
1.38	1.05
.93	.69
.99	.67
.79	.62
.94	1.05
.86	.50
1.06	
.82	
.87	
.90	
.74	
1.04	
.90	
1.43	
1.09	
.77	
1.04	
.60	
1.12	
1.15	
.51	

Source: Data from Table 3.1, presented in the same order.

than one million. Other things being equal, one might expect a bigger state to have more inmates. We could create a ratio, then, which is a percent of the total population of a state who are inmates of care or custodial institutions. Table 3.9 shows these ratios in the same order for the rural and urban states as in Table 3.1. By inspection, it is hard to reach a definite conclusion about whether rural or urban states have a higher ratio (percentage) of their population as inmates in institutions, but it would appear that rural states have a higher percentage in institutions than urban states—a result, if true, which would be opposite to our earlier prediction. At this point we need some further means for statistical comparison between these two sets of percentages. These measures will be developed in Chapter 5.*

3.2.5   Time-Based Ratios

Some specialized ratios are especially useful for measuring the amount of some variable characteristic that occurs in a given time period or the change from one period to the next. Two of these time-based measures are the *rate* and *percentage change.*

3.2.5a   Rates.   One way of defining a **rate** is as a ratio of the number of events which actually occurred in a given time period to the number of such events which might potentially have occurred during the same period. Thus we have a formula which, stated in prose, looks like this:

(3.4)

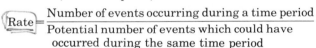

$$\text{Rate} = \frac{\text{Number of events occurring during a time period}}{\text{Potential number of events which could have}}$$
$$\text{occurred during the same time period}$$

The birth rate is one such use of a rate. The *crude birth rate* is simply the ratio of the number of births in a given year divided by the total number of people in a given society at the middle of that year. The midyear population is used because it is probably a good average of the number of people in the society during the year; (in times of increasing population, for example, this number would exceed the actual population early in the year but be below the population achieved by the end of the year). The total population is used as an estimate of the potential number of births in a society.

Unfortunately, the birth rate defined above does not take account of the fact that some societies have an unusually large number of pre-puberty females, males, or older people, which makes the total population a poor estimate of the potential number of births. A better measure of the extent to which a society is producing a maximum number of births would be the number of births divided by the number of women in that society, or, better yet, divided by the number of women aged 15 to, say, 45. In each instance, the improvement in the rate results from finding a more refined estimate of the number of *potential* births in a society

---

*By way of preface to Chapter 5, you could compute the summary ratio called the average (arithmetic mean). The average percentage of inmates for the 33 rural states is 1.05% and for the 18 urban states it is .96%. The average is but one of several simple ratios which greatly facilitate comparisons of groups of scores such as these.

in a given time period. Specialists in population use rates such as the *age-specific fertility rate* (defined as the number of births per 1000 women in a specific age group in a year), or the *fertility ratio* (defined as the number of children under 5 per 1000 women in the 15–45 childbearing period) for these reasons.*

Often rates, like proportions, result in small decimal values, and it is traditional to multiply the rate by some power of ten so that the result is a comfortable whole number. The death rate from cancer in the U.S. general population during the first half of 1971 was 162.4 deaths per 100,000 population. The suicide rate for the same period was 11.8 per 100,000. (Metropolitan Life, 1971).

A somewhat different use of the rate is illustrated in Table 3.10. Is there an increasing chance for people to go to college? Is the educational system retaining more people, longer than before? The *retention rate* shown in Table 3.10 is the ratio of the number of first-time college students in a given year to the number of students in the fifth grade eight years before. Of those who were in fifth grade eight years ago, how many entered college?

It should be clear by now that any summary measure is useful only if one is clear about the components which make it up. This is not so much a comment on the obscurity of summary measures as it is on the need for a clear understanding of what one wants to know and what the information permits him to infer, and it is not a problem particularly unique to statistics. Some time ago, an investigator, T. N. Ferdinand, illustrated how a seeming contradiction between statements based on rates could arise if one is not rather clear about what the

TABLE 3.10   RETENTION RATE FOR FIRST-TIME COLLEGE STUDENTS PER 1000 STUDENTS STARTING AT GRADE 5 IN THE U.S.

1924	118
1926	129
1928	137
1930	148
1932	160
1934	129
1936	121
1938	—
1940	—
1942	205
1944	234
1946	283
1948	301
1950	308
1952	328
1954	343
1956	357

Source: U.S. Bur. Census, *Statistical Abstract*, 1966:112.

*An interesting example of the problem of defining and refining ratios in the area of crime statistics may be found in an article by Chiricos and Waldo, (1970). They develop ratios to measure certainty of punishment and severity of punishment plus measures of percent change, which are discussed later in this chapter.

rate is designed to represent (Ferdinand, 1967). Federal reports for some time had been reporting increases in the number and also the rate of crimes in the United States, but in Ferdinand's careful study of criminal patterns in Boston since 1849, he found declines in crime rates. How could this be so? Ferdinand explained it this way. Using a society with a population of some given size, say 1 million, for illustration, in one year, 800,000 people (80%) might live in villages and the rest might live in urban areas. It is known that villages have a lower crime rate than urban areas, so the following crime rates might hold:

RESIDENTIAL DISTRIBUTION AND CRIME RATE, YEAR ONE

Location of the Population	Percent	Crime Rate
Villages	80%	40 per 1000 population
Urban Areas	20%	100 per 1000 population

Overall crime rate for this year = 52 per 1000 population

In a following year two things could happen. First there might be a shift of population from low-rate areas (villages) to higher-rate areas (urban areas), but there might also be a decrease in crime rates in, say, the urban areas, as shown below.

RESIDENTIAL DISTRIBUTION AND CRIME RATE, YEAR TWO

Location of the Population	Percent	Crime Rate
Villages	10%	40 per 1000 population
Urban Areas	90%	60 per 1000 population

Overall crime rate = 58 per 1000 population

The result of these two shifts, a drop in rate in urban areas and a shift of population to the higher-rate areas, results in an overall increase in crime rate. Rates of sub-populations have gone down, but the overall rate has increased.

3.2.5b Percentage Change. A further ratio which is sensitive to time and change, and the last of those we will discuss in this book, is called **percentage change.** It is defined as the ratio of the amount of change between two time periods to the amount at the start multiplied by 100.

(3.5)
$$\text{Percent change} = \frac{(\text{Amount at Time 2}) - (\text{Amount at Time 1})}{(\text{Amount at Time 1})}(100)$$

It is used to express the amount of change in a variable relative to the starting value of that variable. For example, the population of the United States changed (increased) by +13.3 percent between the 1960 and 1970 censuses. This is computed by using the 1960 population of 179,323,175 and the 1970 population of 203,184,772 as follows:

$$\text{Percent change} = \frac{203,184,772 - 179,323,175}{179,323,175}(100) = +13.3\%$$

The logic of this ratio is that the amount of change, the difference in the numerator, should take account of the size at the starting point. It is one thing for a society of 179,323,175 to increase in ten years by 23,861,597, but it would be much more startling if a society starting with only 40 million people made this amount of change in the same ten year period. If the change is a reduction, then the percentage change will turn out to be negative.

There are situations where it might make more sense to measure change in terms of an ending point rather than in terms of change from a starting point. Hans Zeisel points out some of these situations in his excellent book, *Say It With Figures* (1957). If, for example, we were interested in measuring percentage change in a student's grade-point average (GPA) from his freshman to senior year, we might reason that it is harder to make an increase of 1.0 overall if the student started out with a 3.0 as a freshman than if he started out with a 1.5 GPA as a freshman. In the latter case, several A's might make the change up to 2.5, but no amount of A work would be sufficient to raise the 3.0 to an overall GPA of 4.0. Students are approaching an upper limit, and the closer one approaches the limit the more difficult it is to make any given percentage change. In such a case one might use the ending GPA rather than the beginning GPA as the figure in the denominator of the percentage change formula. Of course such a computation would have to be clearly explained, since the percent change is usually computed with the beginning amount in the denominator.

Zeisel makes a similar point for change in sales volume from one year to the next for businesses that already control most of the market versus those who are just starting in business. It may be harder for one of the largest companies to double their sales volume than it is to double the sales of a very small business. Percentage change in the population of states or regions provides the basis for some migration studies.

3.3   SUMMARY

In this chapter we have considered the basic problem of making valid comparisons in order to reach important substantive conclusions. Almost any thoughtful inquiry involves a *comparison* of one group with another, an individual with the rest of his group, or the outcome of a study with some previously established standard or prediction. Just *what* should be compared and *how* it might be compared are the major topics we have introduced here. The following chapters in descriptive statistics have as one basic theme the formulation of procedures for making meaningful and valid comparisons. Often these comparative procedures involve some form of the simple idea of a *ratio*.

Some of the procedures, such as those for creating distributions, involve organizing data in such a way that certain information contained in the data is made more apparent in order to permit comparisons to be made more readily. *Frequency, percentage,* and *cumulative* distributions were discussed in this light, as well as *tallies, arrays,* and *unordered lists* of data. Where *grouped distributions* are used, detailed knowledge of individual scores is lost, and scores within a category are referred to by their *class midpoint*. Among the problems which confront a person making a comparison is the problem of irrelevant information. Loss of irrelevant detail is often helpful in exposing the desired information that the data contain.

BOX 3.4 SOME GUIDELINES FOR MAKING VALID COMPARISONS

1. *Know what you want to compare,* what variable(s) should be compared for which groups. Is the comparison to be made between groups, between an individual and a group, or between the study group and some standard (previous study, predicted value, etc.)? A good line of reasoning or theory helps immensely at this point.
2. *Have comparable measures on comparable cases.* Training observers, providing standard interview schedules, questions that have been pretested, or special recording devices, etc. generally help assure comparability. The same scale of measurement should generally be used on all groups to be compared and the rules for "sameness" should be such that this claim can be checked. Furthermore, cases that are measured should be the same across groups. If individuals are measured in one group, individuals should be measured in other comparison groups. In general, the sweetness of apples and the sweetness of sweethearts are not comparable.
3. *Research design* is an important topic here, too. We will not go over design possibilities here, but you should consult a research methods text on design *before* you become deeply involved in your own study.
4. Where there is a shifting base, consider taking account of this in terms of a *ratio* of some type.
5. Where the features to be compared are "buried" in accurate but irrelevant information, consider some of the *data summary* operations discussed in this chapter and in the rest of the book.

A second source of problems for those who would make comparisons is the *shifting base of comparison.* The number of inmates in rural states could not be directly compared with that for urban states, (a) because the totals involved more states classified as rural and fewer states classified as urban, and (b) because the urban states had larger populations to start with than did rural states, so that on this basis alone one might expect differences between states in the number of inmates. The solution was to create and examine a number of ratios which took out the effect of different kinds of incomparability. In one instance, we computed percentages of rural (and urban) states with lower or high numbers of inmates. In another, we computed the percentage of a state's population that were inmates of institutions so that we could compare these percentages for rural and urban states. The point is that a ratio was the mechanism by which we arrived at summaries which could be properly compared only when certain distorting irrelevancies were taken into account.

There are a number of different kinds of ratios. Two time-based ratios discussed in this chapter are the *rate* and the *percentage* change.

The next chapter will introduce graphic procedures for making comparisons. You will notice that often ratios, percentages, and rates are used in a graph, and graphic analysis provides some additional analytic insight which is useful in making valid comparisons.

CONCEPTS TO KNOW AND UNDERSTAND

types of comparisons	distributions
array	frequency
grouped frequency distribution	percentage
class	cumulative frequency
midpoint	cumulative percentage
cell or class frequency	percentile
interval width	ratio
real limits	rate
grouping error	percentage change

QUESTIONS AND PROBLEMS

1. Find an interesting article from one of the sociological journals (*American Sociological Review, American Journal of Sociology, Social Forces, Sociometry, Sociological Quarterly,* etc.) and analyze the kinds of contrasts or comparisons its line of reasoning implies. What kind of comparisons are they? If standards are involved, where do the standards come from? What kinds of values might be computed to aid in the comparison? A statistical workbook is likely to contain reprints of several journal abstracts which might be used to locate interesting articles for this problem.*

2. Using a newspaper or magazine, find illustrations of individual-group, group-group, and study-standard types of comparisons. How are these contrasts made, and how would you make them if you were the investigator on the case?

3. Find illustrations of each of the summary measures we have discussed thus far: ratios, rates, distributions, percentiles, and percentage change.

GENERAL REFERENCES

Zeisel, Hans, *Say It With Figures,* New York, Harper and Row, 1957.
    This book contains some clear discussion of the idea of comparison and some of the ways ratios and percentages may be used. Chapter 1 deals with percentages, another chapter illustrates how the "don't know" category might be handled, and Chapter 5 explains how index numbers might be constructed for comparison purposes.
Hagood, Margaret, and Daniel Price, *Statistics for Sociologists,* New York, Holt, 1952.
    Chapter 6 is a useful introduction and organization of the field of descriptive statistics. Chapter 7 deals with rates, ratios, proportions, and percentage change.
Hammond, Phillip E., *Sociologists at Work,* New York, Basic Books, 1964.
    This book is a collection of discussions about the background of some significant sociological research by a baker's dozen of sociologists. In addition to being a very readable and useful insight into research, the book presents the lines of reasoning

*See H. J. Loether and D. G. McTavish, *Statistical Analysis for Sociologists: A Student Manual.*

which result in a need for data on specific kinds of contrasts between individuals, groups, and standards.

OTHER REFERENCES

Brotman, Herman B., "Facts and Figures on Older Americans," Administration on Aging, U.S. Department of Health, Education and Welfare, Publication No. 182, 1970. (Data were originally from U.S. Census publications.)

Chiricos, Theodore G., and Gordon P. Waldo, "Punishment and Crime: An Examination of Some Empirical Evidence," *Social Problems*, 18 (Fall, 1970) p 200–217.

Contact, a newsletter published by Congressman Joseph E. Karth, (Summer, 1971).

Datta, Lois-Ellin, "Birth Order and Potential Scientific Creativity," *Sociometry*, 31 (March, 1968), p 76–88.

Erskine, Hazel, "The Polls: Freedom of Speech," *Public Opinion Quarterly*, 34 (Fall, 1970), p 491.

Ferdinand, Theodore N., "The Criminal Patterns of Boston Since 1849," *American Journal of Sociology*, 73 (July, 1967), p 84–99.

Huff, Darrell, *How To Lie With Statistics,* (New York, Norton), 1954.

Kolko, Gabriel, *Wealth and Power in America: An Analysis of Social Class and Income Distribution,* (New York, Praeger), 1962.

Mendelsohn, Harold, "Election-Day Broadcasts and Terminal Voting Decisions," *Public Opinion Quarterly,* 30 (Summer, 1966), p 212–225.

Metropolitan Life Insurance Company, *Statistical Bulletin,* December, 1968.

Metropolitan Life Insurance Company, *Statistical Bulletin,* September, 1971.

Petersen, William, *Population,* (New York, Macmillan), 1961, (note 4, p 72).

Population Reference Bureau, *Population Bulletin,* 27 (April, 1971), p 6.

Riley, Matilda White, *Sociological Research: A Case Approach,* (New York, Harcourt, Brace and World), 1963.

Stouffer, Samuel A., "Some Observations on Study Design," *American Journal of Sociology,* 40 (January, 1950), p 355–361.

U.S. Bureau of the Census, *Statistical Abstract of the United States: 1966* (87th Edition), (Washington, D.C.), 1966.

————, *Current Population Reports,* No. 154, (Washington, D.C.).

————, *Current Population Reports,* Series P-23, No. 34, (Washington, D.C.), 1971.

————, *U.S. Census Report* PC (V1)–1 (*Final Population Counts for the 1970 U.S. Census*), (Washington, D.C.), 1971.

————, *U.S. Census Report* PC (V2)–1 (*Final Population Counts for the 1970 U.S. Census*), (Washington, D.C.), 1971.

————, *Population Characteristics, (Current Population Reports),* Series P-20, No. 217, (Washington, D.C.), 1971.

Zeisel, Hans, *Say It With Figures,* (New York, Harper and Row), 1957.

4

GRAPHIC PRESENTATION
AND ANALYSIS

The sex ratio (number of males for every 100 females) declines steadily with increasing age not only in the United States, but in all other societies for which there is information. In the United States, slightly more males are born (104.2 males per 100 females in 1970), but by the early 20's the sex ratio begins to reverse, and for those over the age of 75, in 1970, there were only 64.0 males per 100 females.*

4.1 RATIOS—A GRAPHIC EXAMPLE

The line graph in Figure 4.1 shows sex ratios by age for each of three years, 1950, 1960 and 1966. In general the line for each of the three years shows a decline in the sex ratio with older age-groups, but past age 40 the difference between the three lines shows that there has been a rather marked drop in the sex ratio between 1950 and 1966. Why?

The graphic technique used in Figure 4.1, in this case a line graph, displays changes in the sex ratio very clearly, permitting both overall comparisons and comparisons for specific age-segments of the population. Such vivid contrasts help focus further research. Perhaps the greater drop in the mortality rate for females than for males is a factor, and this in turn might be traced to changes in medical techniques and social norms concerning births. The changing sex composition of the post-40 age brackets might also be related to the way sex roles are defined in the U.S. (*e.g.* male mortality from wars, or perhaps occupation-related

*See Table 3.7.

stress and disease). The consequences of such changes in composition would then begin to show up in data as an age cohort. A **cohort** is defined as those people experiencing a similar event in the same period or year — in this case, those *born* in the same year. (See Riley, 1973.) Such graphic comparisons also help focus research questions about possible *consequences* of an increasing sex imbalance with advancing years for such areas as housing, types of role relationships, and various types of medical and social services which may be used by older age-groups in our society. Each of these possibilities suggests further avenues of related research. Graphic presentation in this case probably communicates more relevant information more clearly and accurately than would be immediately evident if the same information were to be presented in a table.

An important aim of statistics is that of making clear the relevant kinds of information a collection of measures may contain. In a sense, statistical handling of data helps highlight the "information" contained in data so that an investigator and his audience may examine it and draw appropriate conclusions in an efficient way. Graphic analysis has much to offer when it comes to clarifying complex relationships, and with the advent of computer-controlled plotting systems, there is an opportunity to exploit this means of analysis more than has been possible in the past. In this chapter we will discuss some of the basic techniques of graphic analysis and illustrate some of the more useful alternatives.*

4.2 BASIC TECHNIQUES FOR GRAPHING DISTRIBUTIONS

Histograms, polygons, ogives, and line graphs are basic graphic procedures used in statistics, and they provide a useful way to introduce some of the techniques and cautions of graphic analysis. The first three of these techniques illustrate how the distributions discussed in Chapter 3 may be handled graphically. A later section in this chapter will apply some of these techniques to other styles of graphic presentation and introduce some important and useful alternative approaches to graphic analysis.

Basic to any graphing is the idea of a **reference system** or **coordinate system.** The usual coordinate system for graphing consists of lines or "dimensions" at right angles to each other called a Cartesian Coordinate system.† The reference system in Figure 4.2 is two-dimensional but the idea can be generalized to three or more reference axes or dimensions. Traditionally, the vertical line is called the Y-axis or **ordinate** and the horizontal line is called the X-axis or **abscissa.** This divides a plane into four **quadrants.** The **origin** or zero point on both axes is the point where the axes cross and numerical scales extend outward from this point. Scores upward from the origin on Y are positive scores,

---

*For an excellent reference for graphic presentation, see Schmid, (1954), in the General References.
†René Descartes (1596–1650), the French philosopher and mathematician, is said to have devised the coordinate system named after him while he was in bed watching a fly. He could locate the fly's travels in terms of three lines perpendicular to the walls and floor. In two dimensions, on a page, points can be exactly located by two axes at right angles to each other and thus by a pair of numbers (X and Y) shown in the graph above. Descartes went on to combine graphing and algebra by expressing the location of points in terms of formulas or functions such as $Y = 3 + 2(X)$, ideas we will use in Chapter 7. Descartes published this important work as an appendix to a 1637 book on the solar system. For an interesting discussion of Descartes' work, see Asimov (1964:83–4). There are other kinds of reference systems, some of which will be introduced later in this chapter.

those downward are negative. Scores to the left on X are negative and to the right are positive. Since most social measurements are on scales that extend from zero in a positive direction only, quadrant one is frequently the only one needed, and the other quadrants are then simply omitted from a graph as a matter of aesthetics and convenience.

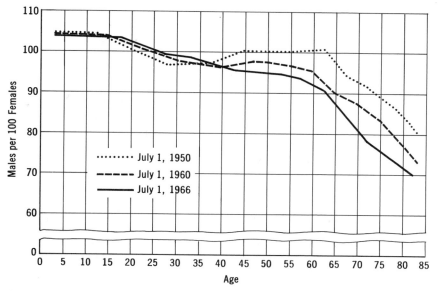

Sources: Riley and Foner, 1966; U.S. Bur. Census, 1966.

FIGURE 4.1 Line Graph Showing the Sex Ratio by Age for Three Years, 1950, 1960 and 1966 (Total population including Armed Forces overseas.)

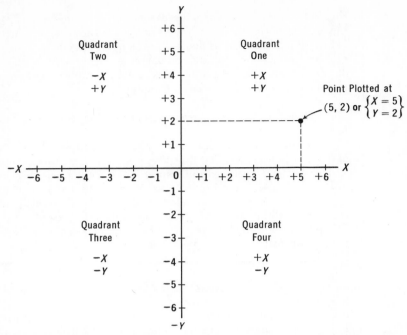

FIGURE 4.2 Cartesian Coordinate Reference System, Two Dimensional

4.2.1 Histogram

A histogram is a plot of a frequency or percentage distribution in which the frequency (or percentage) of cases in each category is represented by a bar as wide as the plotted score category on the X-axis and to a height which is proportional to the frequency (or percentage) of cases falling in that category as shown on the Y-axis. The scale of categories of the variable being plotted is laid out on the X-axis with equal physical distances corresponding to equal differences in scores. The frequency (or percentage) scale is arranged on the Y-axis, again with equal physical distances corresponding to equal frequency (or percentage) amounts. The Y-axis always begins with the origin or zero point to avoid distortions in comparing different columns, but the X-axis or score axis typically begins with any convenient low score. The objective is to create a figure with a total area corresponding to a total frequency, N (or total percent, 100%), which is distributed among the different categories of the variable on the X-axis in a way that correctly represents the relative number (percentage) of cases in each category or interval. A step-by-step discussion of the construction of a histogram is presented in Diagram 4.1.

Figure 4.3 illustrates the use of a histogram. In this case it shows the number of U.S. households in 1970 which have different numbers of persons in them. There are nearly eleven million households of size one, 18 million of size two, and so forth. The histogram clearly shows that most households are of size one, two or three. The average number of persons per household in the U.S. in 1970 is 3.17 persons.

Some variations of the basic histogram are used to reflect certain characteristics in the data. For example, if the variable is a *nominal* one, the bars in the histogram may be separated somewhat to visually carry the image that they are separate and distinct categories. This is usually called a "bar chart" or "bar graph," and the bars are drawn with equal widths.

For *ordinal* variables, where equal distances are not defined, one may choose to separate bars slightly to emphasize this fact (particularly if the variable is discrete rather than continuous). Alternatively, one might rely on the "stair-step" impression of the histogram to carry this message and still preserve the impression of rank order of categories by placing columns immediately next to each other (incorporating the lines between each column). For ordinal variables, it is customary to adopt a standard category width for plotting purposes, in spite of the fact that distances are not defined. This helps avoid distractions and apparent distortions from arbitrarily varying width. In this respect, one may want to treat ordinal variables by the same rules that apply to plotting interval-level variables.

For *interval* variables the basic procedures for plotting a histogram in Diagram 4.1 can be followed. A histogram may be particularly appropriate for discrete, interval variables. If the variable being plotted is continuous, one may prefer to turn to another type of basic graphing technique, the polygon.

A number of variations on the histogram are discussed in Section 4.3.

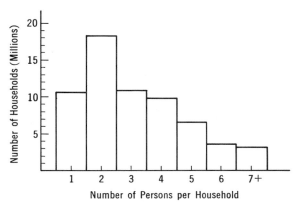

Source: U.S. Bur. Census, 1970, P-60: Table 6.

FIGURE 4.3 HISTOGRAM OF SIZE OF HOUSEHOLD, U.S., 1970

DIAGRAM 4.1   How to Construct Basic Graphs

THE PROBLEM

Select an appropriate graphic technique and plot the following data on age of 223 grade-school children. Notice that we will illustrate all of the basic graphic techniques on the same set of data for comparative purposes. In practice, an investigator would choose one appropriate technique and *not* draw all possible graphs.

Age of Grade School Child	Frequency Distribution	Percentage Distribution	Cumulative Frequency Distribution	Cumulative Percentage Distribution
4 years	21	9.4	21	9.4
5	53	23.8	74	33.2
6	69	30.9	143	64.1
7	47	21.1	190	85.2
8	33	14.8	223	100.0
	$N = 223$	100.0%		

Step 1: Using graph paper, lay out the X- and Y-axes so that the Y-axis is three-fourths to equally as long as the X-axis. Use standard arithmetic graph paper (10 lines per inch is often a useful type of ruling to use).

Step 2: Lay out the score, or X-axis. Choose a standard size physical unit to represent a standard size score step. Start near the origin on the X-axis with a score that is one score interval lower than the lowest score category to be plotted. This permits one to leave a small space between the Y-axis and the left-hand side of the graph you plot. Notice in the examples that one year of age is represented by a fixed physical distance in a graph, and that age scores start with age 2 or 3, even though the lowest age category for which there are data is age 4. Label the X-axis and create a descriptive heading for the graph (and figure number for reference if there are several graphs).

The remaining steps depend upon the type of graph used.

HISTOGRAM

Step 3: After steps 1 and 2 above, lay off the frequency scale on the Y-axis. Begin with zero at the origin and lay off frequency intervals so that a fixed physical distance stands for a given jump in frequency. Make the height of the Y-axis correspond to somewhat more than the maximum frequency in the category with the greatest frequency of cases. Label the Y-axis clearly.

Step 4: Using a ruler, construct rectangles to a height which corresponds to the frequency in a given category as indicated on the frequency axis; (see note below). Sides of each rectangle should come down exactly at class boundaries. In this case, there are 21 cases in the age-four category, so

DIAGRAM 4.1 *(Continued)*

the height of that column is plotted at 21 and the sides of the column come down at 3.5 and 4.5, which are the class boundaries. This is done for each category, although the vertical lines may be omitted or erased, leaving only the outside lines of the enclosed figure.

Note: If a category is twice as wide as most of the others, its frequency and the height of the column should be reduced proportionately (to half) so that the area reflects the number of cases in that interval (*i.e.* so that the area of each column is proportional to the cases in that interval). For discrete, ordinal, or nominal data, one may want to separate bars somewhat to reinforce this impression of the data.

The *percentage* histogram is constructed in the same way, except that the Y-axis represents percentage points and is as tall as the largest cell percentage.

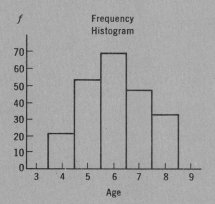 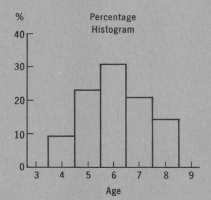

POLYGON

Step 3: After steps 1 and 2 above, lay off the Y-axis in frequency or percentage units in exactly the same way as discussed in step 3 under histograms.

Step 4: Plot the cell frequency (or percentage) as a dot at a height above the X-axis which corresponds to the frequency (or percentage) in that category as indicated on the Y-axis scale; (see note below). The point should be plotted directly above the *midpoint* of the class.

Step 5: Now plot two added points. Plot a zero at the next lower class midpoint below the lowest plot point on the X-axis. Then plot a zero at the midpoint of what would be the class just higher than the highest plotted point.

Step 6: Using a ruler, connect all of the dots so that there is a closed polygon—closed with the X-axis.

Note: If a category is wider than others, reduce the height of that

DIAGRAM 4.1 *(Continued)*

category proportionately. For example, if the category is twice as wide as others, plot the frequency (or percentage) above the midpoint of the class, but at a height which is equal to one half of the frequency (or percentage) in that class.

A percentage polygon is constructed in the same way as the frequency polygon, except that the Y-axis is laid out in percentages.

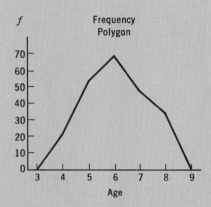

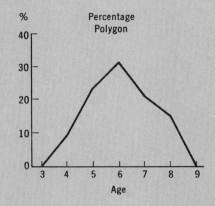

Ogive

Step 3: After steps 1 and 2 above, lay off the frequency or percentage scale on the Y-axis in a way similar to that indicated in step 3 under histogram. The scale should extend up to N, the total number of cases (or 100 percent, in the case of a cumulative percentage scale).

Step 4: Plot a zero at the *lower* real limit of the first (lowest) score category. Then plot each successive cumulative frequency (or percentage) just above the upper real limit of the class to which it corresponds; (see note below). A cumulative distribution shows the number (percentage) of cases below the upper real limit of each successive class up to N or 100 percent.

Step 5: Connect all dots with a straight line, ending at the last dot which is N or 100 percent. The graph should go up and to the right without any dips. A frequency in the next higher category can not be any lower than it was at the last category (although it may be the same height if there are no further cases in that next category).

Note: Always plot above the upper real limit of a category regardless of the widths of classes. The percentage ogive is the same as the frequency ogive, except that the Y-axis is laid off in percentages from zero to 100%. An added use of the percentage ogive is that it permits one readily to find any percentile (*i.e.* the score below which some percentage of the cases happen to fall).

DIAGRAM 4.1 *(Continued)*

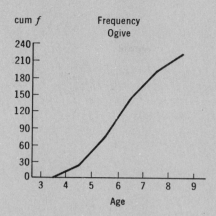

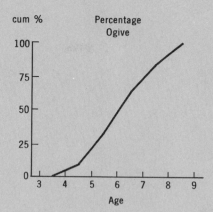

LINE GRAPHS

Step 3: The Y-axis is laid out in terms of the scale of the dependent variable that is being plotted, and the X-axis is laid out in terms of the scale of the independent variable. For example, the X-axis may represent time or age or regions of the country, etc. The Y-axis may be a sex-ratio, the number of crimes in a given year, etc. Label each axis. Again, equal physical distances correspond to equal score distances, and the Y-axis starts with zero.

Step 4: Plot with a dot, the value of the dependent variable above the appropriate category midpoint on the independent variable.

Step 5: Join the dots, using a ruler, without closing the figure with the X-axis. Where more than one line is plotted on the same graph, use a different type of line for each (dotted, solid, dot and dash, etc.). Clearly label each line.

An example of a line graph is as follows:

TOTAL BIRTHS EXPECTED PER 1000 WIVES 18–39 YEARS OLD, 1971*

Age	*Births Expected per 1000 Wives*
18–24	2,384
25–29	2,617
30–34	2,996
35–39	3,255

*Source: U.S. Bur. Census, 1972:P-20, No. 232.

DIAGRAM 4.1 *(Continued)*

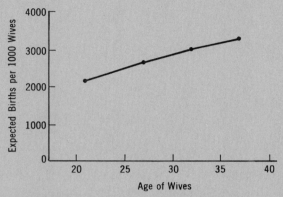

TOTAL BIRTHS EXPECTED PER 1000 WIVES 18–39 YEARS OLD, 1971*

*Data from the above table.

CAUTIONS

1. Use the three-fourths rule, creating the Y-axis about three-fourths the length of the X-axis (or equally long).
2. Always begin the frequency or percentage axis with zero at the origin. The score axis may begin with any convenient score to make an aesthetically balanced but accurate diagram.
3. Be sure that equal numeric differences are represented by equal physical distances on all scales.
4. Label the graph adequately to include all scales, the source of data, a heading explaining what is shown, and keys to explain different kinds of lines or symbols, etc.
5. To avoid confusion, do not attempt to show too many different graphs on the same axes.

4.2.2 Polygons

The frequency (or percentage) polygon is a closed figure connecting points plotted above the *midpoint* of each category at a height corresponding to the frequency (or percentage) of cases in each category. Figure 4.4 shows two percentage polygons of the age distribution of enrolled and not-enrolled people aged 3 to 34 years in the United States in October, 1971. Figure 4.4a is the age distribution for those enrolled in school and Figure 4.4b shows the age distribution for those not enrolled in school. Note that each figure is closed by extending the line down to the X-axis at the next midpoint beyond the extreme categories of the distribution. Diagram 4.1 presents step by step procedures for constructing a polygon.

A comparison of the two age distributions for those enrolled and those not enrolled, as in Figures 4.4a and 4.4b, shows marked differences in their form. Among those enrolled in school the distribution is concentrated around the 10–13 year ages, with smaller percentages enrolled shown on either side. For those not enrolled, the distribution is concentrated at both ends of the age range and the distribution forms a "U-shape."

The polygon gives the visual impression of more gradual shifts in frequency (or percentage) from category to category, while the histogram highlights shifts between categories. The frequency (or percentage) polygon also relies on distances between categories, and for this reason it is most appropriate in graphing interval-level variables.

Figure 4.5 shows an analytic use of the polygon to present the overlap between distributions of income for blacks and for whites in the United States in 1968. The area of overlap of the two distributions is used as one measure of *integration* which is computed by finding the percentage (or proportion as shown

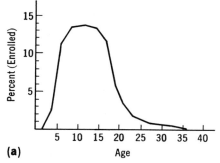
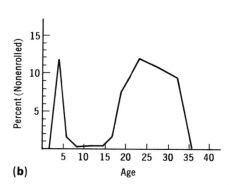

Source: U.S. Bur. Census, 1972, P-20, No. 234.

FIGURE 4.4

(a) Percentage Polygon of the Age of 3 to 34 Year Olds Who Were Enrolled In School: U.S. October, 1971

(b) Percentage Polygon of the Age of 3 to 34 Year Olds Who Were Not Enrolled In School: U.S. October, 1971

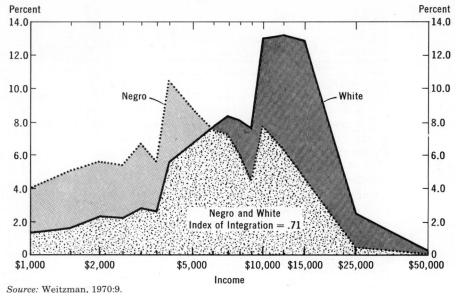

Source: Weitzman, 1970:9.

FIGURE 4.5 PERCENT DISTRIBUTION OF NEGRO FAMILIES AND WHITE FAMILIES BY TOTAL MONEY INCOME: 1968

in Figure 4.5) of overlap out of the total area under both curves (*i.e.,* the total shaded area). In this example, there is a 71 percent overlap, or the "index of integration" for blacks and whites on family income in 1968 is equal to .71. Complete segregation, where the index of integration is equal to 0.0, would be shown by a graph in which the income distributions of blacks and whites do not overlap at all. Complete integration, where the index of integration would equal 1.0, would be shown by two identical distributions exactly "overlapping" or corresponding to each other. Both polygons are plotted on the same graph for easier comparison, and essentially two bits of information are presented. Ultimately two measurements had to be made on each family, race, and income, for the graph to be prepared. The distribution of income was then plotted separately for the two racial groups.

4.2.3 Ogives

A third basic graphic technique is a plot of a cumulative distribution (either percentage or frequency). This kind of graph shows the frequency (or percentage) of cases falling below the upper boundary of each successive class.* Ogives are

---

*Note that we are accumulating from low scores to high scores for consistency throughout this book. Obviously one could accumulate from high to low, too, in which case statements like this one would have to be reversed or changed to the "lower" boundary. High to low accumulation would be useful in the analysis of waiting times in a queue, for example, where one would be interested in the percentage of people waiting a given number of minutes "or more."

used with ordinal or interval-level variables to aid in the examination of the overall shape of a distribution, and to aid in finding various percentiles. Diagram 4.1 illustrates the steps in drawing an ogive. Notice that the plot points are directly above the *upper boundary* of each class, so that the line connecting them extends from the *X*-axis up and to the right, ending at the total frequency (or total percentage, 100%, in the case of a percentage ogive).

Figure 4.6 illustrates one use of the ogive in sociology. Abbott Ferriss was interested in the rate of divorce and whether or not the percentage of couples who divorced within the first nine years of marriage was changing through time (Ferriss, 1970:363). He used a percentage ogive to plot the cumulative percentage of divorces among those married in the same year. That is, Ferriss gathered data on a given marriage cohort, calculating the percentage of that cohort who divorced each year for the first nine years of their marriage. These percentages were then accumulated and plotted above December 31st of each successive year of marriage. This was done for each of the annual marriage cohorts from 1949

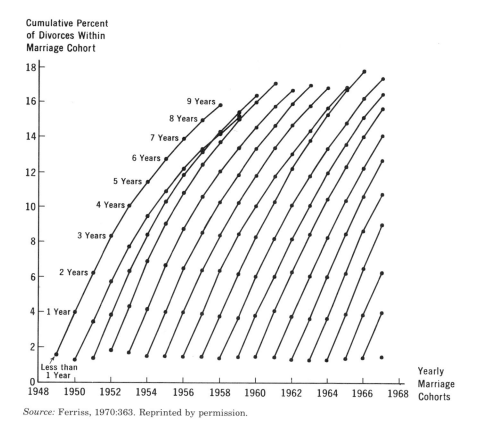

Source: Ferriss, 1970:363. Reprinted by permission.

FIGURE 4.6 Cumulative Percent of Divorces within Yearly Marriage Cohorts, by Duration of Marriage (through 9 years), 1949–1967.

to 1967. For couples married in 1949, for example, about 1.5 percent divorced in less than a year. By the end of the first year about 4 percent had divorced, and so on, until by nine years nearly 16 percent had divorced. The ogive in this case does not extend to 100 percent because the base of the percentage was all marriages of a given cohort, a more meaningful figure in this instance, rather than the final number of divorces of a given cohort (which would still be unknown at the time of Ferriss' study).

From the ogives in Figure 4.6 one can see that the percentage of married couples who divorce after a given number of years of marriage is relatively constant from cohort to cohort. There is some suggestion that the percentages might be rising for later-married cohorts (shown by taller ogives in later years) and the 1950 marriage cohort had a lower than usual percentage of divorces after the fifth year of marriage. This latter point is shown by the ogive bending to the right rather than extending upward as steeply as other cohort ogives.

BOX 4.2 THE DISTRIBUTIONS BEHIND THE GRAPHS

The basic graphic techniques discussed so far — histograms, polygons and ogives — are used to present the distributions which were discussed in Chapter 3. Do you understand the following?

Frequency distribution (if not, see Section 3.2.3a).

Percentage distribution (if not, see Section 3.2.3b).

Cumulative distributions (if not, see Section 3.2.3c).

Percentiles (if not, see Section 3.2.3d).

4.2.4 Line Graph

A fourth type of basic graph is the line graph, which shows the value of some dependent variable (scaled along the Y-axis) for each of several categories of another variable, usually an independent variable, (scaled along the X-axis). The plotted points are connected by a straight line, and the figure is not closed with the X-axis, since the area under the curve has no particular meaning as it does in the case of the frequency or percentage histogram or the polygon. Diagram 4.1 provides a step-by-step discussion of the way these graphs are constructed.

Figure 4.7 is an example of a line graph, where time is represented on the X-axis. The dependent variable, rate of marital dissolution through death, is plotted on the Y-axis, and the line extends from 1860 to 1964. This is often called a **trend line** because it is a plot of some characteristic through time. The graph shows rather clearly the overall decline in marital dissolutions through death during the century, with minor fluctuations from this trend for most years. The year 1918 stands out as a major departure from the trend. It was during 1918 that

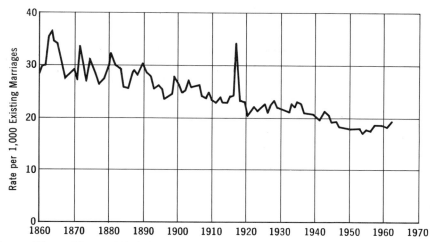

Sources: Riley and Foner, 1968:19; Jacobson, 1959:118; and Jacobson, 1966: Fig. 1. Used by permission

Note: Includes Armed Forces overseas during 1917 to 1919 and 1940 to 1964; excludes civilian population of Alaska and Hawaii prior to 1960.

FIGURE 4.7 MARITAL DISSOLUTIONS BY DEATH, U.S., 1860–1964

there was a major epidemic of influenza, an epidemic which also claimed German sociologist Max Weber in 1920.

Line graphs are particularly appropriate where one of the variables (on the X-axis) is a continuous, interval-level variable, such as age or time. A bar graph could be used instead of a line graph for situations where the variable on the X-axis is nominal or ordinal. Figure 4.8 provides an example where columns represent the number of children desired for two groups of countries, those with relatively low birth rates and those with higher birth rates, as recorded in a study by W. Parker Mauldin (1965). The graphic technique clearly shows the author's conclusion that "the number of children desired by people in countries with low birth rates is generally lower than in countries with higher birth rates." Interesting, too, is the difference between the two collections of countries. Those with lower birth rates in this graph are generally considered more industrialized than those with higher birth rates.

4.2.5 DISTORTIONS IN GRAPHING

Whichever form of graph is selected, the key criterion should be the accuracy with which it communicates the aspects of the data of interest to an audience or to the investigator himself. The investigator has the opportunity and a wide range of techniques for selecting the specific part of the data which is of interest in his study. To communicate properly requires clear knowledge of what is there

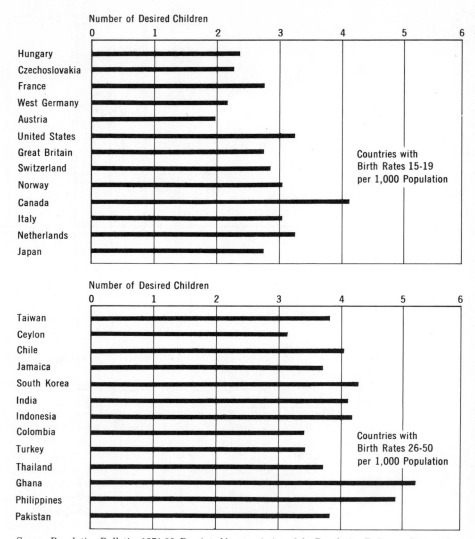

Source: Population Bulletin, 1971:20. Reprinted by permission of the Population Reference Bureau, Inc.

FIGURE 4.8   DESIRED FAMILY SIZE, SELECTED COUNTRIES

to communicate, and of possible misinterpretations and qualifications which should be taken into account, along with a healthy sensitivity for the ways people interpret and understand evidence. Clearly, too, there are vast possibilities for doing mathematically or technically correct manipulations which may intentionally or inadvertently misrepresent the state of affairs being investigated. Some cautions and rules for careful representation are given in this book, but there are always exceptional situations, and the responsibility for clear communication is not solved by mere rules for technical accuracy.

There are several ways of graphing which are numerically accurate but which give a distorted impression of the data. These are illustrated in Figure 4.9. The series of graphs, Figure 4.9a through 4.9c, illustrates the distorting effects of extending or shortening one of the axes. Although the data are accurately plotted in each graph, the impression of the steepness of change from category to category is greatly altered. A partial corrective is the three-quarters rule discussed in Diagram 4.1.

Similar in effect to the distortion involved in changing scale length is the distortion involved in not starting with zero on the frequency (or percentage) scale on the Y-axis in a histogram or polygon. Figure 4.1 illustrates a helpful

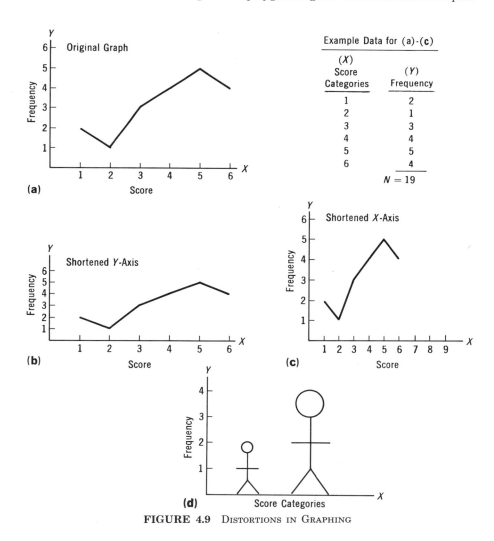

FIGURE 4.9 DISTORTIONS IN GRAPHING

procedure to use where a graph would be awkwardly tall if all values from zero were included. In Figure 4.1 sex ratios were plotted in the 70 to 110 range, and in order to have the graph large enough so that values could be read off the Y-axis, physical units on the Y-axis were made relatively large. In this case, Riley did not include all score values from zero to 70, because this would have resulted in a graph longer than the printed page (Riley and Foner, 1966). Rather, she skipped some values between zero and 60, but clearly indicated in her presentation that this had been done and the reader should beware. This warning is expressed by "breaking" the graph and the Y-axis to show that part of the table is missing. In general, it is a poor practice to omit values on the frequency or percentage axis.

A further potential distortion of graphs is the use of figures which differ in area or volume as well as height. In Figure 4.9, graph (d) illustrates the problem. While the stick figures are drawn so that the taller is twice as high as the shorter to indicate a doubling in frequency, the figures, if drawn aesthetically, also cover an area, and the ratio of these areas is likely to be about 1 to 4 rather than 1 to 2 as intended. It is often not clear to a reader which of these possible comparisons correctly represents the data. If a figure is a square or circle, a doubling of its height or diameter results in an area that is four times larger. If a figure in a graph is illustrated as a cube or sphere, a doubling of its diameter or height results in an eight-fold increase in volume. To solve this possible distortion, investigators generally prefer to adopt a standard-sized figure to represent a given number or percentage of cases and merely use as many of these figures as is necessary to indicate different category values. Figure 4.10 illustrates this more careful procedure. Called a **pictograph** because of its use of small pictures to represent a standard quantity of the variable being studied, Figure 4.10 shows the relationship between birth and death rates for seven world areas and for the world as a whole. Notice that each figure represents two births or deaths per 1000 population, and that fractional figures are used to represent fractional amounts.

4.3 VARIATIONS ON BASIC GRAPHIC TECHNIQUES

There are a number of other graphic techniques which are useful either for analysis of data or presentation of results or both. In this section of the chapter we will illustrate some useful variations of the basic graphing techniques we have been discussing thus far. In the following sections we will discuss techniques involving somewhat different approaches, and illustrate new applications of analytic graphing in sociology.

4.3.1 The Bar-Chart

The **bar-chart** is a variation of the histogram often used for nominal variables or when emphasis is on categories of a variable (see Figure 4.8). Figure 4.11 shows bar-charts of "place of physician visits" for four age categories (0–4 years, 5–14,

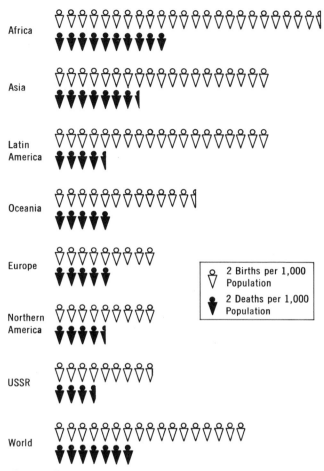

Source: Population Bulletin, 1971:6. Reprinted by permission of the Population Reference Bureau.

FIGURE 4.10 BIRTH AND DEATH RATES BY AREA, 1971

15–24 and 25 and over). Data from monthly interviews by the U.S. Public Health Service are shown for a year ending June, 1958, in the top graph and for the year 1968 in the bottom graph. In this application each bar represents 100 percent of the physician visits made by a given age group in a given year, but the bars are divided differently to show the percentage breakdown of visits by where they occurred—in the physician's office, a hospital, home, or "other" places. For ease in interpretation, percentages are also entered on each of the shaded portions of each bar. Notice that in both graphs, older age groups are more likely to visit physicians in their office, and between 1958 and 1968 there was a shift to greater relative use of the physician's office than alternative sites. Between the two years, home visits nearly disappeared, while hospital visits remained relatively con-

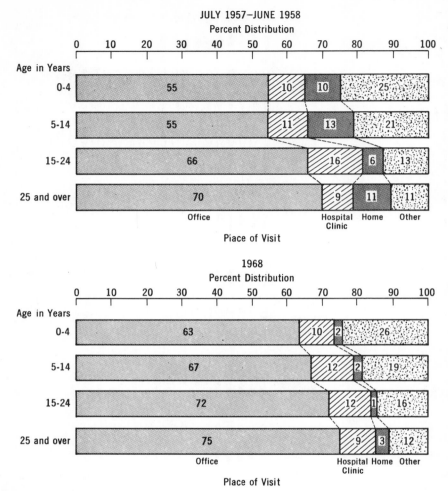

FIGURE 4.11 PERCENT DISTRIBUTION OF PHYSICIAN VISITS BY PLACE OF VISIT, ACCORDING TO AGE: JULY 1957–JUNE 1958 AND 1968.

stant both over age groups within a given year and between 1958 and 1968. Generally this form of graph is adopted to facilitate comparison of the size of separate components within several bars.

Figure 4.12 provides another illustration of a bar-chart, where again each bar is the same length, representing 100 percent of the cases in a category (*e.g.* number of crimes of a given type known to the police). In this instance, however, the bars are adjusted so that the part extending to the right of a vertical line represents the percentage of that type of crime which has been "cleared" by an

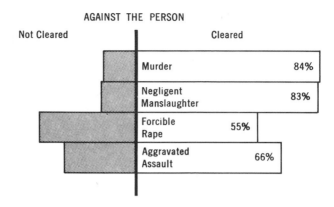

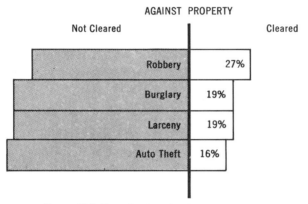

Source: U.S. Dept. Justice, 1971:32.

FIGURE 4.12 CRIMES CLEARED BY ARREST, U.S., 1971

arrest having been made. The top graph presents a group of crimes "against persons" and the bottom graph presents similar data for crimes "against property." It is obvious in these graphs that crimes against persons are much more likely to be cleared by an arrest than are crimes against property—at least among those crimes known to police.

4.3.2 The Population Pyramid

The **population pyramid** is somewhat more complex in design, while again illustrating some simple graphing procedures discussed in connection with the histogram. Figure 4.13 provides an illustration. Each bar in the graph represents the percentage of the population in a specific age-sex category. The bars are

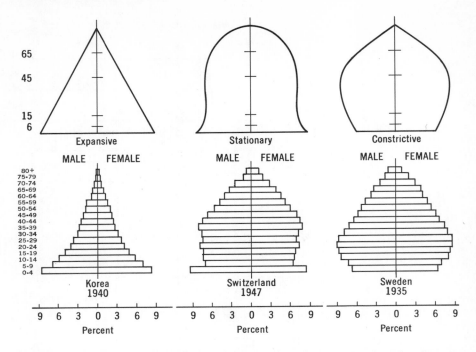

Source: Petersen, 1961:628. Reprinted by permission of the publishers, The Macmillan Company. Copyright © William Petersen, 1961.

FIGURE 4.13 THREE ANALYTIC POPULATION PYRAMIDS SHOWING DIFFERENT POPULATION STRUCTURES AND THREE ACTUAL POPULATION PYRAMIDS.

organized with those for males on one side and those for females on the other and are stacked from youngest to oldest ages. The population pyramid is used chiefly by demographers to show the overall distribution of a population and to make comparisons of the populations of different countries. Figure 4.14 shows the population pyramid for the United States in 1969 (shaded pyramid) and, on the same axis, a pyramid which is a projection of the population of the U.S. in the year 2037 under the assumption of a stable population just producing enough children to replace itself. Compared with the stable population pyramid, the 1969 pyramid shows a relatively greater percentage of younger people and a relatively smaller percentage of older people. Notice too that the imbalance of males and females in the older age brackets is clearly shown, as are the effects of the depression of the 1930's (shown by the "notches" in the 30- and 35-year bars for the 1969 pyramid), and the "baby boom" is shown by the percentage of population in the 20- and-younger age brackets. Sometimes one can see traces of the effects of disease or war on a cohort.

A similar idea has been used in the study of organizational hierarchies. Figure 4.15 shows several hypothetical and actual "pyramids" drawn symmetrically so that ratios between the number of people at different levels in an organi-

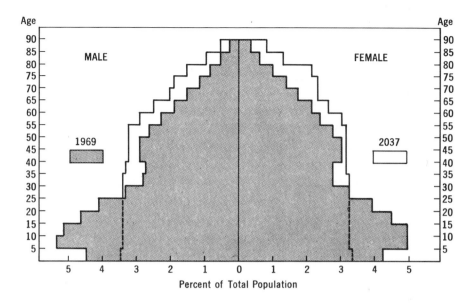

Source: U.S. Bur. Census, 1970, P-25.

FIGURE 4.14 POPULATION PYRAMIDS FOR THE U.S. IN 1969 AND FOR A STATIONARY 2037 PROJECTION; by percent of total population.

zation are accurately shown. Kaufman and Seidman (1970), whose data are shown in Figure 4.15, conclude from their study of 25 federal agencies and 4 county health departments that "line-personnel" tend to form pyramid structures with a broad base and a narrow top but "staff-personnel" tend to form an inverse pyramid-shaped organization with the base narrower than the top.

4.3.3 The Pie Chart

A **pie chart** is shown in Figure 4.16, where an entire circle represents the total of some characteristic such as the total world population. In this example, the world population at different dates is shown by larger and larger sized circles (the area representing the changing total size). The "pie" is divided into segments with different kinds of shading, where each segment represents a component of the total. In this figure, the components are four general continental population areas of the world. Each wedge has an angle at the center which represents its relative share of the 360 degrees in a circle. Each 3.6 degrees represents one percent of the total. In 1970, the Americas held about 14 percent of the world's population and its "wedge" of the pie is represented by 50.4 degrees of the circle, ($14\% \times 3.6° = 50.4°$).

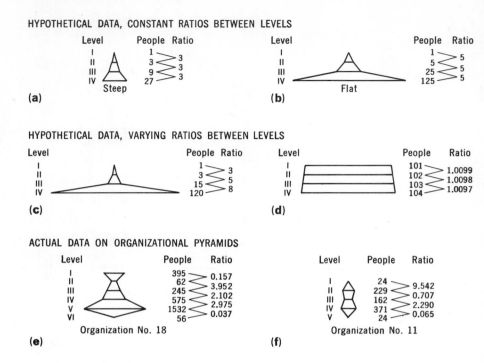

Source: Kaufman and Seidman, 1970:440. Reprinted by permission.

FIGURE 4.15 Organization Hierarchy Pyramids with Varying Ratios between Levels

4.4   OTHER APPROACHES TO GRAPHIC ANALYSIS IN SOCIOLOGY

In addition to the methods discussed above for graphing distributions, there are four further graphic techniques which we will introduce here because they offer some special advantages for the examination of data and because they suggest some of the types of contrasts an investigator may be interested in making. These techniques include statistical maps, scatter diagrams, triangular charts, and semilogarithmic graphs.

4.4.1   Statistical Maps

Statistical maps have been widely used in ecological studies in sociology and three somewhat different approaches will be presented here. A statistical map shows the distribution of a variable over a geographic area. In Figure 4.17 a base map (the outline map of some area) of Chicago was divided into community areas for which data on suicide rates had been gathered for the 1959–1963 period. Often

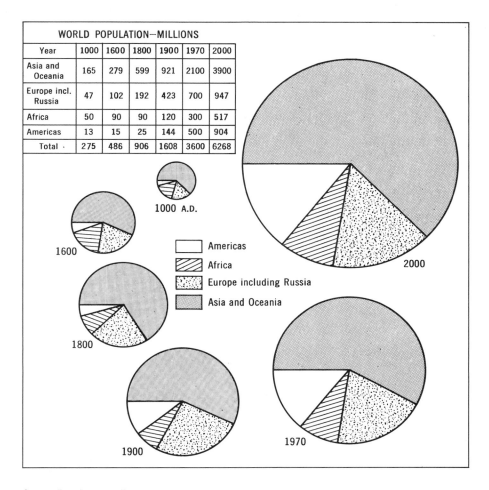

Year	1000	1600	1800	1900	1970	2000
Asia and Oceania	165	279	599	921	2100	3900
Europe incl. Russia	47	102	192	423	700	947
Africa	50	90	90	120	300	517
Americas	13	15	25	144	500	904
Total ·	275	486	906	1608	3600	6268

Source: Population Bulletin, 1971:9. Reprinted by permission of the Population Reference Bureau.

FIGURE 4.16 ONE THOUSAND YEARS OF POPULATION GROWTH

statistical maps report data by states, counties, or census tracts. Each area is shaded or "cross-hatched" in a way which illustrates the value of the variable in that area. In Figure 4.17, the more dense shading is used for higher suicide rates (12 to 23.1 per 100,000 population) and a *key* explains what each type of shading means. Usually variables with only a few categories are plotted, and shading or coloring is selected to reflect gradations of a variable by brightness or density. The suicide rate map prepared by Maris shows that rates tend to increase toward the center of the downtown area (Maris, 1969). Where other characteristics of community areas are known, clues to the pattern of suicide rates can be found, and changes over time can be studied by comparing similar maps for successive years.

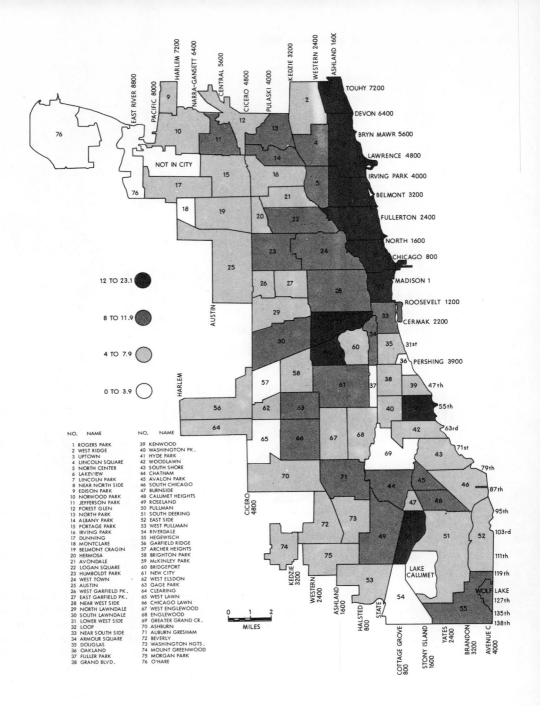

Source: Maris, 1969:139. Reprinted by permission of the author and publishers.

FIGURE 4.17 SUICIDE RATES BY COMMUNITY AREAS, CITY OF CHICAGO, 1959–1963

The following labels appear around the map:

EAST RIVER 8800
PACIFIC 8000
HARLEM 7200
NARRA-GANSETT 6400
CENTRAL 5600
CICERO 4800
PULASKI 4000
KEDZIE 3200
WESTERN 2400
ASHLAND 1600

TOUHY 7200
DEVON 6400
BRYN MAWR 5600
LAWRENCE 4800
IRVING PARK 4000
BELMONT 3200
FULLERTON 2400
NORTH 1600
CHICAGO 800
MADISON 1
ROOSEVELT 1200
CERMAK 2200
31st
PERSHING 3900
47th
55th
63rd
71st
79th
87th
95th
103rd
111th
119th
127th
135th
138th

NOT IN CITY
AUSTIN
HARLEM
CICERO 4800
KEDZIE 3200
WESTERN 2400
ASHLAND 1600
HALSTED 800
STATE
COTTAGE GROVE 800
STONY ISLAND 1600
YATES 2400
BRANDON 3200
AVENUE C 4000
LAKE CALUMET
WOLF LAKE

Legend:
12 TO 23.1
8 TO 11.9
4 TO 7.9
0 TO 3.9

NO.	NAME	NO.	NAME
1	ROGERS PARK	39	KENWOOD
2	WEST RIDGE	40	WASHINGTON PK.
3	UPTOWN	41	HYDE PARK
4	LINCOLN SQUARE	42	WOODLAWN
5	NORTH CENTER	43	SOUTH SHORE
6	LAKEVIEW	44	CHATHAM
7	LINCOLN PARK	45	AVALON PARK
8	NEAR NORTH SIDE	46	SOUTH CHICAGO
9	EDISON PARK	47	BURNSIDE
10	NORWOOD PARK	48	CALUMET HEIGHTS
11	JEFFERSON PARK	49	ROSELAND
12	FOREST GLEN	50	PULLMAN
13	NORTH PARK	51	SOUTH DEERING
14	ALBANY PARK	52	EAST SIDE
15	PORTAGE PARK	53	WEST PULLMAN
16	IRVING PARK	54	RIVERDALE
17	DUNNING	55	HEGEWISCH
18	MONTCLARE	56	GARFIELD RIDGE
19	BELMONT CRAGIN	57	ARCHER HEIGHTS
20	HERMOSA	58	BRIGHTON PARK
21	AVONDALE	59	McKINLEY PARK
22	LOGAN SQUARE	60	BRIDGEPORT
23	HUMBOLDT PARK	61	NEW CITY
24	WEST TOWN	62	WEST ELSDON
25	AUSTIN	63	GAGE PARK
26	WEST GARFIELD PK.	64	CLEARING
27	EAST GARFIELD PK.	65	WEST LAWN
28	NEAR WEST SIDE	66	CHICAGO LAWN
29	NORTH LAWNDALE	67	WEST ENGLEWOOD
30	SOUTH LAWNDALE	68	ENGLEWOOD
31	LOWER WEST SIDE	69	GREATER GRAND CR.
32	LOOP	70	ASHBURN
33	NEAR SOUTH SIDE	71	AUBURN GRESHAM
34	ARMOUR SQUARE	72	BEVERLY
35	DOUGLAS	73	WASHINGTON HGTS.
36	OAKLAND	74	MOUNT GREENWOOD
37	FULLER PARK	75	MORGAN PARK
38	GRAND BLVD.	76	O'HARE

0   1   2
MILES

There are now a number of computer programs which permit an investigator to have his data automatically plotted in some graphic form, either by using printed characters or by creating instructions which can be used on a separate plotting device or shown on a television-like computer terminal. This greatly facilitates visual inspection of data and permits an investigator to examine even more complex plots which show several variables simultaneously.* Figure 4.18 shows a statistical map of the percentage of blacks in community areas of Chicago in 1964; in this case, the map was prepared on a computer. The concentration of blacks in three areas on this map shows the geographic segregation of this group. It is interesting to note that areas with a high percentage of blacks in 1964 are generally not the areas with a high suicide rate shown in Figure 4.17.†

A second illustration of statistical maps is shown in Figures 4.19 and 4.20, which were created in a study by Thomas Donnelly, F. Stuart Chapin, Jr., and Shirley F. Weiss, showing land use in Greensboro, North Carolina (Chapin and Weiss, 1965). Instead of using existing and often irregular community areas, they divided Greensboro into arbitrary but equal-sized land areas and created a "land development" index which was divided into ninths and used to shade in the grid map. The darkest areas are the areas of greatest development as of 1960. The authors also developed a statistical model (*i.e.*, a set of equations) using scores on some variables for each of the land areas in 1948 and "simulated" the process of development of land use. That is, their equations helped them project the land use patterns in 1960 on the basis of earlier development patterns. Figure 4.20 shows this "expected" or "computed" 1960 outcome. Differences between the two statistical maps help identify factors which perhaps should be taken into account in developing a better predictive model. Models of this sort (*e.g.* voting prediction models) will not be discussed in this book, but they represent some exciting applications of both sociological theory and statistical technique. A computer-controlled plotter could have produced maps such as those in Figures 4.19 and 4.20, although in this example the maps were prepared by hand.

The third statistical mapping technique is illustrated in a study by Hoiberg and Cloyd (1971) in which they show the distribution of social class throughout a community by "isolines." These are lines drawn in such a way that they connect geographic areas with the same values of a variable, creating closed figures which do not cross or meet. Lines are drawn for each of several values of a variable and the values are usually picked at equal intervals along a scale of that

---

*Some computer-driven devices will create a three-dimensional plot by pushing small wires through a board (which represents two of the dimensions) to a height above the board which represents the value of a third dimension. The result is similar to a patch of grass that has been clipped in an uneven pattern to represent the distribution of some characteristic. Such plots might be useful in showing the distribution of social class in areas throughout a city, for example, a graphic alternative to the two-dimensional plots in Figure 4.17 and 4.18.
†This is probably a good place to caution the reader about making direct inferences about the relationship between two characteristics which describe groups, such as percentage black *vs.* suicide rates in "community areas." It would be an error (called the "ecological fallacy") to make any direct simplistic inference from these patterns for community areas such as, for example, that white people rather than black people may be more likely to commit suicide. It is entirely possible, for example, that in largely white areas it is blacks who commit suicide and in largely black areas it is the whites who commit suicide (or vice versa). The general point is that conclusions about *community areas*, generally cannot be inferred from data collected only on *individual people* (or subgroups), and conversely conclusions on individuals are not warranted from community (or group) data.

B. VARIATIONS IN THE PERCENTAGE OF POPULATION BLACK IN CHICAGO, 1964[a]

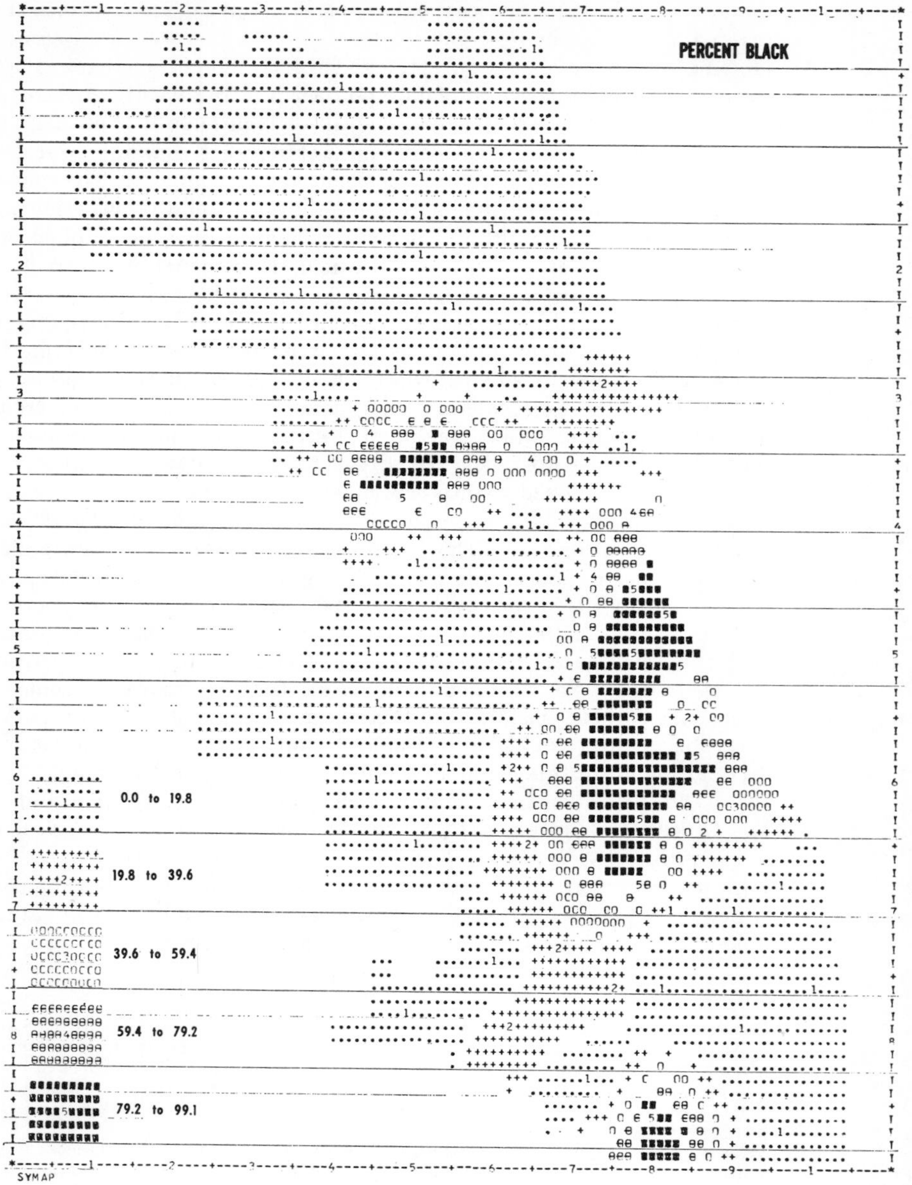

SYMAP

Source: Berry, 1971. Reprinted by permission.

FIGURE 4.18 Variations in the Percentage Black in Community Areas of Chicago in 1964, a Computer-Created Statistical Map

variable. Isolines are like lines on a contour map showing the elevation of hills and valleys (or pressure and temperature lines on a weather map) except, in this case, they reflect not elevation but social class (or some other selected social characteristic).

Figure 4.21 was created by laying a grid over a base map of a midwestern community of some 150,000 population. Values of social class were determined for residences in the grid areas and the isolines were then drawn. The value of the social class measure through which a given line is drawn is indicated on the line itself and, in this case, larger numbers represent higher social class. Notice that the "peak" of social class appears to be in the central and southern edge of the town. Where isolines are very close together this indicates a rather steep gradient (like a cliff in physical characteristics). Again, as with other statistical maps, this map helps an investigator consider a pattern of geographic distribution for some characteristic, and his comparison of this pattern with maps of other characteristics is often useful in producing insight into reasons underlying the pattern. Where isolines (a more general term) refer to similar values of *ratios or indices* they are generally called "isopleths." More precisely, the isoline map shown in Figure 4.21 would be a map where a social class index provided the information for drawing "isopleths."

BOX 4.3 A PAUSE FOR REFLECTION

The expressed purpose of this chapter has been a discussion of different ways to graphically present and analyze data. The "hidden" purpose, which is also important, has been to provide exercise in the idea of scores and distributions of scores on a variable. You have probably seen examples of most of the graphic techniques presented thus far in the newspaper or in other texts. Most of these techniques are rather direct expressions of ideas contained in some kind of distribution. If you feel somewhat confused at this point, we suggest that you "loop back" for a quick review of distributions in Section 3.2.3 ff. All of the techniques described there are useful because they permit some of the kinds of comparisons and contrasts discussed in Section 3.1 ff. The following three analytic graphs are also part of this same theme.

4.4.2 The Scatter Diagram

A particularly useful form of analytic graph is the scatter diagram, where individual cases (cities, states, people, organizations, etc.) are plotted as points on Cartesian coordinates. In this graph there are as many dots as there are cases, and the dots are *not* joined by lines. Each dot is placed on the plot in a way that reflects the standing of an observed unit on two variables, one scaled on the Y-axis and the other scaled on the X-axis. We will make extensive use of scatter plots later on, but for now we will illustrate their use in detecting deviant cases and in seeing how cases bunch together in various ways.

Ninths of Development

■	9
▓	7 - 8
▨	5 - 6
▒	3 - 4
░	1 - 2
□	0

Source: Chapin and Weiss, 1965: Fig. 3. Reprinted by permission.

FIGURE 4.19 LAND IN RESIDENTIAL USE, GREENSBORO, NORTH CAROLINA, 1960

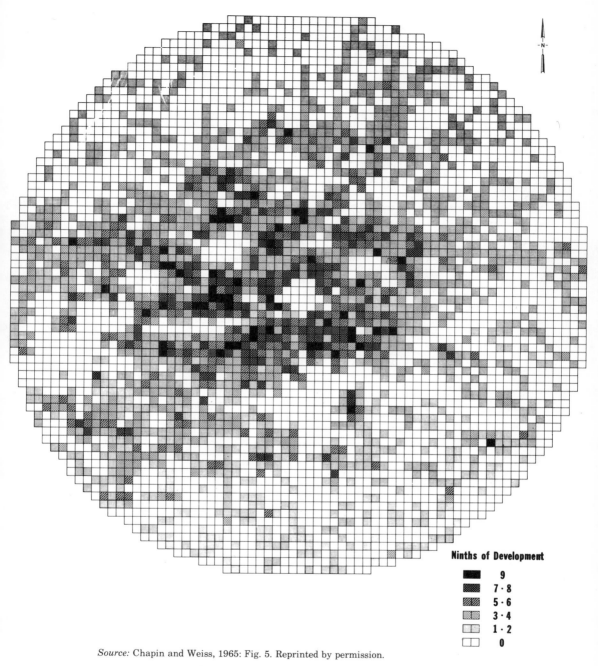

Ninths of Development

■	9
■	7 · 8
▨	5 · 6
▨	3 · 4
▨	1 · 2
□	0

Source: Chapin and Weiss, 1965: Fig. 5. Reprinted by permission.

FIGURE 4.20 EXPECTED RESIDENTIAL LAND USE, GREENSBORO, NORTH CAROLINA, 1960, BASED ON USE OF PROBABILISTIC MODEL—MEDIAN OUTCOME OF 50 RUNS

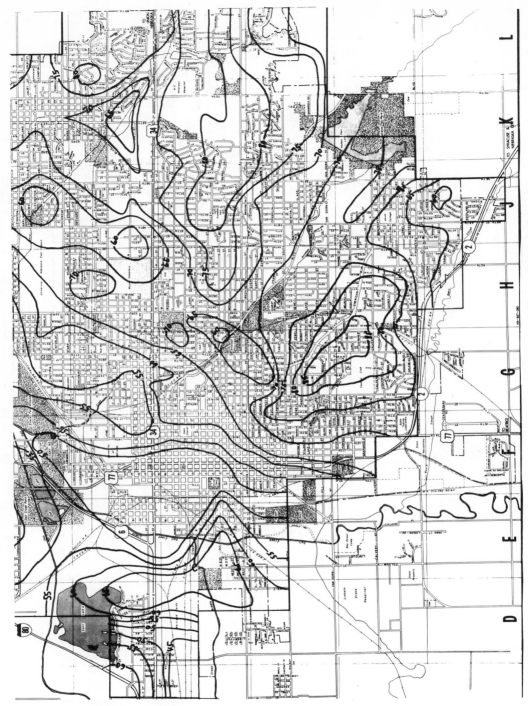

Source: Hoiberg and Cloyd, 1971. Reprinted by permission.

FIGURE 4.21 AN ISOLINE MAP OF SOCIAL CLASS VARIATION IN A MIDWESTERN CITY

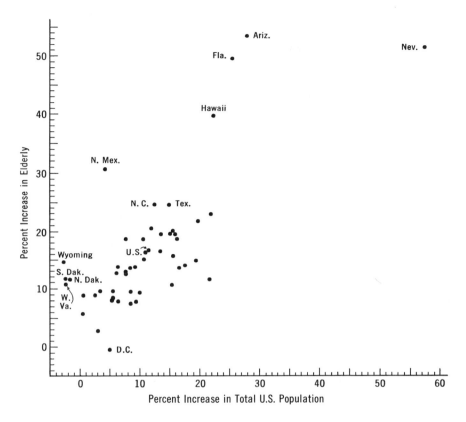

Source: U.S. Senate: 1969:326.

FIGURE 4.22 SCATTER PLOT OF PERCENT INCREASE IN TOTAL POPULATION AND IN POPU-
LATION AGED 65 AND OVER BETWEEN 1960 AND 1968 FOR STATES AND THE DISTRICT OF
COLUMBIA

Figure 4.22 shows a scatter plot of the fifty states plus the District of
Columbia. Each dot represents one of these areas. The dot is placed to show on
the X-axis the percentage change in its population overall between 1960 and
1968, and on the Y-axis the percentage change in the state's elderly population
aged 65 and older between 1960 and 1968. As shown on the scatter diagram, most
states show a total population increase of 10 to 20 percent, and most likewise
show a 10 to 20 percent increase in the elderly population. The dots tend to bunch
around the overall U.S. average of an 11 percent population increase and a 16
percent increase in the elderly. Yet several states show an unusually large increase in the elderly, or in both elderly and total population. Some of the deviant
states are labelled on Figure 4.22. Nevada, Arizona, Florida, Hawaii, and New
Mexico show a larger percentage increase in the elderly population than in the
total population. Wyoming, North and South Dakota, and West Virginia show
a total population decline coupled with a 10 to 15 percent increase in the elderly

population. Only the District of Columbia showed a decline in the elderly and an increase in total population between these two years.

An examination of these deviant cases which are made evident in an examination of a scatter diagram may lead to other important insights into migration trends. Likely population processes are relatively obvious for the first two groupings of states noted above. The first group consists of states which are often defined as "retirement areas" with large villages developed mainly for the elderly. The second group of states are those where other population groups are moving out, leaving the elderly behind. The District of Columbia presents an interesting reversal of this pattern of increase in the 65-plus population. Isolation of such deviant cases often serves as the focus for productive future research to better understand and explain the sociological phenomenon of migration, in this instance. Other examples of the use of the scatter diagram will be presented in Chapter 7.

Scatter diagrams are useful to show how individual cases are spread out in a "space" formed by the two dimensions or variables scaled along the X- and Y-axes. Diagram 4.2 provides a further explanation of the mechanics of creating scatter diagrams.

4.4.3 Triangular Plot

A triangular plot is like a scatter diagram in that each case or individual is located by a dot in the space of the graph so that clusterings and distances between the dots on measured variables may be examined. The triangular plot, however, locates dots on a graph which is the shape of an equilateral triangle. It is used in situations where a variable has three meaningful categories (or can be regrouped to have three), and where a case can be characterized in terms of a percentage in each category totalling to 100 percent for each case (*i.e.* it is composed of three parts that include all the possibilities being considered in the case). Usually the "cases" plotted are groups, like "male graduate students," "members of a certain religious denomination," "the leading crowd in a highschool," etc., where each case can be characterized in terms of a total percentage (100%) made up of those for example, who have a "favorable," "unfavorable" or "no opinion" attitude on some issue. Other variables with three categories, in addition to some opinion questions, might be marital status (single, currently married, other); residence (in the central city, in suburbs, in rural areas); judgments (other jobs are better, the same, or worse than mine), and so forth.

The graph paper, which is available commercially, is an equilateral triangle with scales extending from each side to the opposite corner. Each scale is marked from zero percent at the opposite side to 100 percent in the corner. A point that is one third of the way toward a corner from each of the three sides falls exactly in the middle of the graph at the point which is 33⅓% on each of the scales. Thus a dot's location reflects three percentages which total to 100 percent. Figure 4.23 illustrates this type of graph and Diagram 4.2 discusses the mechanics of construction.

DIAGRAM 4.2 How to Construct Scatter Plots, Triangular Plots and Semi-Log Graphs

SCATTER DIAGRAMS

Step 1. Data on at least two variables for each case are needed to construct a scatter diagram. For a 2-dimensional scatter plot, two scores per case are needed. In the following example, large cities have been measured using a health facility measure (number of hospital beds per 100,000 population in 1970) and an economic measure (that city's per capita personal income as a percentage of the national average per capita income).*

	Selected Cities	No. Health Facilities	Economic Measure (%)
a	Youngstown, Ohio	366.8	100
b	Trenton, N.J.	525.1	115
c	Springfield, Mass.	437.5	97
d	St. Louis, Mo.	496.4	108
e	Newark, N.J.	436.9	129
f	New Orleans, La.	507.2	97
g	Huntington, W. Va.	593.5	87
h	Erie, Pa.	397.5	96
i	Cleveland, Ohio	418.3	119
j	Cincinnati, Ohio	370.7	106
k	Chicago, Ill.	436.9	127
l	Charleston, W. Va.	619.1	93
m	Birmingham, Ala.	493.3	87

Step 2. Set up coordinates and mark the scale of each variable on one of the axes. Axes should be about the same physical length, and the scales should be marked so that the highest and lowest scores are nearly as far apart as the axis is long. Equal physical units on the scale, of course, should correspond to equal distances on the variable. Label the axes clearly.

Graph paper is usually used. It is commercially available with different numbers of lines per inch, but for much of the graphing in sociology a 10-line-per-inch graph paper is most useful.

Step 3. Plot each case as a dot, located so that it is just opposite the proper point on both axes correctly showing its score on both variables. One dot is plotted per case. Often, in this descriptive usage, the dots will be identified by some sort of coding system such as the small letters used below.

Step 4. Analysis. The scatter diagram can then be examined to see to what extent the dots tend to cluster. By looking at other characteristics of cases in a cluster, often additional insight into possible reasons for the cluster-

*These cities all are Standard Metropolitan Statistical Areas with 200,000 population or more in 1970. All areas chosen have a death rate of 10.0–10.2 (the national death rate is 9.7). The U.S. average on the health facilities measure is 414.6 and for the economic measure it is 100%. Both variables are interval level. *Source:* U.S. Bur. Census, 1971; Stat. Abstract.

DIAGRAM 4.2 *(Continued)*

ing can be found. Some investigators used this technique to identify
types of cities, for example.

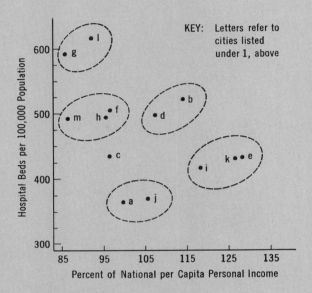

KEY: Letters refer to cities listed under 1, above. Scatter plot with vertical axis "Hospital Beds per 100,000 Population" (300 to 600) and horizontal axis "Percent of National per Capita Personal Income" (85 to 135).

TRIANGULAR PLOTS

Step 1. Data for a triangular plot must have three parts for each case that is to
be plotted, and, for each case, the sum of the three parts must equal 100
percent. Thus we could plot a series of questions or *items* if they all were
characterized by the same three-part response scale such as "agree,"
"disagree," and "undecided," and each item could be scored in terms of
the percent of people who gave these three responses so the sum of percentages for any item would be 100 percent. Alternatively, one could
measure *cases* on a specific variable where, again, that variable has three
categories and each case is measured in such a way that the sum of the
measures for a case is always 100 percent. Cities, for example, might be
characterized in terms of percentage of their population which falls in
three inclusive general ethnic categories.

For this illustration we will use data from a Gallup poll in which
the question was asked for several years, "Do you think Communist
China should or should not be admitted as a member of the United
Nations?" The answers were either "favor," "oppose," or "no opinion."
For each poll the percentage responding in each category is given below,

DIAGRAM 4.2 *(Continued)*

and the total of these percents is 100 for any given poll. Here we can examine change through time.

Poll Date	% Favor	% Oppose	% No Opinion	Total
1954, July	7	78	15	100
1954, Sept.	8	79	13	100
1955, June	10	67	23	100
1955, Sept.	17	71	12	100
1956, July	11	74	15	100
1957, Feb.	13	70	17	100
1958, Feb.	17	66	17	100
1958, Sept.	20	63	17	100
1961, March	20	64	16	100
1961, Oct.	18	65	17	100
1964, Feb.	15	71	14	100
1964, Nov.	20	57	23	100
1965, March	22	64	14	100
1966, Jan.	22	67	11	100
1966, April	25	55	20	100
1966, Oct.	25	56	19	100
1969, Feb.	33	54	13	100
1970, Oct.	35	49	16	100

Source: Erskine, 1971. Used by permission of George Gallup.

Step 2. *Set Up Coordinates* and mark one of the corners of the triangular chart with each response alternative. The perpendicular from the opposite side to a corner is laid off on a scale of percents with 100 percent the value in a corner and 0 percent the value at the opposite side. Label the graph clearly.

  Graph paper is available from most engineering supply stores. It is called "triangular coordinate" paper.

Step 3. *Plot each case* as a single dot. The dot is located in terms of percentages. For example, the July, 1954 poll outcome would be represented by a dot at the 7% point on the scale that ends in the corner labeled "favor" where that line crosses the line at 78% out toward the corner marked "oppose." This will be at a point which is 15% out from the side opposite the corner marked "no opinion." (See graph on following page.)

Step 4. *Analysis.* Two comments are relevant. First, it would be a mistake to examine only percentages in favor without also taking account of whether the rest of the cases were "oppose" or whether there was merely a shift from favor to "no opinion," for example. Secondly, by connecting dots with a line, we can show the direction of the shift through time. It appears, overall, that there has been a shift toward the "favor" corner.

DIAGRAM 4.2 *(Continued)*

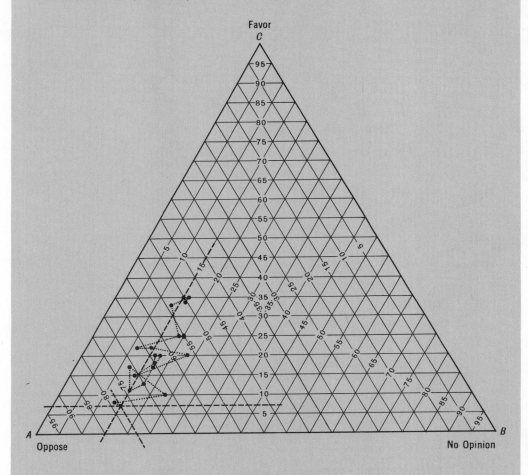

SEMI-LOGARITHMIC CHARTS

Step 1. Data used in semi-logarithmic charts are usually measures for a series
of different years made on one case, such as a society. There are excep-
tions, of course, but the usual use of semi-logarithmic charts is to show
rate of change through time. The following data are median (a kind of
average which is discussed in the next chapter) income for families in
the United States and these measurements were made for a number of
different years. What is the rate of change in median income of families?

DIAGRAM 4.2 *(Continued)*

Year	Median Income
1947	$3,031
1950	3,319
1958	5,087
1959	5,417
1960	5,620
1961	5,737
1962	5,956
1963	6,249
1964	6,569
1965	6,957
1966	7,500
1967	7,974
1968	8,632
1969	9,433
1970	9,867

Source: U.S. Bur. Census, 1971:P-60.

Step 2. Set Up Coordinates. A semi-logarithmic chart could be created by marking an arithmetic scale with the logarithms of numbers. Instead, semi-log graph paper is available, where the rulings are in terms of original scores rather than their logs, so that scores need not be converted to logs prior to plotting. This is the reason for the unequally spaced appearance of semi-log graph paper; it has lines more closely spaced together toward the top of the paper.

Paper is available with several tiers or "cycles" of lines numbered from 1 to 10. One-cycle paper is used to plot scores where the largest is no more than 10 times the smallest. If the largest number is 10 to 100 times the smallest, two-cycle paper is needed, and so on. The X-axis is a standard arithmetic scale (although double-logarithmic paper is available and used for some specialized purposes not discussed in this text).

In the example above, the largest median income figure is less than 10 times the smallest so one-cycle paper is needed. The log-scale is labeled in score units, in this case $1000's of dollars. Notice that the starting point is some convenient power of ten (.01, .1, 10, 100, 1000, etc.) rather than zero because the rate of increase from zero can not be determined (recall that percentage change is the difference between a starting and ending figure divided by a starting figure and division by zero is not a defined operation). We chose $1,000. and proceeded upward in $1,000. increments.

The X-axis is labeled in terms of time, in this case years between 1947 and 1970.

Step 3. Plot the value of the score above the proper X-axis score. Here, we are plotting each median income figure above the year to which it refers.

DIAGRAM 4.2 *(Continued)*

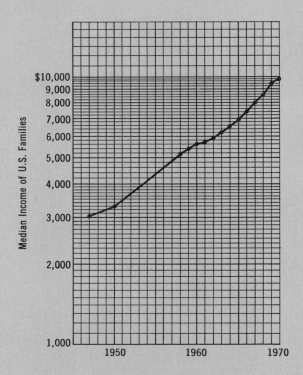

These dots are connected with straight lines and the figure is *not* closed
with the X-axis.

Step 4. Analysis. A straight line indicates a constant rate of change. The more
steeply the line goes up or down, the more rapid the rate of change, and
by inspection of these graphs one can determine whether there is a
change at an increasing rate or a decreasing rate of change.

In the example, the rate of increase has been relatively constant,
overall, but there have been periods of decreasing-rates-of-increase prior
to 1950, just after 1960, and just before 1970. In the mid-60's there was a
slightly increasing rate of increase, as shown by the arching upward of
the line into a steeper ascent.

Figure 4.23 is from a study of adolescent society by James Coleman (1961) in which he studied ten highschools selected from northern Illinois in 1957 and 1958. Data for the triangular graph came from a question in his study which asked boys what they most wanted to be—jet pilot, nationally famous athlete, or atomic scientist. For each school two sets of percentages were computed: the percentage of all boys selecting each of the three "ideals," and the percentage of boys who were among the "elite" or leading crowd who selected each of the three

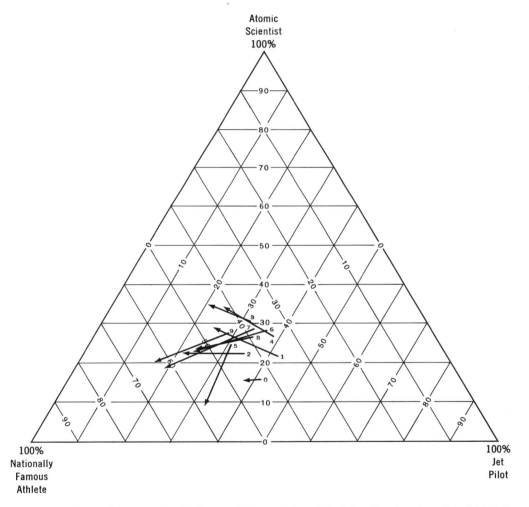

Source: Coleman, 1961:132. Reprinted by permission of The Macmillan Company. Copyright © The Free Press, A Corporation, 1961.

FIGURE 4.23 TRIANGULAR PLOT OF THE RELATIVE ATTRACTIVENESS OF "NATIONALLY FAMOUS ATHLETE," "ATOMIC SCIENTIST," AND "JET PILOT" TO BOYS IN EACH SCHOOL (tail end of arrow) AND LEADING CROWD OF BOYS IN EACH SCHOOL (point of arrow)

ideals. Most triangular plots stop with this display of results, but Coleman took an additional step which highlights the relative attractiveness of the "nationally famous athlete" category among the leading crowd in each school. He connected each overall percentage for each school with the dot representing the elite's position in that school with the arrow pointing toward the elite's dot. The length of the arrow reflects the difference between boys in general and the leading crowd and the direction of the arrow indicates the category toward which this difference is directed. Notice that most leading crowds are "further out" than boys in general, and that they are different in the direction of finding "nationally famous athlete" a more attractive ideal category. This triangular plot, and others that Coleman presents, greatly aid in his analysis of the social trends and pressures of highschools he studied.

4.4.4 The Semi-Logarithmic Chart

The last graphic technique we will discuss here is the semi-logarithmic chart. This is a graph plotted on rectangular coordinates which are similar to the Cartesian coordinates we have used before. The X-axis is a numeric scale often showing time or age. The Y-axis, however, is laid off in terms of the logarithms of

TABLE 4.1 AN ILLUSTRATION OF RATE OF CHANGE AS REFLECTED IN DIFFERENCES BETWEEN RAW SCORES AND DIFFERENCES BETWEEN LOGS OF SCORES

(a) Data Illustrating a *Constant Rate* of Increase

Year	Raw Scores	Amt. of Change	Percent Change	Log of Scores	Amt. of Change in Logs
1930	12.00			1.079	
1935	15.00	+3.00	+25%	1.176	+.097
1940	18.75	+3.75	+25%	1.273	+.097
1945	23.44	+4.69	+25%	1.370	+.097

(b) Data Illustrating an *Increasing Rate* of Decrease

Year	Raw Scores	Amt. of Change	Percent Change	Log of Scores	Amt. of Change in Logs
1950	8.00			0.903	
1955	6.00	−2.00	−25%	0.778	−.125
1960	4.00	−2.00	−33%	0.602	−.176
1965	2.00	−2.00	−50%	0.301	−.301

(c) Data Illustrating a *Decreasing Rate* of Increase

Year	Raw Scores	Amt. of Change	Percent Change	Log of Scores	Amt. of Change in Logs
1970	2.00			0.301	
1975	6.00	+4.00	+200%	0.778	+.477
1980	10.00	+4.00	+66%	1.000	+.222
1985	14.00	+4.00	+29%	1.146	+.146

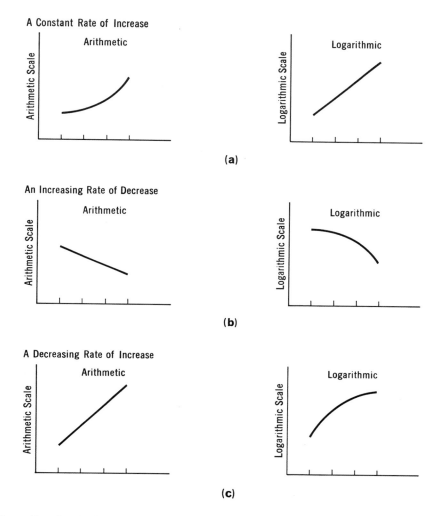

Source: Data from Table 4.1.

FIGURE 4.24 GRAPHIC ILLUSTRATION OF THE DIFFERENCE BETWEEN AN ARITHMETIC AND LOGARITHMIC CHART TO PORTRAY RATES OF CHANGE

numbers rather than their arithmetic value. The semi-log chart is especially useful in an analysis of *trend lines,* because equal numeric differences between logarithms indicate equal *rates of change.** Table 4.1 and Figure 4.24 illustrate this useful feature of logarithms. Notice that a constant rate of change shown in Figure 4.24 can be quickly detected on a semi-logarithmic chart by a straight line rather than a curved line.

*There are charts with logarithmic scales on both axes, and these are called "log-log" charts. They are used for more complex plots of rates against each other and will not be included in this discussion.

BOX 4.4 LOGARITHMS AND THEIR USE IN STATISTICS

Common logarithms are a system of exponent numbers for the base-number 10, that is, exponential powers to which 10 may be raised to produce any given original number. For example, the common logarithm (base 10) of 100 is 2.0 because $10^{2.0}$ is 100; the $\log_{10}$ of 1000 is 3.0, and so on, with the majority of log numbers being a fractional power of 10. Logarithms are convenient for calculation because the process of *adding* these logarithmic exponents amounts to a process of *multiplying* the original numbers produced by the logarithms (and subtracting amounts to dividing). Thus the relatively simple process of adding or subtracting can be used to show more complex multiplying and dividing variations. In statistical graphing, logarithms can thus be used to exaggerate certain effects.

The usual fractional common logarithm has two parts: a whole number to the left of the decimal point called the *characteristic*, and a fractional number to the right of the decimal point called the *mantissa*. The value of the characteristic may be positive or negative and depends on the location of the decimal point in the original number; the value of the mantissa is normally read from a table of common logarithms (usually in reference sections of mathematics texts or in some statistics workbooks). The table below has been developed to show both the characteristic and the mantissa.

Original Number	Logarithm	Original Number	Logarithm
0.01	−2.0000	50	1.6990
0.1	−1.0000	100	2.0000
1	0.0000	200	2.3010
2	0.3010	500	2.6990
5	0.6990	1000	3.0000
10	1.0000	2000	3.3010
20	1.3010	5000	3.6990

Notice that the characteristic for original numbers less than one is negative and is equal to the number of zeros between decimal point and first digit, plus one. For original numbers greater than one, the characteristic is a positive number which is one less than the number of integers in the original number (*i.e.*, zero for ones, 1 for tens, 3 for thousands, etc.). Thus the complete common logarithm is formulated with the appropriate characteristic for the original number plus its mantissa as shown in a standard reference table. *Anti-logarithms* are found by reversing the procedure to find the original number from a logarithm.

Since commercial logarithmic graph paper is available, conversion of statistical scores or frequencies to logarithms by calculation is not normally necessary, and the scale of the original scores can be placed within a labeled sequence in the unequally (*i.e.*, logarithmically) spaced Y-axis scale points. Original scores are then plotted directly on the scale.

Logarithms are quite useful in statistics in a number of ways. They simplify the computation of the specialized mean called the geometric mean (see Chapter 5); they greatly aid in the study of trends, as indicated in this chapter; and they are sometimes used to transform scores to simplify a study of relationships between variables (see Chapters 7 and 8).

Two studies will serve to illustrate uses of the semi-logarithmic chart and Diagram 4.2 provides details about their construction. Figure 4.25 presents data on infant mortality for the United States during the period from 1915 to 1967. The Y-axis is a logarithmic scale labeled in terms of death rates for infants. The trend line shows a general decline which is almost a straight line but not quite. The rate of decline from year to year is nearly but not quite constant. In years prior to 1945 the rate of decline slowed up slightly and the rate of decline dropped more rapidly again in the few years after about 1945. Again around 1960 there was a slowing in the rate of decrease in infant mortality shown by a leveling off of the trend line. More recently the steep rate of decline has been resumed. Demographers sometimes use infant mortality figures as an indicator for changes in the quality of health care in a country. Research could be focused on explanations for the increasing or decreasing rate of decrease in mortality in the U.S. over this half-century period. The semi-logarithmic chart makes these changes in rates more apparent. In Figure 4.25, the fact that this is a semi-logarithmic chart can be readily detected by the characteristically unequal spacing on the Y-axis and the constant size of the unit on the X-axis.

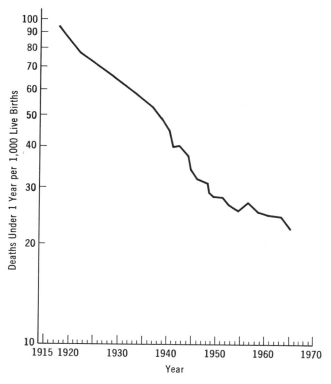

Source: Chase and Byrnes, 1972: Fig. 1.

FIGURE 4.25 INFANT MORTALITY RATES, U.S. 1915–1967 (a semi-logarithmic chart)

The second example of the use of a semi-logarithmic chart is from a study of population growth by Wray (1971) which matched infant death certificates with the corresponding birth certificates for the 1.3 million births in England and Wales in 1949–1950 (an example of the use of recorded data). The graph in Figure 4.26 shows infant mortality ratios on the logarithmic scale on the Y-axis. A mortality ratio is the ratio between the mortality rate for infants in a given population sub-group divided by the overall mortality rate for all infants. The value 100 on the Y-axis indicates that the sub-group mortality rate and the overall mortality rate are the same; higher values indicate that the sub-group mortality rate is higher. In this graph, the sub-groups which are examined reflect different social classes (I and II are upper classes, III is middle class, and IV and V are lower classes in these data) of the infant's mother. Within social class groupings mortality ratios are computed for infants of different birth order. That is, infants who are first-born, second- or third-born, and fourth- or later born are handled separately in the graphic presentation. Thus there is a separate line on the graph for each birth order within each of three social classes. Each line shows the mortality ratio of infants in a given birth-order and social class category by the age of its mother at the time of its birth. From this semi-logarithmic chart a large number of conclusions may be drawn. In virtually all cases the mortality ratio drops with increases in the mother's age until some time around the 30's where the rate of decline slows up and gradually changes direction. Toward the 40's the mortality ratio shows an increasing rate of increase, in most instances with the increasing age of the mother. The mortality ratio (and, by the way, the infant mortality rate as well) is higher for later-born infants than for early-born infants, and this finding holds up within each of the social class categories. Furthermore, looking across the three social class categories for the latest-born category of infants, the mortality ratio is higher among infants of upper-class mothers of a given age than it is among infants of lower-class mothers of that age. The investigators conclude that high mortality rates among infants of young mothers with large families occurs in all social classes and the concentration of young mothers with large families in lower social classes can not totally account for higher mortality rates among infants in lower classes.

BOX 4.5 TRENDS AND TREND LINES

The study of *trends,* or change in some characteristic through a period of time, is one of the important areas of sociology. It is an area which poses many problems for research design, for measurement, and for statistical analysis. (For example, see Harris, 1967, for a discussion of several methods for handling change with techniques which are referred to in the chapters of this present volume.)

The study of change via *trend lines* was first discussed in Section 4.2.4. Up to this point we have discussed four methods for describing change: (a) rates (Section 3.2.5 a), (b) percentage change (Section 3.2.5 b), (c) time-line graphs (Section 4.2.4), and semi-logarithmic graphs (Section 4.4.4). In Chapter 5 some methods for "smoothing" trend lines will be discussed.

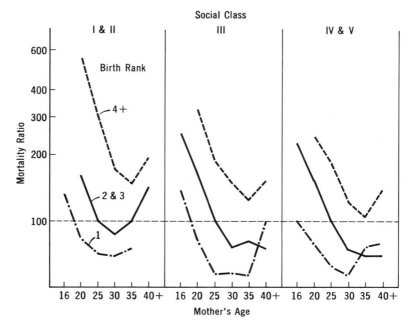

Source: Wray, 1971:414. Reprinted by permission.

FIGURE 4.26 MORTALITY RATIOS BY BIRTH RANK, MOTHER'S AGE AND SOCIAL CLASS, ENGLAND AND WALES, 1949–1950; A SEMI-LOGARITHMIC CHART

4.5 SUMMARY

In this chapter several basic illustrative and analytic graphing techniques have been discussed and their principles analyzed. Graphic techniques, properly used, constitute a very useful and powerful means for communicating more involved comparisons in data and for analyzing complex relationships. They are particularly useful in showing the overall form of a distribution (a feature to be discussed at greater length in Chapter 5) and in showing trends through time.

It seems to be characteristic of more useful procedures that they also have a potential for distortion as well as a potential for more accurate and helpful displays of interesting features of data. A number of possibly distorting practices have been pointed out in this chapter.

The next chapter returns us again to the basic univariate distribution discussed in Chapter 3, which is graphed by techniques such as the histogram and polygon as shown in this chapter. Chapter 5, however, will approach the description of whole distributions of scores in terms of a few summary index numbers which will communicate key features of a univariate distribution. Later chapters will address similar problems for bivariate and multivariate distributions.

CONCEPTS TO KNOW AND UNDERSTAND

reference system
  ordinate
  abscissa
  origin
  quadrants
histogram
polygon
ogive
line graph
bar chart

cohort
population pyramid
pie chart
pictograph
triangle plot
scatter diagram
statistical map
semi-logarithmic chart
trends
cautions about graphic distortions

QUESTIONS AND PROBLEMS

1. Find several examples of graphic presentation of data in popular magazines and newspapers. For each graph describe its strengths and weaknesses in presenting relevant features of the data for the reader. Are there flaws in the graphic presentation? If so, what corrective measures would you suggest, and what possible distortions might your changes promote?

2. If you are assigned a project or piece of research in this course, now is a good time to decide upon the kinds of phenomena you are going to study. This often means selecting an interesting dependent variable. After you have selected your dependent variable and found relevant data, begin your analysis by creating a distribution of the dependent variable. Select an appropriate graphic technique and graph the distribution.

3. Using data in a journal research article or from a statistics workbook, select two scores on each of several cases. Create a scatter diagram with scales for the two variables along the X and Y axes. Explain in your own words what it is that the graph shows.

GENERAL REFERENCE

Schmid, Calvin F., *Handbook of Graphic Presentation,* (New York, Ronald Press), 1954. This is a carefully explained and illustrated book on different types of graphic presentation and how to solve some of the presentational problems an analyst encounters.

OTHER REFERENCES

Asimov, Isaac, *Asimov's Biographical Encyclopedia of Science and Technology,* (Garden City, N.Y., Doubleday and Company), 1964.

Berry, Brian J. L., "Problems of Data Organization and Analytical Methods in Geography," *Journal of the American Statistical Association,* 66 (September, 1971), p 510–523.

Chapin, F. Stuart, Jr., and Shirley F. Weiss in collaboration with Thomas G. Donnelly, *Some Input Refinements For A Residential Model,* a project of the Center for Urban and Regional Studies, University of North Carolina at Chapel Hill, in cooperation with the U.S. Bureau of Public Roads, July, 1965, p 28.

Chase, Helen C., and Mary E. Byrnes, "Trends In 'Prematurity': United States: 1950–1967," Vital and Health Statistics Series 3, Number 15, (U.S. Department of Health, Education and Welfare, Public Health Service, Washington, D.C.), 1972.

Coleman, James S., *The Adolescent Society: The Social Life of the Teenager and its Impact on Education,* New York, The Free Press of Glencoe), 1961.

Erskine, Hazel, "The Polls: Red China and the U.N." *Public Opinion Quarterly,* 35 (Spring, 1971), p 125.

Ferriss, Abbott L., "An Indicator of Marriage Dissolution By Marriage Cohort," *Social Forces,* 48 (March, 1970).

Harris, Chester W., (ed), *Problems in Measuring Change,* (Madison, Wisc., University of Wisconsin Press), 1967.

Hoiberg, Eric O., and Jerry S. Cloyd, "Definition and Measurement of Continuous Variation in Ecological Analysis," *American Sociological Review,* 36 (February, 1971) p 65–74.

Jacobson, Paul H., *American Marriage and Divorce,* (New York, Rinehart), 1959, p. 118.

————, "The Changing Role of Mortality in American Family Life," *Lex et Scientia,* vol 3, no. 2, 1966.

Kaufman, Herbert, and David Seidman, "The Morphology of Organizations," *Administrative Science Quarterly,* 15 (December, 1970).

Maris, Ronald W., *Social Forces in Urban Suicide,* (Homewood, Illinois, Dorsey Press), 1969.

Mauldin, W. Parker, "Fertility Studies: Knowledge, Attitude, and Practice," *Studies in Family Planning* #7, (New York: The Population Council), June, 1965.

Petersen, William, *Population,* (New York, Macmillan), 1961.

[Population Reference Bureau] "Man's Population Predicament," *Population Bulletin,* vol. 27, no. 2, April 1971.

Riley, Matilda White, and Anne Foner, *Aging and Society: An Inventory of Social Research Findings,* (New York, Russell Sage Foundation), 1968.

Riley, Matilda White, "Aging and Cohort Succession: Interpositions and Misinterpretations," *Public Opinion Quarterly,* 37 (Spring, 1973), p 35–49.

Schmid, Calvin F., *Handbook of Graphic Presentation,* (New York, Ronald Press), 1954.

U.S. Bureau of the Census, *Current Population Reports,* P–25, No. 352, (Washington, D.C.), 1966, p 4.

————, "Projections of the Population of the United States by Age and Sex (interim projections): 1970 to 2020," *Current Population Reports,* P–25, No. 448, (Washington, D.C.), 1970.

————, "Consumer Income," *Current Population Reports,* P–60, No. 72, (Washington, D.C.), 1970, Table 6.

————, "Consumer Income," *Current Population Reports,* P–60, No. 78, (Washington, D.C.), 1971, Table 1.

————, "Metropolitan Area Statistics," *Statistical Abstract of the United States, 1971,* (Washington, D.C.), 1971.

————, "Birth Expectation Data: June 1971," *Current Population Reports,* P–20, No. 232, (Washington, D.C.), 1972.

————, "School Enrollment in the United States, 1971," *Current Population Reports,* P–20, No. 234, (Washington, D.C.), 1971.

U.S. Department of Health, Education, Welfare: Public Health Service, "Children and Youth: Selected Health Characteristics," *Vital and Health Statistics,* Series 10, No. 62 (Rockville, Md.), 1971, p 31.

U.S. Department of Justice, *Uniform Crime Reports for the United States,* (Washington, D.C.), 1971, p 32.

U.S. Senate, Committee on Aging, "Developments in Aging," (Washington, D.C.), 1969, p 326.

Weitzman, Murray S., "Measures of Overlap of Income Distributions of White and Negro Families in the United States," *Technical Paper* No. 22, U.S. Bureau of the Census, (Washington, D.C.), 1970, p 9.

Wray, Joe D., "Population Pressure on Families: Family Size and Child Spacing," Chapter 11, *Rapid Population Growth: Consequences and Policy Implications,* vol. 2, (Baltimore, Md., Johns Hopkins Press), 1971, p 414. (Prepared under direction of Dr. Roger Revelle.)

5

SUMMARY MEASURES OF THE LOCATION, VARIATION AND FORM OF UNIVARIATE DISTRIBUTIONS

A very basic type of research continually pursued by all quantitative disciplines is research on measurement instruments. Some of this research is to develop new or better measurement procedures for some interesting characteristic. Other research is for the purpose of identifying possible biases which may enter into the use of a measurement procedure, and also for identifying those conditions under which the measurement will produce valid and reliable scores.

5.1 UNIVARIATE DISTRIBUTIONS—AN EXAMPLE AND OVERVIEW

Cloud and Vaughn conducted research of the kind described above, using the Wilson-Patterson "Conservatism Scale," (1970). The Wilson-Patterson scale includes 50 words or catch phrases which, in many Western contexts, reflect ideas held by more "liberal" or more "conservative" people. A respondent is asked to indicate which words represent ideas he favors or believes in. Ten of the 50 items are given below, and agreement with the odd-numbered items is thought to indicate a conservative attitude.

Which of the following do you favor or believe in?

1	death penalty	Yes	?	No
4	striptease shows	Yes	?	No
7	patriotism	Yes	?	No
12	birth control	Yes	?	No
22	legalized abortion	Yes	?	No
29	royalty	Yes	?	No
33	apartheid	Yes	?	No

35	church authority	Yes	?	No
36	disarmament	Yes	?	No
50	pyjama parties	Yes	?	No

An individual's "conservatism" score is created first by assigning numeric weights to the answer alternatives, and then by summing up the weights for a respondent's answer alternatives for all 50 items. A weight of 2 was assigned to the most conservative response to each item, which means that the "Yes" response on the 25 conservative words, or the "No" response on the 25 liberal words, were each assigned the weight 2. The undecided, question-mark response was assigned a weight of 1, and the liberal response was assigned a score of zero. Thus, individual respondents could get a total score for all 50 items from zero (for those giving all "liberal" responses) to 100 (for those giving all "conservative" responses). This scale is "balanced" because there were an equal number of conservative and liberal items, and by using the scoring procedure discussed above, the final score should be one which eliminates acquiescence bias and produces a "true" content score. To say the same thing somewhat differently, any tendency an individual may have to give a "yes" answer regardless of the content of an item will occur equally often both for liberal items (and be scored zero) and for conservative items (and be scored 2), thus balancing any bias toward conservativism or toward liberalism in the overall score.

Cloud and Vaughn then developed two other ways of scoring the same kind of scale which would represent acquiescence bias. One scoring procedure, called a "yeasaying" score, is simply the sum of weighted responses as before, except that the "yes" response always was weighted 2 regardless of the content of the item. The score zero would be for those who never checked "yes" to any of the 50 items and the score 100 would go to those who always checked "yes." The other score, called a "style" score, is somewhat more complicated. It is a ratio created by taking the difference between the proportion of agreements to conservative items and the proportion of agreements to liberal items, divided by the proportion of all items the subject agrees with.* Both the yeasaying scores and the style scores are measures of response style of the kind called acquiescence.

*As an example of the three scores, suppose that there were only a scale of six (rather than 50) items, alternating liberal and conservative, as follows:

	One Person's Answers
Item 1 (conservative item)	Yes
Item 2 (liberal item)	No
Item 3 (conservative item)	Yes
Item 4 (liberal item)	Yes
Item 5 (conservative item)	Yes
Item 6 (liberal item)	No

One person's answers to these six items is given above and his three scores are computed as follows:
(a) Conservativism Score (C), in this example would count 2 for each conservative item answered "yes" or each liberal item answered "no." Here, the total would equal 10, two points for the answer to items 1,2,3,5, and 6.
(b) Yeasaying Score (Y), counts two points for each yes regardless of whether the item is a liberal or conservative item. Here there are four yes answers for a score of 8.
(c) Style Score (S) is a ratio made up of the following proportions:

Proportion of conservative items that the subject agreed with. Here he agreed with all three of the conservative items for a score of 1.00.

5.1a   Features of a Distribution.   Figure 5.1 shows frequency polygons for content (C), yeasaying (Y), and style (S) scores from the Wilson-Patterson

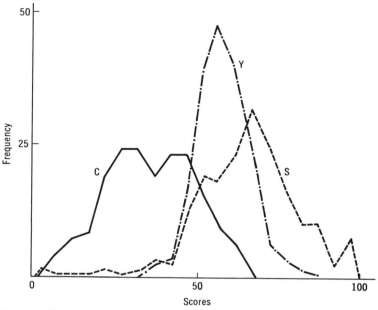

Source: Cloud and Vaughn, 1970: 199. Reprinted by permission.

FIGURE 5.1   FREQUENCY DISTRIBUTIONS OF CONTENT (C), STYLE (S), AND YEASAYING (Y) SCORES FOR 183 NEW ZEALAND COLLEGE STUDENTS ON THE WILSON-PATTERSON CONSERVATISM SCALE.

scale for 183 New Zealand college students. The three distributions are clearly different in a number of respects. First, they differ in their *location* or concentration along the score scale. The "lowest" score distribution is the C, next the Y, and the highest is the S distribution. Secondly, the distributions differ in their relative *concentration.* The Y distribution is much more "piled up" in the center of the distribution, with fewer cases at the extremes, than is the case for the

---

Proportion of liberal items that the subject agreed with. Here, he agreed with one out of the three liberal items for a score of .33.

Overall proportion of items agreed with. Here four of the six items were agreed with for a score of .67.

Combining these three components, the Style score is:

$$\text{Style} = \frac{1.00 - .33}{.67} = \frac{.67}{.67} = 1.00$$

While the construction of this type of score need not be understood to handle material in this chapter, it does provide an illustration of a use of statistical summaries in combination to create an index which may get at the phenomena one wants in a useful fashion. Index formation and "scaling" techniques are topics usually reserved for a course in research methods.

other two distributions. Both C and S distributions are much more spread out, with lower frequencies in any one category than is true of Y, but greater frequencies in more categories than is true of Y. Thirdly, the ③ *form* of the distributions differ in several respects, such as the number of peaks, extent of "lop-sidedness" etc. These three features of distributions are referred to as **central tendency** (or, sometimes, *location*), **variation,** and **form.**

In the case of Cloud and Vaughn's research (1970), the C distribution represents acquiescence-free conservatism content scores. The Y and S distributions represent somewhat different approaches to relatively pure "acquiescence" score distributions. Their point is that unbalanced tests, those which do not include equal numbers of "opposite" items, would result in a distribution of some type of combination of the C and Y (or C and S) distributions. The effect of not eliminating acquiescence bias would not only be a change in the *location* or *central tendency* of the distribution of conservatism scores, but it would likely also be a change in the the amount of *variation* among scores and the *form* of the distribution of conservatism scores—rather complex biasing of scores from a measurement procedure. They naturally recommend that attitude scales, such as the Wilson-Patterson scale, be carefully "balanced" as they were able to do in their research.

In this case, differences between three distributions were shown by the graphic technique of the frequency polygon discussed in Chapter 4. In this chapter we will discuss the possibilities of an even more compact characterization of distributions than the graphic technique permits. We will do this by using a very few summary "index numbers" which will indicate central tendency, variation and form of a distribution. We will then be in a position to compare distributions both more efficiently and in terms of some of the specific ways in which distributions differ from each other.

5.1b.   On the Need to Drop Detail.   Cloud and Vaughn (1970) could have compared each of the three scores (*i.e.* the C, the Y and the S scores) for each of the 183 students in their study and based a judgment of differences on this type of detailed search. This would be tedious, unnecessary, and probably misleading in their research. The myriad differences between *individual* scores would probably serve to obscure differences between the three **sets** of scores, and the researchers were interested in differences between the three whole distributions. Furthermore, examining individual score differences for all combinations of scores would probably focus attention on differences person-by-person, and

---

BOX 5.1

The idea of a **distribution** of scores—in frequency or percentage form—is basic to the discussion in this chapter. The objective of this chapter is to describe whole distributions in compact ways. The idea of distribution is introduced in Section 3.2.3 and graphic presentations of distributions are shown in Figures 4.3 and 4.4.

would neglect statistical comparisons between sets of different scores. Their research question is at the level of differences in the overall **distribution** of a variable, and the possible effects one kind of bias may have.

The typical interest of investigators is in distributions rather than individual scores. Thus it is very helpful to have ways to describe whole distributions and drop real but nonetheless distracting information about specific individual scores. As we noted in our discussion of distributions of raw scores, one of the helpful procedures in the analysis of data may be selective elimination of distracting detail in order to permit a clearer focus on differences which are important to the research question at hand.

5.1c. Three Features of a Distribution. Thus it turns out that there are three main ways that distributions differ from each other, and the point of this chapter is to develop accurate ways to measure the features of a univariate distribution for various kinds of data. There are several different approaches to each feature, and the approach one selects in any specific instance will depend on such things as the level of measurement of the variable, the research question in which one is interested, and, sometimes, on the way the variable happens to be distributed. Separate sections of this chapter will deal with approaches to measuring *central tendency* (Section 5.3 ff.), *variation* (Section 5.4 ff.) and *form* (Section 5.5 ff.) of distributions.

5.2 THE FORM OF A DISTRIBUTION—I

The feature of a distribution most readily apparent from a histogram or polygon is its form—the overall shape of the distribution. For many purposes a simple verbal description is sufficient, but single summary "indices" can be developed to reflect certain aspects of the form of a distribution. These numeric indices will be presented in Section 5.5 at the end of this chapter after some of the basic notions of location and variation have been developed. For now, we will call attention to aspects of the form of distributions and introduce some of the terminology by which these features can be expressed.

5.2.1 Number of Modes

A first characteristic of the form of a distribution readily picked up from a histogram or frequency polygon is the number of high points or peaks (modes) the distribution has. In Figure 5.1, for example, the distribution of conservatism scores (C) has two high points with a low between them, and it would be called a **bimodal** distribution. The other two distributions (S) and (Y) in Figure 5.1 are **unimodal** since they have only one main high-point. Notice that the determination of the number of peaks depends to some extent upon one's judgment of the importance of differences in the frequency in categories. For example, the curve (S) has some slight dips and peaks on each side of the main peak, but these are clearly minor when compared to the main peak in the distribution. If they were judged important, comparatively and absolutely, one would refer to a many-moded distribution or "multimodal" distribution. It seems to be true that very many distributions actually encountered in research are unimodal, overall.

5.2.2   Symmetry

A second aspect of the form of a distribution is the extent to which it is symmetrical rather than lopsided or "skewed." The "skew" in a distribution refers to the trailing off of frequencies toward extreme scores in one direction, away from the bulk of cases. Figure 5.2 shows various curves skewed to the left (negatively), in Figure 5.2f, or right (positively), in Figure 5.2d.

A symmetrical curve is one in which two sides of the distribution would exactly correspond, if the figure were to be folded over at its central point. Income is a variable that is usually positively skewed, there are a few extremely high scores (incomes) which are not "balanced" by equally extreme low scores and most individuals have modest to moderate incomes. Ability or experience test scores very often have a nearly symmetrical shape.*

5.2.3   Kurtosis

This aspect of the form of a distribution refers to the extent to which cases are piled up closely around a point in the distribution or are distributed rather widely among categories. As indicated in Figure 5.2, an unusually concentrated distribution of scores is called a **leptokurtic** distribution, one which is flatter than "normal" is called a **platykurtic** distribution. A "normally" concentrated distribution of scores is called **mesokurtic.** Here "normal" has a technical and precise meaning which will be discussed later on. For the time being it is sufficient to know the terminology and be able to compare curves in an approximate way.

There are some terms which refer to the overall shape of a distribution and are handy to know. A **"J-shaped"** distribution has almost all cases piled up at one end of the scale and then tails off uniformly in one direction from the concentration as indicated in Figure 5.2j. **Rectangular** distributions have equal frequencies in all categories so the distribution has a flat top.† A **"bell-shaped"** distribution is unimodal and slopes gently off in both directions from the mode to form the general shape of a bell. Finally, a **U-shaped** distribution is bimodal, with modes at both extremes and a low-frequency area in the center of the distribution.

---

*A shape which is generally a function of the way scores are defined.
†It is interesting to note that pseudo-random numbers are a good example of a *rectangular distribution,* where the likelihood of any of the ten digits from 0 to 9 appearing is equal. Computers sometimes are used to create pseudo-random numbers for random sampling purposes, and one check on such computer programs is to see if they indeed produce a rectangular distribution of numbers. Sampling and the use of random numbers is a topic in the area of inferential statistics (see H. J. Loether and D. G. McTavish, *Inferential Statistics for Sociologists*).

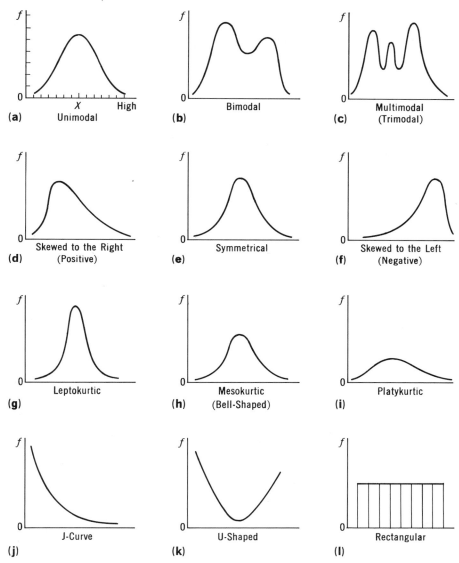

FIGURE 5.2 VARIETIES OF OVERALL FORM OF DISTRIBUTION

5.3  OF A DISTRIBUTION

The location or "central tendency" of a distribution refers to the place on the scale of score values where a particular distribution is centered. Consider the following five sets of scores on height of people, measured in feet. The five individuals in group (c) generally have lower heights than those in (a) or (b), while individuals in (d) and (e) are generally taller. Notice this is generally true even

group a	2	3	4	5	6	N = 5
group b	2	4	4	4	6	N = 5
group c	2	2	2	4	6	N = 5
group d	2	4	6	6	6	N = 5
group e	5	6	7	8	9	N = 5

though some individuals in the group with the tallest heights (e) have heights that are no taller than the highest individuals in the group with the shortest individuals (c). Location is usually measured in terms of some center point or "typical" score in the distribution around which the scores tend to center or cluster in some defined way. There are three main location measures we will use frequently throughout this book.

5.3.1 Mode (Mo)

The **mode** is the value of the score which most frequently occurs in a collection of scores. It would be represented by the tallest column or peak on a histogram or frequency polygon. For grouped data, the mode is the midpoint of the *class* which has the largest frequency of cases in it. The mode of group (b), above, is the score "4," for example, and the modal category of education for 20–21 year old whites in Table 5.1 is "one-year-of-college-or-more." One may choose to designate several modes, as explained in the previous section on the form of a distribution (Section 5.2.1), even though not all "modes" are of exactly equal frequency.

The mode has the virtue of being relatively easily discovered by inspection, and therefore it is often used as a first, quick index to the location of a distribution. In fact, the mode is almost never "computed" by any formula.

The mode can be used with nominal variables (*e.g.* at birth, the modal sex is "male") since it does not depend upon the ordering of scores. Stated differently, the mode ignores score information about rank order and interval size, even if they are available in the data. Distributions (f) and (g), below, have the same mode even though they are located at seemingly quite different points on a score scale if the distances between scores are taken to be meaningful.

| group f | 1 | 3 | 3 | 3 | 3 | 4 | N = 6 |
| group g | 3 | 3 | 50 | 75 | 100 | 119 | N = 6 |

If the variable is ordinal or interval, important locational information may be ignored by using the mode, and this loss of information is usually not desirable. The mode does not require a closed-ended, grouped distribution, provided that the modal category is not the open-ended category (so that a midpoint can be computed). As in (g), above, there may be (and, generally there are) more scores that are *not* equal to the mode than those that *are* equal to the mode. The mode is merely the particular score that most frequently occurs in the data.

TABLE 5.1 PERCENT DISTRIBUTION OF YEARS OF SCHOOL COMPLETED FOR PERSONS 20 YEARS OLD AND OVER, BY AGE AND RACE: U.S. 1970

Age and Race	Total	Less Than 4 Years High School	High School, 4 Years	College 1 Year or More	Median Years of School Completed
WHITE					
20 and 21 years old	100.0	17.7	39.5	42.8	12.8
22 to 24 years old	100.0	17.1	45.9	37.1	12.7
25 to 29 years old	100.0	22.2	45.0	32.8	12.6
30 to 35 years old	100.0	25.8	44.8	29.4	12.5
35 to 44 years old	100.0	33.1	41.9	25.0	12.4
45 to 54 years old	100.0	38.8	40.0	21.2	12.3
55 to 64 years old	100.0	53.6	28.2	18.2	11.2
65 to 74 years old	100.0	67.0	18.4	14.6	8.9
75 years old and over	100.0	75.0	13.8	11.2	8.6
NEGRO					
20 and 21 years old	100.0	32.5	43.5	24.1	12.4
22 to 24 years old	100.0	36.9	41.6	21.4	12.3
25 to 29 years old	100.0	43.9	39.0	17.1	12.2
30 to 34 years old	100.0	50.0	37.6	12.4	12.0
35 to 44 years old	100.0	58.5	29.4	12.2	11.2
45 to 54 years old	100.0	70.9	19.8	9.3	9.3
55 to 64 years old	100.0	83.1	10.7	6.3	7.9
65 to 74 years old	100.0	90.0	4.7	5.4	6.1
75 years old and over	100.0	92.5	4.4	3.1	4.6

Source: U.S. Bur. Census, 1970, P-60:9, Table 7.

5.3.2 Median (Mdn)

The median is the score value below which (and above which) half the scores in a distribution fall. It is the 50th percentile. In group (e), above (in Section 5.3), the median is 7, since this score value exactly divides the odd number of scores ($N=5$) into high and low halves. Group (g) has a median falling between the two center scores, since there are an even number of scores ($N=6$). In this simple case, the usual procedure is to take the average of the two center scores as the median. In this case, the median would be:

$$\text{Mdn} = \frac{50+75}{2} = 62.5$$

In a **grouped distribution,** the median is usually computed on the assumption that cases in the category containing the median are evenly distributed throughout that interval (and, in fact, on the assumption that the interval width is a meaningful value). Diagram 5.1 below illustrates the steps involved in computing the median from grouped data by use of the following formula:

(5.1)
$$\text{Mdn} = L_{\text{mdn}} + \left(\frac{\frac{1}{2}N - \text{cum} f_{\text{mdn}}}{f_{\text{mdn}}}\right) w$$

BOX 5.2 PERCENTILES

The 50th percentile is the *score* below which 50 percent of the scores in a distribution fall. In general, the *n*th percentile is the *score* below which *n* percent of the scores in a distribution fall. You may want to review percentiles by looking back at Section 3.2.3d. Diagram 3.2 illustrates how percentiles may be computed from grouped data. Diagram 5.1 also explains in somewhat more detail the computation of the median itself.

---

where: L_{mdn} is the lower limit of the category containing the median, N is the total number of cases, cumf_{mdn} is the cumulative frequency up to but *not* including the frequency in the median category, f_{mdn} is the frequency in the median category, and w is the width of the median category.

This formula is identical to the formula for computing percentiles since, after all, the median is merely the 50th percentile, although symbols appropriate to the median have been inserted. We will postpone explaining the rationale behind this simple interpolation until Diagram 5.1, since most computations of the median are made by computer directly from raw data. Grouped-data formulas like the one above provide a very good approximation if the number of categories is relatively large (15 or more, for example).

From this definition, it is clear that scores must be at least ordinal before the median can be computed, since the concept of a median implies direction (ranking above and below the median). The median is an index of location that does not imply knowledge of distance, however.* This means that it, like the mode, loses some information contained in interval-level scores. This is sometimes a strength since the median, for example, is little influenced by wild and erratic extreme scores; it is simply the point on the scale of scores dividing all cases into an upper and lower half. Like the mode, the median does not require that extreme classes in a grouped distribution be closed, provided that the median does not fall in one of the open, extreme classes (in which case a category width could not be identified for use in Formula 5.1, above).

To illustrate the median, we have taken data from Reiss concerning the variable, "attitude toward premarital sexual permissiveness"—clearly an ordinal variable (Reiss, 1967:36). Reiss used five attitude questions reflecting permissiveness attitudes, and he asked a sample of college students and a national sample of adults to indicate the extent to which they agreed with each of the five questions. An individual's answers were combined, and he was assigned a "permissiveness score" using a scaling technique called Guttman scaling. The scores ranged from a conservative or low permissiveness score of zero to a high permissiveness score of 6. The percentage distribution of students and of adults is given in Table 5.2, below.

From an examination of the cumulative percentage distributions it is clear that slightly over half (51%) of the students have permissiveness scores of types 0, 1, or 2. The median, therefore, could be some value between 2 and 3 on the

---

*The exception is the width of the median interval when the grouped-data formula for the median is used.

TABLE 5.2 Percentage Distribution of Attitudes Toward Premarital Sexual Permissiveness for a College Student and Adult Sample

College Student Sample

	Permissiveness Scale Types	Percent	Cumulative Percent	
	0 (low)	15	15	
	1	17	32	
Median →	2	19	51	←
(2.4)	3	18	69	
	4	16	85	
	5 (high)	15	100	
		100		
		(844)		

National Sample of Adults

	Permissiveness Scale Types	Percent	Cumulative Percent	
	0 (low)	37	37	
Median →	1	11	48	←
(1.6)	2	31	79	
	3	5	84	
	4	6	90	
	5 (high)	10	100	
		100		
		(1399)		

Source: Reiss, 1967:36. Reprinted by permission of Holt, Rinehart, and Winston, Inc. Copyright © 1967 by Holt, Rinehart, and Winston, Inc.

ordinal scale of types of permissiveness, below which (about) half of the scores fall. The value of 2.5 might be chosen as a convenient median. If the grouped formula were used, the median for these grouped data would turn out to be a value of 2.4.* For the national sample, however, it is clear that subjects are much more concentrated toward the low-permissiveness scale types, and in fact nearly half (48%) have scale type scores of 0 or 1. Again, we could use a convenient value between 1 and 2 as the point on the scale below which (about) half of the cases fell. If this were computed by the grouped formula for the median, the value would be 1.6 for the median. These two values can be compared; the national sample of adults are "located" at a lower point on the permissiveness scale than are the college students. The median is a useful measure of location for a distribution of cases on an ordinal variable.

*It should be noted that the Guttman scaling procedure can result only in integers as score values. Thus the score 2.4 is not defined within the operations of that procedure. Nevertheless, the variable "permissiveness attitudes" is defined as a continuous variable, so that fractional values are conceptually meaningful. Use of the grouped data formula also implies that the width of the median interval is a meaningful concept. This is not defined in an ordinal variable, so the median computed by this formula should be considered an approximation. Investigators generally are willing to make this approximation, and they use fractional values for the median of ordinal variables or of interval variables which are defined as discrete. Other than the assumptions about the category containing the median, the median uses only the ranked aspect of scores.

TABLE 5.3 PERCENTAGE DISTRIBUTION OF HOUSEHOLD HEADS ON 1969 INCOME, BY EDUCATION, IN THE UNITED STATES (Households as of March, 1970)

Educational Attainment of Head	All House-holds (Thousands)	Total	Total Household Income										
			Under $1,000	$1,000 to $1,499	$1,500 to $1,999	$2,000 to $2,499	$2,500 to $2,999	$3,000 to $3,499	$3,500 to $3,999	$4,000 to $4,999	$5,000 to $5,999	$6,000 to $6,999
ALL HOUSEHOLDS												
Total	62 874	100.0	3.2	3.4	3.4	3.4	2.8	3.1	3.1	5.7	6.0	6.4
Elementary: 0 to 7 years	9 203	100.0	7.7	9.2	8.6	6.9	5.8	5.8	4.9	8.3	7.5	6.1
8 years	8 274	100.0	4.5	6.0	5.4	5.3	4.8	4.3	4.7	8.3	7.3	6.7
High School: 1 to 3 years	10 505	100.0	3.1	3.1	3.5	3.9	3.1	3.2	3.3	6.7	7.1	7.4
4 years	19 522	100.0	2.0	1.7	1.7	1.9	1.7	2.2	2.6	4.8	5.9	7.0
College: 1 to 3 years	7 146	100.0	1.7	1.6	1.6	2.2	1.4	2.2	2.2	4.5	4.9	6.3
4 or more	8 225	100.0	1.1	0.6	1.0	1.3	0.9	1.3	1.4	2.3	3.1	3.6
HOUSEHOLDS WITH HEAD AGED 25 OR OVER												
Total	58 570	100.0	3.2	3.5	3.5	3.3	2.7	3.0	3.0	5.5	5.7	6.1
Elementary: 0 to 7 years	9 086	100.0	7.7	9.3	8.7	6.9	5.7	5.9	4.9	8.2	7.4	6.0
8 years	8 123	100.0	4.5	6.0	5.4	5.3	4.8	4.3	4.6	8.3	7.2	6.5
High School: 1 to 3 years	9 737	100.0	2.9	3.1	3.5	3.6	3.0	3.0	3.3	6.4	6.6	7.2
4 years	17 605	100.0	1.9	1.7	1.7	1.9	1.5	2.1	2.3	4.4	5.4	6.7
College: 1 to 3 years	6 249	100.0	1.5	1.5	1.6	1.8	1.3	1.7	1.7	3.8	4.0	5.9
4 or more	7 770	100.0	1.0	0.5	0.9	1.0	0.7	1.1	1.2	2.0	2.7	3.2

TABLE 5.3 (Continued)

Educational Attainment of Head	Total Household Income								Median Income (Dollars)	Mean Income (Dollars)
	$7,000 to $7,999	$8,000 to $8,999	$9,000 to $9,999	$10,000 to $11,999	$12,000 to $14,999	$15,000 to $24,999	$25,000 to $49,999	$50,000 and Over		
ALL HOUSEHOLDS										
Total..............	6.8	6.7	6.2	11.3	11.8	13.4	2.8	0.4	8 389	9 544
Elementary: 0 to 7 years.	5.3	4.8	4.1	5.5	4.9	3.8	0.6	(Z)	4 108	5 494
8 years	6.9	6.3	5.7	8.7	7.8	6.5	0.7	(Z)	5 928	6 951
High School: 1 to 3 years .	8.1	7.0	6.3	11.4	11.3	10.3	1.1	0.1	7 687	8 454
4 years	8.0	8.3	7.4	14.2	14.2	14.0	2.1	0.1	9 275	10 003
College: 1 to 3 years .	6.7	6.8	7.0	12.7	14.7	18.8	4.2	0.5	10 145	11 314
4 or more....	4.2	4.9	5.0	12.1	16.1	29.0	10.4	1.8	13 362	15 452
HOUSEHOLDS WITH HEAD AGED 25 OR OVER										
Total..............	6.6	6.6	6.1	11.5	12.2	14.2	3.0	0.4	8 614	9 755
Elementary: 0 to 7 years .	5.3	4.8	4.1	5.5	5.0	3.9	0.6	(Z)	4 097	5 501
8 years	6.8	6.4	5.7	8.8	7.9	6.6	0.7	(Z)	5 936	6 979
High School: 1 to 3 years .	8.1	7.0	6.5	11.7	11.8	11.0	1.1	0.1	7 919	8 667
4 years	7.6	8.2	7.4	14.6	15.0	15.3	2.3	0.2	9 640	10 329
College: 1 to 3 years .	6.4	6.4	7.0	13.5	15.9	21.0	4.7	0.6	10 836	11 960
4 or more....	4.0	4.9	4.9	12.2	16.5	30.2	11.0	1.9	13 756	15 916

Source: U.S. Bur. Census, 1970: Table 2.

Table 5.3 shows another use of the median, in this instance, used on an interval variable,—income,—which usually has extreme or erratic scores. Table 5.3 is the income distribution for the U.S. as a whole and for household heads who have attained differing amounts of formal education. Notice that the *median* income for all households in 1969 was $8,389. and that the median increases markedly as the amount of formal education increases. In fact, for households whose head had four or more years of college, the median income ($13,362) was about three times the median income for families whose head had completed no more than seven years of elementary school. The median greatly aids in making these kinds of contrasts between the location of different income distributions. In each case, half the individuals have scores below the median income for that group, and half above.

5.3.3 Arithmetic Mean ($\overline{X}$)

The common average or **arithmetic mean** is simply the sum of all scores divided by their number, as in Formula 5.2, below.* You have used this average for some time in computing your grade point average, batting averages, etc.

(5.2)
$$\overline{X}=\frac{\Sigma X_i}{N}$$

It has some other interesting and useful characteristics beyond its value as the most commonly known and widely used measure of central tendency.

To start with, it is another example of the statistical use of the ratio as an aid to valid comparison. The aggregate or total of scores is "standardized," so to speak, in terms of the number of scores that are included in the sum. This permits one to compare "averages" for groups of different sizes, whereas a direct comparison of totaled-up scores would be misleading. Sometimes, however, the number of scores contributing to a sum is not the only source of distracting differences one may want to take into account in making comparisons of central tendency. In arriving at a sum, each score contributes a different amount depending upon its numerical value. Big scores count more than small ones in the sum, and this means that extremely large (or small) scores will tend to have a stronger influence on the mean than more modest, single scores. The arithmetic

*Two comments are relevant. First, the symbol for the arithmetic mean is traditionally $\overline{X}$ or μ (the Greek letter *mu*). The X-bar symbol is used for the statistic—the arithmetic mean computed on sample data—while the symbol μ is used for the parameter—the arithmetic mean computed for the population. Since sample data are generally used in sociology, we will use symbols appropriate for sample statistics throughout this volume. In the field of inferential statistics, where the distinction becomes critical, the two different symbol usages must be made plain and observed carefully. (See H. J. Loether and D. G. McTavish, *Inferential Statistics for Sociologists*.) Secondly, we should note that the summation operator, sigma, correctly includes limits of summation (see Box 3.2) written below and above the symbol as follows:

$$\overline{X}=\frac{\sum_{i=1}^{N} X_i}{N}$$

However, in statistics, summations are nearly always over all N cases, so we will simplify our notation by omitting the limits where this is true. Limits will be introduced when they are needed for clarity.

mean is "pulled" toward unbalanced, extreme scores in a distribution. To state it differently, the mean is pulled toward the tail of skewed distributions; it is pulled higher in positively skewed distributions and lower in negatively skewed distributions. The median, on the other hand, uses the numerical value of the score merely to establish the rank order of a point so that the "upper" and "lower" half of the scores can be identified. Extreme scores would have a minimal effect on the median (each score has the same weight in determining ranking) but a larger effect on the arithmetic mean (where each score contributes different amounts according to its magnitude).

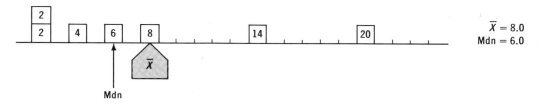

The arithmetic mean is like a balancing point or fulcrum of a lever where uniform blocks are placed on the lever at distances representing their score value. Extreme scores are farther out in both directions on the lever. If the top score in the diagram above were larger, say 30 instead of 20, the balancing point would move to a higher score point on the scale, as shown below.

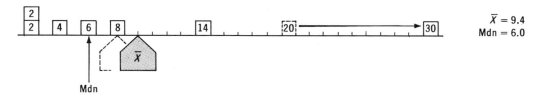

If the extreme score were 200 instead of 20, the fulcrum would have to move to the right even farther as illustrated below, a value for the mean which is quite different from the bulk of scores and perhaps gives too much weight to the single extreme score, 200. The median, on the other hand, would be the same (Mdn = 6), in all three of these situations, since the center of the distribution in the 50%–50% sense has not changed.

If one were to compute the difference between the arithmetic mean and each of the scores in the group upon which it was based as in Table 5.4, and sum

TABLE 5.4 DEVIATION OF SCORES FROM THE ARITHMETIC MEAN AND FROM THE MEDIAN OF A DISTRIBUTION

Raw Scores X_i	Difference $(X_i - \overline{X})$	Absolute Difference $|X_i - \overline{X}|$	Difference $(X_i - \text{Mdn})$	Absolute Difference $|X_i - \text{Mdn}|$
2	$2-8 = -6$	6	$2-6 = -4$	4
2	$2-8 = -6$	6	$2-6 = -4$	4
N = 7 4	$4-8 = -4$	4	$4-6 = -2$	2
6	$6-8 = -2$	2	$6-6 = 0$	0
8	$8-8 = 0$	0	$8-6 = +2$	2
14	$14-8 = +6$	6	$14-6 = +8$	8
20	$20-8 = +12$	12	$20-6 = +14$	14
$\Sigma X_i = 56$	0	36	+12	34

$$\overline{X} = \frac{56}{7} = 8.0$$

$$\text{Mdn} = 6$$

these differences algebraically, another interesting and useful property of this measure of location would be evident. The algebraic sum of deviations of scores from their arithmetic mean is zero, and this is always the case, since the mean is defined as that value around which scores balance or cancel each other's effect.* Notice that the sum of deviations from the median bears out this rule. It is not zero. On the other hand, the median has an interesting property of being the point on the scale for which the sum of absolute deviations is a minimum value. In Table 5.4, the sum, 34, is smaller than the sum of absolute deviations from the mean, which is 36 in this case.

For grouped distributions, the arithmetic mean can be computed only if the distribution is "closed" so that midpoints can be computed for each and every class (so that the total of all scores can be computed). This is because the midpoint is used to stand for the value of each of the scores in a class, since information on the exact value of scores is lost when a grouped frequency distribution is created. Formula (5.3) is for the mean for grouped data, and computing Diagram 5.1 explains the computational procedures involved. Note that X_i is the class midpoint and f_i is the frequency in the ith class.

(5.3)
$$\overline{X} = \frac{\Sigma f_i X_i}{N}$$

The arithmetic mean for household income is shown in Table 5.3 in addition to the median income. Notice that in each case, the mean is higher than the median, even though it, too, increases as one moves toward higher educational attainment categories. This difference between the mean and median indicates a positive skew in the distribution of income; some extremely high scores are evident.

*It is also a property of the arithmetic mean that it is the value for which the sum of squared deviations of scores is a minimum value. The sum of squared deviations from any other point will be larger.

DIAGRAM 5.1   Measures of Central Tendency

MODE (Mo)

The mode is almost always found simply by inspecting for the most frequent single raw score or, in the case of grouped distributions, the midpoint of the class which has the highest frequency of cases in it.

MEDIAN (Mdn)

Raw Scores:

If N, the number of cases, is *odd:* the median is the value of the middle score. This would be the Kth score in the array of scores, where:

$$K = \frac{N+1}{2}$$

For the following seven scores, the median is 8, which is the value of the $K = (7+1)/2 = 4$th score in the array.

$$2, 3, 5, \underset{\uparrow}{8}, 8, 10, 12$$

If N is *even:* the value of the median is the average of the two center scores (or, said differently, the score which is exactly mid-way between them). This would be the point on the score scale between the Kth and $K + 1$st scores in the array, where this time $K = N/2$.

For the following six scores, the median is $(5+8)/2 = 6.5$. This is the value between the $K = 6/2 = 3$rd and the $K + 1 = 3 + 1 = 4$th scores in the array.

$$2, 3, 5, \underset{\uparrow}{8}, 8, 10$$

Grouped Scores:

Step 1: Create a cumulative frequency distribution, starting with the lowest score category as shown in the illustration below.

Scores	f	cum f	Real Limits	Class Width
22−26	18	88	21.5−26.5	5
17−21	21	70	16.5−21.5	5
12−16	26	49	11.5−16.5	5
7−11	15	23	6.5−11.5	5
2−6	8	8	1.5−6.5	5
	$N = 88$			

Step 2: Find $N/2$, the *number of cases* that fall below the median score. Here this is 44 cases (88/2).

DIAGRAM 5.1 *(Continued)*

Step 3: Using the cumulative frequency distribution of step 1 and the results of step 2, find the category within which the median falls. This is the category with a cumulative frequency equal to or bigger than (but closest to) $N/2$.

In this example, the class 12-16 is the median category because the 44th case falls in that class. The "cum f" of 49 is just bigger than $N/2 = 44$.

Step 4: If the cumulative frequency in a class exactly equals $N/2$, then the upper class boundary is the value of the median.

If the median falls some place within a category as is usually the case; it is traditional to "interpolate" to find a median value within the median class on the assumption that cases are distributed in an even (rectangular) fashion within the median interval.

The logic is that we want to locate a median score within the median class, which is a certain distance into that class. The distance depends upon the proportion of the frequency in the median class that needs to be added to the cumulative frequency below the median class, in order to equal $N/2$, or the number of cases that should fall below the median score. This proportion is found by asking how many additional cases are needed:

$$\frac{N}{2} - \text{cum}f_{\text{mdn}}$$

($\text{cum}f_{\text{mdn}}$ is the cumulative frequency up to but *not* including the frequency in the median category.)

or,
$$\frac{88}{2} - 23 = 21$$

This is .81 or 81 percent of the cases in the median category (21 divided by 26, which is the number of cases in the median category itself, f_{mdn}).

Since the median class is 5 score units wide, 81 percent of the way through that width is:

$$.81 \times 5 = 4.0$$

Adding this 4.0 points to the lower real limit of the median class yields a median of 15.5,

$$11.5 + 4.0 = 15.5$$

a score below which 50% or 44 of the 88 cases should fall. These relationships are shown in the "off-set" bar chart diagram below. In practice, the formula for computing the median of grouped data is used directly. It is a specific case of percentiles discussed in Section 3.2.3d.

DIAGRAM 5.1 *(Continued)*

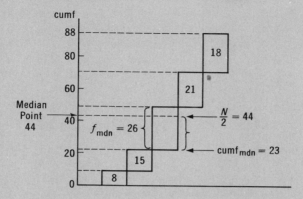

$$\text{Mdn} = L_{mdn} + \left(\frac{\frac{1}{2}N - \text{cum}f_{mdn}}{f_{mdn}}\right) w$$

where: L_{mdn} is the lower limit of the median class; N is the number of cases; $\text{cum}f_{mdn}$ is the cumulative frequency up to *but not including* the frequency in the median class; f_{mdn} is the frequency in the median class; w is the width of the median class interval.

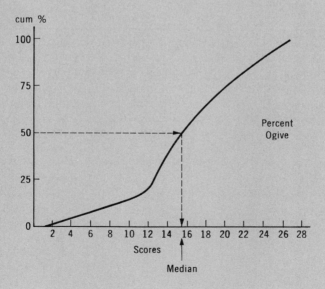

DIAGRAM 5.1 *(Continued)*

Graphically, the median could be found from a percentage ogive (plot of a cumulative percent distribution) by extending a line from the 50 percent point to the ogive and dropping down to the score axis to read off the 50th percentile or median score.

ARITHMETIC MEAN ($\overline{X}$)

Raw Scores:

Simply add up the scores, algebraically, and divide by N, the number of cases.

$$\overline{X} = \frac{\Sigma X_i}{N}$$

For example, the mean of the 8 scores at the right is:

$$\overline{X} = \frac{23}{8} = 2.88$$

X_i	
0	
2	
3	
3	
−4	$N = 8$
6	
10	
3	
$\Sigma X_i = 23$	

Grouped Scores:

Step 1: Create a column of class midpoints. Scores in a class will be treated as if they have the value of the midpoint of a class since no other information on their specific values is known.

Scores	X_i	f	$f(X_i)$
22–26	24	18	432
17–21	19	21	399
12–16	14	26	364
7–11	9	15	135
2–6	4	8	32
		$N = 88$	1362

Step 2: Multiply, for each class, the class midpoint times the frequency in that class, $f(X_i)$.

Step 3: Sum the products in Step 2, $\Sigma f X_i$, and compute the mean by dividing by N.

$$\overline{X} = \frac{\Sigma f X_i}{N}$$

The mean is, thus, 15.5 since $1362/88 = 15.5$.

5.3.4 Special Kinds of Means

There are other measures of central tendency designed for special situations, although most of these measures do not find frequent use in the social sciences. One might, for example, weight scores unequally, before combining them into a mean, by multiplying each score times some previously arranged weighting factor. If, for example, a score were simply too wild or unusual, it might be considered to be due to errors in recording information or making measurements and, accordingly, weighted zero (*i.e.* dropped). If this were done, the base of the ratio, the number of scores, would usually be reduced accordingly. Other weighting schemes take account of over- or under-represented segments of samples.

Two somewhat different kinds of means are the **geometric mean** and the **harmonic mean,** neither of which is widely used as a measure of central tendency, but both of which have specific uses. The geometric mean is the nth root of the product of all scores (or, using logarithms, the antilog of the average logarithm of the scores). It is used in averaging rates or scores where one expects a constant rate of change.

$$\text{(5.4)} \qquad \text{Geometric Mean} = \sqrt[N]{(X_1)(X_2)(X_3) \cdots (X_N)}$$

We will use this average in Chapter Seven to combine two summary statistics. The harmonic mean is the reciprocal of the average reciprocal of scores and it is used to average ratios in which the numerators are constant but the denominators vary.

$$\text{(5.5)} \qquad \text{Harmonic Mean} = \frac{N}{\Sigma(1/X_i)}$$

Both the geometric and the harmonic mean turn out to be somewhat smaller than the arithmetic mean.*

5.3.5 Selecting the Most Appropriate Measure of Central Tendency

Generally speaking, in analyzing the distribution of a variable only one of the possible measures of central tendency would be used. Its selection is largely a matter of judgment based upon the kind of data, aspect of the data to be examined, and the research question. Some of the points that might be considered are the following.

Central tendency for interval-level data is generally indexed by the arithmetic mean, which takes into account the available information about distances between scores. For ranked data, the median is generally most appropriate, and for nominal data, the mode or modes.

If there are several modes, then the mode may be useful alone, or in addition to one of the other two measures, even for ordinal or interval data. If the

---

*Wallis and Roberts (1956) discuss these means and provide several suggestive examples of their application. A somewhat more detailed, illustrated discussion of the geometric and harmonic means is presented in Newman (1956: v 3, 1489–1493).

BOX 5.3 FEATURES OF A DISTRIBUTION

At this point you have made it through essentially two thirds of the different kinds of features of a univariate distribution one might describe: form and central tendency. The third feature, variation, will be discussed next, followed by a bit more on form. Check yourself at this point to see if you are ready to go on. The idea of *variables* and *level of measurement* is discussed in Sections 2.1 and 2.1.1. The different kinds of distributions are defined and illustrated in Section 3.2.3 and the following few pages. The graph in Figure 4.5 illustrates differences in form and location, and Figure 5.1 illustrates differences in form, location and the degree of concentration of scores. After a comment on the use of the arithmetic mean to "smooth" curves, our next main topic will be measures of the concentration of scores.

---

distribution is badly skewed, one may prefer the median to the mean, because the median would not be affected as much by unusual extreme scores. For this reason, for example, the median income of people is usually reported rather than the arithmetic mean.

If one is interested in prediction, the mode is the best value to predict if an *exact* score in a group has to be picked. More cases occur at the value of the mode than at any other *single* score value one could pick. The median has the property of exceeding and being exceeded by half of the scores, so the result of guessing the median would be an over-prediction as frequently as an under-prediction. Overall, the median produces the smallest absolute error (*i.e.* the sum of absolute deviations is less from the median than from any other point). The arithmetic mean is the score around which the aggregate of deviations (algebraically considered) is zero, so the result of guessing or predicting the value of the mean would always be an algebraic deviation which balances out. In each case, a certain kind of predictive error is minimized, and one would pick a measure of central tendency to use in prediction which depends upon the kinds of predictive error one wants to minimize.

Finally, it should be noted that it is possible to have median or arithmetic-mean measures which do not correspond to any specific score in a distribution. There may be a gap at that point where the median or mean happens to fall, but the score at that gap would still be the result of the computation. This is, of course, quite appropriate, since we are trying to develop an index which characterizes the *distribution* of scores — not a single number which will be close to each individual case. The mode, of course, is an actually observed score, and the most frequent one, at that.

The arithmetic mean is probably the most important measure of central tendency only in the sense that it appears repeatedly as a part of the logic of other statistical procedures you will encounter in this book; procedures such as the variance and standard deviation, standard scores, correlation, regression and factor analysis.

5.3.6 Smoothing Trend Lines: The Moving Average

In Chapter 4 we introduced the idea of a line graph which might be used to plot the value of some variable through time. This would result in a trend line, but often the trend line shows a confusing picture. In addition to the general trend, most plots of real data show a "saw-toothed" pattern of cyclic or minor variations which tend to obscure the overall trend. This is shown in Figure 5.3 by the dotted lines, showing components of population change by month for the 1968 to 1972 period in the United States. If an investigator wants to show the general trend, he may want to "smooth out" some of the minor ups and downs. The arithmetic mean is sometimes used to smooth trend lines, and in this application it is called a "moving average."

A moving average is an average of a fixed number of scores over successive periods of time. In Figure 5.3, the heavy line represents the result of using successive 12-month periods. In our example in Table 5.5, annual net growth rate figures are given, one for each year between 1935 and 1966. We would create a moving average by deciding upon a fixed time period over which to average, say, five years. We would then add together and average the rates for the first five years (*i.e.* for 1935 through 1939), and place this value, 8.2, at the midpoint of that time span, the year 1937. This is the first of our five-year averages.

The second five-year average is created by dropping the earliest year's rate and adding in the following year's rate. Thus the rate for 1935 would be dropped, and the rate for 1940 would be added, and again these five figures would be averaged; then the resulting average would be placed by the year which is mid-way in the five-year period. Successive sets of five years are averaged in this way until the last period, 1966, is reached, as shown in Table 5.5. Notice that the two years at the extreme ends of the distribution do not have five-year average figures, be-

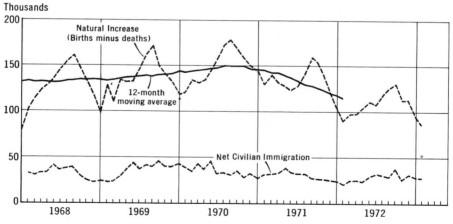

Source: U.S. Bur. Census, 1972.

FIGURE 5.3 Components of Population Change by Month, U.S. 1968 to 1972.

TABLE 5.5 Illustration of a Five-year Moving Average for Annual Rates of Net Growth, U.S. 1935–1966

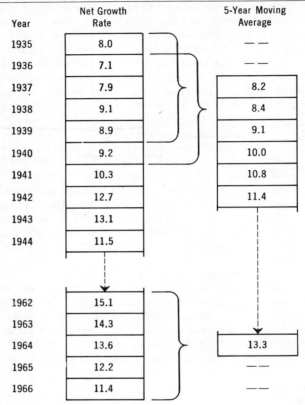

Year	Net Growth Rate	5-Year Moving Average
1935	8.0	— —
1936	7.1	— —
1937	7.9	8.2
1938	9.1	8.4
1939	8.9	9.1
1940	9.2	10.0
1941	10.3	10.8
1942	12.7	11.4
1943	13.1	
1944	11.5	
1962	15.1	
1963	14.3	
1964	13.6	13.3
1965	12.2	— —
1966	11.4	— —

Source: U.S. Bur. Census, 1971.

cause they are not the middle year for an average. The moving averages are then plotted, and the result is a smoothed trend line.

The longer the period over which the average is taken, the smoother the trend line. By careful choice of the time period over which averages are taken, an investigator can remove or smooth out cyclic or seasonal variations in data. This is very clearly indicated in Figure 5.3, where the 12-month moving average removes the seasonal fluctuation in the rate of natural increase over a year. The result shows the trend as it changes year by year, with seasonal variation removed.

Moving averages tend to "anticipate" marked changes in the direction of the un-smoothed graph; that is, the moving average begins to drop or rise somewhat before the point where a marked shift occurs. You will recognize this as one of the properties of the arithmetic mean; it tends to be influenced in the direction of extreme scores. This method of smoothing trend lines is useful in analytic graphing.

5.4 VARIATION

Adams (1953), in a study of the occupational origins of physicians, sent mailed questionnaires and did interviews with physicians in four northeastern cities. Their "occupational origin" was measured by using the North-Hatt occupation prestige scale on their reported father's occupation. Needless to say, physicians tend to come from families where the father also has a relatively highly prestigious occupation (lawyer, banker, physician, etc.). Separating his data by the date of birth (age) of sampled physicians, he noted that the prestige of father's occupation tended to decrease. For physicians born between 1875 and 1895 the mean of father's prestige was 79.8, and it dropped to 74.6 for the later period, 1895 to 1920. He also found an interesting second feature in the data, namely that there seemed to be more variation in the backgrounds of physicians born more recently. That is, their mean prestige rating not only dropped somewhat through time, but there was more variation in father's occupational prestige scores; they were not as similar to each other at the end of the time period as they were before. How can this feature be measured?

The third of the three characteristics of a univariate distribution, for which we are developing simple measures, is the characteristic of spread, or dispersion of scores. Some groups of scores are wide-ranging; others are more bunched together, as the following illustrations show, quite apart from their location or the distinctive features of the distribution's form.

group a	2	3	4	5	6	N = 5
group b	5	6	7	8	9	N = 5
group c	51	52	53	54	55	N = 5
group d	52	53	53	53	54	N = 5
group e	47	50	53	56	59	N = 5

In the first three groups, (a), (b), (c), each has the same amount of variability between scores. Notice that the scores are all consecutive integers. Group (d), however, has less variability since the scores are more closely grouped, many of them identical in value. Group (e) is even more dispersed than group (c), yet (c), (d), and (e) all have the same mean and median, 53. (As far as the other measure of central tendency is concerned, only group (d) could be usefully described as having a mode which is 53.)

There are several different approaches to the measurement of variability in a group of scores, and the basic distinction between measures appropriate for nominal (categorical) data and interval data is needed here as well. Variation in ordinal data is often treated by techniques used for interval-level data even though the distance idea is not defined. Ordinal data could also be treated by measures of variation appropriate to nominal data.* Diagram 5.2 (below, near

---

*To the authors' knowledge, there is no measure of variation designed specifically for ordinal data.

Section 5.4.6.) provides the step-by-step procedures for computing each measure. We will begin with some of the measures for interval-level data.

For interval-level scores where the idea of distance on a score scale has meaning, there are two general approaches to the measurement of variation in a distribution. First, one could think in terms of the range of the scale over which the scores in a distribution actually fall. Secondly, one could think of measures of variation describing the extent to which scores in a distribution differ from some single score, such as a central-tendency score for the distribution.

5.4.1   Range

The **range** is simply the score range over which scores actually fall. It is the difference between the lower real limit of the lowest score category and the upper real limit of the upper score category in a distribution.

(5.6)
$$\text{Range} = U - L$$

In Formula (5.6), U refers to the upper real limit of the highest class in the distribution, and L refers to the lower real limit of the lowest class. Usually the range, like the mode, is quickly computed by inspection of a distribution, and this is one of its chief claims to fame.

Unfortunately, the range only depends upon the two extreme scores in a distribution, and it ignores completely the way the data between these extremes are distributed. In practical research and everyday life we often expect that extreme scores will be undependable. They may be due to some gross measurement error or, perhaps, a very rare and unusual score.

For example, if one were interested in studying multiple births he might examine birth records. In most modest-sized samples of these records he would undoubtedly yield scores from one to three (single-birth to triplets) or a range of 3. With much larger samples, or by unusual luck in small samples, an investigator might observe a range of 5 (from single-birth to a quintuplet-birth). Only seven quintuplet births (where all survived infancy) are known in the world in the decade of the 60's.

If sample size is increased, the crude range can only stay the same or increase, regardless of the concentration or dispersion of the rest of the scores. For these reasons, a more refined measure of variation is generally preferred.

5.4.2   Interquartile Range (Q)

The **interquartile range** is defined as the range which includes the center fifty percent of cases in a distribution or the distance between the first and third quartiles.

(5.7)
$$Q = Q_3 - Q_1$$

Although, again, this range measure is based on the difference between two points in a distribution, these points are determined in a way that is sensitive to the concentration in the data itself.

The first quartile is the point on the score scale below which 25 percent of the cases fall, and the third quartile is the point on the score scale below which 75 percent of the cases fall. These are determined in ways quite similar to the way the median (point below which 50 percent of the cases fall) is computed. (See Diagram 5.2 and the discussion of percentiles in Chapter 3.)

The interquartile range avoids the exclusive use of the two extreme scores, and it is thus less subject to the erratic variation in extreme scores. Distance between other points on a distribution may be used instead of quartiles. For example, the interdecile range would be the difference between the 9th and the 1st decile (the difference between the point below which 10 percent of the cases fall and the point below which 90 percent fall). Sometimes the semi-interquartile range is used, which is simply half the interquartile range. Its virtues and properties are the same as those of the interquartile range itself.

5.4.3 Average Absolute Deviation (AD)

Another kind of measure of variation is that in which the deviation of scores is measured from a central point in a distribution, usually the arithmetic mean. Although seldom used, the **average absolute deviation** illustrates nicely the principles involved in this approach.

A portion of Table 5.4 provides a good illustration of the logic of this dispersion measure.

Raw Scores X_i	Absolute Difference $\|X_i - \bar{X}\|$	
2	6	$N=7$
2	6	
4	4	$\bar{X}=\frac{56}{7}=8.0$
6	2	
8	0	
14	6	
20	12	
56	36	

You will recall from our discussion of the arithmetic mean that one of its properties is that the sum of algebraic deviations of scores from it is always zero. Thus, as a measure of dispersion, the average deviation shifts to the use of the absolute value of the deviation of each score from the mean, as shown above. The average absolute deviation is simply the arithmetic mean of absolute deviations, another ratio.

(5.8)
$$AD=\frac{\Sigma|X_i-\bar{X}|}{N}$$

$$AD=\frac{36}{7}=5.1$$

On the average, these seven scores deviate 5.1 points from the arithmetic mean of this distribution. The larger the average deviation, the more variability there is between scores in the distribution. If all the scores are identical to the mean, the numerator becomes zero and the average absolute deviation is, appropriately, zero. The average deviation can become quite large; in fact, its upper limit depends upon the unit of measurement and the magnitude of variation in the data themselves.

While the average deviation is easily interpreted and relatively easily computed, another measure is generally preferred, simply because of its mathematical uses in other areas of statistics. This measure is the variance, or its square root, the standard deviation.

5.4.4 Variance and Standard Deviation (s^2 and s, respectively)*

The **variance** and **standard deviation** are similar to the average deviation in that differences between the mean and each score are used, but instead of taking the absolute value of these deviations, the square of the deviation is used. This has a similar effect to side-stepping the zero-sum-of-deviations property of the arithmetic mean, and results in a measure of dispersion for interval data that has wide applicability and some interesting connections with other topics in statistics.

The variance is simply an average of squared deviations of scores from the arithmetic mean, and the standard deviation is the square root of the variance.†

(5.9)

$$s^2 = \frac{\Sigma (X_i - \overline{X})^2}{N}$$

(5.10)

$$s = \sqrt{s^2}$$

Using the illustrative data below from a portion of Table 5.4, the variance and standard deviation can be computed. Computing diagram 5.2 (below, near Section 5.4.6) presents the step-by-step procedures and more convenient formulas for computation.

---

*Again, we should note that there are, conventionally, two sets of symbols for the variance and for the standard deviation, one for the statistic (s^2 and s) and one for the parameter (the lower-case Greek letter sigma, σ^2 and σ). In this book we will use the symbols for sample statistics (s^2 and s), whereas in the field of inferential statistics, both sets are introduced when contrasts between them are important.

†Although the variance is defined as the simple "average" of squared deviations from the mean (and thus it has N in the denominator as in Formula 5.9, above), this is a biased estimate of the population standard deviation if Formula 5.9 is used on sample data from small samples. Since we are dealing in the area of description rather than inference at this point, we will use the formula with N in the denominator. It simplifies some later computations in this book, and the "unbiasing" can be better explained and treated in inferential statistics. (See H. J. Loether and D. G. McTavish, *Inferential Statistics for Sociologists*.) The square root of the variance is called the "standard deviation," a term coined by Karl Pearson (1894). As an aside, the sample variance as computed in Formula 5.9 yields a slight *under*-estimate of the population variance, especially for small, probability samples. This under-estimate bias is usually corrected by using $N-1$ in the denominator for the sample variance rather than N. In most sociological studies the sample size is sufficiently large so that the effect of this correction is nil.

	Raw Scores X_i	Differences $(X_i - \overline{X})$	Squared Differences $(X_1 - \overline{X})^2$
	2	$(2-8) = -6$	$(-6)^2 = 36$
	2	$(2-8) = -6$	$(-6)^2 = 36$
$N = 7$	4	$(4-8) = -4$	$(-4)^2 = 16$
	6	$(6-8) = -2$	$(-2)^2 = 4$
$\overline{X} = 8.0$	8	$(8-8) = 0$	$(0)^2 = 0$
	14	$(14-8) = +6$	$(6)^2 = 36$
	20	$(20-8) = +12$	$(12)^2 = \underline{144}$
	56	0	272

$$s^2 = \frac{272}{7} = 38.9$$

$$s = \sqrt{38.9} = 6.2$$

In the study of the occupational origins of physicians discussed at the beginning of this section, Adams actually chose the standard deviation as a measure of variation to show what has been happening from 1875 to 1920 in terms of variation. Table 5.6 shows his data. The standard deviation shows the variation in physician's father's occupational prestige in units of the North-Hatt occupation prestige scale. In the earliest period the standard deviation was 7.5 North-Hatt units, while in the last period, 1915–1920, the standard deviation was nearly double, 13.6 North-Hatt score points. The average standard deviation prior to 1895 was 9.2 and the average standard deviation from 1895 on was 11.3.* There is clearly an increased variation in the prestige backgrounds of phy-

---

TABLE 5.6 Trend in the North-Hatt Occupation Prestige Scores for the Occupation of Fathers of Physicians by Date of Birth of Physicians.

Date of Birth	Number	Mean Prestige Rating	Standard Deviation of Prestige Rating
1875–1879	9	78.7	7.5
1880–1884	9	77.9	6.7
1885–1889	7	81.6	8.8
1890–1894	15	80.9	7.0
1895–1899	19	74.8	10.4
1900–1904	22	74.6	8.7
1905–1909	24	74.2	14.2
1910–1914	23	74.0	10.6
1915–1920	9	76.4	13.6
Overall	137	76.1	10.7

Source: Adams, 1953: 406, Table 2. Reprinted by permission.

*These averages cannot simply be computed by adding up standard deviations and dividing by their number, because each standard deviation is based on a different number of cases. The averages quoted in the text are weighted averages.

sicians in addition to a slightly declining average level of father's occupational prestige. This finding is backed up by other data Adams collected. Physicians have a 93 on the 100-point North-Hatt rating scale, and if many physicians had fathers who were also physicians, the average prestige score would be higher (and the standard deviation smaller). There has been, however, a decline in the percentage of physicians who come from families where their father is also a physician. For physicians born in the 1870–1879 period, 22 percent came from physician-families, while the figure drops to 9.4 percent from physician-families among those born in the 1910 to 1920 period.

Apart from its interpretation in terms of sheer difference in magnitude, the standard deviation has a number of interesting properties and may be interpreted in at least two different ways. To start with, the standard deviation and variance will both be zero where all scores have the same value (*i.e.*, the value of the mean), and they reach a maximum magnitude for a given set of data when scores are divided between the extreme ends of the scale. These conditions are illustrated in Figure 5.4. Given some difference between scores, the value of the variance can be interpreted in terms of a scale extending from a minimum possible value which equals the range divided by the square root of twice the sample size, to a maximum which is the square of half the range. The standard deviation could be interpreted in terms of a scale extending between values which are simply the square root of the values given above.

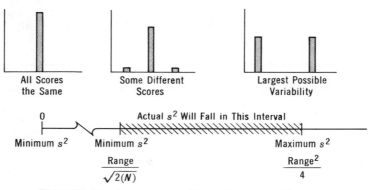

FIGURE 5.4 Limits on the Magnitude of the Variance

For most curves, the range is approximately equal to six times the standard deviation as a rough rule of thumb.

The variance and standard deviation can be interpreted in a somewhat different way too; in terms of the area under a curve within z standard deviations of the mean of a distribution.* This central area, between z standard de-

---

*The number of standard deviations a score is from the mean of its distribution is called a "standard score" or z-score. If all scores in a distribution were expressed in terms of the number of standard deviations they are from their mean, the distribution of z-scores which would result would have a mean of zero and a standard deviation of one. This simply follows from the definition of the standard score or z-score. We will discuss standard scores somewhat further later in this chapter (Section 5.4.7).

viations below the mean and z standard deviations above the mean, is always, and for any shape of distribution, at least as follows:

$$\begin{array}{l}\text{Minimum percent of cases}\\ \text{within } z \text{ standard deviations}\\ \text{above and below the mean}\\ \text{of a distribution of any}\\ \text{shape}\end{array} = 100\left[1-\left(\frac{1}{z^2}\right)\right]$$

Thus at least 75 percent of the area under a curve will fall within 2 standard deviation units of the mean: $100\left[\,1-(1/2^2)\,\right]$. This is called Chebyshev's Theorem (or Tchebycheff's inequality), and it has applicability especially in inferential statistics. In descriptive statistics it provides a useful interpretation of the standard deviation. For many curves, particularly those more concentrated around the mean, the percentage of cases within a given number of standard deviation units is much larger than the minimum given by Chebyshev's Theorem. For curves which are unimodal and symmetrical, for example, the minimum percent within $(\overline{X}+z)$'s and $(\overline{X}-z)$'s is at least as follows:

$$\begin{array}{l}\text{Minimum percent of cases}\\ \text{within } z \text{ standard deviations}\\ \text{above and below the mean}\\ \text{of a unimodal, symmetrical}\\ \text{distribution}\end{array} = 100\left[1-\left(\frac{4}{9}\right)\left(\frac{1}{z^2}\right)\right]$$

The minimum percentage of cases within two standard deviations above and below a unimodal, symmetrical distribution would be 89 percent rather than 75 percent, which is the general figure for any shaped distribution.

TABLE 5.7 PERCENT OF AREA UNDER A CURVE BETWEEN THE MEAN PLUS z AND THE MEAN MINUS z STANDARD DEVIATIONS

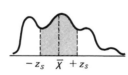 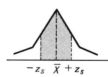 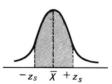

(z) Number of Standard Deviations From $\overline{X}$	Minimum for any Distribution (Chebyshev's Theorem)	Minimum for any Unimodal and Symmetrical Distribution	Value for a Normal Distribution
.67	0%	1%	50%
1.00	0	56	68
2.00	75	89	95
3.00	89	95	99.7
4.00	94	97	99.99 . .
10.00	99	99.6	99.999 . . . .

In fact, the special bell-shaped curve called the "normal curve" has considerably more area within z standard deviations of the mean, as is shown in Table 5.7. The normal curve has 95 percent of its area within two standard deviations above and below the mean. The normal curve will be discussed further in Section 5.5 on the form of a distribution, since it is an important shape which is used in other topics in statistics.

5.4.5   Index of Dispersion (*D*)

The measures of variation discussed above all imply the knowledge of distance and thus are most appropriate for interval-level measures. The idea of variation in scores is not limited, however, to interval-level data. The index of dispersion is suggested as a measure of variation for nominal (or ordinal) variables by Hammond and Householder (1962: 136–142).*

The **index of dispersion** is a ratio whose numerator and denominator are counts of the number of pairs of scores. The denominator is the maximum number of unique pairs that could be created out of the scores such that each member of the pair is different. It turns out that this condition is met where the N scores are evenly distributed among the k categories into which the scores are grouped. This corresponds exactly with our idea of maximum variability in a nominal (and ordinal) variable.

To illustrate the logic behind this measure, suppose we consider the following nine scores on marital status, classified into three categories ($k=3$):

	f
Married	5
Single	3
Other	1
Total	9

If variability among the 9 scores were a maximum, there would be three scores in each of the three categories. The number of pairs of cases where the members of a pair came from *different* categories would be 27. That is, three pairs could be formed by pairing each of the three married people with the single people. Since there are three married people this means $3 \times 3 = 9$ pairs. The same pairing could occur between married and "other," and between single and "other" categories, yielding a total of $9+9+9=27$. In this example, however, cases are not evenly distributed over categories; they are more concentrated than that. The 5 married people could be paired with the 3 single (15 pairs) and with the 1 "other" person (5 pairs), and the single people could be paired with the "others" (yielding 3 pairs), or a total of 23 pairs. The D statistic is simply a ratio of the number of different pairs that could be made out of the data at hand, compared with the maximum number of unique pairings that could be created if cases were evenly spread over all available categories. Here $D=.85$.

If all scores were in a single category of a variable that has several possi-

---

*Another expression of this measure is called the 'index of qualitative variation' (IQV), in Mueller and Schuessler (1961: 177-179).

ble categories, then there is maximum concentration or minimum variability, and D would equal zero. On the other hand, if cases were evenly distributed among the possible categories, there would be a maximum variability, and the numerator and denominator of the D ratio would be the same, and D would equal 1. D varies, then, from zero to one and is a useful measure of variation for nominal or ordinal variables.

The computational formula for D is given below and the step by step procedures for computing D are discussed below in Diagram 5.2.*

(5.11)
$$D = \frac{k(N^2 - \Sigma f_i^2)}{N^2(k-1)}$$

where: N is the number of scores; k is the number of categories of the variable into which data might be classified (apart from whether all categories are used or not); f_i is the frequency of cases in the ith category; and the summation is over the squared category frequency of all categories.

An application of the index of dispersion might be made on data presented by Linn (1971), who studied the career patterns and preferences of 785 women dentists in the United States. Among the questions asked in the 1968 mail questionnaire was one requesting the subject to check items which were found to be most satisfying, second most satisfying, etc. from a list Linn provided. He subsequently compared the distribution of sources of satisfaction for women dentists who were married and those who were separated, single, divorced, or widowed.

Table 5.8 shows that the modal activity giving the most satisfaction shifted from family relationships for married dentists to career or occupation for the dentists who were not married, and the percentage checking the mode in each case was 68 and 64 percent, suggesting a good deal of agreement on priorities. As D, the index of dispersion, indicates, the variation in sources of satisfaction is also greater among those not currently married as compared to currently married women dentists, suggesting a focusing of sources of satisfaction around fewer areas for the latter.

The D statistic (with slightly different symbols used to express it) was proposed by Rushing and Davies (1970) as a measure of the concept, "division of labor." The concept of division of labor refers to the difference or variability there is among individuals in their sustenance activity. Generally this can be thought of in terms of the different kinds of occupations there are in a society, and the extent to which individuals are spread out among them rather than all concentrated in, say, laboring or farming or housewifing. Division of labor, then, could be measured by D, using information about the number of individuals in different occupational categories. The more evenly spread they are among the

---

*Maurice G. Kendall defined a measure of variation which examined all pairs of scores in a set of data. The measure is equal to one half of the average squared difference between all possible pairs of scores. This one can be computed as:

$$\text{Variation} = (N^2 - f_1^2 - f_2^2 \cdot \cdot \cdot - f_k^2)/2N^2$$

where f_1^2 is the frequency squared in category one of the variable and the square of the frequency in each of the "k" categories is subtracted in the numerator. This is a slightly different expression of the identical formula, above (number 5.11), and it has several useful implications for sociological analysis, as shown in Hawkes (1971).

DIAGRAM 5.2   Computing Measures of Variation and Form

As is true of central tendency, measures of variation and form may be computed on raw scores or on grouped frequency distributions. Both procedures are illustrated below using the same set of scores on number of items correct on a 20-item exam in arithmetic. The 32 scores are listed below and the same scores are shown in a grouped distribution below:

Raw scores:

$$\underset{Q_1}{2\ 3\ 4\ 4\ 5\ 6\ 6\ 7\ \Big|\ 7\ 7\ 8\ 8\ 8\ 8\ 9\ 9\ 9\ 9\ 9\ 10\ 10\ 10\ 11\ 11\ \Big|\ \underset{Q_3}{11\ 11\ 12\ 12\ 12\ 12\ 15\ 16}}$$

$\Sigma X_i = 281$ $\Sigma X_i^2 = 2791$

Grouped distribution: (Using the data, above)

	Class	X_i Midpoint	f_i	cum f_i	$f_i X_i$	$f_i X_i^2$
	2–3	2.5	2	2	5.0	12.50
Class	4–5	4.5	3	5	13.5	60.75
Containing $Q_1 \rightarrow$	6–7	6.5	5	10	32.5	211.25
Class	8–9	8.5	9	19	76.5	650.25
Containing $Q_3 \rightarrow$	10–11	10.5	7	26	73.5	771.75
	12–13	12.5	4	30	50.0	625.00
	14–15	14.5	1	31	14.5	210.25
	16–17	16.5	1	32	16.5	272.25
	Total		$\Sigma f_i = 32$		$\Sigma f_i X_i = 282.0$	$\Sigma f_i X_i^2 = 2814.00$

1. RANGE (Formula 5.6)

$$\text{Range} = U - L$$

where: U is the upper real limit of the highest score (or class), and L is the lower real limit of the lowest score (or class).

For raw data: Range $= 16.5 - 1.5 = 15$
For grouped data: Range $= 17.5 - 1.5 = 16$

The difference between the two values for raw and grouped data is due to the way data were grouped. The U value of the grouped data is 17.5.

2. INTERQUARTILE RANGE (Formula 5.7)

$$Q = Q_3 - Q_1$$

where: Q_3 is the *score value* below which 75 percent of the cases fall, and Q_1 is the score value below which 25 percent fall.

DIAGRAM 5.2 *(Continued)*

For raw scores, Q_3 and Q_1 may be found by creating an array as shown in the raw data above, and counting up the array to the respective score values. If a quartile falls between two actual scores, it is traditional to simply take as the quartile score value the average of the two adjacent scores. In this example:

$$Q_3 = 11$$

$$Q_1 = 7$$

$$Q = 11 - 7 = 4$$

For grouped data, quartiles are found in the same way that any percentile is found. This is discussed with respect to the median (the second quartile) in Diagram 5.1 and in Diagram 3.2.

(D1)
$$Q_3 = L_{Q_3} + \left(\frac{{}^{3}/_{4}N - \text{cum} f_{Q_3}}{f_{Q_3}} \right) w$$

(D2)
$$Q_1 = L_{Q_1} + \left(\frac{{}^{1}/_{4}N - \text{cum} f_{Q_1}}{f_{Q_1}} \right) w$$

where L_{Q_3} and L_{Q_1} are lower limits of the classes containing the third and first quartiles; N is the number of cases; w is the width of the class containing the quartile of interest; $\text{cum} f_{Q_3}$ and $\text{cum} f_{Q_1}$ are cumulative frequency of cases *up to but not including* cases in the class containing the quartile being computed; f_{Q_3} and f_{Q_1} are frequency of cases in the quartile class being computed. In these data:

Step 1: Find the class containing the quartile of interest by using a cumulative frequency distribution and finding the class below which the $3N/4$-th case would fall for the third quartile, or the $N/4$-th case for the first quartile. For the first quartile that class is the $6-7$ score class (since the $\frac{1}{4}$ of the 32 scores is 8, and the 8th score falls in the $6-7$ class). The third quartile is the $10-11$ score class because it contains the 24th score out of 32.

Step 2: Substitute values in the formulas for Q_3 and Q_1 and compute the estimated third and first quartiles.

$$Q_3 = 9.5 + \left(\frac{{}^{3}/_{4}(32) - 19}{7} \right)(2) = 10.9$$

$$Q_1 = 5.5 + \left(\frac{{}^{1}/_{4} \, 32 - 5}{5} \right)(2) = 6.7$$

Step 3: Compute the interquartile range.

$$Q = 10.9 - 6.7 = 4.2$$

A similar procedure could be used to compute other percentiles (or other "fractiles"), and other ranges, such as the interdecile range, could be used.

DIAGRAM 5.2 *(Continued)*

3.3 Variance and Standard Deviation

The definitional formulae for variance and standard deviation are as follows:

$$s^2 = \frac{\Sigma(X_i - \bar{X})^2}{N} \qquad \text{Variance* (Formula 5.9)}$$

$$s = \sqrt{s^2} \qquad \text{Standard Deviation (Formula 5.10)}$$

These formulae are rarely used in computational work because they require the extra step of computing the arithmetic mean and finding the deviation of each score from the mean — steps which may result in extensive rounding error. Computational formulae given below make use of raw scores (or category midpoints and frequencies in the case of grouped data) and are mathematically identical to the definitional formulae above.

For raw data:

(D3)
$$s^2 = \frac{\Sigma X_i^2 - (\Sigma X_i)^2/N}{N}$$

where: ΣX_i^2 is the sum of *squared scores;* $(\Sigma X_i)^2$ is the square of the *sum of scores;* N is the number of cases.

As before, the standard deviation is the square root of the variance.

In the example above, where $\Sigma X_i = 281$, $\Sigma X_i^2 = 2791$, and $N = 32$

$$s^2 = \frac{2791 - (281)^2/32}{32} = \frac{323.47}{32} = 10.1$$

$$s = \sqrt{10.1} = 3.2$$

For grouped data:

The formula for the variance of grouped data is similar to that given above, except that category midpoints and frequencies are used rather than raw scores. The formula for the variance is this:

(D4)
$$s^2 = \frac{\Sigma f_i X_i^2 - (\Sigma f_i X_i)^2/N}{N}$$

where $\Sigma f_i X_i^2$ is the square of the category midpoint times the category frequency summed up over all categories; $(\Sigma f_i X_i)^2$ is the sum of category midpoint and category frequency products, squared.

---

*See the first two footnotes in Section 5.4.4 in this chapter. The variance given here is a "biased" estimate of a population variance. Where inferences to population variances on the basis of sample variances is of interest, the unbiased sample variance is used. It simply substitutes $N-1$ in place of N in the denominator of the variance. Where N is large, this makes little numeric difference, but the resulting variance and standard deviation are then referred to as "unbiased." This topic is explored in the field of inferential statistics (see Chapter 12). Here we will use the somewhat simpler formula given here.

DIAGRAM 5.2 *(Continued)*

In this example, these two sums can be found by creating two columns of products as shown above. The result is this:

$$s^2 = \frac{2814 - (282)^2/32}{32} = \frac{328.88}{32} = 10.3$$

$$s = \sqrt{10.3} = 3.2$$

4. INDEX OF DISPERSION (Formula 5.11)

$$D = \frac{k(N^2 - \Sigma f_i^2)}{N^2(k-1)}$$

where k is the number of categories of the variable; Σf_i^2 is the sum of squared frequencies; N is the number of cases.

In the example, above, the scores would be grouped into a frequency distribution prior to computing D, and a new column of f_i^2 values, not shown above, would be created and summed as follows:

f_i	f_i^2
2	4
3	9
5	25
9	81
7	49
4	16
1	1
1	1
32	186

D is then computed as:

$$D = \frac{8(32^2 - 186)}{32^2(8-1)} = \frac{6704}{7168} = .94$$

5. BETA-1 (β_1), A SKEWNESS MEASURE (Formula 5.14)

$$\beta_1 = \frac{m_3^2}{m_2^3}$$

where m_3 is the third moment, and m_2 is the variance or second moment, defined under part 3, above. The third moment may be computed from raw scores by the following formula.

$$m_3 = \frac{\Sigma X_i^3 - [3\Sigma X_i \Sigma X_i^2/N] + [2(\Sigma X_i)^3/N^2]}{N}$$

The grouped-data formula is similar with the substitution of category midpoints and category frequencies for raw scores. In the example, above, where $\Sigma X_i^3 = 29125$

DIAGRAM 5.2 *(Continued)*

$$m_3 = \frac{30149 - [3(281)(2791)/32] + [2(281)^3/32^2]}{32} = \frac{-40.4}{32} = -1.26$$

$$\beta_1 = \frac{(-1.26)^2}{(10.1)^3} = \frac{1.59}{1030.30} = -.0015$$

The sign of the third moment is attached.

6. Beta-2 (β_2), A Kurtosis Measure (Formula 5.15)

$$\beta_2 = \frac{m_4}{m_2^2}$$

where m_4 is the fourth moment, and m_2^2 is the square of the variance.

The fourth moment may be computed from raw scores by the following formula.

$$m_4 = \frac{\Sigma X_i^4 - [4\Sigma X_i \Sigma X_i^3/N] + [6(\Sigma X_i)^2\Sigma X_i^2/N^2] - [3(\Sigma X_i)^4/N^3]}{N}$$

In this example, where $\Sigma X_i^4 = 347887$

$$m_4 = \frac{347887 - [4(281)(30149)/32] + [6(281)^2(2791)/32^2] - [3(281)^4/32^3]}{32}$$

$$m_4 = \frac{9376.72}{32} = 293.02$$

$$\beta_2 = \frac{293.02}{(10.6)^2} = 2.61$$

TABLE 5.8 Activities Indicated by Women Dentists as Those Which Provide the Most Satisfaction

Activities Listed	Married Women Dentists		Separated, Single, Divorced, or Widowed Women Dentists	
Your career or occupation	27%	(101)	64%	(133)
Family relationships	68%	(253)	24%	(50)
Leisure time recreational activities	3%	(11)	4%	(8)
Religious activities	2%	(7)	5%	(10)
Participation in the public affairs of your community	0%	(0)	1%	(2)
Others (written in)	0%	(0)	2%	(4)
Totals	100%	(372)	100%	(207)
	$D = .56$		$D = .63$	

Source: Linn, 1971: 401, Table 4. Reprinted by permission.

different possible occupations, the greater the "division of labor." The amount of division of labor could be expressed for societies, cities, states, and within organizations. It could also be expressed for different groups of people. Undoubtedly the division of labor for women in the United States is less than it is for men. Besides noting the relative concentration of individuals within occupational categories, it would be useful to note the number of different categories (k) that exist for given organizations or societies, as Rushing and Davies note. The Rushing and Davies suggestion indicates a rather important usage of statistics: to measure an interesting characteristic of social organization. In addition, of course, statistics are used to summarize collections of such scores.

5.4.6 Selecting the Most Appropriate Measure of Variability

Several criteria might enter into the selection of a measure of variability. One, of course, is the meaning of the scores one has. For interval-level scores, the interquartile range or, more likely, the standard deviation (or variance) would be chosen. Since range-based measures tend to be sensitive to only two scores or points on the distribution, they would probably not be selected if the standard deviation could be computed. If a distribution is severely skewed, so that the mean is thought not to give an appropriate indication of central tendency, the range-based measures may then be preferred.

Ordinal data present something of a problem. The index of dispersion, D, is not sensitive to the ordering of categories implied in ordinal variables; thus D loses some information. On the other hand, measures which rely on distances, such as the interquartile range or the standard deviation, imply information in data which are not defined into the scores. The usually recommended halfway house is to use the median for central tendency and the interquartile range for variation of ordinal data, interpreting the interquartile range as the range of ranked categories which include the middle fifty percent of cases.

For nominal, and perhaps ordinal variables, the index of dispersion provides a nice solution to the problem of measuring the variation in scores, D has another feature which recommends its use. It can be interpreted more readily because it varies on a scale from zero (for no variation) to 1.0 (which corresponds to the maximum amount of variation possible in the data at hand). Although the other measures of variation indicate greater amounts of variation by larger magnitudes, the maximum possible magnitude of the variation measures, other than for D, varies depending upon the size of the score units used (*e.g.* years or decades) and the spread of the scores. Zero may indicate no variation (for the range and for the variance and standard deviation), but beyond that the magnitude of the number has little meaning in an absolute sense.

5.4.6a The Variation Ratio.   This state of affairs has led to the development of some relative measures of variation. For example, the variation ratio is the standard deviation divided by the arithmetic mean.

(5.12)

$$V = \frac{s}{X}$$

This serves to take into account the units of measurement (*e.g.* years or decades) and the location of the distribution. This measure is not used very frequently, in part because it also does not have defined limits (unlike the D statistic). Re-

---

BOX 5.4 REVIEWING FEATURES OF A DISTRIBUTION

Form, central tendency, and variation, the three features of a univariate distribution, may each be measured in several different ways. Thus far only verbal descriptions of the form—kurtosis (Section 5.2.3), symmetry (Section 5.2.2) and number of modes (Section 5.2.1)—of a distribution have been discussed, but the next section will introduce some indices for these features as well. For the central tendency of a distribution we have discussed the mode (Section 5.3.1), the median (Section 5.3.2) and the arithmetic mean (Section 5.3.3), plus a couple of special types of means which are not too frequently seen. Finally, variation measures included the range (Section 5.4.1), the interquartile range (Section 5.4.2), the average absolute deviation (Section 5.4.3), the variance and standard deviation (Section 5.4.4), the index of dispersion, D (Section 5.4.5) and the variation ratio (Section 5.4.6a).

An important point you should be clear about is the three different ways that the standard deviation (and variance) can be interpreted: (a) in terms of sheer magnitude (Section 5.4), (b) in terms of the minimum and maximum values it could take for a given set of data (Section 5.4.1), and (c) in terms of the proportion of the area under curves between points defined in terms of the number of standard deviations out on either side of the mean (Section 5.4.4).

cently two sociologists developed a relative measure of variation which does vary between the limits 0.0 and 1.0 (this is known as a "normed" measure of variation, since its maximum and minimum possible values are fixed at zero and 1.0). (See Martin and Gray, 1971.*)

5.4.7 Standard Scores

Early in Chapter 3 we discussed the various types of comparisons that one might well want to make, statistically. Many of our procedures in Chapters 3, 4, and 5 were designed to facilitate the group-group or group-standard types of comparison. One could also make use of what we have described up to this point to indicate the relative standing of an individual in his group. One of these ways is to compute an individual's *percentile rank* (*i.e.* the percentage of all scores equal to or less than his score). Another way to make this individual-group comparison is to create **standard scores** which are also called *z-scores.* A standard score is merely the number of standard deviation units an individual falls above (or below) the mean of his group.

(5.13)
$$z = \frac{(X_i - \overline{X})}{s}$$

The standard score takes out the effect of the mean (by subtraction) and expresses the difference in standard deviation units (by dividing by the standard deviation). It is a simple re-scaling of scores so that the mean of z-scores is zero and the standard deviation is one—a change from dollars and years, for example, to "standard" units.† Because of this, one could compare z-scores of an individual on different distributions (*i.e.*, he may be 2 standard deviations above the mean on one score distribution and only 1 standard deviation above on another). More will be said about standard scores later in this chapter.

5.5 FORM OF A DISTRIBUTION—II

Thus far, we have described the form of a distribution only in terms of some general verbal labels which pointed to symmetry, kurtosis, and a number of peaks in a general way. In this section we will introduce some approaches to summary measures of form that might be expressed as single numbers, which are similar in purpose to the summary index numbers used to describe central

---

*Their measure, called $s(d)$, is simply a ratio of the actual value of V, the variation ratio computed in Formula 5.12, above, divided by the maximum possible V.

$$s(d) = \frac{V}{V_{max}}$$

where $V = s/\overline{X}$ and $V_{max} = \sqrt{N-1}$. They also propose a variation ratio which is the average absolute deviation divided by the arithmetic mean. Its maximum, and the denominator of $s(d)$ where it is used is $2(1 - 1/N)$.

†An interesting property of z-scores, which will be used later on in Chapter 7 when we discuss a correlation coefficient, is that the sum of squared z-scores always equals the number of cases, N. $\Sigma z^2 = N$

tendency and variation in a distribution. In the process, we will discuss the idea of standard scores (z-scores) and special kinds of curves such as the standard normal curve.

As a matter of fact, we already have a number of tools at hand which would be useful in creating an index of skewness. If the mean and median are different, for example, we would conclude that the distribution is skewed in the direction of the mean and, for the same range of scores, bigger discrepancies would indicate more skewness. We could also examine differences between quartiles in a distribution. If the distance between the first and second quartiles is greater than the distance between the second and third, we would conclude that the distribution is negatively skewed. In this section, however, we will develop more useful and interpretable measures of skewness and kurtosis.

5.5.1 The Moment System

When one is dealing with interval-level data, it is often useful to describe the data in terms of its balance around some central point. The arithmetic mean, for example, is the point around which the algebraic "balance" of scores is perfect in the sense that the algebraic sum of deviations of scores is zero. Deviation of scores from the mean of a distribution is often expressed by the small letter x.

$$x = (X_i - \overline{X})$$

The **first moment** about the arithmetic mean, then, is simply the average of the first power of deviations from the mean, or:

$$m_1 = \frac{\Sigma x}{N}$$

Since the sum of deviations around the mean is always zero, the first moment is always zero, a defining characteristic of the mean. If higher powers of deviations about the mean are examined, however, additional information about a distribution is revealed. The **second moment,** for example, is the variance:

$$m_2 = \frac{\Sigma x^2}{N}$$

Statisticians generally consider only the first four moments. The **third** and **fourth moments** are simply the average of the third and fourth power of deviations from the mean.

$$m_3 = \frac{\Sigma x^3}{N}$$

$$m_4 = \frac{\Sigma x^4}{N}$$

The advantage of each of the moments stems from two factors: (a) the fact that even powers have the effect of eliminating negative signs but odd powers preserve negative signs in the numerator of the moments, above, and (b) the fact that higher powers tend to emphasize larger deviations from the mean, as illustrated below:

(x) Deviation	Power To Which x Is Raised			
	1st	2nd	3rd	4th
−9	−9	+81	−729	+6561
+1	+1	+ 1	+ 1	+ 1
+1	+1	+ 1	+ 1	+ 1
+2	+2	+ 4	+ 8	+ 16
+5	+5	+25	+125	+ 625
Totals	0	+90	−594	+7204

The third moment provides an index of skewness because it is an odd moment; thus if the high and low scores do not balance out around the mean (as they do not in the example above), it will not be equal to zero. Also, it is a higher moment, and thus it emphasizes the extreme deviations there may be from the arithmetic mean. The fourth moment is an even moment, thus it does not distinguish between deviations above or below the mean. It is a higher moment, so that it emphasizes the deviation of scores which fall in the tails or extremes of a distribution. Thus the fourth moment is useful in measuring the degree of kurtosis in a distribution.

None of the moments are relative measures. That is, they range in magnitude over a scale which starts at zero and extends upward to a value which depends upon the units of measurement and the variability of scores. For this reason, skewness and kurtosis measures are sometimes created in such a way that the range of index values is over a defined scale. This would for example, permit one to compare skewness and kurtosis scores regardless of units of measurement. Two such measures, called Beta-one (β_1) and Beta-two (β_2), are sometimes created out of the moment system:

(5.14)
$$\text{Beta-one } (\beta_1) = \frac{m_3^2}{m_2^3} \qquad \text{(Skewness)}$$

(5.15)
$$\text{Beta-two } (\beta_2) = \frac{m_4}{m_2^2} \qquad \text{(Kurtosis)}$$

5.5.1a Skewness (Beta-one) The *skewness* measure, called *Beta-one* (β_1), is the ratio of the square of the third moment divided by the cube of the second moment. If the distribution is symmetrical, the third moment will be zero and thus the β_1 measure will be zero. If the distribution is skewed to the right, β_1 will be a positive value, and if it is skewed to the left, β_1 will be negative. The magnitude of β_1 expresses the relative amount of skewness and can be compared between distributions of different units of measurement.

5.5.1b Kurtosis (Beta-two) The *kurtosis* measure, *Beta-two* (β_2), is the ratio of the fourth moment to the square of the second moment, and it too is a relative measure. Small values of β_2 indicate a platykurtic (flatter than normal) distribution, and high values indicate a leptokurtic distribution. The normal or mesokurtic distribution has a β_2 value of three, as does a curve called the standard normal curve.

5.5.2   The Standard Normal Distribution

The so-called "normal curve" is only one possible shape of a distribution, but it is a frequently used shape in statistics because it usefully describes a large number of chance distributions which are explored at great length in the field of inferential statistics (see Chapter 12 and the chapters following). Here it is useful to mention for two reasons, first, because it is the "mesokurtic" normal curve, and secondly, because it is helpful in explaining some of the usefulness of the standard deviation as a measure of variation. Platykurtic and leptokurtic distributions are, quite aptly, less peaked and more peaked than this normal one. As noted above, the normal curve has a β_2 value of 3.0 and, because it is a symmetrical curve, it has a β_1 value of zero. It is a unimodal, bell-shaped distribution which can be precisely described in terms of the following formula:

(5.16)
$$Y = \frac{N}{s\sqrt{2\pi}} \exp\left[-\frac{(X-\overline{X})^2}{2s^2} \right]$$

where Y is the value on the ordinate of a graph; X is the score value on the abscissa; N is the number of observations; "exp" represents e, the base of the natural logarithms (2.71828), raised to the power indicated in brackets; and π is pi (3.14159).

Notice that the formula includes s, the standard deviation, as well as the squared deviation of scores from their mean. It is not at all necessary to remember this formula; it is only introduced to indicate that the normal curve is a specific form of curve which is a function of the mean and standard deviation.

5.5.2a   The Normal Curve.   In statistics it is often useful to think of a normal curve where scores are expressed as standard scores (z-scores) rather than in terms of original units (*e.g.* tons, pounds). Such a normal curve is called a **standardized normal curve.** It has a mean of zero, a standard deviation of 1.0, and an area which is set as equal to 1.0. Figure 5.5 shows a standard normal curve.

Notice that the percentage of area under a normal curve falling between a point which is one standard deviation below the mean ($z=-1$) and one standard deviation above the mean ($z=+1$), is about 68 percent of the total area under the curve. Since 50 percent of the area under the curve is on either side of the mean (it is a symmetrical curve), there is only about 16 percent of the area under a curve falling above a z-score of $+1.0$.

5.5.2b   Area under a Normal Curve.   Since the normal curve is used rather frequently in inferential statistics, tables of areas under the normal curve have been prepared. Table B in the Appendix of this book is such a table. The first column in Table B is the z-score value. Notice that it is necessary to list only positive z-scores, since we know that the normal curve is symmetrical and thus identical values would be given for negative z-scores. The second col-

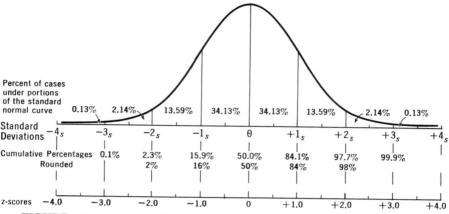

FIGURE 5.5 AREAS AND PERCENTAGES UNDER THE STANDARD NORMAL CURVE

umn in Table A shows the proportion of the area under the entire normal curve which falls between the mean and a point which is a given number of standard deviation units away in a given direction. Column 3 in Table A gives the proportion of the area under the curve falling beyond a given z-score in one direction. With this table, it is possible to compute quickly the proportion of the area under a normal curve between any two z-scores.* The following table lists some of the more frequently used z-score values from Table A and corresponding percentages of the area under a normal curve.

	Percentage Of The Total Area In:	
z-score	One-Tail	Both Tails Combined
1.64	5%	10%
1.96	2.5%	5%
2.33	1%	2%
2.58	0.5%	1%

To illustrate the use of the table of areas under a normal curve and z-scores, let us consider the case of an achievement test with normally distributed scores, with a mean of 50, and with a standard deviation of 15. What proportion of the scores in the distribution will fall above the score of 66? To solve this we compute the z-score for the score 66:

$$z = \frac{66 - 50}{15} = \frac{16}{15} = +1.07$$

Looking up this value in the z-score column of Table A in the Appendix, we will take the value in column C, which is the proportion beyond a given z-score. For the z-score of +1.07, this table value is .1423. Slightly more than 14% of the area under the curve is above this z-score or, in terms of the problem, slightly more

---

*Tables are also available which give the height of the ordinate on a normal curve at various points represented by z-scores. See, for example, Hagood and Price, 1952:558.

than 14% of the scores in this test distribution are above the score 66. Using similar procedures, we could compute the percent of the area under a curve "below" a given z-score, between z-scores of different values, or we could compute the scores at the first and third quartiles.

5.5.3   Other Mathematical Descriptions of Form

Although the standard normal curve is a useful curve in statistics and one which can be described mathematically, it is but one form of curve. It was once thought that many characteristics were distributed in this way, but it is clear that this is not particularly true. The main use of the normal curve will be as a description of a certain kind of probability of sampling outcomes. For most other distributions, a description in terms of central tendency, form, and variation adequately expresses what the distribution is like. Where a mathematical description of a curve is possible, a clearly powerful tool for description is available. Examples in the social sciences include a curve describing the likelihood of the end of wars and strikes, the Lorenz curve in demography, and the J-curve hypothesis concerning adherence to social norms. Some examples of these may be found in various sociology texts, or illustrated in the data section of a workbook (such as the one designed for use with this text: *Statistical Analysis for Sociologists: A Student Manual*, by H. J. Loether and D. G. McTavish).

5.6   SUMMARY

In this chapter we have discussed ways of describing distributions of univariate data. Three overall features of distributions were described—*form, central tendency* and *variation*—and several indices of each feature were presented. The form of a distribution varies in terms of *kurtosis, skewness,* and number of *modes* or peaks, and it is often simply described in terms that are broad and descriptive such as a "bell-shaped" distribution. Measures of kurtosis and skewness were developed, and mathematical formulas can be used to describe precisely the shapes of distributions. Measures of central tendency and variation were also discussed, and some of the reasons one might prefer one measure over another were presented. Typically, an investigator would describe his data in terms of one index of variation, one index of central tendency, and measures of form (kurtosis, skewness and modes). The specific measures used depend on the type of data and research interests.

Comparisons of individuals and between individuals and their group are facilitated by using standard scores, and, if the curve happens to be a normal curve, tables of areas under the normal curve would permit one to readily convert a z-score into an expression about the proportion of cases in a group falling below a given z-score. In any case, measures presented in this chapter are highly useful in making valid comparisons between individuals, groups, or outside standards as dictated by one's problem.

Thus, looking back at the Cloud and Vaughan study of the control of acquiescence bias in the measurement of attitudes (Figure 5.1), we can describe the content curve (C) as bimodal, unlike the other two which are unimodal, and we can describe it as located lower on the score scale than the other two. The "yeasayer" curve (Y) is unimodal, leptokurtic, and has much less variability than the other two; also it is located between the others on the score scale. The highest curve (S) for style, is unimodal and of an average amount of variation and kurtosis. Numeric indices for these features of the distributions would have greatly aided our overall comparisons and would have aided us in drawing clearer conclusions about the differences between these distributions.

The next section of this book also deals with description, but instead of describing and contrasting univariate distributions, it will confront the problem of describing sets of univariate distributions where each individual is simultaneously characterized by scores on two different variables. This is called a bivariate distribution. Although specific tools of description vary from those we have covered, the essential principles remain: — the selective losing of information with more pointed and powerful summary measures; the utility of the idea of a ratio; the description of location and variation in a dependent variable across subgroups defined in terms of the second variable; and, finally, the importance of clearly identifying the contrasts and comparisons one wants to make.

CONCEPTS TO KNOW AND UNDERSTAND

three features of a distribution
    central tendency (location)
    variation (dispersion)
    form
kurtosis
    platykurtic
    mesokurtic
    leptokurtic
unimodal, bimodal, multimodal
skewness
    negative
    positive
    symmetry
arithmetic mean
mode

median
other specialized means
range
interquartile range
average absolute deviation
variance, standard deviation
index of dispersion
variation ratio
moving average
standard scores (z-scores)
standard normal distribution
area under a normal curve
moment system
Beta-1
Beta-2

QUESTIONS AND PROBLEMS

1. Select data on an interesting variable from the U.S. Census sources available to you, or from the data section of a workbook (such as the one designed for use with this text: *Statistical Analysis for Sociologists: A Student Manual,* by H. J. Loether and D. G. McTavish). Compute appropriate measures of central

tendency, variation and form. Justify your selections and explain in your own words what each of the measures means.

2. Sometimes it is helpful at this point to set up a chart which organizes the main differences between the measures included in this chapter. Computing formulae and interpretations could be entered on such a chart for each measure. See if you can set up a chart which helps you select and interpret measures.

3. Sociology often deals with the idea of "normal" or "average" and with the idea of similarity and difference. Find one research article in a sociology journal which uses statistical measures of central tendency and variation to discuss these concepts. Explain how the authors use and interpret these measures in their work.

GENERAL REFERENCE

Hagood, Margaret Jarman, and Daniel O. Price, *Statistics for Sociologists,* revised edition, (New York, Holt), 1952.
See especially Chapters 9 and 14.

OTHER REFERENCES

Adams, Stuart, "Trends in Occupational Origins of Physicians," *American Sociological Review,* 18 (1953), p 404–409.

Cloud, Jonathan, and Graham M. Vaughn, "Using Balance Scales to Control Acquiescence," *Sociometry,* 33 (June, 1970), p 193–202.

Hagood, Margaret Jarman, and Daniel O. Price, *Statistics for Sociologists,* revised edition, (New York, Henry Holt and Company), 1952, p 558.

Hammond, Kenneth R., and James E. Householder, *Introduction to the Statistical Method* (New York: Alfred A. Knopf), 1962, p 136–142.

Hawkes, Roland K., "Multivariate Analysis of Ordinal Measures," *American Journal of Sociology* 76 (March, 1971), p 908–926.

Linn, Erwin L., "Women Dentists: Career and Family," *Social Problems,* 18 (Winter, 1971), p 393–404.

Martin, J. David, and Louis N. Gray, "Measurement of Relative Variation: Sociological Examples," *American Sociological Review,* 36 (June, 1971), p 496–502.

Mueller, John H., and Karl F. Schuessler, *Statistical Reasoning in Sociology,* (Boston, Houghton Mifflin), 1961, p 177–179.

Newman, James R., *The World of Mathematics,* vol. 3, (New York, Simon and Schuster), 1956, 1489–1493.

Reiss, Ira L., *The Social Context of Premarital Sexual Permissiveness,* (New York, Holt, Rinehart, and Winston, Inc.), 1967, p 36.

Rushing, William A., and Vernon Davies, "Note on the Mathematical Formalization of a Measure of Division of Labor," *Social Forces,* 48 (March, 1970), p 394–396.

U.S. Bureau of the Census, "Consumer Income," *Current Population Reports,* P-60, No. 72, (Washington, D.C.), 1970, Table 2.

————, "Estimates of the Population of the United States and Components of Change:

1940 to 1971," *Current Population Reports,* P-25, No. 465, (Washington, D.C.), 1971.

⸻, "Selected Characteristics of Persons and Families, March, 1970," *Current Population Reports,* P-20, No. 204, (Washington, D.C.), 1970, p 9, Table 7.

⸻, "Estimates of the Population of the United States to September 1, 1972," *Current Population Reports,* P-25, No. 491, (Washington, D.C.), 1972.

Wallis, W. Allen, and Harry V. Roberts, *Statistics: A New Approach,* (New York, The Free Press of Glencoe), 1956, p 226–230.

DESCRIPTIVE STATISTICS: TWO VARIABLES

6

CROSS CLASSIFICATION OF VARIABLES

Sociologists concerned with urban styles of life have theorized that people living in larger cities will have greater tolerance of racial and ethnic differences, for example, than people living in smaller cities or rural areas. This is thought to be due to a number of features of the urban environment such as the greater impersonality, greater variety of contacts between people, greater concern for utility of others, and the greater use of universalistic standards for making judgments and decisions. Does the evidence support this prediction? To examine this question, Fischer (1971) used data from five Gallup polls taken between 1958 and 1965 in the U.S.

6.1 BIVARIATE DISTRIBUTIONS: AN EXAMPLE

In these polls, the question was asked, "If your party nominated a generally well-qualified man for president and he happened to be a (Negro or Jew or Catholic), would you vote for him?" Tolerance was measured by counting the number of these three minority groups for which the respondent would agree to vote (*i.e.* none, one, two, or all three). Table 6.1 presents the overall frequency and percentage distribution of tolerance scores for the 7,714 cases in the combined polls.

It is interesting to note that about 41 percent of the respondents would vote for all three minority groups—that is, they show high tolerance for ethnic and racial minorities as measured by this type of question.[*] It is clear, however,

---

[*] It is important to distinguish between tolerance views expressed in polls and behavior indicative of tolerance which may be expressed in the privacy of an election booth or in other situations.

TABLE 6.1 Tolerance Scale for 7,714 Respondents of Five Gallup Polls Taken between 1958 and 1965 in National Samples of the U.S.

Tolerance Level	f	%
3 (High)	3,147	40.8
2	2,317	30.1
1	1,229	15.9
0 (Low)	1,021	13.2
Totals	7,714	100.0%

Source: Fischer, 1971: 849. Used by permission.

that this overall distribution does not permit one to say whether the theory is supported, simply because it does not provide necessary information which would permit us to make a comparison between cities of different sizes. We need to know whether tolerance scores are distributed differently for people residing in places of different sizes, and if they are, we also need to see whether the percent of respondents in the high tolerance categories of the tolerance scale is higher in larger cities compared to smaller ones. We need to compare this univariate distribution of tolerance scores for small and medium and large cities to see if the differences are in the predicted direction.

Table 6.2 provides the detail we need. Here four separate univariate distributions (both frequency and percentage) are shown: one for only those respondents who live in rural areas; one for small places; one for medium places,

TABLE 6.2 Tolerance Scales for Respondents in Table 6.1

6.2A TOLERANCE SCALE FOR FARM OR COUNTRY RESIDENTS

Tolerance Level	f	%
High	597	26.2
2	700	30.7
1	497	21.8
Low	485	21.3
Total	2,279	100.0%

6.2B TOLERANCE SCALE FOR SUBJECTS LIVING IN TOWNS UNDER 25,000

Tolerance Level	f	%
High	483	36.0
2	396	29.5
1	272	20.3
Low	191	14.2
Total	1,342	100.0%

6.2C TOLERANCE SCALE FOR RESPONDENTS LIVING IN PLACES 25,000 TO 500,000

Tolerance Level	f	%
High	738	43.4
2	536	31.5
1	242	14.2
Low	185	10.9
Total	1,701	100.0%

6.2D TOLERANCE SCALE FOR SUBJECTS LIVING IN CITIES OVER 500,000

Tolerance Level	f	%
High	1,328	55.5
2	684	28.6
1	220	9.2
Low	160	6.7
Total	2,392	100.0%

Source: Fischer, 1971: 849, Table 2. Used by permission.

and one for large cities. In each case, however, we are looking at the distribution of the dependent variable, tolerance scores.* Comparing the "high-tolerance" end of the scale of tolerance, for example, we see that the predictions seem to be borne out: 26.2% have "high-tolerance" among rural and country people; this percentage increases to 36.0% for people living in places of under 25,000 population; it increases again to 43.4% for people living in the next larger category of cities; and reaches 55.5% scored as "high-tolerance" among people living in the largest cities. A comparison of the "low-tolerance" category reflects this trend also. Smaller places have a bigger percentage of people with "low-tolerance," and the percentages decrease as city size increases. Thus far, then, it seems to be the case that the theory holds for these data.† Notice that we arrived at this conclusion by comparing percentages rather than absolute frequencies, since it is clear that the number of respondents differs between tables we want to compare. Chapter 3 discussed this use of percentages as one means by which valid comparisons could be made in just such circumstances.‡

Up to this point we have discussed the problem of comparing tolerance scores for each category of city size as a comparison of several univariate distributions. The dependent variable is common to each of the distributions, and separate tables are distinguished in terms of categories of the independent variable, size of place. It happens to have four categories, and thus there are four separate distributions of the dependent variable to examine. A more efficient way to reach conclusions under these conditions would be to combine all of the

TABLE 6.3 PERCENTAGE DISTRIBUTION OF TOLERANCE SCORES FOR RESPONDENTS IN A COMBINED SAMPLE CONSISTING OF FIVE GALLUP POLLS OF U.S. NATIONAL SAMPLES CONDUCTED BETWEEN 1958 AND 1965, BY SIZE OF PLACE OF RESIDENCE

Tolerance Level	Size of Place of Residence				Total
	Farm & Country	Under 25,000	25,000 to 500,000	Over 500,000	
High	26.2%	36.0%	43.4%	55.5%	40.8%
2	30.7	29.5	31.5	28.6	30.1
1	21.8	20.3	14.2	9.2	15.9
Low	21.3	14.2	10.9	6.7	13.2
Totals	100.0%	100.0%	100.0%	100.0%	100.0%
	(2279)	(1342)	(1701)	(2392)	(7714)

Source: See Tables 6.1 and 6.2

*Recall from Chapter 2 that a dependent variable is either the primary variable whose variation one is interested in, or the effect or outcome of variation in an independent or causal variable. The role variables play in a study depends upon the investigator's theoretical reasoning about what influences what.
†Actually Fischer presents a more exciting analysis, tracing out differences in the distribution of tolerance by such other variables as occupation, race, region, and religion. These appear to be important conditions which govern the distribution of tolerance, and this leads to important questions about the explanatory importance of city size alone.
‡We might also have made the comparisons from table to table in terms of some set of measures of central tendency, form, and variation, as discussed in Chapter 5. Certainly a comparison of medians, for example, would have reduced some of the detail involved in comparing all of the percentages shown in Table 6.2 above.

separate tables (*i.e.* Tables 6.2A, 6.2B, 6.2C, 6.2D and Table 6.1) into one overall table as shown in Table 6.3. This table permits us to compare the separate groups more readily and it leads to a type of summary of the whole table in terms of a relationship between the two variables in general. Table 6.3 is known as a **bivariate percentage distribution** because it permits one to examine the percentage distribution of one variable (the dependent variable) within the different categories of the other variable. The comparison ideas behind such cross-classifications are the basis of analysis in sociology, because the science attempts to develop theoretical statements about the relationship of variables and the conditions under which these occur.

6.2 CONDITIONAL DISTRIBUTIONS

A bivariate distribution, such as that shown in Table 6.3, permits one to examine not only the overall distribution of some dependent variable, but also some of the conditions which may be thought to influence how that variable is distributed. The theory suggested that under certain conditions tolerance would be higher than under other conditions. In Table 6.3 these conditions corresponded to different sizes of place of residence, but one could think of other conditions which may have a bearing upon the level of tolerance. In fact, one could think of a scientific discipline as one which is searching for the kinds of conditions which help predict and explain the level of some kind of phenomenon. A table merely puts together a related set of **conditional distributions** and an overall total distribution of some dependent variable.

Our objective in this chapter is to explore some of the characteristics of bivariate distributions or cross-classifications of two variables. The following chapter will discuss some of the more useful index numbers which can be used to summarize variables that are related to each other. This is a road we have already traveled once before in previous chapters. In univariate descriptive statistics we started with a set of raw scores or a distribution, and then we asked if there were ways it could be summarized in terms of a few overall index numbers. We developed several measures for each of the three features of a distribution: central tendency, form, and variation. Our objective in bivariate description is quite similar, and, in many respects, simpler, more interesting, and more useful in sociological inquiry.

6.3 HOW TO SET UP AND EXAMINE TABLES

A cross-classification of two variables requires a table with rows and columns. The categories of one variable are labels for the rows, and the categories of the other variable are used to label the columns. Usually, where there is a dependent variable, it is used as the row variable, and the independent variable is used as the column variable, but this tradition is sometimes broken.

6.3.1 Creating a Bivariate Frequency Distribution

To illustrate how a table is constructed, we could think of 13 sets of scores. Figure 6.4 shows a tolerance score and a sex score for each of 13 individuals. The bivariate distribution is set up as shown, with the categories of tolerance (here two categories, high and low) down the **stub** or side of the table, and the categories of sex across the **heading** at the top.

This table is a **2 by 2 table,** or **fourfold table,** because it has two rows and two columns (or four cells in the **body** of the table where the rows and columns intersect). Tables can, of course, have any number of rows or columns (in general we refer to an *r* by *c* table where *r* refers to the number of rows and *c* refers to the number of columns); *r* and *c* depend upon the number of categories which are distinguished for row and column variables.

The problem now is to count the number of cases which have various possible combinations of values on the two variables, and to enter these totals into the table to form a bivariate frequency distribution. Notice that three of the 13 cases in this sample are males who are "high" on tolerance. Three are males who are "low" on tolerance, five are females who are "high" on tolerance, and two are females who are "low" on tolerance. These numbers are written in the

TABLE 6.4 A FREQUENCY TABLE

Score Key	Case I.D.	Tolerance Score	Sex Score
M = male	A	L	M
F = female	B	L	M
H = high	C	H	M
L = low	D	H	M
	E	H	F
	F	L	F
	G	H	F
	H	H	M
	I	L	F
	J	L	M
	K	H	F
	L	H	F
	M	H	F

TABLE OF TOLERANCE LEVEL BY SEX

Tolerance Level	Sex		Row Totals
	Male	Female	
High	III 3	JHT 5	8
Low	III 3	II 2	5
Column Totals	6	7	13

Source: Hypothetical data.

boxes or cells in the body of the table corresponding to the appropriate row and column labels as shown in Table 6.4. Sometimes it is helpful to create a tally within each cell as a workmanlike way to assure accuracy.

Each of the boxes in the table is called a **cell** and the frequency in a cell is called a **cell frequency.** Cell frequencies are sometimes symbolized by the small letter n_{ij}, where the first subscript indicates the number of the row and the second subscript indicates the number of the column, as follows:

	column 1	column 2	row totals
row 1	n_{11}	n_{12}	$\sum_j n_{1j}$
row 2	n_{21}	n_{22}	$\sum_j n_{2j}$
column totals	$\sum_i n_{i1}$	$\sum_i n_{i2}$	N

They indicate the number of cases in the total sample which fall in a certain category of the row and column variable as indicated by the row and column labels.* The cell frequencies indicate the number of cases with two characteristics simultaneously. Row and column totals each add up to 13, which is the total number of cases there were. The cell frequencies constitute the conditional distributions, and the row and column totals reflect the marginals or univariate distribution of each variable.

6.3.2 Traditions of Table Layout

Usually tables are set up so that the dependent variable is the one with categories listed down the *stub,* or left side of the table, and the independent variable is listed across the top in the *heading.* This convention, of course, is not always kept, but it does tend to aid in the examination of conditional distributions in each column to have it set up this way. Table 6.3 illustrates proper labeling of a table. Notice that low categories of the independent variable, where there are low categories on that variable, are listed at the left and the high category is at the right. For the dependent variable the high categories are at the top of the table and the low categories are at the bottom. This is similar to the labeling of other graphs, although in the case of tables the convention is not as rigidly adhered to, and the investigator would do well to double-check the table layout before proceeding to make any interpretation.

A table usually has a title which lists the dependent variable, whether the table contains frequencies or percentages (or some other measure), the independent variable(s), and the kind of case upon which the measurements were taken. Table 6.3 contains data on 7,714 individuals. If the table is a percentaged table,

---

*Some authors use a different set of symbols for row and column totals, where a dot is used in place of a subscript for totals. Thus $n_{.1}$ would be the sum of column 1 over all of the rows in the table (the row subscript is replaced by a dot) instead of $\sum_i n_{i1}$ and $n_{1.}$ would symbolize the total of row one, instead of $\sum_j n_{1j}$. One could use n rather than N or $\sum\sum n_{ij}$ to indicate the grand total number of cases.

it is important to indicate the base upon which the percentage was computed in brackets, at the bottom by the column total percentages*; otherwise cell frequencies are omitted from a percentaged table. The source of data is indicated, typically, in a footnote to the table, and both the stub and heading are clearly marked with the variable and the name of each of the categories of each variable.

Table 6.4 is a frequency table. It has categories of the tolerance variable down the side (the stub), and categories of the variable, sex, across the top. In this case, tolerance played the role of dependent variable.

Notice that cell frequencies in columns are summed, and the sums are put at the bottom of the table. Rows are also summed, and the totals put at the right hand side. These row and column totals are called **marginals,** or simply row totals and column totals, and they are merely the univariate distribution of each variable separately.

If the table shows percentages it is called a bivariate percentage distribution, and if frequencies are shown, it is called a bivariate frequency distribution.

6.3.3 Percentaged Tables

Probably the most often used type of table is the percentaged table. Its value lies in the way it helps one to make comparisons across the conditional distributions one wants to compare. The basic rule for computing percentages on a table is as follows:

> *Compute percentages in the direction of the independent variable.*

This means that percentages should sum up to 100% for each category of the independent variable. For tables set up such as Table 6.3, the percentaging rule leads to computation with column totals as the base of the percent; thus column percents add up to 100% for each column. If the independent variable and the dependent variable were switched around, the percentages would have to be run in the other direction. There are three ways that a table can be percentaged, as shown in Table 6.5, using the hypothetical data from Table 6.4. Tables could be percentaged with *column totals* as the base of percentages, with *row totals* as the base of percentages, and with the *grand total* as the base of percentages. Since the dependent variable is down the stub of Table 6.4. the proper table to examine to see what differences there may be between categories of the sex variable would be to percentage with column totals (the number of males or the number of females) as the base of the percentages. One wants to contrast the distribution of the dependent variable between men and women, and the only way to do this is to take out the effect of different numbers of men and women by percentaging down (in the direction of the independent variable). This type of operation permits one to make comparisons in the *other direction. Comparisons are made* (made possible) in the *opposite direction from the way percentages are run.*

*This is true if column totals are the bases of percentages. If rows sum to 100% then row total frequencies are given.

TABLE 6.5 ILLUSTRATION OF DIFFERENT WAYS PERCENTAGES CAN BE COMPUTED ON TABLES

ORIGINAL FREQUENCY DISTRIBUTION FROM TABLE 6.4

Tolerance Level	Sex Male	Female	Total
High	3	5	8
Low	3	2	5
Total	6	7	13

6.5A PERCENTAGING TO COLUMN TOTALS AS THE BASE

Tolerance Level	Sex Male	Female	Total
High	50%	71%	62%
Low	50	29	38
Total	100%	100%	100%

6.5B PERCENTAGING TO ROW TOTALS AS THE BASE

Tolerance Level	Sex Male	Female	Total
High	38%	62	100%
Low	60%	40	100%
Total	46%	54	100%

6.5C PERCENTAGING TO OVERALL GRAND TOTAL AS THE BASE

Tolerance Level	Sex Male	Female	Total
High	23%	39%	62%
Low	23%	15%	38
Total	46%	54	100%

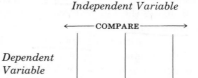

Independent Variable

←——COMPARE——→

Dependent Variable

100%   100%   100%

Comparisons are made in a percentaged table by examining differences between percentages. In Table 6.5a, for example, the difference between percentage "high" on tolerance among men and women is 21% (71%−50%=21%). This value is called **epsilon,** the percentage difference in a table, and it is symbolized by the Greek letter ϵ. For tables larger than a two by two table, there are a number of percentage contrasts or epsilons which may be computed and used in interpretation. Epsilon will be discussed further later on in this chapter.

Sometimes an investigator will compute percentages, as in Table 6.5c, with the total number of cases (N) as *the base for all cell percentages*. Where this is done, we no longer can compare conditional distributions, but we can express the percentage of cases which have each of the different combinations of characteristics labeled by the rows and columns.

If it is not clear which variable is dependent or independent, or if we could think of the data in both ways, we might compute percentages to *both row and column totals* (as in Tables 6.5a and 6.5b) and *examine each table*. Table 6.5a would permit us to say that females are more likely to be higher on tolerance than are males. Table 6.5b would permit us to say that high-tolerance people are more likely to be female than are low-tolerance people—a subtle shift with worlds of import, as we shall soon see.

As shown in Table 6.5, percentaging *down* permits an examination of any influence sex may have on the distribution of tolerance; percentaging *across* shows the possible recruitment pattern into tolerance levels from each sex, and percentaging to the *grand total* permits us to examine the joint percentage distribution of tolerance levels and sex.

6.3.3a THE EFFECT OF SAMPLING DECISIONS ON PERCENTAGING TABLES

Sometimes an investigator will decide to draw a sample in such a way that he guarantees himself, say, equal numbers of cases in each study category or condition he wants to examine. This means, of course, that the marginals for that variable do not necessarily reflect or represent the way that variable is distributed in the population from which he drew his sample. This happens, for example, in situations where the phenomenon being studied is quite rare. Only a small percentage of the population of the U.S. is classified as alcoholic, and it would be easy to draw a sample and completely miss this kind of person. If one were interested in comparing alcoholics and non-alcoholics on some characteristic, the whole study would collapse if alcoholics were not sampled in sufficient numbers to analyze. To protect himself, an investigator may sample in a way that is called *stratified sampling;* (sampling techniques are introduced and discussed in research methods texts or inferential statistics books).* That is, the investigator may divide a population list up into alcoholic and non-alcoholic and deliberately draw an equal (or specified) number of cases from each condition into his sample.

This procedure results in the distribution of alcoholism which may not reflect the way that variable is distributed in the population as a whole (*i.e.* alcoholics would be over-represented in the sample). This procedure would mean that alcoholism would be an "unrepresentative" variable. Because of this essentially arbitrary changing of the distribution of a variable in a sample, we must follow procedures which take this into account; namely, the table must be percentaged so that the category totals of the unrepresentative variable are used as the base of percentages. This is called **percentaging in the direction of the non-representative variable.** If the non-representative factor happens also to be an independent variable, then the percentages we have to examine are in-

*See H.J. Loether and D.G. McTavish, *Inferential Statistics for Sociologists*, Chapter 2.

deed the percentages we need to use in drawing conclusions. If, however, we stratify or make non-representative in some way a dependent variable, then the percentages have to be run the "wrong" way for this analysis, and we are unable to make the contrasts we need to make.

6.3.3b ILLUSTRATION OF PERCENTAGED TABLES

Table 6.6 provides data on the bivariate distribution of income and ethnicity in the U.S. in 1970. The table clearly shows differences in the distribution of income for the different ethnic groups. Whites are less likely to be in the lowest income categories as compared to those of Spanish origin or blacks. Epsilon, the difference between percentages, is 3.2% between whites and those of Spanish origin, and 14.1% between whites and blacks. This table would be quite useful to answer the question: What is the consequence of ethnicity for the distribution of income? Had the percentages been run the other way, we could answer the question: What is the consequence of different income levels on the ethnic distribution of the United States? The first question is probably much more sensible and useful to answer than the second; thus percentaging down, as has been done in Table 6.6, would be the appropriate way to percentage this table.

Table 6.7 provides a somewhat different example of percentaged tables which also highlights one of the problems involved in comparison of percentages. These data are from a summary of questions asked in a number of public opinion polls concerning the role of women. One of the questions asked over several years by the Gallup Poll is: "If your party nominated a woman for President, would you vote for her if she were qualified for the job?" The response categories are, basically, "yes" and "no," and the percentage giving these two responses out of the total number of men and women sampled is shown in the table.

Notice that for men and to some extent for women, the percentage saying that they would vote for a woman increases over the years between 1937 and 1969. The percentage saying they would not vote for a woman also tends to decline. Using these data, we could answer the question: "What is the difference in percent agreeing to vote for a woman from year to year?"

Notice too that the comparison is contaminated by the troublesome "no opinion" or "no response" category. Where percentages include these cases, the

TABLE 6.6 PERCENT DISTRIBUTION OF INCOME IN 1970 FOR MALES WITH INCOME, AGED 25 YEARS OLD AND OVER, BY ETHNIC ORIGIN, U.S., MARCH 1971

	Ethnic Origin		
Income	White	Spanish	Black
Less than $3000	14.0	17.2	28.1
$3000 to $5999	18.2	30.3	31.9
$6000 to $9999	32.0	35.1	29.6
$10000 and over	35.9	17.3	10.4
Total	100.0	100.0	100.0
Number in millions	(45.9)	(1.8)	(4.4)

Source: U.S. Bur. Census, 1971.

TABLE 6.7 Percentage Indicating Support for a Woman President in Gallup Polls in the United States between 1937 and 1969, by Sex

"If your party nominated a woman for President, would you vote for her if she were qualified for the job?"

| | | FOR MEN | | | | | FOR WOMEN | | |
Time	Would	Would Not	No Opinion	Total*	Time	Would	Would Not	No Opinion	Total
1937	27%	69%	4%	100%	1937	40%	57%	3%	100%
1945	29	58	13	100	1945	37	51	12	100
1949	45	50	5	100	1949	51	46	3	100
1955	47	48	5	100	1955	57	40	3	100
1963	58	37	5	100	1963	51	45	4	100
1967	61	34	5	100	1967	53	44	3	100
1969	58	35	7	100	1969	49	44	7	100

Epsilons between Men and Women on Percentage Saying They *Would* Vote for a Woman for President

Time	ϵ†
1937	+13%
1945	+ 8
1949	+ 6
1955	+10
1963	− 7
1967	− 8
1969	− 9

Source: Data from Erskine, 1971:278. Used by permission of George Gallup.
*Total number of cases was not given in the source.
†Epsilons here are computed by subtracting the percentage who would vote for a woman president among men from that among women in any given year. Minus signs indicate that the male percentage is higher and plus signs indicate that the female percentage is higher.

percentage comparisons of voting intention between one year and another are distorted because they also reflect differences in the level of "no opinion." This is particularly important to watch for in comparisons involving the year 1945, where the percentage of men and women giving no opinion increased a very great deal. Among men, there is little difference in percentage who would vote for a woman between 1937 and 1945, but there is a big drop between these years in percent saying they would not vote for a woman. Apparently, overall, there was a shift to "no opinion" from the "would not vote for a woman" category. Between 1945 and 1949, however the percent "no opinion" drops back to a modest level, and there is a corresponding increase in the percentage who would vote for a woman. In this case, then, epsilons computed between years on one response category of the dependent variable (*e.g.* willingness to vote for a woman as president) would be misleading without taking account at the same time of the shift in the "would not" and "no opinion" categories.* We need some descriptive device which will permit an overall examination of a table rather than

*Other procedures for handling the "no response" or "no opinion" categories in research of this sort are discussed by Davis and Jacobs, 1968.

only a contrast of individual pairs of percents, (although these too are interesting for some purposes).

BOX 6.1

Thus far in Chapter 6 we have discussed the way in which bivariate distributions may be created (Sections 6.1, and 6.2, and 6.3.1) and the use of percentages to examine the distribution of a variable within categories of some other variable (Section 6.3.3. ff). Percentaging rules which are useful in this process are: (a) percentage in the direction of the independent variable and compare in the other direction (Section 6.3.3), (b) percentage in the direction of the non-representative variable, if any (Section 6.3.3a), and (c) percentage to the grand total to examine the joint percentage distribution (Section 6.3.3). These uses of percentages should be understood before you go on into some further applications of these rules under somewhat more detailed conditions, and before we discuss the measures of association which follow.

6.3.4   More Complex Conditional Distributions

It is often the case that investigators look at percentage tables which are a good deal more complex than those we have just been examining. That is, they may be interested in conditional distributions which are distinguished by more than one independent variable. We will have more systematic things to say about such tables later on in this book, but for now we should indicate how we might begin to approach the interpretation of such a table.

Often a table is set up so that the focus is on either the *dependent variable alone* under various kinds of conditions, or on some basic set of conditional distributions — *a basic table,* — which is examined in another set of conditional situations.

Table 6.8 illustrates a more complex table of the first kind. Four variables, education of mother, education of father, I.Q. of the child, and sex of the child, define the conditions within which a student's plans regarding college can be examined. The dependent variable is, as the title suggests, the percentage *planning on going to college.* Actually, there could be two tables presented here instead of one. One table would show the percentage *planning* on college and the other would show the percentage *not planning* on college. Since these two percentages would total to 100 percent, it is sufficient to look at only one of the two possible tables. The other table would be a mirror image of the first. There is a relatively orderly way to go about reading such a table, and we will discuss these procedures here.

The *first step* in examining a table as complex as this one is to clearly *identify the dependent variable* and the kind of *unit* (*i.e.* family, person, parent) upon which it has been measured. In this table it is "expressed plans to go to college"

TABLE 6.8 Percentage Who Planned on College by Sex, Intelligence, Father's Education, and Mother's Education†

Father's Education	MALES Mother's Education				FEMALES Mother's Education				TOTAL Mother's Education			
	High	Middle	Low	Total	High	Middle	Low	Total	High	Middle	Low	Total
a. High Intelligence												
High	89.3(186)	87.8(115)	55.6(36)	85.2(337)	86.0(186)	74.5(102)	68.6(35)	80.5(323)	87.6(372)	81.6(217)	62.0(71)	82.9(660)
Middle	85.7(63)	66.0(241)	53.5(144)	64.7(448)	62.7(75)	50.0(238)	40.5(131)	49.3(444)	73.2(138)	58.0(479)	47.3(275)	57.1(892)
Low	55.1(78)	54.8(210)	45.3(415)	49.2(703)	62.0(100)	37.3(220)	28.1(438)	35.2(758)	59.0(178)	45.8(430)	36.5(853)	42.0(1461)
Total	80.4(327)	66.3(566)	47.9(595)	62.0(1488)	74.5(361)	49.5(560)	33.1(604)	48.9(1525)	77.3(688)	57.9(1126)	40.5(1199)	55.4(3013)
b. Middle Intelligence												
High	71.0(69)	50.0(84)	36.1(36)	55.0(189)	79.5(78)	56.9(58)	38.2(34)	63.5(170)	75.5(147)	52.8(142)	37.1(70)	59.1(359)
Middle	51.1(47)	39.5(218)	30.9(139)	37.9(404)	49.0(49)	31.7(205)	17.1(152)	28.3(406)	50.0(96)	35.7(423)	23.7(291)	33.1(810)
Low	36.0(50)	32.7(211)	26.8(598)	28.8(859)	37.2(78)	24.1(232)	17.1(679)	20.3(989)	36.7(128)	28.2(443)	21.6(1277)	24.2(1848)
Total	54.8(166)	38.4(513)	27.9(773)	34.7(1452)	56.1(205)	31.1(495)	17.9(865)	27.1(1565)	55.5(371)	34.8(1008)	22.7(1638)	30.8(3017)
c. Low Intelligence												
High	48.6(35)	32.1(53)	21.4(28)	34.5(116)	50.0(34)	26.2(42)	30.8(26)	35.3(102)	49.3(69)	29.5(75)	25.9(54)	34.9(218)
Middle	43.3(30)	16.6(181)	15.8(101)	18.9(312)	43.3(30)	20.6(136)	13.4(142)	19.5(308)	43.3(60)	18.3(317)	14.4(243)	19.2(620)
Low	27.3(44)	14.2(211)	0.5(765)	11.3(1020)	30.8(39)	8.3(193)	7.6(887)	8.5(1119)	28.9(83)	11.4(404)	8.5(1652)	9.8(2139)
Total	38.5(109)	17.3(445)	10.6(894)	14.8(1448)	40.8(103)	14.8(371)	8.9(1055)	12.5(1529)	39.6(212)	16.2(816)	9.7(1949)	13.6(2977)
d. Total												
High	80.0(290)	63.5(252)	39.0(100)	67.1(642)	80.2(298)	59.4(202)	47.4(95)	67.9(595)	80.1(588)	61.7(454)	43.1(195)	67.5(1237)
Middle	65.0(140)	43.0(640)	35.4(384)	43.1(1164)	54.6(154)	36.6(579)	23.1(425)	34.0(1158)	59.5(294)	40.0(1219)	28.9(809)	38.6(2322)
Low	42.4(172)	33.9(632)	23.7(1778)	27.4(2582)	47.5(217)	23.9(645)	15.3(2004)	19.6(2866)	45.2(389)	28.8(1277)	19.2(3782)	23.3(5448)
Total	65.8(602)	42.6(1524)	26.4(2262)	37.4(4388)	63.7(669)	34.1(1426)	17.8(2524)	29.5(4619)	64.7(1271)	38.5(2950)	21.8(4786)	33.3(9007)

Source: Data from Sewell and Shah, 1968:198, Table 2. Used by permission.

†The base of percentages is shown in parentheses by each percentage. Data are based on a large, randomly selected cohort of Wisconsin highschool seniors who were followed for a seven-year period.

which is the dependent variable asked of individual people who are the school-aged sons and daughters of parents who have differing amounts of formal education.

The *second* step is to identify the variables involved in the table and the categories of each. In the education variables, three categories are used in this table, and they are labeled "low," "medium," and "high." One education variable has to do with father's education and one has to do with mother's education. There is also an intelligence variable which has three values: "high," "middle," and "low." Finally, female students and male students are distinguished.

Thirdly, the structure of the table should be clarified. In the case of Table 6.8, categories of sex are reflected in the left two strips of percentages down the table. The right strip down the table shows percentages for all cases, regardless of sex, in the total sample. Father's education appears in rows of the table; three rows for father's education within the "high intelligence" category, three in the "middle intelligence" category and three within the "low intelligence" category. The bottom general row of numbers combines together students of all intelligence categories but distinguishes (in rows, again) the father's education. Mother's education is indicated across the top of the two sex and total strips down the table, and there are "total" columns which summarize over father's education or over mother's education, etc. In Table 6.8, rows of figures around the bottom and right hand sides of the table indicate totals, and more detailed breakdowns are concentrated in the rows and columns in the middle and upper left areas of the table. Having identified the structure of the table, we can examine percentages.

The percentage 89.3% in the upper left corner of the table means that 89.3 percent of students plan on going to college among those students who are (a) male, (b) of high intelligence, have (c) a father with "high" education, and (d) a mother with "high" education. Pick another percentage and express its meaning in your own words.

At this point, it is a good idea to find the overall percentage planning on college regardless of education of parents, I.Q., or sex; that is, find the *overall* distribution of the dependent variable without any conditional distribution being considered separately. That figure can be found in Table 6.8 in the lower right hand corner—the total column which summarizes all of the conditional distributions. This figure is 33.3%. Then we can look at the distribution of this variable by each of the other variables one at a time, making contrasts between the percentages, perhaps in terms of epsilon. For example, 67.5% of those with high father's education plan on college, but only 23.3% of those students with low father's education have similar plans. For mother's education the figures are 64.7% and 21.8% respectively. For males, overall, the percentage is 37.4% and for all females it is 29.5%. Finally, among those with high measured intelligence, 55.4% plan on college, but only 13.6% of those with low measured intelligence plan to attend college.

The next step would be to look at the various combinations of variables two at a time, three at a time, and four at a time to see what the effect of various conditional distributions is. The highest percentage planning on going to college is the 89.3% in the upper left corner of the table, and this corresponds to high I.Q. males with parents each of whom has high education.

At the other extreme, 7.6% of the female students with low intelligence and with parents who have low educational backgrounds plan on going to college. Notice that percentage planning on college increases uniformly as one moves from the less advantaged conditions to the more advantaged. Each improvement in advantage seems to be related to an increase in the percentage planning on college.

We could draw several conclusions from these data. First, it seems to be the case that the higher the educational background of the mother or of the father, the higher the percentage of students who plan on college becomes. This will later be called a *positive* relationship, since increases in one variable tend to go along with increases in the other. Males are more likely to plan on college, and the higher the measured intelligence, the higher the percentage planning on college. These findings seem to hold up even within various categories of other variables shown in the table. Furthermore, all of these conditions seem to be cumulative in the sense that individuals with two sources of "advantage" do better than those with only one, and so forth.

At this point we should recall our initial purpose. We wanted to examine the distribution of a *dependent* variable under conditions which are defined in terms of other variables singly or in combinations.

While many investigations call for the examination of conditions based on one variable at a time (*i.e.* by sex or separately by education, etc.), many of our core interests are posed in terms of more complex conditions defined in terms of more than one variable, as was the case in Table 6.8. In many instances the examination of percentaged tables provides the kind of summary and the kinds of contrasts we need for the problem at hand. They are easily understood and direct. On the other hand, it is clear that even simple percentaged tables may contain more details than we want, and some of these may interfere with the analysis. The solution, as it was in the case of univariate summary statistics, is to try to create overall indices which summarize the aspect of the distributions we are most interested in examining.

6.4   FOUR CHARACTERISTICS OF AN ASSOCIATION

Going back to a bivariate distribution such as that shown in Table 6.3, we can think of that distribution as a relationship between two variables, and we want to know how the distribution in the dependent variable varies as we move from category to category of the other variable. The way two variables relate to each other is called an **association** between the two variables. In Table 6.3, as city size increased, the percentage of individuals showing higher tolerance began to increase. The two variables were associated in that particular fashion.

We can speak of the association of any two variables and describe that association in terms of a percentaged table, as we have shown. There are other ways to summarize the association between two variables, however, and, in fact, there are four characteristics of an association which we will single out for summary, just as there were three characteristics of a univariate distribution which we summarized in terms of different index numbers (*i.e.*, central tendency, variation, and form). The four aspects of a bivariate association are:

(a) Whether or not an association *exists*.
(b) The *strength* of that association.
(c) The *direction* of the association.
(d) The *nature* of the association.

Each of these characteristics will be discussed in turn, and in the next chapter we will develop several alternative measures of them. In fact, we will create a single number which will be used to describe the first three features of an association listed above and in some cases a simple formula can be used as an efficient description of the last of the features above.

6.4.1   The Existence of an Association

An association is said to exist between two variables if the distribution of one variable differs in some respect between at least some of the categories of the other variable. This rather general statement can be pinned down in a number of ways, the first of which we have already discussed. If, after computing percentages in the appropriate direction in a table, there is *any* difference between percentage distributions, we would say that an association exists in these data. In the first table, below, the distribution of education is slightly different for men compared with women. We know this by percentaging in the direction of the

Education	Men	Women	Total
High	40%	38%	38%
Low	60	62	62
Total	100%	100%	100%
	(43)	(56)	(99)

(fictitious data)

independent variable and comparing across. In the second table, below, there is *no* association between "toe-nail length" and "education," and this is shown by

Education	Toe Nail Length Short	Long	Total
High	33%	33%	33%
Low	67	67	67
Total	100%	100%	100%
	(521)	(1756)	(2277)

(fictitious data)

the fact that there is no difference in the percentage distribution of education (the dependent variable) regardless of the category of the independent variable within which we examine the dependent variable. In the following table it is clear that there *is* an association between social class and the number of arrests, because the percentage distributions, comparing across the way percentages were run, are different.

Number of Arrests	Social Class		
	Low	Medium	High
None	11%	28%	45%
Few	11	18	35
Many	66	54	20
	100%	100%	100%
	(129)	(260)	(73)

(fictitious data)

There is a name for these comparisons: **epsilon** (ϵ), which is the percentage difference computed across the way percentages were run in a table. In a table where *all* of the epsilons are *zero*, there is *no* association. If any epsilon is non-zero, there is an association in the data even though we may not choose to consider the very small differences important enough to talk about.

The second way to tell whether or not there is an association in a table is to compare the **actual observed table frequencies** with the frequencies we would expect if there were no association, or **expected frequencies.** If the match between actual data and our model of no association is perfect, then there is no association in the actual data between the two variables which were cross tabulated in the table.

6.4.1a No Association Models. A **model of no association** can be set up for a specific table as follows. Usually in setting up a model of the way frequencies in a table should look if there were no association, we assume that the marginal distribution of each variable is the way it is in the observed data table, and that the total number of cases is the same. The problem is to specify the pattern of cell frequencies in the body of the table in a way which shows no association. As an example, suppose the marginals on variables X and Y are as follows:

(Y)	(X)		Total
	Low	High	
High	a	b	57
Low	c	d	50
Total	34	73	107

The problem is to find a pattern of frequencies for cells a, b, c and d such that they exhibit no association between X and Y. The reasoning goes like this. If there is no association in the table, then the ratio of "high" cell frequencies for variable Y as related to the corresponding column totals should be the same throughout the table, as it is in the overall distribution of Y itself, namely 57 to 107. In the table above, we would expect 57/107ths of the 34 cases in the "low" category of X to be in the "high" category of Y. Furthermore, we would expect the same ratio, 57/107ths of the 73 cases in the high column of X to be in the top row. This would mean that, relatively speaking, there is no difference between the proportion of cases in the top row for any column of the table.

$$\frac{57}{107}(34) = .533(34) = 18.1 \text{ cases } \textit{expected} \text{ in cell } a$$

$$\frac{57}{107}(73) = .533(73) = 38.9 \text{ cases } \textit{expected} \text{ for cell } b$$

Given that one of the above cell frequencies in a 2×2 table is computed, the other expected cell frequencies could be determined by subtraction. The resulting table of expected cell frequencies (expected if there were no association between the two variables, X and Y for these 107 cases) is shown below.

	"EXPECTED" CELL FREQUENCIES		
	(X)		
(Y)	Low	High	Total
High	18.1	38.9	57.0
Low	15.9	34.1	50.0
Total	34.0	73.0	107.0

This is a hypothetical tabulation showing no association and thus fractional frequencies are appropriate.

Expected cell frequencies (f_e) can be computed for a given cell by multiplying the row total for that cell by the column total for that cell and dividing by N, which is the operation explained above.

(6.1)
$$f_{e_{ij}} = \frac{(n_{i.})(n_{.j})}{N}$$

Where $f_{e_{ij}}$ refers here to the expected cell frequency for the cell in the ith row and jth column of the table, $n_{i.}$ is the total for the ith row and $n_{.j}$ is the total for the jth column, and N is the total number of cases. An expected cell frequency is computed for each cell in the table.

Now, the difference between the table of observed data and the model we could construct of how this table would look if there were no association can be compared. This comparison is made by subtracting an expected cell frequency, f_e, from an observed cell frequency, f_o. The difference is called **delta,** and in this text we will symbolize delta with the upper case Greek letter Delta (Δ).

For a given cell,

(6.2)
$$\Delta = f_o - f_e$$

A delta value can be computed for each cell in a table, regardless of the size of the table. If any of the deltas are *not* zero, then there is at least some association shown in the table. Whenever all deltas are zero, all epsilons will also be zero. Later we will discuss summary measures of association based on these ideas.

In summary, whether or not an association exists in a table of observed frequencies can be exactly determined in a number of ways. One way is to compute percentages in one direction and compare across in the other direction, using epsilon. The other way we discussed is to create a table of expected cell frequencies and compare the observed and expected cell frequencies, cell by corresponding cell, using delta. If all of the epsilons that can be computed in a table, or if all of the delta values for a table amount to zero, then there is no association between the two variables cross-tabulated in the bivariate distribution. This is called **statistical independence.** If, on the other hand, there is any epsilon or any delta which is not zero, then to that extent there is an association in the observed frequency table, however slight or large that association might be.

6.4.2 Degree (Strength) of Association

Where the differences between percentages (epsilons) are large, or where the deltas are large, we speak of a strong **degree of association** between the two variables; that is, the dependent variable is distributed quite differently within the different conditional distributions defined by the independent variable. This can be contrasted with a weak association where there is very little difference or where the epsilons and deltas are very small, approaching or equalling zero.

Often investigators use epsilon (or delta) as a crude first indicator of the strength of association. The problem with both delta and epsilon is that it is difficult to determine what a given sized delta or epsilon means, other than that there is some association in the table. The reason for this is that both delta and epsilon values for any cell(s) can vary from zero or near-zero up to a magnitude which is not, in general, fixed. They are not "normed" or standardized. Later, in this chapter and the next, the problem of creating good standardized measures of the strength of association will be discussed and several alternative measures will be described. Suffice it to say here that some tables show a strong relationship between independent and dependent variables, and some show a weak association or no association at all.

6.4.3 Direction of Association

Where the dependent and independent variables in a table are at least ordinal variables, it makes sense to speak about the **direction** of an association that may exist in a table. If the tendency in the table as shown by the percentage distribution is for the higher values of one variable to be associated with the higher values of the other variable (and the lower values of each variable also tend to go together), then the association is called a *positive* association. Height and weight tend to have a positive association, since the taller a person is, the heavier he tends to be, in general across the people in a general population.

On the other hand, if the higher values of one variable are associated with the lower values of the other (and the lower values of the first with the higher values of the second), the association is said to be *negative*. Sociologists generally expect that the higher the educational level of people, the lower their degree of normlessness will be—a negative association.

The association between city size and tolerance scores (see Table 6.3) is positive because the larger the city, in general, the higher the tolerance level becomes (*i.e.* the higher the percentage of people who have high tolerance scores). The older a person's age, in general, the lower the chances of living another half century, a negative association.

6.4.4 The Nature of Association

Finally, the **nature** of an association is a feature of a bivariate distribution referring to the general *pattern* of the data in the table. This is often discovered by examining the pattern of percentages in a properly percentaged table. Often the pattern is irregular, and an investigator would cite many epsilons in describing where the various concentrations of cases are in the different categories of the independent variable. Sometimes there is a rather uniform progression in concentration of cases on the dependent variable as we move toward higher values of the independent variable. If, with an increase of one step in one variable, cases tend to move up (or down) a certain number of steps on the other variable we might call the nature of the association "linear." That is, the concentrations of cases on the dependent variable (the mode, for example) tends to fall along a straight line that could be drawn through the table.

The nature of association will be discussed at length later, in the next chapter. Simple linear associations have an intrinsic interest to investigators as one of the simplest natures of association, but some associations are curvilinear in nature, or of some more complex patterning. In most cases the nature of association will be determined from a percentage table or a scatter plot, but in some cases nature can be described in terms of an equation.

At this point we should pause to examine several tables and describe them in terms of these four features of an association. Table 6.9 presents a series of examples together with brief summary statements.

TABLE 6.9   Illustrations of the Existence, Strength, Direction, and Nature of Association

6.9A   PERCENTAGE DISTRIBUTION OF SEVERITY OF DISABILITY BY EDUCATION FOR DISABLED, NON-INSTITUTIONALIZED ADULTS AGED 18–64, UNITED STATES, SPRING, 1966

Severity of Disability	Education				Total
	No School	Elementary	Highschool	College	
Severe	65.6%	43.8%	28.0%	21.2%	34.4%
Occupational	11.2	29.1	29.6	24.3	28.2
Secondary Work Limitations	23.2	27.1	42.4	54.4	37.4
Total	100.0%	100.0%	100.0%	100.0%	100.0%
Number in millions	(0.5)	(6.9)	(7.5)	(2.5)	(17.8)

Source: Treitel, 1972:Table 5.

(1) *Existence of Association.* This table is percentaged down in the direction of the independent variable, education, so that comparisons may be made across. The percentages across are different from zero so that there is an association evident in the table. Com-

TABLE 6.9 *(Continued)*

pare any row, say the row for "Severe" disability; percentages range from a high of 65.6% down to 21.2%, all different from 34.4%, the total percentage for that category.

(2) *Strength of Association.* Overall, if education makes any difference in severity of disability, we should find the largest percentage difference (epsilon) between the "no-school" and "college" groups for the extreme categories of disability — namely the "severe" category or the "secondary work limitation" category. The epsilon for the "severe" disability comparison is 44.4%, and for the "secondary work limitation" category it is 31.2%. Both epsilons are substantial percentage differences, although they are not equal to 100%, which in some tables is the largest that epsilon could be.

(3) *Direction of Association.* As an aid in finding the direction of an association between variables each of which is at least ordinal, a useful procedure is to make comparisons across the way percentages are run, underlining the highest percentage for each comparison. In this table, we could make three comparisons, one for each row. In the "severe" row, 65.6% is clearly the largest percentage. In the "occupational" row, 29.6% is largest, but it is virtually tied by 29.1%, so we will underline both of these largest percentages. In the "secondary work limitations" row, 54.4% is again clearly the largest. One could draw a line through the underlined percentages in the table. In this case, the line would extend from the "severe/no school" corner down to the "secondary work limitation/college" corner. This is the major diagonal along which cases tend to concentrate. Notice that the more extreme disabilities tend to go with less education, and the more mild types of disabilities tend to go with higher educational categories, with intermediate stages on both variables falling in between. This is a *negative* direction of association: the higher the education the less severe the disability tends to be.

(4) *Nature of Association.* In this table, the nature of association, that is, the pattern of concentration in the table, tends to be almost linear. There is a relatively uniform shift toward less education as one shifts toward the more severe disability categories. There are no "reversals" in this general trend of concentration. Because the variables are ordinal, it would be more appropriate to speak of this nature of association as "*monotonic*" rather than linear. If distances were defined then one could determine whether in fact there is a *constant* amount of shift in values of one variable, given a fixed amount of change in the other. In ordinal variables one can only say that the value of one variable remained the same or shifted in a fixed *direction* with increases in the other variable — a monotonic nature of association. Contrasted with this type of nature are those shown in later tables here.

6.9B PERCENTAGE DISTRIBUTION OF EARNINGS OF U.S. WORKERS IN 1967, BY AGE

	Age of Worker				
Annual Earnings	*Under 25*	*25–44*	*45–64*	*65 and over*	*Total*
Under $2,000	60.7%	21.4%	20.6%	55.9%	32.7%
2,000–3,499	18.3	13.8	15.1	12.2	15.3
3,500 and over	21.0	64.8	64.3	31.9	52.0
Totals	100.0	100.0	100.0	100.0	100.0
(in millions)	(22.2)	(33.5)	(26.4)	(3.6)	(85.5)

Source: Data from U.S. Dept. H.E.W., 1971:Table 1. Data are for earnings of covered employment in the old-age, survivors, disability and health insurance program which covers virtually all work categories. Income refers to taxable wages or salaries.

(1) *Existence of Association.* After percentaging down, comparisons across reveal differences in percentage; thus there is an association.

TABLE 6.9 *(Continued)*

(2) *Strength of Association.* Although we do not have formal ways to measure the strength of association yet (they will be discussed later), it is clear that some of the percentage differences are relatively large. Take, for example, the 40.1 percentage point difference between the "under 25" and the "45–64 year old" workers on percentage earning under $2,000 per year.

(3) *Direction of Association.* In this table the direction of association is somewhat confused. Among those aged 44 or less, the association is positive – the older the person the more likely his income will be higher. Among those aged 45 and over, however, the association is negative – the older the age of worker, the more likely he is to earn less.

(4) *Nature of Association.* This association is curvilinear in nature since both extremes of age tend to earn less, while those in the middle tend to earn more.

6.9C PERCENTAGE DISTRIBUTION OF COLLEGE ENROLLMENT OF PERSONS AGED 18–21 YEARS OLD, BY RACE, OCTOBER, 1970

| College Enrollment | Race | | | |
	White	Black	Other	Total
Enrolled	36%	21%	44%	34%
Not Enrolled	64	79	56	66
Total	100%	100%	100%	100%
(Number in Millions)	(11.3)	(1.6)	(0.1)	(13.1)

Source: Data from U.S. Bur. Census, 1972:Table 15.

(1) *Existence of Association.* In this table, percentages enrolled and not are computed down, within race categories. Comparing across, there is a difference in percentages and thus, an association exists between race and college enrollment.

(2) *Strength of Association.* Using epsilon, we might note that $\epsilon = 8\%$ between "white" and "other," and it is 15% between "white" and "black," and 23% between "black" and "other." In general, other races are more likely to be enrolled in college, but the percentage differences are not very large. Notice that at this point we do not have tools for saying how strong some kind of difference in percentages is. Clearly, however, these are not zero, nor are they 100 percent differences.

(3) *Direction of Association.* Since race (and enrollment) are generally considered nominal variables, it would not make sense to talk about the direction of association, so this feature can be ignored.

(4) *Nature of Association.* The pattern of percentages in the table can be described at length. Here the percentage differences cited under #2, above, seem to cover all we can say about a 2×3 table, but in larger tables or for tables with ordinal or interval variables, much more description of patterning is generally possible.

6.5 CREATING MEASURES OF ASSOCIATION

It is possible to create single summary index numbers which will indicate the existence, degree, and direction of association all in the same number. Typically these measures are set up so that they will vary along a scale from a minus value, indicating a negative relationship, to zero, indicating no association, to a positive value, indicating a positive association. The larger the magnitude of the index number, the stronger the association.

Ideally a measure of association would also have the characteristic of varying between two *fixed limits* such as −1.00 and +1.00, where 1 indicates a **perfect association** or a maximally strong one in some sense, and zero indicates statistical independence.

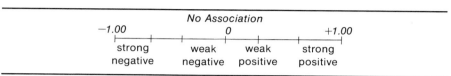

SCALE OF STRENGTH OF ASSOCIATION WITH FIXED LIMITS OF −1.00 AND +1.00

A measure of association which varied over a scale with fixed limits, such as that shown above, is called a **normed** or **standardized measure of association.** Its value lies in the fact that normed measures can be validly compared. If a measure of association computed on one table was −.56, and the same kind of measure computed on another table was −.13, both could be interpreted as falling between the highest possible negative value of −1.00 and zero (no association). They could be compared. The first table has a stronger negative association (about four times stronger) than the second, and the difference between the two measures is substantial. If the limits on a scale were not fixed or known, then an index number such as −.56 would be very difficult to interpret and it would be essentially impossible to use the index in making comparisons of strength of association between two different tables. Since comparison and interpretation are important to sociologists, normed measures of association are important.

Table 6.10 illustrates the problem of norming with epsilon, an unnormed measure of association. Notice that the marginals of a table may be such that an epsilon of 100% could not be achieved regardless of the way cell frequencies are rearranged.

TABLE 6.10 Epsilon, an Illustration of the Norming Problem in Developing Measures of Association

Two illustrative tables are given below. The first shows a 2 × 2 table with balanced marginals (both row and column totals are the same) and it is possible in this particular table to fix cell frequencies so that, computing percentages down, an epsilon could equal zero or 100 for this table. Thus, the achieved epsilon of 17% can be interpreted as falling on the scale from 0% to 100%. In the second illustration, however, it is *not* possible to adjust cell frequencies (given fixed marginals, as before) so that zero or 100 could be achieved for epsilon. The epsilon in this second table 19%, thus has to be interpreted in terms of a more limited scale extending from 3% to 83%. It would not be appropriate to compare the two epsilons because they not only reflect the pattern of frequencies in a table, but they are also constrained by the way the marginals are distributed, and this confounds the intended comparison. About all one is able to say is that epsilon indicates that there is an association in both original tables.

TABLE 6.10 *(Continued)*

ILLUSTRATION 1

	Weakest Possible Association				*Original Table*				*Strongest Possible Association*		
		X				*X*				*X*	
		Low	*High*			*Low*	*High*			*Low*	*High*
Y	High	9	6	15	*Y* High	10	5	15	*Y* High	15	0	15
	Low	6	4	10	Low	5	5	10	Low	0	10	10
		15	10	25		15	10	25		15	10	25
		$\epsilon = 0\%$				$\epsilon = 17\%$				$\epsilon = 100\%$	

ILLUSTRATION 2

	Weakest Possible Association				*Original Table*				*Strongest Possible Association*		
		X				*X*				*X*	
		Low	*High*			*Low*	*High*			*Low*	*High*
Y	High	8	7	15	*Y* High	9	6	15	*Y* High	13	2	15
	Low	5	5	10	Low	4	6	10	Low	0	10	10
		13	12	25		13	12	25		13	12	25
		$\epsilon = 3\%$				$\epsilon = 19\%$				$\epsilon = 83\%$	

In order to create a measure of association which is normed and interpretable, it turns out that we need to define 0 and 1, that is, we need to define what no association and perfect association are supposed to mean. We have already discussed two ways to identify the situation of no association, or statistical independence, in a table, using epsilon or delta. The definition of the opposite extreme is less clear cut.

6.5.1 In Pursuit of a Normed Measure of Association

Measures of association turn out to be rather simple ratios designed to be sensitive to changes in the strength of association and, in some cases, to the direction, nature, and role played by independent and dependent variables. Often the ratios suffer from the usual ailments of ratios: the numerator or denominator may fluctuate because of some irrelevancy, such as the number of cases in the table or the number of rows and columns—things which are generally of no interest when one wants to compare strength of association, and things which prevent the valid comparisons needed in a study. As in the other approaches to refining ratios, better measures of association become better by excluding irrelevant influences on the numerator and denominator. Actually you should be able to think up some of your own measures of association on the basis of the kinds of univariate and bivariate statistics we have discussed thus far.

In the following paragraphs we will illustrate this pursuit with a set of

measures based on delta, the difference between observed and expected cell frequencies in a table. Most of the delta-based measures are not used widely because of the problems they *do not* adequately take into account. On the other
hand, there are not very many measures of association for nominal variables, so
certain of these measures are familiar to and used by investigators in certain
situations. Here they are presented for the purpose of showing the straightforward way measures of association are developed.

To start with, it appears intuitively useful to measure the "distance" between an *observed* set of frequencies in a bivariate table (f_o) and an *expected* set
of frequencies (f_e) which serve as a model for statistical independence or no association. Clearly, if there are no differences between observed and expected
tables, the association in the observed table is zero, as defined earlier. The larger
the difference in general, the stronger the association. In order for one to characterize a whole table rather than a single cell in a table, the delta values are traditionally summed up over all cells in the table.
Thus:

$$\Sigma\Delta = \Sigma(f_o - f_e)$$

where the summation is over all cells in a table.

Such a measure is deficient for a number of reasons. First, the importance
of any $f_o - f_e$ difference clearly depends upon the size of f_e. After all, a delta of 6
is large if only three cases were expected in that cell, but a delta of 6 is not very
impressive if 300 cases were expected. Secondly, it will always turn out to be
zero, because positive differences between f_o and f_e will be balanced out by negative differences elsewhere in the table. This occurs because row and column totals in the observed and expected tables are identical, so that excesses in one
place have to be offset by deficiencies elsewhere.

To help take account of problems of the total delta above, it is traditional
to compute a different measure. The difference between observed and expected
cell frequencies is squared to eliminate negative differences (and skirt the problem of always totaling up to zero), and this squared difference is divided by the
expected cell frequency to help take out the effects of different numbers of cases
in a category of the row or column variable. This division of the squared difference for each cell by f_e takes out the effect of different marginal distributions in
different tables and results in what is called a "margin-free" measure of association. The measure which sums over all of these cell by cell calculations is called
chi-square (χ^2).

$$\chi^2 = \Sigma\left(\frac{\Delta^2}{f_e}\right)$$

where $\Delta = (f_o - f_e)$, and the summation is over all cells.

Chi-square (χ^2) is used in inferential statistics as a basis for a test of sig-
nificance called the "chi-square test." It is useful in that role, but it is *not* useful
as a measure of degree of association in general, because of norming problems.
To repeat, chi-square is *not* used as a measure of association, it is a test used and
discussed in inferential statistics books.

χ^2 is always a positive number, and it will equal zero if there is no association in the table. However, the upper limit on the magnitude of χ^2 is:

$$N(k-1) = \text{upper limit of } \chi^2$$

where N is the sample size and k is the number of rows or columns in a table, whichever is the smaller number. For a 2×2 table, for example, the upper limit of χ^2 is N. Given two tables with equal association (*i.e.*, in percentaged form, they are identical), where one table has twice the number of cases as the other, the table with twice the number of cases will have a χ^2 value twice as large as the other table.

The advantages of χ^2 (advantages useful in inferential statistics) lie in the fact that it works for nominal variables. Categories of rows or columns can be re-ordered without any effect on delta, and χ^2 will always be zero if there is indeed a perfect match between observed and expected cell frequencies in a whole table.

To begin to take account of the maximum possible χ^2, at least for the table with 2 rows (or 2 columns), another frequently mentioned coefficient has been designed called the "mean square contingency" or **phi squared, ϕ^2**. It is simply the χ^2 value divided by N, the maximum possible χ^2 for a table with two rows (or columns).

(6.3)
$$\phi^2 = \frac{\chi^2}{N} \quad \text{or} \quad \phi = \sqrt{\frac{\chi^2}{N}}$$

Phi varies from 0 (for independence) to a maximum of $+1$ (perfect association) for any $2 \times k$ table (where k is the number of categories in the other variable), and its magnitude can be interpreted as a measure of the strength of association. It also retains the margin-free, nominal variable features of χ^2 itself. So far, so good. The problem with this measure is that its maximum value exceeds 1.0 in tables which have more than 2 categories in both variables, since the upper limit of χ^2, $N(k-1)$ can be larger than N. The maximum value for $\phi^2 = k-1$, where k is the smaller of the number of rows or columns.

A partial solution to this problem was developed by Karl Pearson in his "coefficient of contingency," **Pearson's C**. C can not exceed 1.0 in magnitude, regardless of the size of the table.

(6.4)
$$C = \sqrt{\frac{\chi^2}{\chi^2 + N}}$$

This is so simply because χ^2 appears in both the numerator and the denominator of the ratio. It can always reach zero, which means, again, that there is no association, but its upper limit, while it can not exceed 1.0, likewise can never reach 1.0. In fact, its maximum value varies depending upon the number of rows and columns there are in a table. For a square table (where $r = c$), the maximum value of C can be computed as follows:

$$\text{Maximum } C = \sqrt{\frac{k-1}{k}}$$

where k is the number of rows (or columns) in a square table.

For a 2×2 table, for example, the maximum C is .707 and for a 5×5 table the maximum C is .894. Again, comparisons of this measure of association could not be made between tables of different sizes.

A further refinement on measures of association is called **Tschruprow's T,** which attempts to correct the upper limit problem of C by changing the denominator slightly so that it includes a value reflecting the number of cells in a table instead of χ^2 itself, as in Pearson's C. This new element in the denominator of T is called **degrees of freedom** (df) and it is computed thus:

$$df = (r-1)(c-1)$$

It is the product of the number of rows minus one times the number of columns minus 1.* Tschruprow's T is defined as:

(6.5)
$$T = \sqrt{\frac{\chi^2}{N(df)}}$$

As before, this is an advance in our pursuit of a properly normed measure of strength of association appropriate to any table, in that the upper limit of T is 1.0 and that value can always be achieved regardless of the size of the table—so long as the table is square (i.e. $r = c$). For tables which are not square, T cannot possibly reach 1.0, although if tables to be compared have the same number of degrees of freedom, the maximum possible T is constant, and therefore a valid comparison of T values could be made.

Finally, a different measure of association, called **Cramer's V,** handles the norming problems of T by a slightly different figure, t, in the denominator, in place of degrees of freedom.

(6.6)
$$V = \sqrt{\frac{\chi^2}{Nt}}$$

Here, t is defined as the smaller of the two quantities, $(r-1)$ or $(c-1)$. Cramer's V can always attain a value of +1.0 even if the table is not square, and it equals zero if there is no association. It is, so to speak, a properly normed measure of association for bivariate distributions of nominal variables, it is "margin free" in that the number or distribution of cases in row or column totals does not influence its value, nor is it influenced by the number of categories of either variable.

But norming is only part of the problem of developing a summary index number to stand for the association in a table. There are at least two other desirable characteristics for such measures. *First,* the number should be interpretable in some intuitively useful sense, and, *secondly,* the meaning of 1.0, the "perfect association" norm, should be definable. In the first instance, Cramer's V (and, in fact, most of the other delta-based measures of association) can only be thought of as a magnitude on a scale between zero and 1.0; the bigger the number the stronger the association. It can *not* be interpreted, for example, as the

*Degrees of freedom (df) is a concept used heavily in inferential statistics. Here it can be grasped intuitively by noting that in a 2×2 table, where $df = (2-1)(2-1) = 1$, we could set up an expected frequency table by merely supplying one cell frequency. The rest could then be obtained by subtraction, since the marginals were taken as fixed. We had, so to speak, one degree of freedom in choosing a cell frequency before all other cell frequencies were determined. In a 2×3 table, two cell frequencies can be chosen before others are determined—there are two degrees of freedom, etc.

percentage of variation in one variable explained by another, nor can it be interpreted as the proportion of predictive errors which may be reduced by prior knowledge of one of the variables—interpretations which are especially useful for substantive investigators. More will be said about this criterion, and the next chapter will develop a group of measures called "proportionate reduction in error" ("PRE") measures of association, which have as one of their strengths this kind of ready operational interpretation.

The other criterion for a good measure of degree of association is that the limits be defined in a meaningful way. We have already established the idea of *statistical independence,* or no association. In fact, all of the measures of association discussed here are always zero when there is no association in a table.* What about the upper extreme? What does a *perfect association* mean? What is the pattern in a table when a normed measure of association equals 1.0?

6.5.2 Meanings of Perfect Association

In this chapter we will limit our attention to the 2×2 table in considering alternative meanings of **perfect association.** In the next chapter, this idea will be extended to larger tables. For now, however, we can focus on two somewhat different notions of perfect association: a more restrictive or stringent definition, and a less restrictive one.

6.5.2a The Restrictive Meaning of Perfect Association. The first model, the *more restrictive* meaning of perfect association, is one where all of the cases in a table are in one diagonal of the table. Stated differently, each value of one variable is associated with only one single value of another variable, so that for any category of the independent variable, only one cell of the dependent variable is non-zero. In a 2×2 table, this means that two diagonal cells have frequencies, and the other two cells do not. This condition for a positive and a negative association is indicated by X's (for some frequency) and zeros (for no frequency) in Figure 6.1. The left-hand tables in Figure 6.1 indicate a perfect negative association, and the right hand tables indicate a perfect positive association. The middle table shows symbols for cell frequencies which are traditionally used in expressing formulas for measures of association for a 2×2 table.

If we were testing a theory that stated that the larger the city size the higher the degree of tolerance, this model of perfect association would seem to reflect a situation where this hypothesis held exactly. All individuals living in large cities would have "high" tolerance scores, and all individuals living in smaller cities would have "lower" tolerance scores. Any deviation from this pat-

---

*While it is the case that measures we have discussed will be zero when a table shows no association (when one variable is statistically independent of another), it is not always the case that they will be zero only when two variables are statistically independent of each other. As we shall see later, measures of association are defined to be sensitive to certain features of an association, often depending upon the level of measurement, for example. Variables may be statistically independent with respect to categorical or ranking features, but not independent with respect to the distance features defined into interval-level variables. For this reason selection of an appropriate measure of association again depends critically upon meanings defined into variables and variation in data which an investigator is interested in examining. This will be discussed later, in this chapter and the next, as measures of association are presented and contrasted.

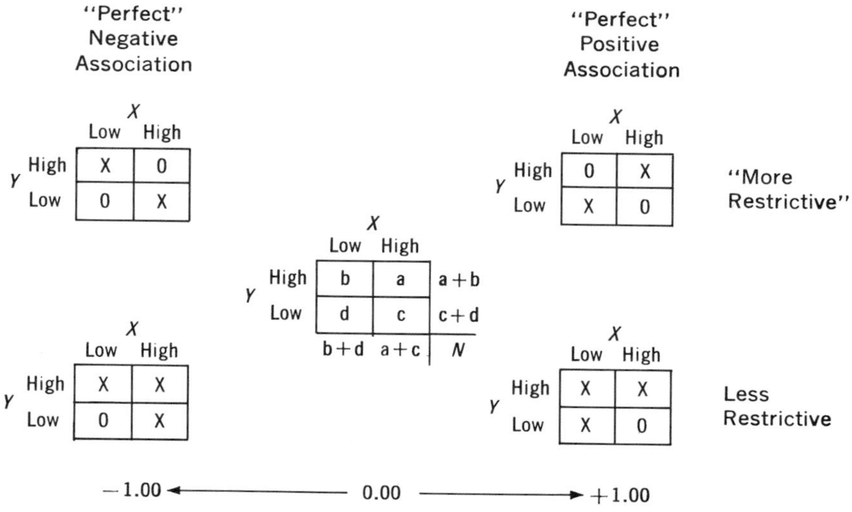

In the notation shown in the middle table, cell *a* is in the high-high corner and *d* is in the low-low corner; thus cells *a* and *d* are on the positive diagonal. This is important simply because it assures the correct sign in computations which follow.

FIGURE 6.1 Two Models of Perfect Association for 2×2 Tables

tern would be less than a perfect association. The *more restrictive* definition of a perfect association would require that all of the data be concentrated in one diagonal of the table for there to be a perfect association, as in Figure 6.1.

Phi, one of the delta-based coefficients discussed above, is a normed measure of association for a 2×2 table in this more restrictive sense. The *phi coefficient* on a 2×2 table can be computed as follows:

(6.7)
$$\phi = \frac{ad - bc}{\sqrt{(a+b)\ (c+d)\ (b+d)\ (a+c)}}$$

where *a, b, c* and *d* refer to cell frequencies in a 2×2 table as indicated in Figure 6.1, and the denominator of ϕ is the square root of the product of the marginals.

ϕ can be interpreted as the degree of diagonal concentration, and it will have values between −1.0 and +1.0. The values of 1.0 will be reached only if all cases are concentrated in the main diagonal of the table, and the magnitude of this coefficient indicates the extent to which this condition is exhibited in the table. For nominal variables, of course, one would use only the magnitude of the coefficient and drop the sign.*

6.5.2b The Second Model of Perfect Association. For a 2×2 table, the second model of perfect association, the less restrictive one, is illustrated by the set of tables in Figure 6.1. Here the requirement is that only one of the four cells need have a zero frequency and the other three, including the two on the

---

*As we will show in the next chapter, the 2×2 table is an interesting situation because many measures of association which are different for larger tables turn out to have the same numeric value for a 2×2 table. Thus $\phi = T = V = r$. Pearson's *r* is a measure of association to be developed in the next chapter.

main diagonal in the table, may have any frequency. Where might this definition be useful? Consider two illustrations.

Social science investigators often measure attitudes in terms of a series of individual items which are carefully graded to indicate different degrees of that attitude. For example, in a study of permissiveness attitudes regarding sex, an individual might be asked to indicate his agreement with statements such as these:

    a) I believe that petting is acceptable for the female before marriage when she is engaged to be married.
        ( ) Agree
        ( ) Disagree

    b) I believe that petting is acceptable for the female before marriage even if she does not feel particularly affectionate toward her partner.
        ( ) Agree
        ( ) Disagree

Now, if these questions do indeed reflect differences in degree of permissiveness attitudes, and if people realize this and respond accordingly, we would not expect anyone to disagree with the first question and agree with the second. If a person's permissiveness attitudes are sufficient to accept or agree with the second statement, then that person should also agree with the first. This expected state of perfect association between answers to these two attitude items would be shown in a table, as follows:

"More Permissive" Attitude Item (b)	"Less Permissive" Attitude Question (a)	
	Disagree	Agree
Agree	O	X
Disagree	X	X

where X indicates some cell frequency.

The scale items may not be graded as we thought, or people responding to the items may not understand them in this light, so any given set of responses may not match this idea of a perfect logical relationship between these "strong" and "weak" attitude items. A measure of association which used this less restrictive definition of perfect association as its definition of 1.0 would be the measure we would need to measure the distance between the data we observe and this idea of perfect association.

Another example is more of a philosophical distinction between "cause" and "effect" conditions. If one is interested in factors which influence the state of other variables, one may think of two kinds of effect. One situation is where the effect does not occur unless and until a given factor is present in a certain amount (called a *necessary* condition). The other situation is where the outcome may occur for other reasons, but it will never be the case that the outcome will not occur if a given factor is present to a certain extent (called a *sufficient* condition).

These states can be illustrated in terms of the two tables below. The first would be the model of a sufficient condition and the second a model of a necessary condition. The third table below is a model of a condition that is *both* necessary and sufficient. To what extent does the real world behave the way we reason that it should? A measure of association using the less restrictive model of perfect association would permit one to contrast actual data with the models for either a necessary or a sufficient condition to help provide the answer.

MODEL OF A "NECESSARY" CONDITION

| Effect | Cause | |
	Absent	Present
Present	O	X
Absent	X	X

where X indicates some cell frequency

MODEL OF A "SUFFICIENT" CONDITION

| Effect | Cause | |
	Absent	Present
Present	X	X
Absent	X	O

where X indicates some cell frequency

MODEL OF A CONDITION WHICH IS BOTH NECESSARY AND SUFFICIENT

| Effect | Cause | |
	Absent	Present
Present	O	X
Absent	X	O

where X indicates some cell frequency

6.5.2c Yule's Q. Yule's Q is one measure of association for a 2×2 table which uses the less restrictive definition of perfect association.* In a 2×2 table, Yule's Q is computed by finding the cross products, the product of the cells on one diagonal, and the product of the cell frequency on the other diagonal in the table.

(6.8)
$$Q = \frac{ad - bc}{ad + bc}$$

where $a, b, c,$ and d are cell frequencies as shown in Figure 6.1.

If one of the cells on the minor diagonal is zero, then the Q value will be

---

*Actually Yule's Q is identical to gamma, a coefficient to be introduced in the next chapter. Gamma is suitable for any size of table, including a 2×2 table. The different name introduced here is again tradition and a usage frequently found in the literature. The formula with its particular notation is not useful for larger tables, but here it nicely indicates one important difference between measures of degree, direction and existence of association.

BOX 6.2 THE THEME

Thus far in this chapter we have (a) discussed the idea of association (end of Section 6.1; Section 6.2; Section 6.4) and how percentages may be computed to examine an association (Section 6.3.3); (b) we then introduced four features of an association — *existence, degree, direction,* and *nature* (Section 6.4ff.); and (c), we considered how to define no association (6.4.1a) and the more and less restrictive models of perfect association (Section 6.5.2ff). Measures of association which, in one index number, can summarize the existence/degree/direction of association are simple ratios. The problem is to select numerator and denominator in such a way that (only) those features of an association which are of interest are revealed. Several delta-based measures were presented to illustrate the pursuit of a properly normed measure of association. Finally, and most importantly, we ended up with two properly normed measures for 2×2 tables, each "normed" at a different but useful definition of perfect association. Other normed measures will be presented in Chapter 7, but two other topics — one caution and one distinction — will be discussed next.

---

either $+1.0$ or -1.0, depending upon the direction of association. In any event, the value 1.0 means that the data meet the less restrictive criteria for patterns of frequencies required for a perfect association. Notice that the Q and ϕ coefficients have the same numerator, but the denominators differ and produce measures which norm at different definitions of perfect association. If ϕ is 1.0, Q will also be 1.0, since the data will at least show the less restrictive pattern of perfect association. On the other hand, if $Q=1.0$, it may be the case that $\phi \neq 1.0$, because the criterion for perfect association for ϕ is more stringent, calling for a different pattern of concentration of cases in the 2×2 matrix. As in the case of ϕ, Q can be used for nominal variables, but the sign of Q would not be used, only its absolute magnitude.* Q can reach 1.0 for any 2×2 table which is identical in pattern with its model of perfect association.

6.6 GROUPING ERROR

Before we proceed, we should update our attention to grouping error. You will recall that grouping error was one possibly distorting factor involved when we wished to group data into a smaller number of categories which might be handy for presentation purposes (See Section 3.2.3b). In univariate statistics, if the midpoint of a grouped class did not reflect the character of scores in that class,

---

*It is true, of course, that the sign of Q or ϕ resulting from their computation on the association of nominal variables would indicate which categories of one variable go with which categories of the other variable. Direction of association would not have meaning, however, and one would have to examine the table layout carefully to determine and express what the sign means. For this reason, Q and ϕ computed on nominal variables are expressed on a scale extending in magnitude from 0 to 1.0.

some grouping error would result. The same type of problem may happen where a bivariate distribution is grouped into fewer categories. Table 6.11 illustrates this possibility. Notice that the original 2×3 table is grouped in two ways to create a 2×2 table. We might want to group data if we preferred to use 2×2 measures of association (usually we would be well advised to pick a measure that works on the table we have), or we might have relatively few cases in some rows or columns of a larger table which might suggest that less precision is called for. In any event, as Table 6.11 shows, different groupings are not necessarily equivalent.

In the first 2×2 table (6.11b) the degree of association is rather strong and negative; in Table 6.11c, the association is zero. Which accurately represents the

---

TABLE 6.11 AN ILLUSTRATION OF GROUPING ERROR IN BIVARIATE DESCRIPTION

(a) ORIGINAL 2×3 TABLE OF FREQUENCIES

Income	Education			
	High	Medium	Low	Total
High	5	2	8	15
Low	2	3	1	6
Total	7	5	9	21

(b) THE SAME DATA WITH "HIGH" AND "MEDIUM" CATEGORIES OF EDUCATION GROUPED TOGETHER TO CREATE A 2×2 TABLE

Income	Education		Total
	Hi/Med	Low	
High	7	8	15
Low	5	1	6
Total	12	9	21

$$Q = -.70$$
$$\phi = -.33$$

(c) THE SAME DATA WITH "MEDIUM" AND "LOW" CATEGORIES OF EDUCATION GROUPED TOGETHER TO CREATE A 2×2 TABLE

Income	Education		Total
	High	Med/Low	
High	5	10	15
Low	2	4	6
Total	7	14	21

$$Q = 0$$
$$\phi = 0$$

relationship between income and education in the original table? Neither one does, and the distortion is called *grouping error*. Generally speaking, it is a useful practice to retain as much precision as possible and to be reluctant to group more precise data.*

6.7   SYMMETRIC AND ASYMMETRIC MEASURES OF ASSOCIATION

One of the distinctions between different measures of association which we have discussed is whether or not they are properly normed. Another distinction was between measures which define perfect association in a more rather than less restrictive fashion. There is a third distinction between measures of association which should be mentioned here. That is the distinction based upon whether or not the measure distinguishes between independent and dependent variables.

Symmetrical measures of association do not distinguish between dependent and independent variables, but merely address themselves to the strength (and direction) of relationship between pairs of variables. The role of variables in a bivariate distribution does not matter as far as the computation of the measures is concerned. Measures such as Yule's Q, the phi coefficient (as well as C, T, V, and some others) are all symmetrical measures of association.

Asymmetric measures of association, by contrast, do require a distinction between independent and dependent variables for their computation. In general, they are oriented toward measuring the usefulness of the independent variable in predicting values of the dependent variable. In general, two different asymmetric coefficients can be computed on a single bivariate table. One of these coefficients measures the value of predicting Y from a knowledge of variable X and the other measures the value of predicting X from a knowledge of Y. Most of the measures of association of this type will be discussed in the next chapter (*e.g.* Lambda, Somers' d, Eta, etc.) but we have used a measure in this chapter which illustrates the asymmetric idea. That measure, crude (not normed) though it may be, is called **epsilon** (ϵ), and it is simply the difference between percentages. If percentages are computed down, epsilon (ϵ) is simply the difference between percentages compared across in the other direction. Traditionally ϵ is computed as the difference between the extreme corners of a table, as shown below, but it is clear that many ϵ's can be computed to compare cells of particular interest. Here ϵ would equal +25%, the difference between 40% in the upper right corner (the high-high corner of this table), and 15% in the upper left corner (the high-low corner of this table).† The reason for taking this particular difference is that if one expects cases to pile up on the main diagonal as the association becomes stronger, the smallest cell should be in one corner and the biggest in the other, so that this difference is expected to be the biggest in the table.

---

*Even where it is decided to group data into a smaller table, it is advisable to preserve at least three categories in each variable. The reason for this is that one is able to identify curvilinear natures of association if at least three categories are preserved. With only two categories, if there is an association, it will always appear to be linear.

†We could have taken the overall difference between 60% and 29% in the bottom row of the table, following the same logic. The ϵ is likely to be different, of course, and this is one reason why other measures of the overall association in a table are generally preferred.

ELECTORAL ACTIVITY OF RESPONDENTS IN A CROSS-SECTIONAL SAMPLE OF THE U.S., BY SOCIAL CLASS

Electoral Activity	Social Class			Total
	Low	Medium	High	
High	15%	24%	40%	26%
Medium	25	31	31	29
Low	60	45	29	45
	100%	100%	100%	100%
	(857)	(871)	(871)	(2599)

Overall $\epsilon = 25\%$

Source: Kim, 1971:900, Table 1. Data are from a cross-sectional study of the United States. Used by permission.

If percentages were computed in the opposite direction (by rows rather than columns as shown here) the percentage comparison would be made the other way, and it would be a different value as shown below.

SOCIAL CLASS OF RESPONDENTS IN A CROSS-SECTIONAL SAMPLE OF THE U.S., BY ELECTORAL ACTIVITY

Electoral Activity	Social Class			Total
	Low	Medium	High	
High	18%	31	51	100% (687)
Medium	28%	36	36	100% (756)
Low	45%	34	21	100% (1156)
Total	32%	34	34	100% (2599)

Overall epsilon $= 45\% - 18\% = 27\%$

ϵ, then, is an asymmetric measure because it is a comparison made after we percentage in the usual manner—in the direction of the independent variable. As we noted earlier, ϵ suffers from norming problems, but it will serve here as a rough and ready measure of overall differences and as an example of an asymmetric measure. Normed asymmetric measures will be presented in the next chapter.

6.8 SUMMARY

A number of key steps in statistical description have been taken in this chapter, and these will be elaborated in the next chapter and later in this book.

One of the first ideas was that of *association* between two variables. This amounted to a systematic way of examining the differences in the distribution of one variable which are associated with differences in a second variable. As values of one variable increase, there is a tendency for there to be an increase (or decrease) in the scores cases have on a second variable. Stated more generally, a table is said to show some association if a variable is distributed differently within the various categories of some other variable.

An association can be described in terms of four features — *existence* of an association, *degree, direction,* and *nature.* These may be examined by percentaging a table properly (and three rules for percentaging were given). Alternatively, the first three features — existence, degree, and direction — may be measured in terms of a variety of different ratios called *measures of association.* A single measure of association may be computed which (a) will indicate whether or not there is an association in the table (measures are generally zero if there is no association); (b) will indicate the degree or strength of association (by a magnitude which is usually between zero and 1.0), and (c) will show direction (by a plus or minus sign), although this is used only for bivariate distributions of ordinal or interval variables.

To permit valid comparison of measures of association computed on different tables, and to aid in the interpretation of these measures, investigators generally prefer *"normed"* measures of association. This means that the numerator and denominator of the measure of association are selected so that the measure could be -1.0 or 0 or $+1.0$ for any table, regardless of the number of cases it contains, the number of rows or columns, or the way the marginals happen to be distributed. Various delta-based measures of degree of association were discussed to illustrate the problem of norming.

Distinctions among measures of association can be made in terms of (a) whether or not they are normed, (b) the model of perfect association and no association the measure assumes, (c) whether the measure is asymmetric or symmetric, (d) whether it is most appropriate for cross-classifications of nominal, ordinal, or interval-level variables, and (e) the size of table for which it may be computed. Chapter 7 will discuss measures of association for nominal, ordinal, and interval-level cross-classifications.

The *nature* of association in a table refers to the patterning of concentration. It is often examined using a properly percentaged table, but Chapter 7 will discuss the use of a regression equation to describe the nature of association between interval-level variables. Sometimes this patterning is monotonic or linear or curvilinear, but often the pattern is more complex. In any event, the description of the existence, degree, direction, and nature of association between pairs of variables provides a powerful means for describing how variables relate to each other and this, after all, is the central activity of any scientific inquiry.

CONCEPTS TO KNOW AND UNDERSTAND

bivariate distribution; conditional distribution
  heading
  stub

body
cell
cell frequency
2×2 or fourfold table
$r \times c$ tables
marginals
percentaging rules
epsilon (percentage difference)
how to examine complex conditional distributions
association
   existence
   degree
   direction
   nature
expected cell frequencies
delta
statistical independence
norming measures of association
definition of perfect association
   more restrictive
   less restrictive
phi coefficient
Yule's Q coefficient
grouping error in tables
asymmetric and symmetric measures of association

QUESTIONS AND PROBLEMS

1. Using data from a statistics workbook or from a piece of research you have been asked to conduct, select a series of cases which have been measured on two variables of interest to you. Construct a bivariate frequency distribution and compute percentages in the appropriate direction. Set up the table with labeling in a form suitable for presentation. Write a paragraph describing the relationship between the pairs of variables shown in this table.

2. Select an interesting percentaged table from the back of a statistics workbook or from a journal article. Compute percentages in each of the three possible ways (to row totals, column totals, and the grand total). Then, in your own words, express what it is that percentages in each of these three tables tells about the existence, degree, direction, and nature of association in the table.

3. Look through one of the professional journals for an example of a properly percentaged table and for a table which was not properly percentaged for the kinds of conclusions the author wanted to make. Discuss the use of percentaged tables in both articles.

4. Find one example of the use of Yule's Q and phi in a statistics workbook or in journals or texts. Examine each usage and discuss the merits of selecting Q or ϕ in each case.

GENERAL REFERENCES.

Weiss, Robert S, *Statistics in Social Research: An Introduction*, New York, John Wiley and Sons, 1968.
See especially Chapter 4 on tables and Chapter 9 on association.

Zeisel, Hans, *Say It With Figures,* New York, Harper and Row, 1957.
Chapter 1 discusses the use of percentages, Chapter 2 presents examples of percentaging rules and Chapter 3 handles the problem of "don't know"s or "no response"s. More complex tables are discussed in Chapter 4. This is a very thoughtful and readable treatment of the use of percentages in tables.

Rosenberg, Morris, *The Logic of Survey Analysis,* New York, Basic Books, Inc., 1968.
Chapter 1 discusses the meaning of relationships.

Riley, Matilda White, *Sociological Research I: A Case Approach,* New York, Harcourt, Brace and World, 1963.
Unit 8 presents brief summaries of several important sociological studies, and commentary discusses their examination of the relationship among variables.

Davis, James A., and Ann M. Jacobs, "Tabular Presentation," in volume 15, p 497–509, David L. Sills (ed), *International Encyclopedia of the Social Sciences,* New York, Macmillan Co. and The Free Press, 1968.
This article discusses appropriate ways to set up tables, how to handle "don't know"s, and how to use percentages in examining tables.

OTHER REFERENCES

Davis, James A., and Ann M. Jacobs in "Tabular Presentation," in volume 15, p 497–509, of David L. Sills (ed.), *International Encyclopedia of the Social Sciences,* New York, Macmillan Co. and the Free Press, 1968.

Erskine, Hazel, "The Polls: Women's Role," *Public Opinion Quarterly,* 35 (Summer, 1971) p 278.

Fischer, Claude S., "A Research Note on Urbanism and Tolerance," *American Journal of Sociology,* 76 (March, 1971) p 847–856.

Kim, Jae-On, "Predictive Measures of Ordinal Association," *American Journal of Sociology,* 76 (March, 1971) p 900.

Sewell, William H., and Vimal P. Shah, "Parents' Education and Children's Educational Aspirations and Achievements," *American Sociological Review,* 33 (April, 1968).

Treitel, Ralph, "Onset of Disability," Report 18, (U.S. Department of Health, Education and Welfare, Social Security Administration, Office of Research and Statistics, Washington, D.C.), 1972.

U.S. Bureau of the Census, "Selected Characteristics of Persons and Families of Mexican, Puerto Rican, and Other Spanish Origin; March, 1971," *Current Population Reports* P-20, No. 224, (Washington, D.C.), 1971.

———, "Characteristics of American Youth: 1971," *Special Studies,* P-23, No. 40, (Washington, D.C.), 1971.

U.S. Department of H.E.W., "Earnings Distributions In The United States: 1967," (U.S. Department of Health, Education and Welfare, Social Security Administration, Office of Research and Statistics, Washington, D.C.), 1971.

MEASURES OF ASSOCIATION FOR NOMINAL, ORDINAL AND INTERVAL VARIABLES

The ecology of Chicago has long been a source of attention and study by sociologists since Park, Burgess and other early investigators at the University of Chicago began to study the patterning of urban phenomena (*e.g.*, social class, ethnic organization, etc.). A recent study by Albert Hunter (1971) examines ecological trends in Chicago, using census data from the 1930's to the 1960's based on 75 community social areas into which the city had been divided by sociologists in the 1920's. Among the interests Hunter had in this longitudinal study was whether there has been increasing or decreasing segregation in the city over these years. One would expect greater assimilation to occur the longer a group has been in an area, so that the area could no longer be distinguished in terms of the kinds of jobs or income level or family status of people living there compared to others in the city in general.

Ecological research in the U.S. has found that there are three main differences between urban areas, namely: social rank, family status, and segregation or ethnic status of the people living in an area. Hunter used percent black and percent foreign-born in each of the 75 Chicago areas to measure segregation or ethnic status. Percent females employed was used as a measure of family status, and median dollar value of homes was used as a social rank measure. Four other variables were measured but are not reported here. The basic statistical measure he used to describe the relationship between ethnic status and each of the other variables was a correlation coefficient or measure of the existence, strength, and direction of association between pairs of variables.

Hunter's reasoning is that if there is low segregation (*i.e.* high assimilation) then there should be little or no correlation between the percentage black in an area, for example, and the percentage of females who are employed—one of the family status measures he uses. Ethnic status should not make a difference in the distribution of that particular variable, nor should it be correlated with the median value of homes if there is no segregation. If correlations become smaller in magnitude over time, there is evidence of decreasing segregation or increasing assimilation. If, on the other hand, there has been no drop or if there is a shift from a lower to a higher correlation through time, then there is evidence of either no change in segregation or increasing segregation in urban Chicago. The data in Table 7.1 indicate some interesting increases and decreases through time, and these changes may be due in part to recent migration from urban to suburban areas which has been occurring across the nation in recent years.

Notice, in Table 7.1, that the correlation measure for the bivariate relationship between percent black and percent females employed in these 75 Chicago areas was +.46 in 1930, and that the correlation drops steadily in magnitude over time to +.42 in 1940, +.13 in 1950, and −.03 (smaller in magnitude but a shift to a negative rather than positive direction of association) in 1960. Com-

TABLE 7.1 Measures of the Bivariate Association between Each of Two Segregation Variables (percent black and percent foreign-born) and Measures of Status in 75 Community Areas of Chicago for the Years 1930–1960.

A. CORRELATIONS BETWEEN PERCENT BLACK AND THE PERCENT FEMALES EMPLOYED.[†]

1930	.46
1940	.42
1950	.13
1960	−.03

B. CORRELATIONS BETWEEN PERCENT BLACK AND THE MEDIAN VALUE OF HOMES.[†]

1930	−.09
1940	−.17
1950	−.22
1960	−.18

C. CORRELATIONS BETWEEN PERCENT FOREIGN-BORN AND PERCENT FEMALES EMPLOYED.[†]

1930	−.28
1940	−.13
1950	.06
1960	.12

D. CORRELATIONS BETWEEN PERCENT FOREIGN-BORN AND MEDIAN VALUE OF HOMES.[†]

1930	−.31
1940	−.41
1950	−.15
1960	−.01

E. CORRELATIONS BETWEEN PERCENT BLACK AND PERCENT FOREIGN-BORN.[†]

1930	−.52
1940	−.63
1950	−.71
1960	−.77

Source: Data from Hunter, 1971: 437, Table 5. Used by permission.

[†]Correlation coefficients are Pearson product-moment correlations (r), described at the end of this chapter. These coefficients vary between −1.00 and +1.00 and, in general, they can be interpreted in terms of their absolute magnitude—the larger the absolute value of the coefficient, the stronger the association or the more closely related are the two variables being compared.

> **BOX 7.1** ASSOCIATION
>
> Double-check yourself. If you are not really clear about the following ideas, go back for a review.
>
> > *Association* of two variables (Section 6.4)
> > Direction of association (Section 6.4.3)
> > Degree of association (Section 6.4.2)
> > Nature of association (Section 6.4.4)
> > Normed measure of association (Section 6.5 and 6.5.1)
> > Statistical independence (end Section 6.4.1a)
> > Perfect association (Section 6.5.2ff)
>
> The purpose of the current chapter is to develop several measures of association which are normed, which are interpretable in an intuitively meaningful way, and which are appropriate for variables defined at various levels of measurement and related in certain characteristic ways.

parison of these correlation coefficients indicates that percent black in an area is becoming less associated with percentage of women employed, and this can be interpreted to mean that assimilation has occurred in this aspect of family status for this ethnic group. Notice that just the opposite pattern characterizes the association of percent black and median value of homes. The small negative association in 1930 becomes larger through time, although there is a reduction to −.18 in 1960. A decline in correlations from 1930 to 1960 is more characteristic of foreign-born than of black, indicating a more general pattern of assimilation for the foreign-born group. Notice too that the association between the two segregation measures, percent black and percent foreign-born for these 75 areas is getting stronger through time, and that it is a negative association. Where one group is concentrated in an area, the other group, increasingly, is absent. This is what one would expect if the foreign-born were moving to suburban areas, leaving higher percentages of black families behind in the central city neighborhoods.

Now for some comments on the coefficients we have been examining. No comparison such as those Hunter made would be possible unless the measures of association he used were comparable, that is, properly normed so that correlations of a given magnitude have the same meaning. This is an important point, because we want to compare across time and across different combinations of variables to reach a conclusion. Secondly, notice that the numbers may be positive or negative, showing direction of association (*e.g.* the *higher* the percentage black in an area, the *higher* the percentage of employed women in the area – a positive association – , rather than the *higher* the percentage of foreign-born in an area the *lower* the percentage black in the area – a negative association). Magnitude of the number varied from a small value, indicating a weak association between the cross-classified variables (a value of zero would mean no association), to a larger number, approaching 1.0, indicating a strong association between the two variables.

This chapter will introduce three families of measures of association which Hunter might have used for the purpose of validly comparing strength and direction of association between variables. There are several other types of measures we could find and use.* In the last chapter, for example, we discussed some of the so-called "delta-based" measures of association. In fact, you could devise your own measures of association after you see what is involved in measures discussed here. The purpose of this chapter is to present some of those measures used more frequently by sociologists and to illustrate the straightforward logic underlying a normed measure of association. We will present measures suitable for the association of nominal, ordinal, and interval variables.

7.1   PROPORTIONATE REDUCTION IN ERROR MEASURES ("PRE")

All of the measures we will discuss in this chapter are of a type called "proportionate reduction in error" measures, or **"PRE"** measures. They are all relatively simple ratios of the amount of error made in predicting under two situations: first, the situation where there is no more information than simply the distribution of the dependent variable itself, and, secondly, a situation where there is additional knowledge about an independent variable and the way the dependent variable is distributed within the categories of that independent variable. PRE measures simply state the proportion by which one can reduce errors made in the first situation by using information from the second situation, above.

$$\text{PRE} = \frac{\text{Reduction in Errors with More Information}}{\text{Original Amount of Error}}$$

The problem of prediction is a common one to the sciences, so it makes some sense to focus a measure of association on the idea of making accurate predictions of the values of some dependent variable. If theoretical knowledge leads us to say that people with a higher social class standing in a society will feel less alienated than those with lower class standing, we are saying, in effect, that knowledge of social class score differences will permit us to make more accurate predictions of differences in alienation scores. If *all* of the errors of prediction can be eliminated by basing predictions on social class, then there is a perfect association between these two variables, and our theoretical basis for expecting this outcome is supported. On the other hand, if the association between social class and alienation is poor or non-existent, then the fact would be indicated in a measure of association which expresses the proportion of the original predictive errors that can be avoided by virtue of the additional knowledge about social class — in this case little or none.

There are three things we might be interested in predicting, depending, essentially, upon the definition of the variables involved in a problem. For *nominal* variables, we are usually interested in predicting the category or exact score

*Among the variety of measures for special situations, a good sampling is presented in an elementary statistics book by Freeman (1965).

of the dependent variable. Often it is sufficient to focus prediction on the most typical or *modal* value of the dependent variable. If the dependent variable is *ordinal,* then we are probably interested in predicting *rank order* of pairs of scores on the dependent variable (although we could think of other possibilities, such as predicting the median or some other percentile). Finally, if the dependent variable is an *interval* level variable, we would probably be interested in predicting the arithmetic *mean* of that dependent variable. These alternatives are shown in Figure 7.1.

Generally speaking, we make errors in predicting modes or rank orders or

The Feature of the Dependent Variable to Be Predicted.	Rules Used in Making Predictions	
	Rule 1: Minimum Guessing Rule	Rule 2: Improved Guessing Rule
A. Predicting Modes (Nominal variables)	For each case to be predicted, predict the modal category of the variable, overall. (Alternatively, predict the category placement at random.)	For each case, first determine the category of the independent variable into which the case falls; then predict the mode of the dependent variable for that category. (Alternatively, predict category placement within categories of the independent variable.)
B. Predicting Rank Order (Ordinal variables)	For each pair of cases for which rank order on a variable is to be predicted, determine which is ranked higher by a flip of a coin (random selection).	For each pair of cases for which rank order on a dependent variable is to be predicted, first determine the ordering on an independent variable, and then, if the overall association is positive, predict "same ordering" on the dependent variable. If the overall association is negative, predict "reverse ordering" on the dependent variable.
C. Predicting the Mean (Interval variables)	For each case to be predicted, predict the overall mean of the dependent variable.	For each case to be predicted, first determine either (a) the category of the independent variable it falls in and predict the mean of that category, or (b) develop a regression equation which permits you to compute a predicted value for the dependent variable, given the score on the independent variable.

FIGURE 7.1 DEVELOPMENT OF PRE MEASURES OF ASSOCIATION*

*There are a number of good references for further discussions of PRE measures of association. See, for example, Costner, (1965) and Kim, (1971).

means, but with the proper theory and proper information we can cut down the amount of predictive error we would otherwise make.* Figure 7.1 indicates the way in which we might make predictions both with and without information. The PRE measures of association we will discuss below are simply a contrast between the errors made in using Rule 1 and those made in using Rule 2 to predict the mode or rank order or mean of a variable that interests us. In each case, the contrast will be formed as follows:

(7.1)
$$PRE = \frac{(\text{Errors made using Rule 1}) - (\text{Errors made using Rule 2})}{(\text{Errors made using Rule 1})}$$

7.2 MEASURES OF ASSOCIATION FOR NOMINAL VARIABLES

PRE measures for each of the situations illustrated in Figure 7.1 will be discussed in turn in the following sections.

7.2.1 Lambda

The **Lambda** measure of association (also called "Guttman's Coefficient of Predictability"), λ_{yx}, is an asymmetric measure of association especially suited to bivariate distributions where both variables are interpreted to be nominal variables. It is a measure which very nicely illustrates the logic of PRE measures.

Suppose that we are interested in marital status as a dependent variable, and we are interested in making predictions about the marital status of individuals who are household heads in the U.S.† Given information in Table 7.2 about how marital status is distributed in the U.S., we would do best to predict that household heads are married. That is, if we know that the modal marital status is "married," then the most rational single score we could predict for a head of household would be that she (he) is married. We will be correct more frequently than we would be if we picked any other single category of marital status for our prediction. Information on the overall distribution of marital status for household heads in the U.S. in 1970 is shown in the total column at the right of Table 7.2.

If we were to guess that the head of the household is married before

---

*In the case of nominal variables, we will also discuss a measure of association which focuses upon predicting the category into which a case may fall, whether or not this category is the modal category. This measure focuses, in a sense, upon the *distribution* across categories of the dependent variable rather than upon an *optimal* single category. The various coefficients are introduced here, not only because they find important uses in sociology, but because they highlight the notion that there are many things about a dependent variable which one might be interested in predicting. The choice among available measures of association involves not only technical or computational matters, but also a basic understanding of what one wants to predict, and this in turn is tied directly to the substantive logic of the research problem itself.

†The U.S. Census defines a head of family as one person usually the person regarded as the head by family members, but women are not classified as heads if their husbands are resident members of the family.

TABLE 7.2 FREQUENCY DISTRIBUTION OF MARITAL STATUS OF HOUSEHOLD HEADS IN THE U.S. IN 1970 BY TYPE OF HOUSEHOLD (IN THOUSANDS).

| Marital Status of Head | *Type of Household* | | | | |
| | *Male Headed* | | *Female Headed* | | |
	Related Children Under 18	*No Related Children Under 18*	*Related Children Under 18*	*No Related Children Under 18*	*Total*
Married	25,776	19,214	313	198	45,501
Separated	79	502	998	425	2,004
Divorced	74	946	1,135	1,105	3,260
Widowed	181	1,199	942	6,457	8,779
Single	64	2,302	349	2,113	4,828
Total	26,174	24,163	3,737	10,298	64,372

Source: U.S. Bur. Census, 1971: 17, Table 6.

knocking on the door for an interview with each of the 64,372 (thousand)* households in the U.S., we would be right 45,501 times and wrong 18,871 times (*i.e.* 64,372 − 45,501 = 18,871). This is the total number of errors of prediction we would make if we merely predicted the overall mode of the marital status of the head of household variable. How many of these errors could be eliminated if we had more information to start with? (See Rule 2 information listed in Figure 7.1.)

The body of Table 7.2 shows the distribution of marital status of the head of household for separate categories of the "type of household" variable. A quick glance at this table suggests that indeed, marital status is distributed different-ly depending upon whether the household is headed by a male and includes re-lated children 18 years of age, is male-headed with no related children under 18, is female-headed with related children under 18, or is female-headed with no children under 18. How much is this added information worth? If we knew the "type of household" before making our prediction of modal marital status, would we be able to refine our prediction and make fewer errors in predicting scores on the dependent variable?

In this example, the answer is "yes." If we knew that the head of house-hold is a male and that the household contained related children under 18 years of age, we would certainly predict the modal marital status for the head of that kind of household—that he would be "married." We would be right 25,776 times out of 26,174 households of this type. We would also predict "married" for the male-headed-no-young-children households—again the mode for that category— and we would be right 19,214 times out of 24,163. If we knew, however, that the household head was female and that there were under-18, related children in the household, we would predict that the household head is "divorced," the mode of marital status for that type of household. We would be right 1,135 times out of 3,737 households of this type. Finally, if the household head were female and if there were no under-18, related children, we would do best to predict "wid-

---

*In Table 7.2, the number of households is expressed in terms of thousands of households—the unit of measurement. It is important, of course, to be consistent in using the same unit throughout our compu-tations and to interpret the result with this unit in mind.

Within-Category Modal Frequency m_y	Category of the Independent Variable(s)
25,776	Households with male heads and related children under 18 years of age.
19,214	Households with male heads and no related children under 18 years of age.
1,135	Households with female heads and related children under 18 years of age.
6,457	Households with female heads and no related children under 18 years of age.
$\Sigma m_y = 52,582$	Total of within-category modal frequencies

owed" as the household head's marital status. Here we would be right 6,457 times out of 10,298.

Have we improved our predictive power by virtue of this added information? We can determine the answer by adding up the correct predictions resulting from within-category prediction (*i.e.* using Rule 2 to predict) and contrast that with the overall frequency in the modal category of the marital status variable.

The more refined prediction would lead to 52,582 correct predictions, which is some 7,081 fewer errors than would be made if we had merely predicted the overall mode of marital status (in which case we would be correct only 45,501 times out of 64,372). That amounts to a reduction of 37.5% in the errors made in predicting marital status of households. This value is called **lambda** (λ_{yx}), and it is a simple substitution of total errors and reduction in errors in the earlier generalized PRE formula. More specifically, λ_{yx} is computed as follows:*

(7.2)

$$\lambda_{yx} = \frac{\Sigma m_y - M_y}{N - M_y}$$

where N is the total sample size, M_y is the *overall* modal frequency of the dependent variable, Y, (45,501 in this case), and Σm_y is the sum of modal frequencies on the dependent variable, Y, *within* separate categories of the independent variable, X, (52,582 in this example). Applied to the current example, the computation is as follows:

$$\lambda_{yx} = \frac{52,582 - 45,501}{64,372 - 45,501} = \frac{7,081}{18,871} = .375$$

The numerator expresses the reduction in error with improved information and

*Lambda could be expressed in terms of the format given earlier for PRE measures as:

$$\lambda_{yx} = \frac{(N - M_y) - (N - \Sigma m_y)}{N - M_y}$$

where the first term in the numerator is the number of errors made in using rule 1, and the second term is the number of errors made in using rule 2. Simplifying the numerator, as shown in the text above, yields a numerator which is the number of *non-errors* under rule 2 (Σm_y) minus the number of *non-errors* under rule 1 (M_y). The denominator is the number of errors under rule 1.

the denominator expresses the error with minimum information. Notice that the symbol for lambda is a lower case Greek letter, and that it has two subscripts: λ_{yx}. The first of these subscripts indicates which variable is the *dependent* variable (variable Y, traditionally), and the second subscript indicates which variable is the *independent* variable (variable X, traditionally).

λ_{yx} is the asymmetric measure of degree of association which expresses the proportionate reduction in errors made in predicting modal values of variable-Y when prior information about variable-X is available to use in refining predictions of modal scores on the dependent variable. λ_{xy} simply reverses the role of the two variables, predicting X from information about Y. Asymmetric measures of association, unlike symmetric measures, always must be labeled in this way because the value of the measure depends upon which variable is predicted from which.

Suppose, to turn the predictive problem in Table 7.2 around, we were interested in predicting scores on "type of household." How much improvement in prediction would result from using marital status as the predictor variable? The formula for lambda is the same as before, with the exception that the x subscript is substituted for the y subscript (and vice versa) in the previous example. We are interested in predicting modes on type of household, overall, and then within categories of the marital status variable. The computations are as follows:

$$M_x = 26{,}174 \qquad \begin{array}{c} \overline{m_x} \\ 25{,}776 \\ 998 \\ 1{,}135 \\ 6{,}457 \\ 2{,}302 \\ \hline \Sigma m_x = 36{,}668 \end{array}$$

$$\lambda_{xy} = \frac{36{,}668 - 26{,}174}{64{,}372 - 26{,}174} = \frac{10{,}494}{27{,}704} = .379$$

Marital status permits one to reduce errors in predicting type of household by 37.9%. The difference between λ_{yx} and λ_{xy} in this example is rather slim. In general, the two different coefficients need *not* be the same for any given table, and they are interpreted quite differently. Using lambda, one could ask which variable(s) permits the greatest reduction in errors in predicting modes of some specific dependent variable, and lambda is a measure of association which helps one assess the utility of certain additional information.* Note that some of the difference between the two lambdas in a table may result from the precision of measurement of the predictor variable. If one wants to predict a dependent variable which has five categories by using a predictor variable which has only four categories, then one could predict only four different modes, not five. Where the predictor variable is more precise than the dependent variable, then more exact-

*Some investigators compute a "symmetrical" lambda coefficient, which is a kind of average of the two asymmetric lambda coefficients shown here. This is believed to be of limited value and its computation will not be discussed. The formula for the symmetrical lambda, however, is:

$$\lambda = \frac{\Sigma m_y + \Sigma m_x - M_x - M_y}{2N - M_x - M_y}$$

TABLE 7.3 PERCENTAGE DISTRIBUTION OF TYPE OF IMPAIRMENT BY AGE, U.S., JULY 1966–JUNE 1967 FOR CHILDREN AND YOUTH AGED 25 OR LESS

(Y) Type of Impairment	Age (X) Under 15	15–24	25 and over	Total
Visual	12.6	10.4	15.2	14.5
Hearing	18.0	11.7	24.4	22.7
Speech	21.0	3.4	2.6	3.1
Orthopedic	48.4	74.5	58.8	59.7
Total	100.0	100.0	100.0	100.0
N (1000's)	(2,601)	(3,952)	(32,560)	(39,113)

$$\lambda_{yx} = .00$$

Note that although λ_{yx} is zero, there *is* a difference in percentages compared across rows of this table, and thus an association not detected by a measure concerned with predicting modes. Here again it is important to select measures which are sensitive to desired features of data.

Source: U.S. Dept. H.E.W., 1971:15, Table 3. Data are from household interviews with a national sample of children and youth aged 25 or under from the civilian, noninstitutionalized population by the U.S. Census. Impairments are defined as chronic or permanent defects which cause a decrease or loss of ability to perform various functions.

ing predictions can be made. This is one reason why investigators attempt to preserve more rather than fewer categories of variables which are to be used in statistical analysis. Note that since lambda is suitable for nominal variables, rows and columns may then be reordered without affecting the magnitude of lambda.

λ_{yx} varies in magnitude from 0.0 to +1.0, and it can take on these values for any table regardless of size or marginals. Assuming that, overall, there is some range of scores on the dependent variable, a perfect association is defined as a condition in which all of the cases in each category of the independent variable fall into only one category of the dependent variable (the modal category).*
λ_{yx} is zero where the *same* modal prediction is made within all categories of the independent variable as would be made if the overall mode were predicted. Here, quite literally, the extra information about the independent variable is not worth anything in refining predictions of the mode of the dependent variable. Table 7.3 illustrates a situation in which λ_{yx} is zero, but from an examination of percentages one can see that an association exists in a sense other than the meaning involved in predicting modes.

It should be noted that lambda tells only part of the story of the association between two nominal variables. In addition to knowledge of the *strength* of association, an investigator would want to examine the *nature* of the association. In this case nature would probably best be discussed in terms of the pattern of percentages in a properly percentaged table such as Table 7.3 or Table 7.1.

*If all scores in the sample are identical, then a perfect prediction could be made with only the overall mode, and λ_{yx} would equal zero, because additional information about an independent variable cannot reduce predictive errors at all. There would be no errors to reduce, in this instance, and thus the independent variable would not be "worth" anything in prediction.

7.2.2 Goodman and Kruskal's tau-y

Another measure of association suitable for nominal variables contrasts some-what different prediction rules than lambda. Like lambda, these taus are asymmetric measures and, again like lambda, they vary from 0.0 for no reduction in error to +1.0 for perfect reduction in error. Goodman and Kruskal's tau-y measures are designed to address the problem of predicting the *distribution* of the dependent variable, Y. Lambda was concerned with predicting an optimal value, namely the *mode* of the dependent variable.

The minimum guessing rule in the case of tau-y is random assignment of cases to categories of the dependent variable so that the marginal distribution of cases is unchanged. Looking back at Table 7.2, we can see this would mean that we would randomly assign 45,501 (1000's) cases to the "married" category, 2,004 to the "separated" category, etc. Such a random allocation of the 64,372 units would, of course, involve some error, and the expected amount of error for this random assignment to categories can be computed for each category of the dependent variable and summed to yield the error expected under this minimum guessing rule. The procedures are as follows:

In Table 7.2, 45,501 are in the "married" category out of 64,372, leaving the difference, 18,871, *not* in the "married" category. We would expect the proportion 18,871/64,372 of the 45,501 cases in the "married" category to be misclassified if 45,501 cases were assigned to this category at random from among the total number of cases.* This results in 13,338.9 expected errors.

$$\frac{18,871}{64,372}\,(45,501) = .293\,(45,501) = 13,338.9 \text{ expected errors}$$

To this are added errors expected to result from random assignment of cases to each other category and, in each case these errors are computed in the same way:

$$\begin{matrix}\text{Expected Category} \\ \text{Error with Random} \\ \text{Assignment}\end{matrix} = \begin{matrix}\text{Proportion } Not \text{ In} \\ \text{A Given Category}\end{matrix} \times \begin{matrix}\text{That Category's} \\ \text{Frequency}\end{matrix}$$

These errors are then summed over all categories of the dependent variable. Symbolically, this can be expressed as:

$$E_1 = \sum_{i=1}^{k} \left[\frac{N - f_i}{N}\,(f_i) \right]$$

where f_i is the frequency in the ith category of the dependent variable, and k is the number of categories of the dependent variable.

Errors in predicting marital status from Table 7.2 would be computed as follows:

*The reasoning here is that by chance a certain proportion of cases will be misclassified, and that this proportion for any category is simply the proportion of cases *not* in that category to cases *in* that category, based on the overall marginal distribution of the dependent variable. Thus, if all cases were in one category, there could be no error if only that category were predicted. Where there is some spread of scores, there is some chance that random assignment will be correct, and some chance that errors will be made. The chance of error will be less for categories which have high frequencies, and greater for categories which have low frequencies in a given distribution.

$$\frac{64{,}372-45{,}501}{64{,}372}\,(45{,}501)=13{,}338.9$$

$$\frac{64{,}372-2{,}004}{64{,}372}\,(2{,}004)\quad=\quad 1{,}941.6$$

$$\frac{64{,}372-3{,}260}{64{,}372}\,(3{,}260)\quad=\quad 3{,}094.9$$

$$\frac{64{,}372-8{,}779}{64{,}372}\,(8{,}779)\quad=\quad 7{,}581.7$$

$$\frac{64{,}372-4{,}828}{64{,}372}\,(4{,}828)\quad=\quad 4{,}465.9$$

$$E_1 = 30{,}423.0$$

The improved guessing rule for predicting the exact distribution of the dependent variable makes use of information about the distribution of the dependent variable within categories of a nominal independent variable. Computational procedures are identical, except that the process is carried out separately for the distribution of the dependent variable *within* each category of the independent variable; thus the formula shown below directs summation over all of the c categories of the independent variable.

$$E_2 = \sum_{j=1}^{c}\sum_{i=1}^{k}\left[\frac{N_j - n_i}{N_j}\,(n_i)\right]$$

where n_i is the cell frequency in the ith category of the dependent variable within one of the c categories of the independent variable and N_j is the total (marginal) frequency for that category of the independent variable. These computations are carried out for each category of the independent variable and then summed over all of the c categories.

For Table 7.2, these computations are totalled as follows:

Computation for male-headed households with related children
under 18   =   788.23

Computation for male-headed households with no related children
under 18   =   8,558.08

Computation for female-headed households with related children
under 18   =   2,829.49

Computations for female-headed households with no related children
under 18   =   5,675.88

      Total $E_2 = 17{,}851.68$

Goodman and Kruskal's tau-y is computed as follows:

(7.3)
$$\text{tau}_y = \frac{E_1 - E_2}{E_1}$$

$$= \frac{(30{,}423.0) - (17{,}851.68)}{30{,}423.0} = .41$$

Goodman and Kruskal's tau-y can be interpreted as the proportion reduction in errors of predicting category placement. Here, the prediction rules involve the overall marginal distribution of the dependent variable (or distributions within categories of the independent variable), rather than only the central-tendency measure which was used in computing lambda. Again, there are two tau-y values which could be computed on the same table if the roles of dependent and independent variable were reversed. In general, these two values do not turn out to be the same value.

Tau-y varies from 0.0 to +1.0. It is +1.0 where all cases within a category of the independent variable are in the same category of the dependent variable, and this can occur only if there are at least as many categories of the independent variable as of the dependent variable. This condition of perfect association would also yield a value of +1.0 for lambda.

7.3 MEASURES OF ASSOCIATION FOR ORDINAL VARIABLES

Prediction of scores on ordinal variables is somewhat different from prediction of scores on nominal variables. Since we are interested in the *ranking* of scores on ordinal variables, it is useful to think of *pairs* of observations. It takes at least two scores before the idea of "rank" is meaningful. For a measure of association we are interested in the rank of pairs of cases on *two* ordinal variables, since we are interested in whether or not knowledge of the rank ordering of pairs of cases on one variable is useful in predicting their rank order on the other variable. If the knowledge of ranking of pairs on one variable is of no use in predicting rank order on the other variable, then we would like an ordinal measure of association to equal zero. This situation is equivalent to predicting the rank order of cases randomly by tossing a coin, half the time guessing that the highest-ranked case on one variable is highest on the second variable, and half the time guessing that that highest-ranked case on the first variable is lowest on the second variable.

Two other prediction rules may prove to be useful, however, in the sense of reducing errors in predicting rank order of pairs of observations on a dependent variable. These rules correspond to situations where there is (a) a positive association, or (b) a negative association between the two variables. In the first instance, we would predict **same rank order** on the *second* variable as the pair had on the *first* variable. The other rule is predicting the **opposite rank order** of cases on the second variable as opposed to the first. Thus if Johnson is higher on social class than Jones, we could probably use the *"same rank order"* rule to predict their rank in terms of prestige of occupation, the second variable, since these two ordinal variables are positively related. Likewise, we could reduce predictive errors in predicting the rank order of their scores on "anomie" by using the "opposite rank order" rule, since social class and anomie are negatively related. In order to express how good these rank-order prediction rules may be, we need to consider the distribution of different kinds of pairings of scores on two variables.

7.3.1   Types of Pairs

The total number of possible, unique pairs of cases which can be formed from N cases can be computed as follows:

$$T = \frac{N(N-1)}{2}$$

where N is equal to the total sample size.* With five cases, ten unique pairings are possible; with $N = 10$, 45 unique pairings of cases can be distinguished. Furthermore, if these "T" unique pairs are measured on two ordinal variables, there are only five possible patterns of ranking on these two variables.

(a) **Concordant pairs** (N_s) are pairs which are ranked in the same order on both variables.

(b) **Discordant pairs** (N_d) are pairs which are ranked in the opposite order on both variables.

(c) Pairs *tied on the independent variable* (X) but not tied on the dependent variable (Y). These are symbolized T_x.

(d) Pairs *tied on the dependent variable* (Y) but not tied on the independent variable (X). These are symbolized T_y.

(e) Pairs *tied on both variables,* symbolized, T_{xy}.

These five types of pairs exhaust the possibilities, and the sum of pairs of these types equals T, the total number of possible, unique pairs of cases. Diagram 7.1 illustrates the computational procedures involved in finding the number of these different types of pairs for a given set of data.

The difference between the frequency of concordant (N_s) and discordant (N_d) pairs is a measure of which rule is the most accurate predictor of rank order. If there are more N_s pairs than N_d pairs, the *same rank order* rule would be more accurate. If there were a preponderance of N_d pairs in a given set of data, then the *opposite rank order* rule would serve best. In fact, the greater the preponderance of concordant (or discordant) pairs, the better the appropriate rank-prediction rule. If there is no difference between the number of concordant and discordant pairs, then neither rule is better and we would not improve our rank-order predictions over simply using a random guess or flip of a coin.

7.3.2   Measures of Association

For ordinal variables **measures of association** can be created as simple ratios of the various types of pairs distinguished here. In every case, however, the numerator of the ratio turns out to be the same, $N_s - N_d$, the preponderance (if any) of like-ranked or opposite-ranked pairs in a set of data. Each of these measures is a PRE measure, indicating the proportionate reduction in error which could be achieved by using one of the rank-order prediction rules ("same rank" or "opposite rank"), as compared to errors involved in making a random guess

---

*The symbol, T, is the total number of unique pairs in a set of N cases. It has nothing to do with a different measure of association, Tschruprow's T, discussed in the last chapter. Unfortunately, traditional symbolism is not altogether consistent, although in context the meanings are generally quite clear.

DIAGRAM 7.1 Ordinal Measures of Association

The Problem:

We want to describe the association between two ordinal variables in this example, mobility-orientation of 10–19-year-old children in 466 households and the mobility-orientation held for them by their parents (See Furstenberg, 1971:598)*. Data were collected from a representative sample of households on the Lower East Side of New York in 1960. The two mobility-orientation scales included items about educational and occupational values, goals, and attitudes about achievement.

The study was concerned with the extent to which attitudes about mobility are transmitted from parent to child as indicated by the similarity of parent and child views. A strong association between the child's view and his parents' view would suggest that mobility-orientation is indeed transmitted between parent and child. The author's hypothesis was that there was little such transmission, and that the association would thus be rather low. We will use these data to show how the various types of pairs of cases (in this example, a "case" is a child, measured on his and his parent's mobility-orientation for him). Several measures of ordinal association may be computed and these are discussed in this chapter. In actuality, only one of these measures of association would be computed; the criteria for deciding on which one are also discussed in Chapter 7. The author reported tau-*b* as the appropriate measure in this instance.

(Y) Child's Own Mobility Orientation	(X) Mobility Orientation a Child's Parents Hold for Him			
	Low	Medium	High	Total
High	ᵈ 29	55	68	152
Medium	59	53	48	160
Low	ₛ 71	37	30	138
Total	159	145	146	450

Computing Number of Pairs of Different Kinds

In practice, if a computer were not used, only those types of pairs needed for the selected measure of association would be computed. Here all five types of pairs will be computed for illustration.

---

*Sixteen cases of "don't know" or "no answer" were excluded from the table in Furstenberg's study.

DIAGRAM 7.1 *(Continued)*

Step 1: Examine the table and determine which diagonal is the "positive" diagonal, that is, the one which extends from the "high-high" cell to the
"low-low" cell on both variables. In this example, that diagonal is from
the lower left to the upper right on the table. Label one end of this diagonal s and label one end of the "negative" diagonal d. This step assures
that N_s and N_d pairings will be computed properly and, thus, that the
coefficient's sign will accurately reflect the direction of association in a
table.

Step 2: Compute types of pairs.
T = total number of unique pairings of cases

$$T = \frac{N(N-1)}{2}$$

$$T = \frac{450(450-1)}{2} = 101,025$$

N_s = number of "concordant" pairs. This is computed by locating the cell
in the "s" corner of the table as indicated in Step 1, above. This is the first
"target cell" and its frequency is multiplied by the sum of cell frequencies
above and to the right of the target cell (in this instance, since "s" is in
the lower left corner of the table). This is illustrated in the schematic
diagram at the left below, where the darkened, single cell is the target
cell which is multiplied by the sum of cell frequencies in cells indicated
by shading. To this first product are added similar products formed
by taking each additional cell in the table (that has cells above and to the
right) as successive "target" cells. In this table, there are four such products which are summed, as follows:

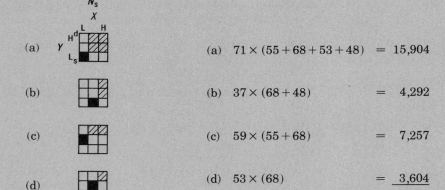

(a)   71 × (55 + 68 + 53 + 48)   = 15,904

(b)   37 × (68 + 48)   =   4,292

(c)   59 × (55 + 68)   =   7,257

(d)   53 × (68)   =   3,604

N_s = 31,057

DIAGRAM 7.1 *(Continued)*

It is helpful to notice the logic involved in these computations. The 71 cases in the first "target" cell have $55 + 68 + 53 + 48$ cases which are ranked differently and also ranked higher on both variables than the target-cell's 71 cases. The number of pairs which could be created would be equal to 71 times the total of $55 + 68 + 53 + 48$, which is 15,904. Likewise, for each target cell, the total pairings of this concordant kind can be computed for it and the sum of all of these computations equals the total number of unique pairs which are concordant.

N_d = number of "discordant" pairs. This is computed in exactly the same fashion as N_s, *except* that target cells start in the "d" corner and work down the negative diagonal. In this case, target cells are multiplied by the sum of cell frequencies for cells which are below and to its right. These computations yield the following sum:

(e)	$29 \times (53 + 48 + 37 + 30) \quad = \quad 4{,}872$
(f)	$55 \times (48 + 30) \quad\quad\quad\quad\quad = \quad 4{,}290$
(g)	$59 \times (37 + 30) \quad\quad\quad\quad\quad = \quad 3{,}953$
(h)	$53 \times (30) \quad\quad\quad\quad\quad\quad\quad = \quad \underline{1{,}590}$
	$N_d \quad = 14{,}705$

It is immediately apparent that there are more concordant pairs in these data, and thus that the association is a positive association. This will result in a plus sign on any of the association measures we eventually compute.

T_x = pairs tied on the independent (X) variable but not on the dependent (Y) variable. These pairs are those formed within the same category of the X variable (*i.e.* tied on X) as indicated in the graphic illustration below at the left. Starting with a target cell at the top of a column, this is multiplied by the sum of cell frequencies for cells immediately below the target cell, etc. The computations are given below:

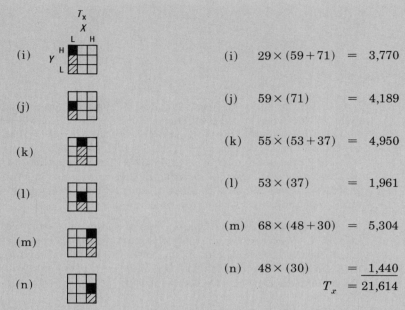

(i)	(i) $29 \times (59+71) = 3,770$
(j)	(j) $59 \times (71) = 4,189$
(k)	(k) $55 \times (53+37) = 4,950$
(l)	(l) $53 \times (37) = 1,961$
(m)	(m) $68 \times (48+30) = 5,304$
(n)	(n) $48 \times (30) = \underline{1,440}$
	$T_x = 21,614$

$T_y =$ pairs tied on the Y variable but not on the X variable. These are computed exactly as T_x pairs are, *except* that products are formed within categories of the Y variable, only. In this case, target cells are multiplied only by the sum of cell frequencies to the right, within rows, as illustrated in the diagram at the left. The computations are as follows:

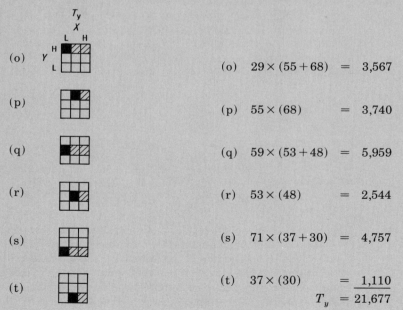

(o)	(o) $29 \times (55+68) = 3,567$
(p)	(p) $55 \times (68) = 3,740$
(q)	(q) $59 \times (53+48) = 5,959$
(r)	(r) $53 \times (48) = 2,544$
(s)	(s) $71 \times (37+30) = 4,757$
(t)	(t) $37 \times (30) = \underline{1,110}$
	$T_y = 21,677$

DIAGRAM 7.1 *(Continued)*

T_{xy} = pairs tied on both the X and the Y variables. These consist of the sum of pairs which can be formed out of cases which fall in the same cell (*i.e.* have the identical value on X and also an identical value on Y). These are computed for each cell as follows:

$$\frac{f(f-1)}{2}$$

where f is the cell frequency for a given cell.

These computations on each cell are then summed over all cells to equal T_{xy}. The computations on this table are as follows:

$$
\begin{aligned}
29(29-1)/2 &= 406 \\
55(55-1)/2 &= 1{,}485 \\
68(68-1)/2 &= 2{,}278 \\
59(59-1)/2 &= 1{,}711 \\
53(53-1)/2 &= 1{,}378 \\
48(48-1)/2 &= 1{,}128 \\
71(71-1)/2 &= 2{,}485 \\
37(37-1)/2 &= 666 \\
30(30-1)/2 &= 435 \\
\hline
T_{xy} &= 11{,}972
\end{aligned}
$$

As a check, you should notice that the sum of these five kinds of pairs equals the total number of possible, unique pairings:

$$
\begin{aligned}
N_s &= 31{,}057 \\
N_d &= 14{,}705 \\
T_x &= 21{,}614 \\
T_y &= 21{,}677 \\
T_{xy} &= 11{,}972 \\
\hline
T &= 101{,}025
\end{aligned}
$$

Step 3: Compute the appropriate ordinal measure of association. These measures are as follows:

tau-a
tau-b
tau-c
gamma
Somers' d_{yx}

and they are discussed in the body of Chapter 7.

about the rank ordering of pairs of cases on some ordinal variable. The different ordinal measures of association we will discuss have different denominators. That is, they differ in terms of the kinds of pairs "at risk," or for which a prediction is attempted. Let us start with the most intuitively meaningful measure of the group, Kendall's tau-*a*.*

7.3.2a Tau-*a*. *Tau-a* (t_a) is defined as the preponderance of concordant (or discordant) pairs out of all possible unique pairs in the data.

(7.4)

$$t_a = \frac{N_s - N_d}{T}$$

Looking back at the example in Diagram 7.1, the tau-*a* (t_a) coefficient would be:

$$t_a = \frac{31,057 - 14,705}{101,025} = \frac{16352}{101025} = +.16$$

Computing Diagram 1 illustrates how the components of t_a would be computed. This coefficient can vary from −1.0 to 0 to +1.0 depending upon whether the association is negative or positive. An association of zero indicates an even split between concordant and discordant pairs (and thus, that neither predictive rule will help in reducing predictive errors over errors one would expect to make just by chance). A t_a of 1.0 would indicate that all of the possible pairs are of one kind (either concordant or discordant depending upon the sign of t_a). This is a symmetrical coefficient since no distinction is made between independent and dependent variables in the computation of N_s, N_d or T, and it is appropriate for any sized table or any number of ranks on either of the two ordinal variables. Unfortunately, if there are ties, as there usually are, t_a cannot reach the magnitude of 1.0, because the denominator which includes ties will always be greater than either N_s or N_d.

7.3.2b Gamma (G). One solution to the problem of actually obtaining a coefficient equal to 1.0 when there are ties is to eliminate the ties from the denominator as well. **Gamma** (*G*) is a frequently used, symmetrical measure for association of two ordinal variables which does just that.† The numerator is the same as that used for t_a and the denominator is simply the sum of pairs which are ranked differently on both variables.

(7.5)

$$G = \frac{N_s - N_d}{N_s + N_d}$$

Gamma (*G*), like t_a, is a symmetrical measure. Unlike t_a, it can always achieve the limiting values of −1.0 or +1.0 regardless of the number of ties. In fact, it would be possible to have a *G* of +1.0 (or −1.0) based on only one pair, where all the rest of the pairs are tied on one or both variables. This may be an undesirable property of *G*, considering it as an overall characterization of the proportionate reduction in errors in predicting rank order of one variable based

---

*An interesting discussion of the relationship between some of the ordinal measures of association is contained in Somers (1962:799–811), as well as original work by Kendall, Kruskal and Goodman, and Kruskal, which are cited in Somers' article.
†Sometimes gamma is symbolized by the lower-case Greek letter (γ). *G* is used here.

on a knowledge of ranking on the other variable. Both t_a and G, however, would be appropriate for an $r \times c$ table. It is interesting to note that G in the 2×2 case is the same as Yule's Q, which was introduced in the last chapter, (Section 6.5.2c), except for the traditionally used symbolism. G is a generalized version of Yule's Q for $r \times c$ tables.

Using the illustration from Diagram 7.1, G would be computed as follows:

$$G = \frac{31057 - 14705}{31057 + 14705} = \frac{16352}{45762} = .36$$

G can be interpreted as the proportionate reduction in errors in predicting ranking that would be made by using the "same" (or "opposite") ranking rule rather than randomly predicting rankings among pairs which are ranked differently on both of the two variables in the table.

7.3.2c Somers' d$_{yx}$. A somewhat different ordinal measure would be appropriate if one distinguishes between independent and dependent variables. If one were predicting the ranking of cases on a dependent variable (variable Y), using variable X as the independent or predictor variable, he would make a prediction about ranking not only for the pairs that are ranked differently on each variable (*i.e.* the N_s and N_d pairs), but he would also make a prediction for the T_y cases which are different on the predictive variable but tied on the dependent variable. The difference on the independent variable permits a prediction even in the T_y cases, although the prediction may not work out, since there may not be any difference on the dependent variable. The denominator of an association measure, then, should include *all* of the pairs for which a prediction would be risked. This is essentially the definition of this next ordinal measure of association, Somers' d_{yx}.

(7.6)

$$d_{yx} = \frac{N_s - N_d}{N_s + N_d + T_y}$$

Notice that the numerator is again the difference between concordant and discordant pairs. Somers' d_{yx} is an asymmetric measure, since it does take account of which variable is the predictor variable and which is the predicted. Ties on the predic*ted* variable are *in*cluded, and ties on the predic*tor* variable are *ex*cluded. Like G, it can vary from -1.0 indicating a perfect negative association (*i.e.* a situation where all pairs are discordant) to $+1.0$. It can be interpreted as the proportionate reduction in errors in predicting ranking on a dependent variable resulting from using the ("same" or "opposite") predicting rule, rather than chance prediction among pairs which are ranked differently on the independent variable. Here again, as was true of other asymmetric measures such as lambda (λ_{yx} and λ_{xy}), there are two Somers' d's which can be computed on any table, depending upon which variable is treated as the independent variable. In general, too, these values may be (and generally will be) different for any given table.

7.3.2d Tau-b(t_b). An investigator might be interested in a measure of degree of association which is symmetrical but, unlike G, takes account of ties on one or the other variable (but not ties on both, T_{xy}). Ties on both variables are considered to be trivial, since they correspond to the number of pairs that could be created out of cases which are identical on both variables and which thus fall within the same cell of a table. In most tables, cell frequencies are greater than one, and it is not the absolute size of any cell frequency, but the *pattern* of frequencies in different cells which is what one means by the association in a table.

Tau-*b* (t_b) is a kind of average of the two Somers' *d*'s which could be computed on a given set of data. In fact, it can be expressed as the square root of the product of these two *d*'s.

$$t_b = \sqrt{d_{yx}d_{xy}}$$

It is usually computed directly from computations of the number of each type of pairs, and it can also be expressed in this fashion as follows:

(7.7)
$$t_b = \frac{N_s - N_d}{\sqrt{(N_s + N_d + T_y)(N_s + N_d + T_x)}}$$

It can take on values from −1.0 to +1.0, depending upon the direction of association, and its magnitude indicates strength of association. t_b cannot achieve a magnitude of 1.0 if a table is not square (*i.e.* if $r \neq c$) since in this case there would have to be more pairs tied on one variable (the one with the fewer categories) than are tied on the other variable.* Unfortunately, the more complicated the denominator the more difficult it becomes to express a clear operational definition in a PRE sense, and this is true of t_b. It is, however, one of the more useful of the ordinal, symmetrical measures, and it is superior to tau-*a* (t_a) because it does take account of the non-trivial ties in expressing the relationship between two variables.

For the illustrative data in Diagram 7.1, t_b would be computed as follows:

$$t_b = \frac{31057 - 14705}{\sqrt{(31057 + 14705 + 21614)(31057 + 14705 + 21677)}}$$

$$= \frac{16352}{67407.5} = .24$$

All of the preceding measures of association for ordinal variables were simply ratios created out of the number of pairs of the several types we distinguished. In each case the balance of concordant and discordant pairs was evaluated in terms of the number of pairs "at risk," so to speak — that is, the number of pairs which constituted a potential number of errors or correct predictions that might have been made. The essential difference between the measures derives from what pool of differences one would be interested in predicting.

7.3.2e Spearman's rho (r_s). The last ordinal measure we will deal with is interesting, because it takes a different approach to the problem of mea-

---

*Another measure of association which can achieve 1.0 for tables where the number of rows and columns is not equal is called tau-*c*. In this formula, *m* is the smaller of the number of rows or the number of columns.

$$t_c = \frac{2m(N_s - N_d)}{N^2(m-1)}$$

As is true of tau-*b*, this measure, although normed, is hard to interpret operationally, and tau-*c* is less frequently used than the other tau measures.

BOX 7.2   ORGANIZING

Often it helps to organize statistical measures in terms of some of their main differences—those differences that might lead to the selection of one measure in preference to another for some particular problem. One organizing scheme is suggested here, and the six PRE measures we have discussed thus far in this chapter are entered for illustration. Your own scheme might have more detailed classifications. Selection of an appropriate measure is discussed later in this chapter.

Level of Measurement	Symmetric	Asymmetric
Nominal		Goodman-Kruskal t_y Lambda (λ_{yx})
Ordinal	Kendall's t_a Kendall's t_b Gamma (G)	Somers' d_{yx}

suring the direction and strength of association. It is primarily used where rankings of individual cases on two variables are available so that rankings range from 1 to N for each variable. Table 7.4 provides an example of two rankings of the same set of sociology departments. One ranking is in terms of degree productivity and the other is in terms of positions held on the editorial board of

TABLE 7.4   RANK OF SELECTED SOCIOLOGY DEPARTMENTS ON PRODUCTIVITY OF DOCTORATES AND REPRESENTATION ON THE EDITORIAL BOARD OF A MAJOR SOCIOLOGY JOURNAL

Sociology Department	(1) Rank on Number of PhDs Produced 1964–8	(2) Rank on No. of Editorial Positions on the ASR for 1948 to 68	Difference Between Ranks D	D^2
Chicago	1	1	0	0
Columbia	2	3	−1	1
Wisconsin	3	4	−1	1
Minnesota	4	5	−1	1
UCLA	5	8	−3	9
Berkeley	6	6.5	−0.5	0.25
Michigan	7	9.5	−2.5	6.25
Ohio State	8.5	6.5	+2	4
Washington (Seattle)	8.5	9.5	−1	1
Harvard	10	2	+8	64
			$\Sigma D = 0$	$\Sigma D^2 = 87.5$

Source: Data from Rossi, 1970, (column 1), and from Yoels, 1971, (column 2). Tied ranks are averaged.

the *American Sociological Review*, official journal of professional sociologists in the United States.

The argument is that the representation of schools on the editorial board of a major journal merely reflects the productivity of these departments. If that is so, then there should be a perfect association – exactly the same ranking – of the departments on both variables, representation and production.

Spearman's rho (r_s) is a measure of association for ordinal variables based on the difference between ranks. If there is no difference, then D will equal zero. Since the sum of the difference between ranks is always zero, as shown in Table 7.4, differences between ranks are squared before summing. In the case of comparisons in ranking of these ten schools, the sum of squared differences between ranks (called ΣD^2) is 87.5. Since this is different from zero we know that the two variables are not identically ranked. But we do not know how to interpret this figure, because we would expect it to vary with the number of individuals ranked in the first place. We could, however, create a ratio of the D^2 obtained and the maximum possible D^2 that could be achieved for a given number of ranked individuals. This maximum D^2 is this: $N(N^2-1)/3$, where N is the number of cases ranked. Then, in order to make it possible for a minus sign to indicate opposite ranking and for the magnitude of 1.0 to be a maximum degree of association, the formula for r_s is written as follows:*

(7.8)
$$\text{Spearman's } r_s = 1 - \frac{6\Sigma D^2}{N(N^2-1)}$$

Rho (r_s) will have a value of +1.0 for a perfect match of ranks, to a value of −1.0 if the ranks are exactly opposite. A r_s of zero indicates no systematic ordering or, rather, no rank pattern between the two variables. In the case of Table 7.4, r_s is as follows:

$$r_s = 1 - \frac{6(87.5)}{10(10^2-1)} = 1 - \frac{525}{990} = 1 - .53 = +.47$$

Intermediate values of r_s can be interpreted in terms of their relative magnitude but r_s does not have a PRE interpretation.

7.4   MEASURES OF ASSOCIATION FOR INTERVAL VARIABLES

As you will recall from the discussion of univariate statistics, the arithmetic mean of an interval-level dependent variable is a useful prediction because the mean has the property that the algebraic sum of deviations of actual scores from it is zero. A measure of how badly wrong this prediction is can be derived from these deviations. The variance (or its square root, the standard deviation) is one such measure which expresses the amount of scatter of scores around this mean.

Thus, as a minimum, one could predict the mean of a dependent variable and measure "errors" made in that prediction in terms of the familiar variance

---

*The formula for Spearman's rho (r_s) is simply a Pearsonian r computed on ranks. Since the ranks for both variables extend from 1 to N, we know that the sum of each variable is $N(N+1)/2$ and the mean of each variable is $(N+1)/2$. The sum of squares becomes $N(N+1)$ $(2N+1)/6$ and the variance in each case is $(N^2-1)/12$. Substitution into the formula for Pearson's r yields the Spearman's r_s formula for the relationship between X ranks on two variables for N cases. The derivation is nicely illustrated in Hammond and Householder (1962:212–214).

BOX 7.3 INTERVAL-LEVEL VARIABLES AGAIN

The following section deals with *measures of association* and a description of the *nature of association* for interval-level variables. It is helpful, at this point, to recall some of the concepts from univariate description which were used to summarize interval level variables. In particular, you should feel quite comfortable with the following:

arithmetic mean   Section 5.3.3
variance and standard deviation   Section 5.4.4
scatter diagram   Section 4.4.2

(s^2) and this, in fact, constitutes the minimum guessing rule for interval variables shown in Figure 7.1, above. How much better can we do? Is there any way that scores on an independent variable could be used to improve the prediction of a dependent variable? As you might suspect by now, the answer is "yes," although the solution to the problem is new to our line of discussion thus far.

Suppose that we were able to derive a formula which would describe the way the mean of variable Y varied as one moved up the scale of variable X. This would, in effect, be a mathematical description of the *nature* of the relationship between two variables and it would also permit us to "compute" an estimate of an individual's score on the dependent variable from information about his score on the independent variable. With a predicted score (called Y', or Y-prime) and an actually observed score (Y), we could then ask how accurate the prediction equation is. This might take the form of a measure of association (usually called a *correlation coefficient* where the variables are interval-level) which would express the amount by which predictive errors could be reduced, given the prediction equation rather than the overall mean of the dependent variable to use in predicting. This is precisely what we will do to create the next measure of association called the **Pearson's Product-Moment Correlation Coefficient, r.** Its square (*i.e.* r^2) will indicate the proportionate reduction in errors resulting from a use of the predictive equation. In order to develop this idea, however, we need to step back and develop a formula for describing the nature of the relationship between two interval variables so as to predict the dependent variable.

7.4.1 Regression Equations

Suppose we start with a small collection of data where two scores are measured on each of six cases.

Case	(X) Years of Education	(Y) Income in ($1000)
A	1	2
B	2	4
C	3	6
D	4	8
E	5	10
F	6	12

These scores could be plotted on a graph, as in Figure 7.2a, where values of the independent variable appear along the X-axis and values of the dependent variable appear along the Y-axis. This is one use of a **scatter diagram** discussed earlier in this book (Chapter 4).

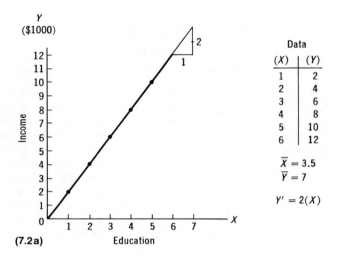

(7.2a)

Data

(X)	(Y)
1	2
2	4
3	6
4	8
5	10
6	12

$\bar{X} = 3.5$
$\bar{Y} = 7$

$Y' = 2(X)$

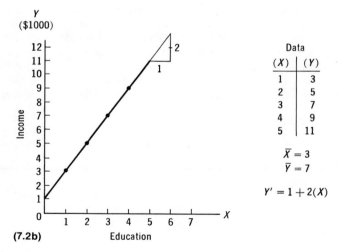

(7.2b)

Data

(X)	(Y)
1	3
2	5
3	7
4	9
5	11

$\bar{X} = 3$
$\bar{Y} = 7$

$Y' = 1 + 2(X)$

FIGURE 7.2 SCATTER DIAGRAMS

Each case is represented by a point on the graph placed above the X-axis and across from the Y-axis at the point which represents that individual's score on each variable. These points can be located by a pair of scores (*e.g.* 1,2 where the first number is the X-score and the second is the Y-score for that point).

7.4.1a In this example, it is clear that the two variables are related in a rather simple and obvious way. In fact, one could predict the Y-score exactly from a knowledge of the X-score merely by doubling the X-score for these cases. This relationship is expressed in the following equation where Y' (called Y-prime) is an estimated or predicted value for that individual on the Y-variable.

$$Y' = 2(X)$$

The predictions fall along a straight line, which is drawn in for Figure 7.2a. The 2 in this equation is called the **slope** of the regression line, and it means that for one-unit increase along the X-axis there will be a predicted increase of two units on the Y-scale. This slope is illustrated in the small triangle shown on the graph, Figure 7.2a. Notice that predictions derived from this equation describe a **straight line,** one of the simplest (*i.e.* easiest to describe) ways in which two variables can be related. One could say that these variables are related in a "linear" fashion; a straight line very nicely describes their relationship. This line is called a linear **regression** line; a regression of the dependent variable, Y, on the independent variable, X.

7.4.1b Let us examine another set of data. Here again we have a very small set of scores for illustrative purposes and, again, we can create a scatter diagram of these five cases as shown in Figure 7.2b.

Case	(X) Years of Education	(Y) Income in ($1000)
A	1	3
B	2	5
C	3	7
D	4	9
E	5	11

The Y-scores for these five cases can also be accurately predicted by a simple formula.

$$Y' = 1 + 2(X)$$

Given an X-score, we can predict a Y-score for that case by merely doubling the X-score and adding a constant, 1. Here too, the equation describes a simple straight line and one would again say that the relationship between these two variables is of a linear nature. The formula, above, describes the specific nature of this relationship for these data. Here again, the 2 expresses the number of

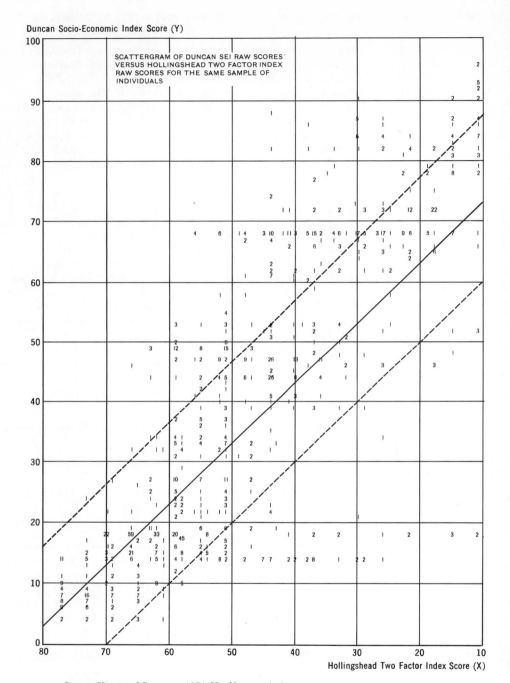

Duncan Socio-Economic Index Score (Y)

SCATTERGRAM OF DUNCAN SEI RAW SCORES
VERSUS HOLLINGSHEAD TWO FACTOR INDEX
RAW SCORES FOR THE SAME SAMPLE OF
INDIVIDUALS

Hollingshead Two Factor Index Score (X)

Source: Haug and Sussman, 1971. Used by permission.

FIGURE 7.3 Scatter Diagram Showing the Relationship between Hollinghead's Two-factor Index and Duncan's SEI as Measures of Social Class Standing

units change in Y given a single unit change in X. The constant, 1, indicates the point at which the straight line crosses the Y-axis in this scattergram in Figure 7.2b and it is called the **Y-intercept.**

    7.4.1c   The general formula for any straight line is expressed as follows:

(7.9)
$$Y' = a_{yx} + b_{yx}(X)$$

where Y' is the predicted or computed value of the dependent variable; a_{yx} is the constant or Y-intercept for this equation; and b_{yx} is the slope coefficient (also referred to as the **b-coefficient**). The first subscript of the a_{yx} and b_{yx} values is the dependent variable, and the second subscript refers to the independent variable. It is immediately clear that these coefficients distinguish between the independent and dependent variables and we might, in fact, expect a different equation if values of X were to be predicted from values of Y. As in the case of asymmetric measures of association, there are two regression equations which could be computed to describe the nature of the relationship between the pair of variables in a scattergram. More of this later.

    Notice that the a_{yx} and b_{yx} coefficients in the last two examples are positive values. This need not be the case for all sets of data. In fact, where the *b-coefficient* is negative, that indicates that the variables are negatively related, since an increase of one unit in the X-value would signal a negative change in the predicted Y-score.

    Now, not all associations between variables are described very well by a straight line, although many come relatively close to this nature of association. A straight line represents in many respects the simplest relationship we could express, and it is usually the one expressed in theoretical statements about how sociological variables are related. As a matter of fact, some relationships between variables are better described by curved rather than straight lines, but these raise the problem of discovering, by some curve-fitting method, what the proper formula for the curve might be, as well as what the particular form of curve might mean, theoretically. Although the problems are not particularly different, we will limit our attention to the simple straight-line relationship and the development of the linear regression equation.

    Figure 7.3 illustrates the more typical scatter diagram. In this instance, individual cases are represented by the placement of the small numbers on the scatter diagram. The number itself indicates how many cases fall at that same point. The relationship is between two different measures of social class. One measure was developed by Hollingshead using occupation and education; the other social class score was developed by Duncan from income and education for different occupation groups. (See Haug and Sussman, 1971.) One would expect that the two measures would be relatively closely related, since they are supposed to measure essentially the same phenomenon. In actual data, however, there is a considerable amount of scatter even though, overall, the data cluster fairly well around a linear regression line. The problem is to place the linear regression line in such a manner that it fits the data as well as possible.

    7.4.1d "Best Fitting" Line. The criterion of "fit" of a regression line is still how well the dependent variable can be predicted by the equation the line represents. Let us take another set of data, where a small number of data

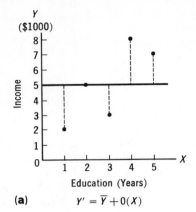

Data

(X)	(Y)
1	2
5	7
3	3
2	5
4	8

$\overline{X} = 3$
$\overline{Y} = 5$

(a) $Y' = \overline{Y} + 0(X)$

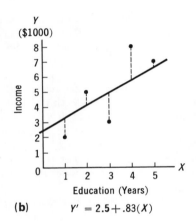

(b) $Y' = 2.5 + .83(X)$

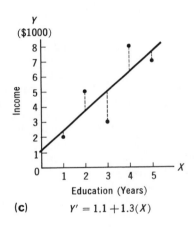

(c) $Y' = 1.1 + 1.3(X)$

	Actual Data		Prediction #1 $Y' = \overline{Y} + 0(X)$		Prediction #2 $Y' = 2.5 + .83(X)$			Prediction #3 $Y' = 1.1 + 1.3(X)$		
	(X)	(Y)	Y'	(Y − Y')	(Y − Y')²	Y'	(Y − Y')	(Y − Y')²	Y'	(Y − Y')	(Y − Y')²
	1	2	5	−3	9	3.33	−1.33	1.77	2.4	− .4	.16
	5	7	5	+2	4	6.66	+ .34	.12	7.6	− .6	.36
	3	3	5	−2	4	5.00	−2.00	4.00	5.0	−2.0	4.00
	2	5	5	0	0	4.17	+ .83	.69	3.7	+1.3	1.69
	4	8	5	+3	9	5.83	+2.17	4.71	6.3	−1.7	2.89
Sum	15	25	25	0	26.0	25.00	.0	11.29	25.0	.0	9.10
Avg	3	5	5	0	5.2	5.0	0	2.26	5.0	0	1.82

Measurement of Prediction Errors

FIGURE 7.4   FINDING THE "BEST" STRAIGHT LINE TO REPRESENT DATA

points are scattered somewhat, and try to discover how one might derive a best-fitting straight line.

The set of five scores shown in Figure 7.4 could be predicted in terms of several different equations. Let us take three to show the kind of error that the "best-fitting" line would help eliminate. First, we could simply predict the mean of Y for every case. This is the regression line shown in Figure 7.4a. Secondly, we could use the prediction: $Y' = 2.5 + .83X$, which is an arbitrarily picked equation (for illustrative purposes) which is *not* the "best-fitting," but it is better than the overall mean of Y as a prediction. Any number of other inadequate equations could be chosen rather than this one, of course. Thirdly, we could use the "best-fitting" regression equation for these data, which happens to be: $Y' = 1.1 + 1.3X$.

7.4.1e Notice in Figure 7.4a that the same prediction will be made for each case, and the inaccuracy of this prediction will be described by subtracting the *predicted* Y-score from the *actual* Y-score, squaring the difference, and dividing this sum by N, the number of cases. You will recall that this is simply the formula for the variance of a set of scores. In Figure 7.4a this variance can be symbolized by s_y^2 to indicate clearly that it is the variance of the Y-variable.

$$s_y^2 = \frac{26.0}{5} = 5.2$$

Using the second prediction equation shown in Figure 7.4b, a different predicted value of Y is shown for each different value of X. Again, we can describe the accuracy of prediction by subtracting predicted from actual Y-score, squaring the difference, summing and dividing by N.* In this case, since the predicted value of Y depended upon the value of X, we will symbolize the variance by $s_{y \cdot x}^2$, which is called the *variance of the estimate;* the square root of this

$$s_{y \cdot x}^2 = \frac{\Sigma(Y - Y')^2}{N}$$

value is called the **standard error of estimate.** Notice that the subscript indicates not only the dependent variable, Y, but the dot followed by the X indicates that different values of X are reflected in predictions upon which this error figure is based. The dotted lines in Figure 7.4a, 7.4b, and 7.4c represent the error of predicted value (on the regression line) and the actual score. These lines are getting shorter as the prediction gets better, and this improvement in prediction is also illustrated by the decrease in the variance figures we have created.

7.4.1f Least squares criterion. Finally, using the third prediction equation shown in Figure 7.4c, we notice that the dotted lines representing inaccuracy in prediction are generally getting shorter. This is reflected in a smaller variance of the estimate, which is again simply the sum of squared differences between actual and predicted scores averaged over the number of cases. This third prediction equation, $(Y' = 1.1 + 1.3(X))$, produces the smallest variance. It happens to be the best prediction, and the regression line in Figure 7.4c is called the "best fitting regression line of Y on X." It is *best* in the sense that the

---

*At this point your attention should again be called to the fact that a better estimate (unbiased estimate) of the population variance includes $N - 1$ in the denominator of the variance computed from sample data. The same principle applies to $s_{y \cdot x}$, which would have $N - 2$ in the denominator.

sum of squared deviations of scores around this line is the smallest it could be for any straight line and thus, this is called the **least-squares** regression line. It is important to notice that the deviations are all figured in terms of Y-scores, since that is the variable we are interested in predicting. Figure 7.5 shows the "least-squares" regression line for the situation where we are interested in predicting X-scores instead, and you will notice that a different equation is needed to minimize errors in predicting X from a knowledge of Y. It is generally true that two different regression equations can be computed for a given bivariate distribution, depending on which variable is to be predicted.

Computation of the coefficients for the least squares regression line is illustrated in Diagram 7.2. The numerator for b_{yx} is a value that expresses how well the two variables go together, and it is formed from the sum of the product of deviations of each score from its mean. The denominator is the sum of squares for the independent variable.

(7.10)
$$b_{yx} = \frac{\Sigma(X-\overline{X})(Y-\overline{Y})}{\Sigma(X-\overline{X})^2}$$

A more convenient formula for hand computation, using only the raw scores themselves, is given in Diagram 7.2.

7.4.1g Since the best-fitting regression line always goes through the point at the mean of both variables (note that this is true of Figures 7.4c and 7.5), the

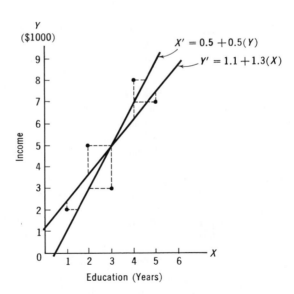

FIGURE 7.5 Least Squares Regression of Variable X on Variable Y taken from Data in Figure 7.4, Superimposed on the Regression Line of Y on X

DIAGRAM 7.2 Regression and Correlation Coefficients

To illustrate the computation of regression coefficients and the Pearsonian correlation coefficient, we will use the illustrative data from Figure 7.4. These are raw data, and $N = 5$.

(X) Education In Years	(Y) Income in $1000's	X^2	Y^2	$X \cdot Y$
1	2	1	4	2
5	7	25	49	35
3	3	9	9	9
2	5	4	25	10
4	8	16	64	32
$\Sigma X = 15$	$\Sigma Y = 25$	$\Sigma X^2 = 55$	$\Sigma Y^2 = 151$	$\Sigma XY = 88$
$\overline{X} = 3$	$\overline{Y} = 5$			

The Problem is to compute coefficients a_{yx} and b_{yx} in the following regression equation: $Y' = a_{yx} + b_{yx}(X)$, and compute the correlation coefficient r. There are a number of different approaches, including using a computer program (which is probably most common and useful), using definitional formulae given in this chapter, or the formula which uses data converted to z-score form prior to computations. Among the hand-computation procedures, the raw-data formulae used below seem most useful.

Step 1: Examine a scatter diagram of the data to determine whether or not a linear regression line is appropriate. Often computer programs provide scatter plots, and computer-driven mechanical plotters also are useful. If a correlation coefficient is low, one reason may be that the linear model does not fit the data very well. (See Figure 7.4.)

Step 2: Find the following sums from the raw data: $\Sigma X, \Sigma Y, \Sigma XY, \Sigma X^2, \Sigma Y^2$. If data are in a grouped frequency distribution form, then X will refer to category midpoints which have to be multiplied by category frequencies to form sums indicated by: $\Sigma fX, \Sigma fY, \Sigma fXY, \Sigma fX^2, \Sigma fY^2$.

DIAGRAM 7.2 *(Continued)*

Computing b_{yx}, the slope coefficient

The slope coefficient, or b-coefficient, of the regression equation expresses the number of units change expected in the dependent variable, Y, given a single unit increase along the scale of the independent variable. Expressed differently, it is the ratio of the co-variation between X and Y, over the variation of the independent variable. Variation is expressed in terms of variances, thus the b-coefficient can be expressed thus:

$$b_{yx} = \frac{\text{Covariance of } X \text{ and } Y}{\text{Variance of } X}$$

The variance of X may be computed by this familiar formula:

$$s_x^2 = \frac{\Sigma X^2 - (\Sigma X)^2/N}{N}$$

The covariance of X and Y may be computed by the following formula where XY is used instead of XX or X^2 and $(\Sigma X)(\Sigma Y)$ is used in place of $(\Sigma X)(\Sigma X)$ or $(\Sigma X)^2$. N is, of course, the number of cases (or pairs of scores).

$$s_{xy}^2 = \frac{\Sigma(XY) - (\Sigma X)(\Sigma Y)/N}{N}$$

Thus, b_{yx} could be computed from raw data by this process:

D 1

$$b_{yx} = \left[\frac{\Sigma(XY) - (\Sigma X)(\Sigma Y)/N}{N}\right] \Big/ \left[\frac{\Sigma X^2 - (\Sigma X)^2/N}{N}\right]$$

$$b_{yx} = \frac{N(\Sigma XY) - (\Sigma X)(\Sigma Y)}{N(\Sigma X^2) - (\Sigma X)^2}$$

Computing for this example, the process would be as follows:

$$b_{yx} = \frac{5(88) - (15)(25)}{5(55) - (15)^2} = \frac{440 - 375}{275 - 225} = \frac{65}{50} = +1.3$$

DIAGRAM 7.2 *(Continued)*

Computing a_{yx}, *the* Y-*intercept constant*

Since a regression line goes through the point which is at the mean of X and the mean of Y, we could substitute these values into the regression equation and solve for a_{yx}, as follows:

D 2
$$a_{yx} = \overline{Y} - b_{yx}(\overline{X})$$

or,

$$a_{yx} = \frac{\Sigma Y - b_{yx}(\Sigma X)}{N} = \frac{25 - 1.3(15)}{5} = \frac{25 - 19.5}{5} = 1.1$$

Thus:

$$Y' = 1.1 + 1.3(X)$$

Computing the Pearsonian Correlation Coefficient, r

The correlation coefficient is defined by the following formula as the ratio of the covariance of X and Y over the product of the standard deviations of X and of Y.

D 3
$$r = \left(\Sigma XY - \frac{(\Sigma X)\ (\Sigma Y)}{N} \right) \Bigg/ \sqrt{\frac{\Sigma X^2 - (\Sigma X)^2/N}{N}\ \frac{\Sigma Y^2 - (\Sigma Y)^2/N}{N}}$$

Simplified, this can be expressed as:

$$r = \frac{N\Sigma XY - (\Sigma X)\ (\Sigma Y)}{\sqrt{[N\Sigma X^2 - (\Sigma X)^2]\ [N\Sigma Y^2 - (\Sigma Y)^2]}}$$

Computing for this example:

$$r = \frac{5(88) - (15)\ (25)}{\sqrt{[5(55) - (15)^2]\ [5(151) - (25)^2]}} = \frac{440 - 375}{\sqrt{(275 - 225)\ (755 - 625)}}$$

$$= \frac{65}{\sqrt{6500}} = +.81$$

Pearson's r can be interpreted in a PRE sense by squaring its value, thus, $r^2 = .65$, meaning that 65 percent of the variation is "explained" by the linear relationship between these two variables.

a_{yx} coefficient can be computed by substituting these mean values in the regression equation and solving for a_{yx}, as follows:

(7.11)
$$a_{yx} = \overline{Y} - b_{yx}(\overline{X})$$

We have now established a simple formula which describes the **nature** of association between two variables and which thus permits us to make use of information about the independent variable to reach a better prediction of the dependent variable. The next problem is to devise a measure of degree of association which will express the proportionate reduction in predictive errors that this formula permits.

7.4.2 Product-Moment Correlation Coefficient (r)

The least-squares regression line computed in Figure 7.4c, permitted us to predict scores on the dependent variable, Y, with somewhat greater accuracy than we could achieve merely by predicting the overall mean of Y. We could say that the regression line helps us "explain" some of the variation in the dependent variable. This left, typically, some of the variation in Y unexplained, and the total of **unexplained** and **explained variation** equals the **total variation** of Y around its mean. This can be shown for Figure 7.4c, as follows:

Actual Scores		Predicted Y-Scores	Unexplained Variation	Explained Variation	Total Variation
X	Y	Y'	$(Y-Y')^2$	$(Y'-\overline{Y})^2$	$(Y-\overline{Y})^2$
1	2	2.4	.16	6.76	9
5	7	7.6	.36	6.76	4
3	3	5.0	4.00	.0	4
2	5	3.7	1.69	1.69	0
4	8	6.3	2.89	1.69	9
15	25	25.0	9.10	16.90	26

$$\overline{Y} = 5$$
$$26 = 9.10 + 16.90$$
$$\Sigma(Y-\overline{Y})^2 = \Sigma(Y-Y')^2 \quad +\Sigma(Y'-\overline{Y})^2$$
$$\frac{\text{Total}}{\text{Variation}} = \frac{\text{Unexplained}}{\text{Variation}} + \frac{\text{Explained}}{\text{Variation}}$$

The objective, of course, is to explain as much of the variation as possible. The square of the **Pearson product-moment correlation** coefficient expresses how well the linear regression line explains the variation in the dependent variable, as follows:

$$r^2 = \frac{\text{Explained Variation}}{\text{Total Variation}}$$

$$= \frac{\Sigma(Y'-\overline{Y})^2}{\Sigma(Y-\overline{Y})^2} \text{ which also equals } \frac{\Sigma(X'-\overline{X})^2}{\Sigma(X-\overline{X})^2}$$

The square of the Pearsonian correlation coefficient could also be expressed in terms of variances:

(7.12)
$$r^2 = \frac{s_y^2 - s_{y \cdot x}^2}{s_y^2} = 1 - \frac{s_{y \cdot x}^2}{s_y^2}$$

The numerator in these instances represents the explained variation using the informed guessing rule. The denominator represents the overall variation.*

The Pearsonian correlation, r, is a PRE measure. If squared (r^2), it expresses the proportionate reduction in error in predicting scores for the dependent variable, given the best-fitting linear regression equation rather than the overall mean to use in prediction. Since the regression of Y on X and the regression of X on Y both have the same amount of scatter around their respective

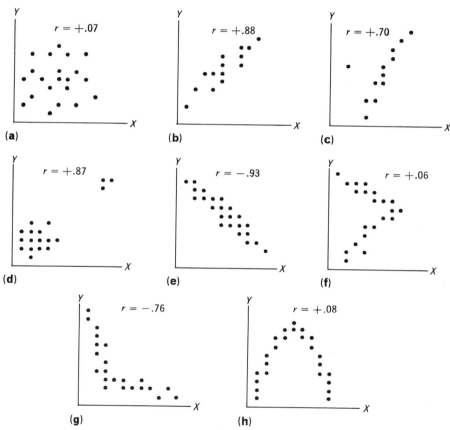

FIGURE 7.6 EXAMPLES OF SCATTERGRAMS AND CORRELATION COEFFICIENTS

*The ratio shown in the second formula above is called the coefficient of nondetermination, or K-squared, since it expresses the proportion of total variation which is unexplained by the regression equation. Thus, $r = \sqrt{1 - K^2}$.

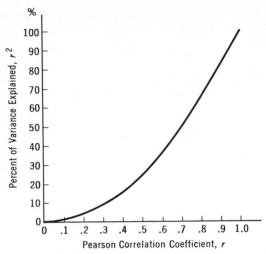

FIGURE 7.7 Percent of Variation Explained by Correlations of Different Sizes

regression lines, the same correlation coefficient will result from either predictive equation. Thus r is a *symmetrical* measure of degree of correlation. Expressed differently, r^2 indicates the proportion of the variation in one variable which is explained by its linear association with the other variable.

Usually, the correlation coefficient is expressed as r, the square root of r^2, although its interpretation is most useful in its r^2 form as indicated above. The actual computational formula of r is given in Diagram 7.2.

Pearson's r is a symmetrical measure of correlation between two interval variables. Its values vary from -1.0 to 0 to $+1.0$, indicating direction and strength of association. Figure 7.6 shows some of the values of r and their related scatter diagrams. Figure 7.7 shows the relationship between r and r^2, that is, the proportion of variation explained for different values of r. Notice in Figure 7.6 that a Pearson r may be quite small, not only where there is a random scattering of cases around the mean of the dependent variable, but also where there is an obvious association, yet the best-fitting straight line is no better than simply the mean of the dependent variable. Where the data are of a nature that is not too close to linear, an alternative, either Eta (symbolized E_{yx}, to be discussed in Section 7.4.4), or a curvilinear regression equation would be more appropriate.*

7.4.3 Another Way to Express Correlation and Regression

Where the data are expressed in terms of z-scores (standard scores), the regression equation and correlation coefficient can be expressed in a somewhat more direct form, although this is true only of the two-variable situation discussed in

*In some cases it is possible to find an equation which expresses in mathematical terms the nature of curvilinear associations. If such an equation can be found, its "fit" to the data can be described by the correlation coefficient, r, by simply substituting the predicted value from the curvilinear equation for the predicted value from the simple linear equation in formulas for Pearson's r, above.

this chapter. When scores are expressed as z_y and z_x rather than Y and X, the correlation coefficient is simply an average of the sum of products of z-scores.

(7.13)
$$r = \frac{\Sigma z_x z_y}{N}$$

BOX 7.4 STANDARD SCORES

If you are a bit rusty on z-scores, refer back to Section 5.4.7. Briefly, a standard score is the number of standard deviation units above or below the mean that a score falls. The mean of a distribution of z-scores is therefore, zero, and the standard deviation of a distribution of z-scores is one.

You will recall from univariate statistics that the sum of squares of z-scores equals the total number of cases, N. If a case has a score which is in the same relative position on both the X and Y variables (and thus the same sized z-score on each variable), the correlation coefficient will equal 1.0, since the numerator will then sum to N. To the extent that the standing of individuals is different on the two variables (as reflected in different z-scores), the numerator of the equation above will not reach N and the correlation will be less than 1.0. If one set of the z-scores tends to be negative, while the other tends to be positive, then the correlation coefficient is negative. The point is that here again a simple ratio expresses one feature of the relationship between two variables, a kind of ratio that was used (with somewhat different components, to be sure) for the arithmetic mean, the variance, ordinal measures of association, and now an interval-level measure of association.

The standard-score form of the simple regression equation is also interesting to note.

$$z'_y = r(z_x)$$

Here the estimated value of the z-score on variable Y can be computed from a knowledge of the z-score on variable X, if an adjustment is made. The adjustment corresponds to multiplication of the z_x score by a constant which (for one independent variable) is the Pearson correlation coefficient, r. This is called a **standardized regression equation**.

One final expression for the correlation coefficient will help show similarities between this measure and some of the other symmetrical measures. The Pearson correlation coefficient can also be expressed as a kind of average* of two asymmetric regression coefficients, b_{yx} and b_{xy}, as follows:

(7.14)
$$r = \sqrt{(b_{yx})(b_{xy})}$$

You will recall that this way of forming a symmetrical correlation coefficient out of two asymmetric measures was also possible for tau-b, which was expressed in terms of Somers' d as follows:

$$t_b = \sqrt{(d_{yx})(d_{xy})}$$

*This average is an example of the geometric mean discussed in Chapter 5.

7.4.4   The Correlation Ratio, Eta (E_{yx}), a Measure of Association for Non-Linear Relationships

If a straight line is not a very useful description of the nature of the association between two interval variables, and if there is no other formula for a curved line available, one might think of falling back on a procedure of making separate predictions of the mean of the dependent variable within categories of the independent variable. This situation is illustrated in Table 7.5.

Here the dependent variable is the number of wage earners in a family and the independent variable is family income, divided up into a series of categories. The overall mean number of wage earners for these data is 1.7 and this would constitute the minimum prediction rule we could use. On the other hand, we could improve our prediction by guessing the category mean for those cases falling in a given income category.

The errors of prediction are calculated as the squared difference between prediction and actual score on the Y-variable. Since there are, again, two predictions, the overall mean and the mean within categories, we have two error

TABLE 7.5 NUMBER OF EARNERS IN FAMILIES IN THE U.S. IN 1970 BY FAMILY INCOME

			(X) Family Income			
Under 1500	1500– 2999	3000– 4999	5000– 7999	8000– 11999	12000– 49999	50000 and up
1	0	0	0	0	1	1
1	0	1	1	1	1	
	2	1	1	1	1	
		1	1	1	1	
		2	1	1	2	
			2	1	2	
			2	1	2	
			3	2	2	
				2	2	
				2	2	
				3	2	
				3	2	
				4	2	
					2	
					3	
					3	
					7	
N_i = 2	3	5	9	14	18	1
$\overline{Y}_i$ = 1	0.7	1	1.4	1.7	2.2	1

$N = 52$
$\overline{Y} = 1.7$
N_i and $\overline{Y}_i$ refer to category size and mean.
N and $\overline{Y}$ refer to the overall size and grand mean.

TABLE 7.5 *(Continued)*

(Y) Number of Earners Per Family	Predictions Overall Mean	Predictions Category Mean	$(Y-\overline{Y})$	$(Y-\overline{Y})^2$	$(Y-\overline{Y}_i)$	$(Y-\overline{Y}_i)^2$
1	1.7	1	− .7	.49	0	0
1	1.7	1	− .7	.49	0	0
0	1.7	.7	−1.7	2.89	− .7	.49
0	1.7	.7	−1.7	2.89	− .7	.49
2	1.7	.7	+ .3	.09	+1.3	1.69
0	1.7	1	−1.7	2.89	−1.0	1.00
1	1.7	1	− .7	.49	0	0
1	1.7	1	− .7	.49	0	0
1	1.7	1	− .7	.49	0	0
2	1.7	1	+ .3	.09	+1.0	1.00
0	1.7	1.4	−1.7	2.89	−1.4	1.96
1	1.7	1.4	− .7	.49	− .4	.16
1	1.7	1.4	− .7	.49	− .4	.16
1	1.7	1.4	− .7	.49	− .4	.16
1	1.7	1.4	− .7	.49	− .4	.16
2	1.7	1.4	+ .3	.09	+ .6	.36
2	1.7	1.4	+ .3	.09	+ .6	.36
2	1.7	1.4	+ .3	.09	+ .6	.36
3	1.7	1.4	+1.3	1.69	+1.6	2.56
0	1.7	1.7	−1.7	2.89	−1.7	2.89
1	1.7	1.7	− .7	.49	− .7	.49
1	1.7	1.7	− .7	.49	− .7	.49
1	1.7	1.7	− .7	.49	− .7	.49
1	1.7	1.7	− .7	.49	− .7	.49
1	1.7	1.7	− .7	.49	− .7	.49
1	1.7	1.7	− .7	.49	− .7	.49
1	1.7	1.7	− .7	.49	− .7	.49
2	1.7	1.7	+ .3	.09	+ .3	.09
2	1.7	1.7	+ .3	.09	+ .3	.09
2	1.7	1.7	+ .3	.09	+ .3	.09
2	1.7	1.7	+ .3	.09	+ .3	.09
3	1.7	1.7	+1.3	1.69	+1.3	1.69
3	1.7	1.7	+1.3	1.69	+1.3	1.69
4	1.7	1.7	+2.3	5.29	+2.3	5.29
1	1.7	2.2	− .7	.49	−1.2	1.44
1	1.7	2.2	− .7	.49	−1.2	1.44
1	1.7	2.2	− .7	.49	−1.2	1.44
1	1.7	2.2	− .7	.49	−1.2	1.44
2	1.7	2.2	+ .3	.09	− .2	.04
2	1.7	2.2	+ .3	.09	− .2	.04
2	1.7	2.2	+ .3	.09	− .2	.04

TABLE 7.5   *(Continued)*

(Y) Number of Earners Per Family	Predictions Overall Mean	Predictions Category Mean	$(Y-\overline{Y})$	$(Y-\overline{Y})^2$	$(Y-\overline{Y}_i)$	$(Y-\overline{Y}_i)^2$
2	1.7	2.2	+ .3	.09	− .2	.04
2	1.7	2.2	+ .3	.09	− .2	.04
2	1.7	2.2	+ .3	.09	− .2	.04
2	1.7	2.2	+ .3	.09	− .2	.04
2	1.7	2.2	+ .3	.09	− .2	.04
2	1.7	2.2	+ .3	.09	− .2	.04
2	1.7	2.2	+ .3	.09	− .2	.04
2	1.7	2.2	+ .3	.09	− .2	.04
3	1.7	2.2	+1.3	1.69	+ .8	.64
3	1.7	2.2	+1.3	1.69	+ .8	.64
7	1.7	2.2	+5.3	28.09	+4.8	23.04
1	1.7	1.0	− .7	.49	0	0
				$\Sigma(Y-\overline{Y})^2=68.37$		$\Sigma(Y-\overline{Y}_i)^2=56.78$

Source: Data are fictitious in this example, but they follow the distribution of number of earners and family income for families in the U.S. in 1970. Each figure is approximately one million families. See U.S. Bureau of the Census, 1971, p-60, No. 80: Tables 1 and 19. The actual average number of earners per family for the above income categories from lowest to highest are: .76, .69, 1.05, 1.44, 1.73, 2.19, and 1.97. The overall average number of earners per family in the U.S. in 1970 was 1.68.

figures to contrast.* Eta squared (E^2_{yx}) is simply a ratio of these quantities, as defined below:

$$E^2_{yx}=1-\frac{\text{variance within categories of }Y}{\text{overall variance of }Y}$$

(7.15)
$$E^2_{yx}=1-\frac{\Sigma(Y-\overline{Y}_i)^2}{\Sigma(Y-\overline{Y})^2}$$

For these data, substituting figures from the second half of Figure 7.5, we get these computations:

$$E^2_{yx}=1-\frac{56.78}{68.37}=1-.83=+.17$$

$$E_{yx}=\sqrt{.17}=+.41$$

This is essentially the same type of measure as r, except that the mean within categories of the independent variable, rather than a regression equation, is used to form the predicted Y-score. Unlike r, however, there are two Etas de-

*The following formula for Eta (E_{yx}) is a more useful computational version.

$$E^2_{yx}=1-\frac{\Sigma Y^2-\Sigma n_k \overline{Y}^2_k}{\Sigma Y^2-N\overline{Y}^2}$$

where $n_k\overline{Y}^2_k$ is the product of the number of cases times the squared mean of the k th sub-category, and these products are then summed over all k sub-categories. ΣY^2 is simply the overall sum of squared scores and $\overline{Y}$ is the overall mean of Y.

pending upon which variable is predicted from which. E_{yx} is asymmetrical. E_{yx}^2 indicates the proportionate reduction in error in predicting the Y-scores if category means rather than the grand mean are predicted. E_{yx} varies in magnitude from 0 (in which case the grand mean is as useful in prediction as category means) up to +1.0, which indicates that category means permit exact prediction. The independent variable may be nominal, ordinal, or interval just as long as the dependent variable is interval-level. Thus sign of the association does not have meaning, or, in other words, E_{yx} will always be a positive value. Since r and E_{yx} have essentially the same form, and differ only in the source of the refined prediction, they can be compared directly. If, for a set of data where both measures are appropriate, E_{yx} is *larger* than Pearson's r, then one can infer that category means do not fall along a simple straight line, and thus, to some degree, the *nature of association is curved* or different from a straight line. If they are identical, then it is clear that subcategory means fall exactly along a least-squares regression line, such as we have developed here. (E_{yx} will never be smaller in magnitude than r.) This provides a rather handy basis for making inferences about the nature of an association.

7.5 THE CORRELATION MATRIX

Because of the interest in comparison, it is not at all unusual for investigators to compute a number of similar association measures, showing the relationship between all possible pairs of a set of items. An example of such a correlation matrix is shown in Table 7.6, where Pearsonian correlation coefficients are used. A matrix consisting of gammas (G's) or any other appropriate measure of association could be used, depending upon the variables being correlated.

In Table 7.6, Marsh and Stafford (1967) present a correlation matrix show-

TABLE 7.6 MATRIX OF CORRELATION COEFFICIENTS BETWEEN ELEVEN MEASURES OF ATTITUDE TOWARD WORK

(Items)	Attitudes	(Items)	1	3	10	12	13	11	9	4	5	7	8
1	Opportunity to be original and creative			.36	.29	.42	.49	.14	.25	.31	.24	.18	.27
3	Relative independence in doing my work				.31	.36	.36	.11	.26	.23	.25	.17	.21
10	Freedom from pressures to conform in my personal life					.35	.31	.26	.37	.17	.34	.23	.33
12	Freedom to select areas of research						.47	.12	.19	.18	.24	.20	.21
13	Opportunity to work with ideas							.29	.31	.29	.24	.24	.26
11	Opportunity to work with people								.43	.39	.35	.44	.27
9	Pleasant people to work with									.29	.45	.36	.39
4	A chance to exercise leadership										.26	.34	.31
5	A nice community or area in which to live											.45	.41
7	Social standing and prestige in my community												.36
8	A chance to earn enough money to live comfortably												

correlation of items 12 and 11.

Source: Marsh and Stafford, 1967. Used by permission. The study is based on an April, 1962 self-administered questionnaire given to some 51,505 professional, technical, and related workers in the U.S. This investigation selected 13 professional fields and limited the analysis to males who had M.A. or Ph.D. degrees. The correlations above are Pearsonian r's between responses to the different items on attitude toward work.

ing the correlation between answers to each pair of eleven questions given male professionals with an M.A. or Ph.D. degree. This was a part of a larger 1962 survey of the U.S. Some respondents were from academic settings and some were from private industry. Agreement with certain of the eleven items was thought to reflect a "professional" orientation and agreement with some of the other items was thought to reflect an "acquisitive" attitude. Examination of the correlation matrix, below, helped them see to what extent these two groups of items — "professional" and "acquisitive" — appeared in their data. Their basic hypothesis in this part of their study was that professionals in academic settings would be more likely to agree with "professional" items and disagree with "acquisitive" items. They thus expected to show that professional and intellectual values of work would serve as "compensation" for the lower incomes academics generally receive as contrasted to professionals in industry. An examination of the correlation matrix in Table 7.6 helped them identify items which could be used to measure these two attitudes.

Table 7.6 is organized so that each row refers to a different item (the numbers at the left are item numbers in the original questionnaire). Columns also refer to the same items, with each item (numbered as they are at the left of the table) being in a different column. The number at the intersection of a given row and column is a correlation coefficient showing the correlation between the items indicated by row and column headings. The items in Table 7.6 appear to fall into two clusters, one being a "professional" cluster including items about independence, creativity, and working with ideas, and the other being a cluster dealing with "acquisitive" items, such as pleasant work, community settings, and prestige.

For convenience, Marsh organized the attitude items into these two clusters and drew lines around the coefficients which refer to the intercorrelation of items within each cluster. The expectation is that items within a cluster would be more highly related than they would be with items in the other cluster. This appears to be the pattern in Table 7.6. Patterns in matrices such as this will be discussed later in this text. For now, the important point is to call your attention to the *comparative* use of measures of association. Notice that the Pearsonian correlation coefficient, *r,* which was used in this instance, is a symmetrical measure. Thus, only half of the matrix in Table 7.6 needs to be given, because the other half would be identical (*i.e.* the correlation between item 3 and item 1 is the same as the correlation of item 1 and item 3).

7.6   SELECTING A USEFUL MEASURE OF ASSOCIATION

There have been a number of criteria discussed which distinguish between the different measures of association and, in general, these are the differences which lead to the selection of one measure rather than another for a particular problem. In a given problem, certain features of these distinctions may take on more importance for the comparisons that are to be made and, thus, these criteria would override other kinds of differences.

BOX 7.5 THE THEME

In Chapters 6 and 7 we have attempted (a) to show how the various measures of association are relatively straightforward solutions to the problem of describing relationships between variables, and (b) to highlight some of the differences between them which may correspond closely to the substantive problem being investigated.

At this point, you should avoid looking for the easy or oversimplified ways to choose an appropriate measure. It might seem easy to recommend only one or two measures out of the variety we have discussed, but the decision on appropriate measures is not that mechanical. The selection depends upon the substantive problem being investigated as well as some "technical" characteristics of each measure. Part of the skill in creating and using statistical information lies in an understanding of the relationship between problem and tools.

7.6.1 Symmetry and Asymmetry

One of the important kinds of differences between coefficients is the way independent and dependent variables are handled. In problems where explanation and prediction of a dependent variable is of particular interest, such as that shown in the following arrow diagram, an asymmetric measure, if one is appro-

priate, would be most useful. If we are interested simply in the way variables covary or relate to each other, which might be the case when we examine the relationship between several indicators of the same concept, then a symmetrical measure provides this information.

Interrelation of social class measures.

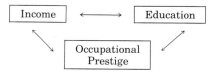

7.6.2 Level of Measurement

The meaning defined into variables also provides an important basis for selecting among the various measures. If only the categorical aspect of a variable is meaningful, then measures suitable for nominal variables would be most appropriate. Diagram 7.3 organizes the measures we have discussed, in this and the

DIAGRAM 7.3   Organization of Measures of Degree and Nature of an Association

Level of Measurement	MEASURES OF DEGREE OF ASSOCIATION		NATURE OF ASSOCIATION
	Symmetric	Asymmetric	
Nominal	C $\lvert Q \rvert$ T $\lvert \phi \rvert$ V	ϵ λ_{yx} t_y	percentaged table
Ordinal	Q G ϕ r_s t_a t_b	d_{yx}	percentaged table
Interval-Ratio	r	E_{yx}	$Y' = a_{yx} + b_{yx}(X)$ or some other, specified form.

last chapter, in terms of level of measurement. As in the case of univariate descriptive statistics, one might find occasion to use lower-level measures on data defined at a higher level of measurement, but this would result in the loss of information contained in the data — a result which is usually undesirable.

In some cases, level of measurement does not make much difference. In a 2×2 table, for example, Pearson's r, tau-b, and the phi coefficient are numerically identical. Spearman's rho is a Pearsonian correlation (a measure designed for interval variables) computed on ranks which may be assigned in the process of measuring an ordinal variable. Generally speaking, however, level of measurement *is* an important consideration in selecting and certainly in interpreting association measures.

7.6.3   Nature versus Strength of Association

Increasingly, sociology is addressing itself to the description of the amount of change a unit change in a given independent variable will likely produce in a dependent variable. "Powerful" variables in this sense are those which produce great effect, and this, of course, has both theoretical and practical importance. If this is the interest, then **regression coefficients** become more interesting than correlation coefficients, or **percentaged tables** more interesting than the various measures of association. Association measures express how well the variables go together, in the sense of scatter around a regression line, or errors in predicting a mode or rank order. A "clean" prediction might be possible in this sense, whenever a predictive variable is relatively so "powerless" that changes in it may not reflect or cause much change in the dependent variable. These two interests go together, of course, but in any given problem one may be more important than the other, and this may influence the selection of measures. Regression equation coefficients and the correlation coefficients are particularly useful if the main focus is on the potency of a variable.* On the other hand, if the nature of association is not relatively linear, then one either would have to find a curvilinear regression equation that fits the nature of the data or shift to some measure which is not tied to a specific nature of association.

7.6.4   Interpretation

Finally, measures of association differ in terms of the features of the association toward which they are most sensitive. Some measures (λ_{yx}, r, E_{yx} for example) are oriented toward predicting an optimal or central value of a dependent variable. Others (*e.g.*, t_y) are oriented toward predicting the distribution of a dependent variable. Some measures (*e.g.*, r, G) contrast observed data with a specific model of perfect association or independence. Some of these differences are organized in Figure 7.8.

Many of the measures discussed have PRE interpretations, which makes

---

*For other models expressing the impact of changes in one variable upon another, see Coleman (1964), Chapters 6 and 7.

Measure	Level of Measrmt.	Table Size	Range	Definition of a Perfect Assn.	Formula	Interpretation
ϵ epsilon	Nominal	$r \times c$	0 up to some x $x \leq 100\%$	More restrictive	Usually, difference of 2 extreme corner pcts. in properly percentaged table	A rough degree of association measure for a table. With care, one can compare across tables of the same size and similar marginals. In a 2×2 table, an epsilon of zero means no association. Asymmetric.
Yule's Q	Ordinal (Nominal if sign dropped)	2×2	-1 to $+1$ $(0$ to $+1)$	Less restrictive	$Q = \dfrac{ad - bc}{ad + bc}$ Hi $\begin{array}{c c} & \text{Lo} \ \text{Hi} \\ \text{Hi} & b \quad a \\ \text{Lo} & d \quad c \end{array}$	Symmetrical measure identical to gamma. Probability of like (opposite) ranking on two variables among cases ranked differently on both variables.
C	Nominal	$r \times c$	0 up to some x $x \leq 1.00$		$C = \sqrt{\dfrac{\phi^2}{1 + \phi^2}}$	Interpret in terms of magnitude.
ϕ Phi	Ordinal (Nominal if sign dropped)	2×2	-1 to $+1$ $(0$ to $+1)$	More Restrictive	$\phi = \dfrac{ad - bc}{\sqrt{(a+b)(c+d)(a+c)(b+d)}}$	Degree of diagonal concentration. A symmetrical measure.
λ_{yx} Lambda	Nominal	$r \times c$	0 to $+1$		$\lambda_{yx} = \dfrac{\Sigma m_y - M_y}{N - M_y}$	An asymmetric measure indicating the percent improvement in predictability of the dependent variable with information about the independent variable classification.
t_y	Nominal	$r \times c$	0 to $+1$	Y all one category for any given X	$t_y = \dfrac{E_1 - E_2}{E_1}$	PRE in predicting category placement. Asymmetric.

Measure	Level of Measrmt.	Table Size	Range	Definition of a Perfect Assn.	Formula	Interpretation
G Gamma	Ordinal	r × c	−1 to +1	Less restrictive.	$G = \dfrac{N_s - N_d}{N_s + N_d}$	A symmetric measure indicating the relative preponderance of like (unlike) ranked pairs among pairs ranked differently on both variables.
t_a Tau-a	Ordinal (No Ties)	r × c	−1 to +1		$t_a = \dfrac{N_s - N_d}{T}$	Symmetric. PRE among all pairs.
t_b Tau-b	Ordinal	r × c	−1 to +1		$t_b = \sqrt{d_{yx}\, d_{xy}}$	Symmetric. For square tables.
d_{yx} Somers'	Ordinal	r × c	−1 to +1		$d_{yx} = \dfrac{N_s - N_d}{N_s + N_d + T_y}$	Asymmetric. PRE among predicted pairs.
E_{yx} Eta	Interval Dependent Variable (Other may be nominal)	r × c	0 to +1	Line of category means.	$E_{yx}^2 = 1 - \dfrac{\sum Y^2 - \sum n_k \overline{Y_k^2}}{\sum Y^2 - N\overline{Y^2}}$	PRE Asymmetric.
r_{yx}	Both interval	r × c	−1 to +1	linear	$r = \sqrt{1 - \dfrac{S_{y \cdot x}^2}{S_y^2}} = \dfrac{\sum z_x z_y}{N}$	PRE. r^2 is the proportion of variation in one variable explained by linear assn. with the other. Symmetric.
r_s Spearman's rho	Ordinal	Two sets of N ranks 2 × c	−1.0 to +1	Identical ranks on two vars.	$r_s = 1 - \dfrac{6\sum D^2}{N(N^2 - 1)}$	Symmetric. Sensitive to large differences in ranks. D is difference between the two ranks for a given subject.

FIGURE 7.8 CHARACTERISTICS OF SELECTED MEASURES OF ASSOCIATION

them more convenient to use in research. Selection among these measures depends upon what one wants to treat "at risk." For asymmetric measures, such as Somers' d_{yx}, the at-risk pairs are pairs which are distinguishable on the independent variable. For gamma (G), they are pairs which are ranked differently on both X and Y variables. Other measures of association do not have PRE interpretations (*e.g.*, C, t_c) but can be interpreted in terms of magnitude between limiting values (often zero and 1.00).

Finally, some of the measures of association we have discussed are most suited to tables which have specific types of layout. Yule's Q and the Phi (ϕ) coefficient from Chapter 6, are oriented toward 2×2 tables, unlike most of the other measures. The contingency coefficient, C, is influenced by the number of rows and columns in a table. Tau-b (t_b) cannot achieve 1.0 in a table which is not square, and measures such as tau-b (t_b), Spearman's rho, and tau-a (t_a), for example, are especially sensitive to ties in data.

Another aspect of interpretability of a coefficient is its familiarity to an audience. At this point in sociology, coefficients such as Pearson's r, G, t_b, lambda (λ_{yx}), percentage difference (epsilon $-\epsilon$), and Somers' d_{yx} are relatively frequently seen in print. If an appropriate measure for one's data happens to be among these, the more widely known and used measure would probably be chosen.

As you might suspect, there is no flat rule which predetermines which coefficient *must* be used. Usually the choice is clear-cut — we would prefer a PRE measure, appropriate for the level of measurement of variables in the study, asymmetric if the independent/dependent role of variables is important, and sufficiently widely known so that it can be used to communicate information about the data. But often the choice is a matter of balance and judgment between coefficients which offer somewhat different strengths. The reasoning process in selecting a coefficient is closely tied to the logic and purpose of a research problem. Probably the only flat rule is that it is *not* appropriate to compute all possible measures and select one measure for the reason that it is numerically, the largest!

7.7 SOME CAUTIONS ABOUT THE INTERPRETATION OF ASSOCIATION MEASURES

The primary purpose of correlation coefficients is, of course, to aid in comparison. Generally we want to know the proportionate reduction in error which can be achieved in some defined respect by using one variable or another. Usually (or hopefully) the contrasts are suggested by some prior reasoning. We expect social class rather than toenail length to have something to do with the distribution of anomie, and a comparison of correlation coefficients bears this expectation out.

7.7.1 Causation and Association

There is sometimes a temptation to attribute more meaning to a measure of association than it really contains. This is particularly likely if the reasoning behind the investigation comes from an interest in explaining the causes of some phenomenon. If knowledge of social class reduces the errors of predicting alienation by quite a large amount, the temptation is to say that social class influences or causes alienation, simply on the basis of the correlation coefficient. Upon reflection, this is not appropriate at all. The correlation may well be the same between doorknob size and education of head of household and we would hardly want to conclude on this basis that knob size has anything particularly to do with education. Even asymmetric measures only state how measured variables relate in the data at hand.

The investigator's theory, however, may lead him to predict that there will be a certain kind of association in the data because of some hypothesized causal link between variables. The data may yield correlations which turn out to be close to predictions, and because of this he may feel that his faith in his theory is well founded, that one of the variables does cause the other to change as his theory stated, and that this is what the static correlation coefficients mean. The cause-effect argument is clearly *in his theory,* however, and *not* something that is included in the correlation coefficient itself. *Correlation is not causation.* More evidence than merely a correlation coefficient is needed to begin to have confidence in a conclusion that one variable influences another under certain conditions.*

7.7.2 Ecological Fallacy

Finally, there are some interpretative problems which arise essentially because an investigator is not clear about the kind of subject or case he is examining. This may be an important source of difficulty in sociology, since the field deals with many different levels of units, from dyads to individual people, to individual roles or self-concepts, to small groups or societies or groups within groups. Correlations between variables measured on *groups* are *not the same* as correlations measured on *individuals,* in spite of the fact that those individuals may form the groups. The error of inferring how two variables are related among *individuals* by examining the correlation of similar variables measured on *groups* is called the **ecological fallacy.**†

A classic example of this problem is illustrated in an article by W. S. Robinson (1950) in which he shows the relationship between "foreign-born" and "illiteracy." The correlation between percent foreign-born and percent illiterate was computed to be −.62, with these two variables measured on each of several regions of the United States. The correlation used geographic regions as the case. This means that the higher the percent of foreign-born in a region, the lower the percentage of "illiterate" we would expect. Does this mean that foreign-born *people* are less likely to be illiterate? No! The correlation between foreign-born or not, and illiterate or not, for individuals in the United States was

*Although one would expect a correlation between a causal variable and its effect, there are several other types of information which need to be examined before a casual interpretation of data begins to become useful. One needs to know time-order (that the cause occurred before the effect), and that the association could not be "explained away" by other factors. The next chapter deals with some of these questions.
†Some of the problems in inference between different levels of phenomena are nicely discussed in a research methods book by Matilda White Riley, (1973: see especially unit 12).

+.12, a low, positive association. In fact, there is little reason why there should be the same correlation between these variables at the group and individual levels. To start with, the variables are different. In one case they are percentage concentration of foreign-born or illiterates, and in the other case they refer to whether or not an individual is or is not foreign-born or illiterate. Secondly, it is quite possible that all of the foreign-born people are illiterate, or none of the foreign-born people are illiterate, in any given area with a given percentage of foreign-born and illiterate. The moral is the same one raised early in this volume: we must be clear about the meaning of statistical observations before statistical results can be meaningfully interpreted.

7.7.3 Built-in Correlations

One final set of alternative interpretations of measures of association should be mentioned before we close this chapter. The possibilities to be mentioned here flow fairly directly from the meaning of specific measures of association we have discussed, but they might be pulled together as a set of possible interpretations of associations. First, a measure of association may be low, not because two variables are not related in some way, but because they are not related in the way to which a given measure of association is sensitive. This was pointed out for Pearson's r, where strong curvilinear associations may show up as a low correlation because r is measuring fit to a simple straight line. It is usually a good idea to examine the nature of an association via a scattergram or table.

Secondly, an association could be "built in," if the original observations are not independent. For example, if a study of income and education of people were designed so that husbands and wives were both measured, then it is likely that some association between education and income would be observed, simply because these variables are probably related for husbands and wives. We would be able to handle the problem in this instance by separating out husbands and wives or by treating them as a pair. Built-in correlations could occur in other ways too—for example, in correlations between a score that is derived from answers to all items and a score that is derived from answers to a sub-set of the same items.

Finally, it is possible to have a correlation affected by a few very extreme cases (as shown for Pearson's r in Figure 7.6d), where, except for these extremes, there may be little or no association (or a very strong association) in the data. It is possible too, that an association may appear very weak (or strong) within a certain restricted range of the variables, but be quite different overall, or within other restricted ranges of the same variables. Unless we are particularly interested in some restricted range of values of a variable, it is good practice to be sure that the full range of possible scores is considered. Grouping variables (or truncating) could also have the effect of distorting a measure of association. This was illustrated in Table 6.1, but it applies to Chapter 7 as well.

7.8 SUMMARY

In this chapter we have developed a series of measures of degree of association for nominal, ordinal, and interval-level variables. In each case our concern was with developing a measure which could be interpreted as an indication of the proportionate reduction in predictive errors to be made by using information about an independent variable, as opposed to using only information about the dependent variable.

We could predict modes, either overall or within categories, for an independent variable. We could predict category placement of cases. We could predict rank orderings, either by chance, or by using a rule based on the direction of association. We could develop an equation to compute a predicted score and compare that prediction with the overall mean of the dependent variable. In each case the association measure amounted to a version of a ratio that expresses the reduction in errors made possible by improved information, as against the total of possible errors that could be accurately predicted.

These measures do not exhaust the range of possible coefficients, and the student may well be able to devise a new coefficient himself. The measures do have utility in sociology, however, because they permit comparisons between tables which would otherwise be difficult to make. By virtue of proper norming and proper selection of measures of association, an investigator is able to raise questions about how well his theory permits him to explain and predict some phenomenon of interest to him.

In addition to the theme of the ratio as a means by which many different kinds of valid comparisons are possible, there has been another theme in this chapter. It points back to the original ideas an investigator has in mind in examining data. Many of the differences in the array of coefficients we have presented are the result of the different kinds of information a collection of data may contain, which may be relevant to some problems and not to others. The difference between asymmetric and symmetric measures, for example, reflects the difference in interest in how the two variables go together, versus how well one variable permits us to predict or explain variation in a dependent variable. We would select between measures according to the nature of the association and, in fact, according to what we want to treat as a perfect association. Clear formulation of a research problem will usually permit a clear selection of the most appropriate coefficient.

Up to this point we have dealt with univariate distributions one by one, and then we compared central tendency and variation, for example, between univariate distributions. Then we packaged a series of these univariate distributions into a single table and developed an overall series of measures on the table itself as a whole. We are about to do this same type of thing again. We have discussed single bivariate distributions. Now we will begin to examine sets of bivariate distributions—one for each special condition or value of a further set of control variables. Then we will again ask whether there is some way to put all of these separate tables together into some overall comparison. At each step, we selectively ignore the more irrelevant information contained in data, and we focus an investigative light on those features which contain the comparative information which gives us the answers to the questions we ask.

CONCEPTS TO KNOW AND UNDERSTAND

PRE measures
regression equation
  intercept
  slope
  b-coefficient
  standardized regression equation
  scatter diagram
linear relationship
curvilinear relationship
nature of association
least squares criterion
standard error of estimate
explained variation
unexplained variation
total variation
lambda
asymmetric, symmetric relationships

concordant, discordant pairs
Kendall's tau-a
Kendall's tau-b
Somers' d
Goodman and Kruskal's tau-y
Gamma
Pearson's product-moment
  correlation r
Eta
Spearman's rho
correlation matrix
selecting appropriate measures
cautions
ecological fallacy
causation vs association
built-in correlations

PROBLEMS AND QUESTIONS

1. Compute Goodman and Kruskal's tau-y for Table 7.2, using "type of household" as the dependent variable and "marital status" as the independent variable. Discuss differences between this computation and the tau-y computed in the text and the two lambda's given in the text. What kinds of different information do each of these coefficients provide? Under what conditions would they be quite different from each other?

2. Develop an analytic organization of measures of association. As a start you might use the guides given in the text and consider the points mentioned in the section on selecting measures of association.

3. Find an interesting pair of scores measured on about 70 cases and compute correlation and regression coefficients. Create a scatter diagram, draw in the regression lines, and interpret the statistics you have computed.

GENERAL REFERENCES

Blalock, Hubert M., Jr., *Social Statistics,* 2nd edition, (New York, McGraw-Hill), 1972.
Costner, Herbert L., (ed.), *Sociological Methodology: 1971,* (San Francisco, Jossey-Bass), 1971.
  See especially the chapter (10) by Robert K. Leik and Walter R. Gove, "Integrated Approach to Measuring Association," which presents a more detailed treatment of the subject.

Mueller, John H., Karl F. Schuessler, and Herbert L. Costner, *Statistical Reasoning In Sociology*, 2nd edition, (Boston, Houghton Mifflin Company), 1970.
See especially Chapters 9, 10, and 11.

Freeman, Linton C., *Elementary Applied Statistics: For Students in Behavioral Science,* (New York, John Wiley and Sons), 1965.
See especially Section C.

Coleman, James S., *Introduction to Mathematical Sociology,* (New York, The Free Press of Glencoe), 1964.
See especially Chapters 6 and 7.

OTHER REFERENCES

Coleman, James S., 1964; see General References.

Costner, Herbert L. "Criteria for Measures of Association," *American Sociological Review,* 30 (June, 1965) p 341 – 353.

Freeman, Linton, *Elementary Applied Statistics for Students in Behavioral Science,* (New York, John Wiley and Sons), 1965

Furstenberg, Frank F., Jr., "The Transmission of Mobility Orientation in the Family," *Social Forces* 49 (June, 1971) p 598.

Hammond, Kenneth R., and James E. Householder, *Introduction to the Statistical Method,* (New York, Alfred A. Knopf), 1962, pp 212 – 214.

Haug, Marie R., and Marvin B. Sussman, "The Indiscriminate State of Social Class Measurement," *Social Forces,* 49 (June, 1971) p 559.

Hunter, Albert, "The Ecology of Chicago: Persistence and Change, 1930 – 1960," *American Journal of Sociology,* 77 (November, 1971) p 425 – 444.

Kim, Jae-On, "Predictive Measures of Ordinal Association," *American Journal of Sociology,* 76 (March, 1971) p 891 – 907.

Marsh, John F., Jr. and Frank P. Stafford, "The Effects of Values on Pecuniary Behavior: The Case of Academicians," *American Sociological Review,* 32 (October, 1967) p 743.

Riley, Matilda White, *Sociological Research: A Case Approach,* vol. 1, New York, Harcourt, Brace and World), 1963. See especially the commentary in unit 12.

Robinson, W. S., "Ecological Correlation and Behavior of Individuals," *American Sociological Review,* 15 (1950) p 351 – 357.

Rossi, Alice, "Status of Women in Graduate Departments of Sociology, 1968 – 1969," *American Sociologist,* 5 (February, 1970) p 4.

Somers, Robert H., "A New Asymmetric Measure of Association For Ordinal Variables," *American Sociological Review,* 27 (December, 1962), pp 799 – 811. See also original work by Kendall, Kruskal, and Goodman and Kruskal, cited in Somers' article.

U.S. Bureau of the Census, "Household Income in 1970" and "Selected Social and Economic Characteristics of Households," *Current Population Reports,* P-60, No. 79, (Washington, D.C.), 1971, p 17, Table 6.

———"Income in 1970 of Families and Persons in the United States," *Current Population Reports,* P-60, No. 80, (Washington, D.C.), 1971, Tables 1 and 19.

U.S. Department of Health, Education and Welfare, Public Health Service, "Children and Youth: Selected Health Characteristics," Series 10, Number 62, (Washington, D.C.), 1971, p 15, Table 3.

Yoels, William C., "Destiny or Dynasty: Doctoral Origins and Appointment Patterns of Editors of the *American Sociological Review,* 1948 – 1968," *American Sociologist,* 6 (May, 1971) p 135.

DESCRIPTIVE STATISTICS:
Three or More Variables

8

ELABORATING THE RELATIONSHIP BETWEEN TWO VARIABLES

8.1 EXAMINING RELATIONSHIPS BETWEEN VARIABLES

Up to this point we have been concerned with the relationship between two variables, often an independent and a dependent variable. The last chapter dealt with a variety of measures of the *nature* and *strength* of their relationship, and these measures were developed so that comparisons could be made either between bivariate associations, in studies involving different sub-groups, or between associations in studies involving different variables. In this chapter we will begin to introduce more systematic differences between tables whose coefficients we want to compare. In fact, we will begin to define sub-populations for which the basic relationship between the same independent and dependent variables can be examined from sub-population to sub-population. Careful comparison will permit us to draw conclusions about the effects of other variables on the *relationship* between the original pair of variables. Let us begin with an example.

8.1.1 Morale and Interaction — An Illustration of Elaboration

What happens to a person's involvement in society as he ages? Does he continue to be engaged pretty much the way he always has been in the round of social activities, perhaps substituting more leisurely for more strenuous pursuits; or does a person typically disengage from society in the normal sequence of his aging? One theory holds that people disengage from society as they enter old age, and that this is a mutually satisfactory process both for the individual and for his society. Such decreases in social interaction would have a positive or at least a minimal impact upon his level of morale or satisfaction. An alternative viewpoint is that individuals attempt to continue to be engaged as they were in middle age, although the form of social engagement may shift. In this view, declines in social interaction have the effect of decreasing the level of morale and satisfaction of an individual. Both lines of reasoning make predictions for the relationship between morale and degree of social interaction for people moving toward the end of life, and data supporting each viewpoint has been presented.

Mark Messer addressed himself to this problem and tried to examine the relationship between morale and interaction in somewhat greater detail (Messer, 1967). He reasoned on the basis of other research that the age concentration of the person's environment is a crucial factor which also has to be considered (*i.e.*, the extent to which older people live only with other older people or with people of a mix of different ages). There is reason to believe, for example, that social interaction rates are higher when a person is in an age-homogeneous environment. This may be because people prefer to interact with age peers. It has been argued that age grouping (especially in the socialization process of young people) helps support transitions from one role to another by insulating an individual from some of his other roles, which may be inconsistent with the new role, until the problems and strains of his role-transition are settled. If this is the case, Messer argues, high morale among those in an age-concentrated environment should be a function of the normative system that this concentration permits rather than a function of the social interaction of an individual. In a mixed-age environment, on the other hand, morale should depend upon a higher rate of social interaction.

To examine his ideas, Messer contrasted 88 older people living in the age-concentrated public housing project for the elderly in Chicago as against 155 elderly people living in a mixed-age public housing project. In each setting, however, he was interested in the relationship between morale and the degree of social interaction, and he expected a stronger positive association in the mixed-age setting. Table 8.1 presents his results.

Interestingly, it does appear that age concentration of the environment has an effect upon the relationship between morale and interaction. In fact, the percentaged tables show a very low and negative relationship between morale and interaction in the age-concentrated environment (Table 8.1b), but the two variables are positively associated in the mixed-age environment. His hypothesis about the effect of age-concentration seems to be confirmed.* The test of his ideas involved an examination of a relationship between two variables within the categories of a third variable. This leads to an important modification and possible linking of the two initial theories.

This kind of examination is called **elaboration** because a basic relationship of interest is examined under a variety of different conditions. In this instance, the introduction of the third variable into the analysis helped *specify*

---

*Messer's hypothesis was that social interaction is causally prior to morale, and he treats his data in these terms. It is possible, however, that morale may have some influences upon future interaction. The importance of theoretical ordering of variables for the way one conducts research will be emphasized later in this chapter in Section 8.2.3.

TABLE 8.1   Percent Distribution of Morale for Elderly in Public Housing

(a) PERCENT DISTRIBUTION OF MORALE BY SOCIAL INTERACTION

(Y) Morale	Interaction (X) Low	High	Total
High	14.3	28.2	21.4
Medium	58.0	50.0	53.9
Low	27.7	21.8	24.7
	100.0	100.0	100.0
	(119)	(124)	(243)

$$d_{yx} = .15$$

(b) PERCENT DISTRIBUTION OF MORALE BY SOCIAL INTERACTION AND AGE OF ENVIRONMENT

(T-1) AGE-CONCENTRATED ENVIRONMENT				(T-2) MIXED-AGE ENVIRONMENT			
(Y) Morale	Interaction (X) Low	High	Total	(Y) Morale	Interaction (X) Low	High	Total
High	26.7	25.9	26.1	High	10.1	30.3	18.7
Medium	60.0	50.0	53.4	Medium	57.3	50.0	54.2
Low	13.3	24.1	20.5	Low	32.6	19.7	27.1
	100.0	100.0	100.0		100.0	100.0	100.0
	(30)	(58)	(88)		(89)	(66)	(155)

$$d_{yx} = -.09 \qquad\qquad d_{yx} = +.25$$

Source: Messer, 1967. Used by permission of the publisher.

conditions under which the relationship would be strong or weak. This kind of examination is not at all uncommon in sociology, and the purpose of this chapter is to show some of these patterns of relationship among three or more variables, to look at some of the ways they might be summarized, and to investigate how the different patterns might be interpreted. Let us start with some of the basic terminology.

8.1.2   Total Tables and Conditional Tables

The overall association between two variables is called a *total association* of the two variables, or a **zero-order association.** Table 8.1a is an example of such a total association. Total tables include, as N, all of the available cases to be examined in terms of the pair of variables. As in the example above, however, analysis of an overall bivariate relationship is usually aided if the cases are divided up into sub-groups corresponding to categories of an additional variable. Tables showing the association between two variables within categories of other variables are called **conditional tables,** or conditional associations.* Table 8.1b

---

*In some texts the "conditional" table is called a "partial" table and the process is called "partialling." We will reserve the term "partial" for the summary coefficients used later in this chapter, which express the relationship between X and Y variables where the effect of a control variable (or variables) has been statistically removed.

BOX 8.1 BASIC IDEAS

Before you get into this chapter very far you should check yourself on the following ideas.

- association of two variables (Section 6.4)
- independent, dependent, and control variables (Section 2.1.4)
- measures of association (Sections 7.2 – 7.7)
- the idea of setting up important contrasts (Sections 3.1 and 3.2)

This chapter has two main parts. The first part deals with comparisons of contrasting associations, that is, associations in several bivariate tables. The second main part concerns ways to make a statistical summary over a set of bivariate tables. In between, topics on experimental design and theory are introduced. These topics are central to an understanding of where and why we would want to use elaboration, standardization, or partial correlation techniques in examining the relationship between three or more variables.

---

above shows two conditional tables. The additional variable that is introduced into the analysis as a basic split in the group of cases is called a "control" variable or "test" variable. We are interested in examining the basic relationship between two variables (X and Y) within categories of control variable(s)—(T). Each conditional table includes only cases which have the same value (or range of values within a category) on that control variable, and there is a different conditional table for each category of the control variable(s). This procedure "controls" or "takes out" variation in that additional variable, permitting a clear focus on the relationship between the original independent and dependent variables within any given table.

The *terminology* goes as follows:

zero-order	*No* control variables (*i.e.* no "test" factors). The basic relationship between two variables is examined *overall*.
first-order *conditional tables*	*One* control variable. The basic $X - Y$ relationship is examined within each category of the control variable.
second-order *conditional tables*	*Two* control variables. The basic $X - Y$ relationship is examined within categories created by all possible combinations of the categories of the *two* control variables.
third-order *conditional tables*	*Three* control variables. The basic $X - Y$ relationship is examined within categories created by all possible combinations of the categories of the *three* control variables.

etc.

TABLE 8.2 Other Tables Made from the First Order Conditional Tables Shown in Table 8.1, above.

(a) FREQUENCY DISTRIBUTION OF MORALE BY INTERACTION AND AGE ENVIRONMENT. Taken from Table 8.1, above.

AGE-CONCENTRATED ENVIRONMENT

(Y) Morale	Interaction–(X) Low	High	Total
High	8	15	23
Medium	18	29	47
Low	4	14	18
Totals	30	58	88

$$d_{yx}=-.09$$

MIXED-AGE ENVIRONMENT

(Y) Morale	Interaction–(X) Low	High	Total
High	9	20	29
Medium	51	33	84
Low	29	13	42
Totals	89	66	155

$$d_{yx}=+.25$$

(b) FREQUENCY DISTRIBUTION OF MORALE BY INTERACTION.

(Y) Morale	Interaction–(X) Low	High	Total
High	17	35	52
Medium	69	62	131
Low	33	27	60
Total	119	124	243

$$d_{yx}=+.15$$

(c) FREQUENCY DISTRIBUTION OF MORALE BY AGE ENVIRONMENT.

(Y) Morale	Age-Environment–(T) Concentrated	Mixed	Total
High	23	29	52
Medium	47	84	131
Low	18	42	60
Total	88	155	243

$$d_{yt}=+.12$$

A second-order conditional table would be one in which, for example, morale and interaction (the basic relationship of interest in Table 8.1) were examined in each category of age-concentration of environment and in public *vs.* private-owned categories of housing. The basic table would then be examined separately for these four categories: (a) age-concentrated public housing, (b) age-concentrated private housing, (c) mixed-age public and (d) mixed-age private housing.* Thus there would be only four tables to compare, since there are only two categories of each control variable.

In general, a statistical analysis of the relationship between two variables

*The four conditional tables in this example could be increased if the control variables had more categories than two each. If one has three categories and the other has four, then there would be $3 \times 4 = 12$ conditional tables to examine, and all 12 tables would be second-order conditional tables because they

TABLE 8.2 *(Continued)*

(d)   FREQUENCY DISTRIBUTION OF INTERACTION BY AGE ENVIRONMENT.

(X)	Age Environment—(T)		
Interaction	*Concentrated*	*Mixed*	*Total*
High	58	66	124
Low	30	89	119
Total	88	155	243

$$d_{xt}=+.23$$

(e)   FREQUENCY DISTRIBUTION OF MORALE BY AGE ENVIRONMENT CONTROLLING FOR INTERACTION.

	Interaction—(X)			
	Low Age Environment (T)		High Age Environment (T)	
(Y) *Morale*	*Concentrated*	*Mixed*	*Concentrated*	*Mixed*
High	8	9	15	20
Medium	18	51	29	33
Low	4	29	14	13
	30	89	58	66

$$d_{yt}=+.28 \qquad\qquad d_{yt}=-.07$$

(f)   FREQUENCY DISTRIBUTION OF INTERACTION BY AGE ENVIRONMENT CONTROLLING FOR MORALE.

	Morale—(Y)					
	Low Age Environment (T)		Medium Age Environment (T)		High Age Environment (T)	
(X) *Interaction*	*Concentrated*	*Mixed*	*Concentrated*	*Mixed*	*Concentrated*	*Mixed*
High	14	13	29	33	15	20
Low	4	29	18	51	8	9
	18	42	47	84	23	29

$$d_{xt}=+.46 \qquad\qquad d_{xt}=+.22 \qquad\qquad d_{xt}=-.04$$

Source: Data from Table 8.1 (Messer, 1967).

proceeds by introducing control variables one at a time, starting from the original zero-order table and proceeding to first-order conditional tables and then to second-order conditional tables, etc. All first-order tables are examined, then second-order, etc.

resulted from a combination of two control variables. In general, the number of conditional tables equals the product of the number of categories of all control variables. Obviously, the higher the order of the conditional tables, the more exacting and refined the analysis, and also the more cases one needs to include in a study to "fill up" the conditional tables. It is a general practice not to compute percentages where the base of the percentage is less than, say, 15 or 20, because such percentages would ordinarily be too unreliable (a topic for consideration in the field of inferential statistics). Where many control variables are used, alternative ways to handle the problem which require fewer cases are usually used. Some of these will be discussed later in this chapter and in the next.

As Table 8.2 illustrates, a number of different total and conditional associations can be created from the basic information given in higher order conditional tables in Table 8.1b (but one cannot create higher order tables out of lower order tables). For example, from the first order conditionals shown in Table 8.1b and reproduced in Table 8.2 as a frequency distribution, we could create three total associations: (a) one between morale and the degree of social interaction, (b) another between age concentration of environment and morale, and (c) a third between age concentration of environment and degree of social interaction. Notice that these total tables are created out of the marginals of the first order conditional tables or, in the case of Table 8.2b, by adding together the two conditional tables cell by cell.

Table 8.2c is created by simply taking the row marginals for the age-concentrated and for the age-mixed environments in Table 8.2a and using these as the frequencies in columns of Table 8.2c. All 243 cases are classified in this total table. Table 8.2d is made up from the column marginals of Table 8.2a and again, all 243 cases appear in this total table.

Table 8.2e is another rearrangement of Table 8.2a. In this case, the control variable is social interaction and the basic relationship under examination is morale and age-concentration. In Table 8.2f, the basic relationship of interaction and age homogeneity of environment is examined within categories of the morale variable. Although 8.2e and 8.2f could be created from these same data, they would not be of central interest to Messer because they do not permit him to focus readily upon the relationship of morale and social interaction, the two key variables in Messer's study. These examples do begin to illustrate, however, the variety of ways a set of data may be examined and, hopefully, the importance of being clear about what it is that we are interested in studying.

8.1.3   The Role of Theory

What other variables may help explain the relationship between morale and interaction? Probably income, sex, cultural background, age, experience in other kinds of interaction settings, whether one is married or not, etc. The list could be rather long. Just which variables to pick is a serious problem and largely unsolvable without a heavy reliance upon prior theoretical work and results of research aimed at explanation of phenomena in a certain area of interest. Clearly, "toe-nail length" would be ruled out immediately as a general explanation of the relationship of morale and interaction. The role of some of the other variables mentioned above is not as clear-cut, and careful theoretical work would point the way toward finding significant variables. In Messer's research he was able to draw upon three kinds of previous theory, the disengagement theory, the activity theory, and ideas which relate age homogeneity to satisfaction and morale. An understanding of these ideas played a critical role in specifying important variables to control and the way results should be interpreted. Without this kind of starting point, an investigator would hardly be able to pick a relevant independent variable, let alone select those which are relevant from an infinity of variables which could be measured and used as control conditions. Even in very small studies, the possible combinations of variables becomes very large indeed, and as purely a practical matter, theoretical guidance in selection of relationships and control conditions becomes important.*

Research which is able to contrast two theories purporting to explain the same phenomenon is particularly fruitful for building scientific knowledge. Usually, however, research leads to an extension of a theory, to an addition of some condition under which the theory is found to lead to somewhat different predictions, or to the refinement of measurements and of "scope conditions" of a theory (*i.e.* the class of phenomena to which the theory pertains). Much research is of an exploratory nature (as sharply opposed to "sloppy" or unplanned investigation), especially when explicit theories have not been developed.† But whether theories are explicit or not, investigators make use of theoretical knowledge in selecting variables and planning their analysis. The more clearly set out these ideas are, the more fruitful the analysis.

The **theoretical order** of variables is important in interpreting the outcome of the process of elaboration. An independent variable, if it is thought of theoretically as a causal variable, comes before the dependent variable (*i.e.*, it changes first) in any time sequence. The "test factor" or control variable, however, may have its effect at different points in time relative to the independent and dependent variables. If a test factor has its effect *before* both independent *and* dependent variables, it is called an **antecedent** test factor. Here is an example:

SEX	SOCIAL INTEGRATION	SUICIDE
(T) ⟶	(X) ⟶	(Y)
Antecedent Variable	Independent Variable	Dependent Variable

If it has its effect *after* the independent *and* dependent variables, it is called a **consequent** test factor, as in this example:

NO. OF DELINQUENT FRIENDS	NO. OF DELINQUENT ACTS SELF-REPORTED	NUMBER OF TIMES ARRESTED
(X) ⟶	(Y) ⟶	(T)
Independent Variable	Dependent Variable	Consequent Variable

If the test factor has its effect *after* the independent variable but before the dependent variable, it is called an **intervening variable** or intervening test factor as below:

NO. OF DELINQUENT FRIENDS	PARENTAL SUPERVISION	SELF-REPORTED NO. OF DELINQUENT ACTS
(X) ⟶	(T) ⟶	(Y)
Independent Variable	Intervening Variable	Dependent Variable

The basic dependent variable of interest will be referred to as variable-Y in this chapter. Variable-X will be the main independent variable of interest, and vari-

---

*For example, in a modest study with only 5 variables, each having 5 categories, there are 10 zero-order tables, 150 first-order conditional tables, 1500 second-order tables, etc. Needless to say, typical research involves many more variables than five, and the problem quickly becomes one of avoiding irrelevant tables and selecting relevant ones.

†There are a number of excellent discussions on theory, on theory construction, and on the role of research. See especially Reynolds, 1971, Blalock, 1969, and Stinchcombe, 1968.

able-T will be used for the control or "test" variable. Where it is important to specify the category of the test variable, we will use subscripts such as: T_1, T_2, etc. The relationship between Y and X within category T_1, then, may be symbolized as: $YX{:}T_1$.

Drawing an arrow diagram of the relationships between variables included in a study is often a useful device for clarifying both the theory and the kinds of statistical analysis needed to answer a research question. For example, in a study of the relationship of organizational involvement and political participation, William Erbe (1964) surveyed the available research literature which suggested that two other variables were relevant. The theoretical relationships between variables used to guide his study were drawn out as follows:

The above model immediately indicates the ordering of the variables, shows which are intervening, and suggests the apparent necessity of taking account of both social class and alienation in examining the "involvement-political participation" relationship.

As we shall see, the theoretical ordering of variables also has a key role to play in the interpretation of results. Virtually identical statistical results may be interpreted as evidence that an hypothesized causal link is spurious, that there is evidence of a causal sequence, or evidence of independent influence, depending upon the ordering of variables.

In many cases, of course, the time order of variables is established simply by the logic of the measurement or the type of variable. If there is any causal relationship between ethnic group and attitudes, the group membership probably is the causal factor. On the other hand, many variables are not clearly time-ordered, especially when the investigator takes measurements of all variables at the same point in time. Where this confusion of time order is likely to occur, an investigator would normally attempt to gather specific information about time order for the effects of the variables he wants to study.

Time order could be established by gathering data at two or more points in time. In voting studies, for example, an investigator may create a "panel," or sample of individuals, who are questioned each month for the two or three months before an election. Measures of attitudes, for example, at "time-point one" could be related to attitudes at "time-point two" and the time order would be clear. This is called a **panel study** design. Other **longitudinal** designs are used, for example, in the study of families or aging individuals over time. Sometimes it is sufficient to ask individuals to report on past events or to use records to establish the time order of variables.*

The centrality of theory as a guide to analysis (and research as a guide to

*Additional information on panel studies and ways they may be statistically examined may be found in Riley, 1963: v. I, 559, in Zeisel, 1957: Ch. 10, and in Lazarsfeld and Rosenberg, 1955:231.

development of theory) will become more evident as we proceed through this examination of statistical elaboration.*

8.1.4 Analysis of Conditional and Total Associations

The statistical analysis of *each* conditional table does not differ in any important respect from the analysis one might do on a total association between two variables. There is the full range of measures of association discussed in Chapter 7 from which to choose, and selection depends upon the character of the variables and the problem at hand. In addition to strength and direction of association, one should examine the *nature* of each association. The only difference in dealing with conditional tables is that comparison between conditional tables takes on a more systematic character than it might otherwise. Tables shown above could be examined in terms of, say, Somers' d_{yx} and percentages. In Table 8.1b the association in the two conditional tables is $d_{yx}=-.09$ in the age-concentrated environment and $d_{yx}=+.25$ in the mixed-age environment. The stronger association between these two variables exists in only one of the two conditions — namely the age-heterogeneous condition — an outcome concerning the relationship between morale and interaction which Messer's logic had predicted.

The relationship in the conditional tables, however, is only part of the story. The more complete story would include the overall relationship in the three total associations (Tables 8.2b, 8.2c, and 8.2d) as a further basis for interpreting these data. Notice, for example, that the original zero-order association between interaction and morale (Table 8.2b) is positive but relatively weak $(d_{yx}=+.15)$. From a look at the conditional tables (Table 2a), it is clear that part of the reason for this overall weakness is that a weak negative association in one conditional (*i.e.* the age-concentrated group) is thrown together with a stronger positive association in the other conditional table (*i.e.* the mixed-age group), and they tend to cancel each other out (in Table 8.2b) to some extent.

Notice, too, that the control variable, T, is positively related to each of the main variables, morale and interaction. The Somers' d for the table of age environment and morale (Table 8.2c) is $d_{yx}=+.12$, and the association of age environment and interaction (Table 8.2d) is $d_{yx}=+.23$. Part of the association observed between morale and interaction is due to the correlation of each of these two variables with the test factor. These outcomes are organized, below.

$\underline{d_{yx}=+.15}$ *Original total association* between morale and interaction is a result of these:

             Conditional Associations:

$d_{yx}=-.09$ a) The association of morale and interaction in the age-concentrated environment

$d_{yx}=+.25$ b) The association of morale and interaction in the mixed-age environment

             Total Associations With the Test Factor:

$d_{yx}=+.12$ c) The association of morale with the test factor, age environment

$d_{yx}=+.23$ d) The association of interaction with the test factor, age environment

---

*A classic statement on the bearing of theory on research and vice versa is made by Merton, 1957:pt. I.

8.1.4a The Lazarsfeld Accounting Formula. The relationship between a total association, a set of conditionals, and another set of total associations has been pointed out in the sociological literature by Paul Lazarsfeld, and it is sometimes summarized in what is called the **Lazarsfeld accounting formula.** This equation states that a total association between X and Y can be accounted for by the conditional associations of X and Y within categories of T (test variables), plus total associations of X and Y separately with the test variables. For the three-variable situation where the variables are all dichotomies and where the degree of association is expressed in terms of delta (Δ),* the Lazarsfeld accounting formula is as follows:

$$\Delta \, XY = \Delta \, XY{:}T_1 + \Delta \, XY{:}T_2 + \frac{N_1 + N_2}{(N_1)(N_2)} (\Delta \, XT)(\Delta \, YT)$$

If the morale variable in Table 8.2 were grouped into only two categories (by putting the "high" and "medium" categories together, for example) and the expected cell frequencies were computed as discussed in Chapter 6, the resulting Δ values would be as follows:

$$+3.62 = -2.13 + 4.88 + \frac{243}{(88)(155)} (3.73)(13.09)$$

$$3.62 = -2.13 + 4.88 + .87$$

Using Δ on a fourfold table, this situation works out nicely: the total association at the left equals the sum of terms expressed in the equation at the right. In general, however, the weighting factor is not resolved, either for other measures of association or for tables larger than 2×2 tables.† The usefulness of Lazarsfeld's formula holds, however; associations between two variables can be accounted for by a set of conditional and total associations.

An examination of the accounting formula quickly yields a rich set of possible outcomes.‡ An association may or may not exist in the total table which is cross-classifying an independent and a dependent variable. If no association exists, then the right-hand side of the Lazarsfeld formula would have to "balance out" to zero. This might happen if the conditional tables yielded a negative and

---

*Recall from Chapter 6 that delta (Δ) is simply the difference between observed and expected cell frequencies. In a 2×2 table the size of Δ is the same, regardless of which cells are contrasted (although the sign may be different). It is traditional (consistency is necessary for the Lazarsfeld equation to work out) to compute Δ on a 2×2 table by subtracting the expected from the observed frequency for only *one* cell, the high-X, high-Y cell in a table. Delta is not a normed measure of association, so it is generally not used except to illustrate how Lazarsfeld's formula works out numerically.

†A slightly different approach using Yule's Q is described in Davis, 1971:188.

‡In addition to the outcomes which are discussed in the chapter, there are other outcomes which should be noted because they are important, although of a different type than those discussed here. First, it is possible that the observed association between two variables is simply due to *chance*. This would be a possible outcome where the data are gathered by sampling procedures from some population. There is some chance that the sample will misrepresent the population from which it is drawn and show an association between two variables when, in fact, in the population there is none. Secondly, an observed association may be due to the research process itself. If observations are related rather than independent, the observed association could be accounted for largely by whatever research steps led to this relatedness. Generally speaking, an investigator tries to design his research so that observations are, in fact, independent observations. Chance can be described by techniques in the field of inferential statistics (see H. J. Loether and D. G. McTavish, *Inferential Statistics for Sociologists*) and they are minimized by careful sampling and the use of relatively large samples.

positive association which, added together in a total table, cancelled each other out. Looking at the right-hand side of the formula, an association may be shown in the total tables, in the conditional tables, or in both. Furthermore, the conditional tables may show the same strength and direction of association, or they may differ among themselves, with some showing a stronger association than other conditional tables, or some showing associations with a different direction or nature than others.

8.2 PATTERNS OF ELABORATION

The interpretation of patterns of outcome revealed by the accounting formula will be illustrated and discussed in the sections that follow.

8.2.1 Specification

Under what conditions does a relationship hold up? Stated differently, under what situations can a given variable (independent variable) explain why a dependent variable is distributed as it seems to be? In Messer's study, discussed above, we used some ideas from theory to suggest a variable, age-concentration of the environment of a person, which we then introduced into the analysis as a control or test factor. The result was that under one condition of the control variable, the relationship remained strong and, in fact, increased but under the other condition the relationship between morale and interaction changed (dropped) markedly. This is a pattern of *specification*. There is a **statistical interaction** between the control variable and the independent variable, and this specifies the level of the dependent variable. The outcome is different for different categories of the test variable and this has helped specify (at least one of the) conditions under which the relationship is maintained.

What other conditions govern the relationship of morale and interaction? We can think of several likely ones just on the basis of our general experience — physical health, whether the move to public housing was voluntary or not, general orientation to life in the past, etc. Does the relationship hold up for younger people? For people in other cultures? For both men and women? These questions suggest a line of further investigation similar to that conducted by Messer. We could select further test factors and examine them for *differences* between the conditional tables.

8.2.2 The Causal Hypothesis

Several astute observers have noticed a curious relationship between dollar loss from fires and whether or not firemen happen to be at the fire. The association, as shown below, is positive, rather strong, and seems to raise a number of embarrassing questions about the activities of those fire departments upon which these data are based. As the hypothesis goes, firemen, rather than reducing the

loss from fire, are actually increasing that loss. Graphically, the hypothesis can
be shown thus:

$$(X) \longrightarrow (Y) \qquad\qquad Model\ 1$$

Number of   Dollar Loss
Firemen at   from the Fire
the Fire

In these data 143 fires are examined in terms of the number of firemen present
and the ultimate fire loss in dollars.

Dollar Loss from the Fire	(X) Number of Firemen None	One+	Total
Over $500	24	61	85
$500 or less	42	16	58
Total	66	77	143

$$Q = +.74$$

Do these data prove that firemen cause fire loss?

While the data are sufficient to raise the suspicions of those who see them,
they are not, for a number of reasons, sufficient to settle the issue. First, there
are the usual questions about bias in collecting the data, sampling procedures,
adequacy of the measurement procedures, and computational accuracy. Secondly,
there is the issue of time-ordering of the variables. Do we have evidence that
the firemen arrived in droves *before* the fire loss became severe? Thirdly, the
idea of *causal* influence includes more than one association. Can the dependent
variable be altered by manipulating the independent variable? Is this possible
under all conditions? Finally, we would expect that the relationship shown
above, if it is indeed a causal one, would be maintained even if other *antecedent*
variables are controlled—even within the categories of other variables.* Is this
the case here?

8.2.2a Testing for Spuriousness. We might suspect that if we could
somehow control for the initial size or threat of the fire, then we could explain
away the apparent support for the causal hypothesis. If, in controlling for this
test variable, the association between loss and number of firemen is *maintained,*
then our causal interpretation would be still *not dis*confirmed, and we would
continue to hold our initial causal model. On the other hand, we might expect
that firemen are rarely called for small fires, and almost always called for larger
ones, so that we would observe an overall association simply because firemen

*The notion of "cause" is a theoretical notion about the way some set of variables are related. A causal
relationship is said to exist if: (a) the independent variable has its effect before, in time, the dependent
variable, (b) there is an association between the independent variable and the dependent variable, and
(c) if this relationship is maintained even when antecedent test variables are controlled. It is often difficult to argue convincingly that all potential test factors have been introduced, and sometimes the time-
order of variables is at issue, particularly in survey research. Generally, too, there are conditions under
which the relationship holds and conditions where it does not. What seems well established today may
well be modified or explained away tomorrow, but this is the state of any explanatory theory in any
field.

and loss are related to the initial threat from the fire (its initial size). We thus have a *competing model* to the causal one above. This model is also a causal model, but it relates each of the original variables to an antecedent variable, and not to each other, as below:

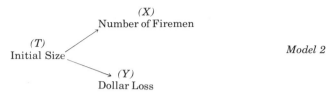

Model 2

Under this model, we would expect to be able to show that by controlling for the test factor, the association of X and Y would drop from its overall association of $Q=+.74$ down to no association, $Q=0.0$. If this happens, we will say that our initial causal interpretation about the link between number of firemen and dollar loss is a **spurious interpretation,** and that Model 2 is a better explanation of the data than Model 1. Let us look at the data.

Table 8.3 shows the relationship of density of firemen and dollar loss separately for the smaller and the larger fires. This is clearly an antecedent variable, because it is measured as the state of the fire prior to any call for firemen and prior to any final determination of loss. The association in the conditional tables does drop to zero. Model 2 works better than Model 1 for these data.

What happened to the association that once was so strong? Lazarsfeld's accounting formula helps explain. If there is an initial association between X and Y and if the association does not exist in any of the conditional tables, then it must exist in the other total associations of each of the other variables and the test variable. This is, in fact, the case, as shown in Table 8.3. Computing delta for these data, the Lazarsfeld equation is as follows:

$$15.2 = 0.0 + 0.0 + \frac{143}{(55)(88)}(27.7)(18.6)$$

Notice that the two conditional tables, added together, do add up to the total association originally observed, and the other total tables can be created from the marginals on the pair of conditional tables in Table 8.3.

This pattern of outcome, when controlling for an antecedent variable, is called "spurious" because the initial causal interpretation of the X-Y relationship is not borne out in these data, and the conditional associations drop to zero. This is another common type of analysis—the search for test factors which might show an hypothesized causal relationship to be spurious. This is the second pattern which would lead an investigator to control for other variables in the process of examining the relationship between two variables.

How much does the association have to drop in the conditional associations before we would conclude that the causal interpretation is spurious? This is hard to say. Any general drop would mean that the test factor helps account for some of the observed, zero-order association between the independent and dependent variables. The more the association drops in the conditional associations, the more the association could be attributed to the test factor. Usually the

TABLE 8.3 Conditional and Total Tables for the Fireman Example*

a FIRST-ORDER CONDITIONAL TABLES

(T-1)
SMALL SIZED FIRE
(X)

(Y) Dollar Loss	Number of Firemen None	One+	Total
Over $500.	4	1	5
$500. or Less	40	10	50
Total	44	11	55

$Q = 0.0$

(T-2)
LARGE SIZED FIRE
(X)

(Y) Dollar Loss	Number of Firemen None	One+	Total
Over $500.	20	60	80
$500. or Less	2	6	8
Total	22	66	88

$Q = 0.0$

b TOTAL TABLES

(T)
Fire Size

(Y) Dollar Loss	Small	Large	Total
Over $500.	5	80	85
$500. or Less	50	8	58
Total	55	88	143

$Q = +.98$

(T)
Fire Size

(X) Number of Firemen	Small	Large	Total
One or more	11	66	77
None	44	22	66
Total	55	88	143

$Q = +.85$

*Data are fictitious.

results are somewhat mixed, and an investigator has to be satisfied with the conclusion that there are several contributing factors to an adequate explanation of the distribution of a dependent variable.

When have sufficient control variables been introduced to assure us that a causal interpretation is the best interpretation? There is never a guarantee that this process is at an end. Many of the advances in the theory of an area come about by introducing a further test factor which alters a favorite causal interpretation. With a reasonably well thought out theory, we can be more confident that all *relevant* test factors have been examined, but this is no ultimate proof or guarantee that controlling on some other variable will not show that a long-held causal hypothesis is, indeed, spurious.

8.2.3   A Causal Sequence of Influence

Why do people plan to vote the way they do? How can we explain their political behavior? This question was raised by Lazarsfeld and others in their research report, *The People's Choice.** They hypothesize that a person's placement in the social class structure of his society explains voting intentions, but that this happens because higher social class individuals are more interested in politics, and this leads them to be more likely to plan to vote. It is a causal sequence from social class standing (as measured here by education level) to interest in politics to vote intentions.

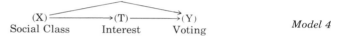

<table>
<tr><td>(X) ─────────→</td><td>(T) ─────────→</td><td>(Y)</td><td rowspan="3">Model 3</td></tr>
<tr><td>Social Class</td><td>Political</td><td>Voting</td></tr>
<tr><td>(Education)</td><td>Interest</td><td>Intentions</td></tr>
</table>

An alternative explanation might be that social class influences political interest but that it also has an independent effect on voting intentions. This could be shown as follows:

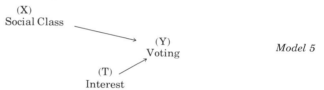

(X) ────→(T)────→(Y)			*Model 4*
Social Class Interest Voting			

A further competing model might be that social class and political interest have independent effects on voting behavior.

(X)
Social Class

(Y)
Voting   *Model 5*

(T)
Interest

Is it reasonable to think of these three variables as forming a causal sequence, or are the other two models more appropriate?

If there is a causal sequence of the kind in Model 3, we might be able to test it by controlling for the intervening variable, "interest," to see if the relationship between social class and voting drops to zero in the conditional tables. This would happen because, if Model 3 is correct, removing the variation in the data in the "interest" variable would also have the effect of removing variation in social class, and thus would eliminate the association of social class and voting. On the other hand, if the association persists at some level, then Model 4 or 5 would more accurately represent the separate and direct contribution of social class to voting. The data are presented in Table 8.4.

Notice that our expectation tends to be supported in the data. What association there was in the data in the original association of social class and voting plans is reduced by half or more in the conditional associations where political interest is controlled. Our conclusion, then, would be that these variables tend to form a causal sequence. Notice, too, that there was not much variation

*This example is cited in an excellent book on partialling and other procedures for handling survey data, by Rosenberg, (1968:59), and comes from Lazarsfeld *et al.* (1948:47).

TABLE 8.4a PERCENTAGE DISTRIBUTION OF VOTE PLANS BY EDUCATION

(Y) Vote Plans	(X) Some High School	No High School	Total
Will not vote	8	14	11
Will vote	92	86	89
Totals	100	100	100
	(1613)	(1199)	(2812)

$$d_{yx} = .06$$

TABLE 8.4b PERCENTAGE DISTRIBUTION OF VOTE PLANS BY EDUCATION CONTROLLING FOR POLITICAL INTEREST

(Y) Vote Plans	(T) Political Interest Great		Moderate		Low	
	Some High School	No High School	Some High School	No High School	Some High School	No High School
Will not vote	1	2	7	10	44	41
Will vote	99	98	93	90	56	59
Totals	100	100	100	100	100	100
	(495)	(285)	(986)	(669)	(132)	(245)
	$d_{yx} = .01$		$d_{yx} = .03$		$d_{yx} = -.03$	

Source: Rosenberg, 1968: Tables 3.3 and 3.4. Copyright © by Basic Books, Inc., Publishers, New York. Used by permission.

in voting plans in the first place and, furthermore, the independent variable as it is measured here does not help explain much of the variation that there is. This would suggest that there may be some separate influence of social class on voting plans, independent of political interest. Model 4 may more accurately reflect the weak streams of influence in this case. The coefficients (.01, .03 and −.03) represent the independent influence of social class (education as measured here) on voting plans when political interest is controlled. Let us examine the association of political interest, controlling for the antecedent variable, social class, to see how much independent influence political interest has for voting plans. These coefficients of association can be computed by using the data in Table 8.4. They are as follows:

$d_{yt} = .15$ The association of political interest (variable T) and voting plans (variable Y) for individuals with *some high-school.*

$d_{yt} = .22$ The association of political interest and voting plans for individuals with *no highschool.*

Our conclusion would be that these coefficients of association are much stronger than those for the independent effects of social class (education). The X-Y stream in Model 4 would be considerably weaker than the T-Y stream. Finally, looking at the conditionals for social class and interest, controlling for the *consequent* variable, voting intentions, we can see to what extent Model 5 would more accurately represent the data. If the conditional associations drop to zero in this case, we would say that Model 5 would be a better fit. The data are as follows (again computed from information contained in Table 8.4, rearranged):

$d_{tx}=.12$ The association of political interest (here called variable T) and social class (variable X), for those with *no plans* to vote.

$d_{tx}=.14$ The association of political interest and social class among those *planning to vote.*

Comparing the coefficients for the three sets of conditional tables, then, the X-T and T-Y links appear to be much stronger than the X-Y link when the third variable is controlled. Since the association between X and Y drops when T is controlled, the conclusion is that the data fit Model 3 best. There is no reason to give up the idea of causal sequence; at the same time, the direct influence of social class on voting plans is considerably less than its indirect influence through political interest. Our hypothesis is confirmed.

8.2.3a   Independent Causation.   The point to be emphasized is that we have contrasted our expectations for three competing models of the relationship between these variables (Models 3, 4, and 5). By controlling on an intervening variable, we are able to conclude that a causal sequence interpretation is *not disproven* if the association in the partials drops to zero. To the extent that it does not drop to zero, there is evidence of some *independent* effect of the independent variable on the dependent variable, irrespective of the test factor which intervenes. By controlling on the other two variables we are able to examine the relative strengths of association. By controlling on X, for example, we can see whether T is related to Y and how strongly, independently of X. By controlling on Y we can see to what extent X and T are related independently of Y. If the partial associations went to zero in this latter test, we would have concluded that the two variables X and T independently influence the dependent variable Y and are related only by virtue of this common influence. Model 5 would have represented the outcome of **independent causation** in this case.

8.2.4   Suppressor Variables

In all of the cases discussed thus far, we have started with some total association between the independent and dependent variables, and the task was to introduce control variables which would help explain the original association further. Is it sufficient to elaborate only those relationships which are not zero to start with? The answer is *no:* It is possible to have a third variable act to *suppress* the observed relationship between two variables and, in fact, to mask it completely as a **suppressor variable.** This sometimes happens with variables such as sex or race when a relationship in one conditional association is equally strong but opposite in direction to the association in another conditional. The result is that one relationship could cancel the other out, so that the overall as-

DIAGRAM 8.1.   Some Strategies of Elaboration

1. Be sure to keep a clear focus on which variable it is that is the *dependent* variable.
2. Contrast explanatory models, if possible, using theory to develop alternatives, and guide the selection of control and independent variables. A useful procedure is to draw out expected relationships in the form of an arrow diagram.
3. Test factors used should be those related to the dependent variable. Take account of the ordering of variables in selecting control variables and interpreting outcomes of analysis.
4. If you are expecting or looking for statistical interaction, examine the conditional tables themselves.
5. Generally, start with a zero-order association and work toward more controls, examining first-order associations, then second order, etc.
6. If you are looking for a general increase or decrease (or no change) in the conditional tables, consider using standardization or the use of an appropriate measure of partial correlation. (See Section 8.3.)
7. In interpreting outcomes, remember where the data came from, the source of measurements, number of cases, reasonableness of contrasts, quality of the data, whether or not multiple measurements of variables were made, and independence of observations.

sociation may be zero. Without some sort of expectation (*i.e.*, a theory) it is, of course, difficult to separate a situation where there is a zero-order association between toe-nail length and number of languages spoken, when one would not expect any association to appear no matter what controls were introduced, as against a situation where there is zero association between sexual permissive attitudes and social class, which is definitely not expected given previous research and theorizing. This latter case will serve as an illustration of a suppressor effect.

Reiss hypothesized, on the basis of prior research and theory, that there

TABLE 8.5a PERCENTAGE DISTRIBUTION OF PERMISSIVENESS ATTITUDES BY SOCIAL CLASS FOR THE STUDENT SAMPLE

Sexual Permissiveness Attitudes	Social Class Low	Medium	High	Total
High	49	46	50	49
Low	51	54	50	51
	100	100	100	100
	(383)	(189)	(225)	(797)

Gamma = .01

TABLE 8.5b PERCENTAGE DISTRIBUTION OF PERMISSIVENESS ATTITUDES BY SOCIAL CLASS AND CHURCH ATTENDANCE FOR THE STUDENT SAMPLE

HIGH CHURCH ATTENDANCE

Sexual Permissiveness Attitudes	Social Class Low	Medium	High	Total
High	42	26	23	34
Low	58	74	77	66
	100	100	100	100
	(262)	(98)	(102)	(462)

Gamma = −.35

LOW CHURCH ATTENDANCE

Sexual Permissiveness Attitudes	Social Class Low	Medium	High	Total
High	64	67	72	68
Low	36	33	28	32
	100	100	100	100
	(113)	(89)	(119)	(321)

Gamma = +.14

Source: Data from Reiss, 1967: Tables 4.1 and 4.2. Copyright © 1967 by Holt, Rinehart and Winston, Inc. Reprinted by permission of Holt, Rinehart and Winston.

would be a negative relationship between social class and permissiveness attitudes, with attitudes toward sexual permissiveness measured by a series of scales (Reiss, 1967: 59 and 61). For the purposes of this study, he dichotomized permissiveness, although the puzzling findings were checked by including more categories of permissiveness attitudes and several different measures of social class. The data were gathered on about 800 students from five schools in the East. Table 8.5 presents these data.

Using gamma (G) as a measure of association, he found that there was no association between permissiveness attitudes and social class. This finding occurred in each of the five schools, with a dozen different social class measures and with a variety of other controls as well. Prior research by Kinsey indicated that religion was an important explanation of variation in sexual relations, so frequency of church attendance was introduced as a control variable, as shown in Table 8.5b. Among the high-church-attenders, the social class-permissiveness association was −.35 (gamma) and it was +.14 among the low-church-attenders. The higher the social class, the lower the level of permissiveness among high-church attenders, and the opposite was true of low-church-attenders. Further investigation indicated that the same kind of outcome occurred whenever the student group was divided into categories of generally "conservative" and generally "liberal" on a number of other variables such as political preference, beliefs about integration of schools, civil rights activity, etc. This and related analyses eventually led Reiss to a general proposition, namely: "The stronger the amount of general liberality in a group, the greater the likelihood that social forces will maintain high levels of sexual permissiveness" (Reiss, 1967:73). Social class standing is one of those forces.

Had he stopped his analysis upon finding no association between social class and permissiveness attitudes, he would have missed an important series of findings about variables which masked the relationship.

8.2.5 Social System Analysis

For many sociological problems an investigator is interested in two levels (or more) of analysis, the *individual* level and the *group* level. He may argue, for example, that differences between groups stem from the different kinds of individuals who compose the group (called structural analysis), or he may feel that individuals behave in certain ways not only because of their own characteristics but because of the character of the group itself of which he may be a member (called contextual analysis). In addition to these two types of analysis are one-level analyses using groups as the unit and one-level analyses using individuals as the unit.*

In a social system analysis involving three variables and two levels, each individual case is characterized by three measured variables. Usually two of these variables, the independent and dependent variables, are individual-level

*In this chapter we will illustrate some of the possibilities that involve conditional tables and an examination for interaction between group and individual level variables, one of the patterns of relationship between three variables. An excellent discussion of social system analysis with some examples from the field of sociology is found in Riley (General References, 1963:V.I, 800, Unit 12).

characteristics and the third variable is a group-level variable which is used to characterize the kind of group context the individual is in. We could consider creating one table cross-classifying the independent and dependent variable for all individuals in a given *kind* of group. One such table would be created for each of the different kinds of groups included in the study, and systematic comparisons would be made within and between groups.

8.2.5a. A **structural analysis** might involve comparison of a specific cell (*e.g.* percent psychotic among foreign-born) across *groups* which differ in some interesting respect (*e.g.* degree of social disorganization of the area), to see what effects the differences between groups might have when the structure of the group is held constant (*e.g.* only foreign-born are compared, or only native-born). Riley points out another kind of structural analysis, used by Durkheim, in which group differences are controlled by examining the association of two variables (*e.g.* religion and suicide) within separate groups (*e.g.* within different types of countries).

8.2.5b. A **contextual analysis** combines information from all three variables, examining the way the relationship between two variables (*e.g.* two individual-level variables, or perhaps an individual and a context variable) may change systematically, for *individuals*, across groups which are set up to differ in a systematic way on a group-level variable. Here the analysis will focus on individuals as the unit being investigated, and it will measure individuals on variables which reflect individual properties as well as some aspect of the kind of group context within which an individual is located. Let us turn to an example at this point.*

In a study of job satisfaction, previous research has supported the notion that older individuals are more likely to be satisfied than are younger workers. It has also been argued that the "age" of the company or department of a company has an influence on job satisfaction (and on the creativity and productivity of the organization), but the data are conflicting and generally show little difference by group age. Is it possible that job satisfaction, for example, is influenced not only by individual age of the worker, but also by the organizational age of the group context within which the worker is situated?

One of the authors examined this question using data on some 235 individuals who worked in 35 branches or departments of a large research and development organization. Each individual was asked his own age and a series of questions designed to measure his degree of job satisfaction. One of these job satisfaction questions was whether or not the individual felt his department was a highly supportive work environment. In addition, the departments themselves were "measured" on organizational age, and this was done by computing the arithmetic mean age of individuals in that department. Each individual, then, was characterized by his own age, the age of the department he worked in, and his job satisfaction.

Both individuals and departments were classified on age into "old," "middle age," and "young" in this analysis. There were, of course, a number of different departments in each age bracket, but rather than examine each organiza-

---

*An excellent example of contextual analysis which makes use of some of the procedures to be discussed in the next chapter is given in McDill *et al.*, 1967. At issue is whether or not the socioeconomic context of the school influences individual achievement. Data came from 20 public highschools.

tion separately as we might do in one kind of structural analysis, we put the data together in three summary tables, one for each kind of group (*i.e.* old, middle-aged, and young groups). These data are presented in Table 8.6, below.

Overall, 48.1 percent of the workers felt their work context to be "highly supportive." Older individuals were more likely to agree that their context was highly supportive, as is indicated in the following distribution. The pattern by group age is reversed in that the percentage is lower for the older-age groups than for younger-aged groups.

PERCENTAGE OF WORKERS FEELING THEIR BRANCH PROVIDES A HIGHLY SUPPORTIVE WORK ATMOSPHERE, BY GROUP AND BY INDIVIDUAL AGE

By Group Age		N(100%)		By Individual Age		N(100%)
31–35yrs	52.2%	(86)	Young	22–32yrs	42.9%	(63)
36–39yrs	46.1%	(89)	Middle	33–39yrs	45.6%	(90)
40–55yrs	45.0%	(60)	Older	40–64yrs	54.9%	(82)

TABLE 8.6 PERCENTAGE FEELING THEIR DEPARTMENT IS A HIGHLY SUPPORTIVE WORK ATMOSPHERE, BY INDIVIDUAL AGE AND ORGANIZATIONAL AGE

YOUNGER DEPARTMENTS

Feelings About Support of Work Context	Individual Age			Total
	Young	Middle	Older	
Highly Supportive	51.4	48.6	64.3	52.2
Not Highly Supp.	48.6	51.4	35.7	47.8
	100.0	100.0	100.0	100.0
	(35)	(37)	(14)	(86)

MIDDLE-AGED DEPARTMENTS

Feelings About Support of Work Context	Individual Age			Total
	Young	Middle	Older	
Highly Supportive	30.4	45.9	58.6	46.1
Not Highly Supp.	69.6	54.1	41.4	53.9
	100.0	100.0	100.0	100.0
	(23)	(37)	(29)	(89)

OLDER DEPARTMENTS

Feelings About Support of Work Context	Individual Age			Total
	Young	Middle	Older	
Highly Supportive	(40.0)	37.5	48.7	45.0
Not Highly Supp.	(60.0)	62.5	51.3	55.0
	100.0	100.0	100.0	100.0
	(5)	(16)	(39)	(60)

Source: Data are from 235 individuals in 35 branches of a research and development organization, collected in 1966, by Robert Biller, who kindly made these data available for the author's study of individual and organizational age. Branch heads and managers have been eliminated in the above data.

Data in the three summary tables (Table 8.6) show an interesting added pattern. Young or middle-aged individuals in middle-aged or older group contexts are less likely to feel their department is a highly supportive work context. Compare these figures to, for example, older individuals in young groups, older individuals in middle-aged groups, or the young or old individuals in their own-aged groups. The differences in percentage feeling their department work context is supportive in Table 8.6 show a pattern of *statistical interaction* between individual and group age. Not only are there differences by individual age or by organizational age, separately, but there are much more impressive differences when specific combinations of these two age measures are examined. This effect can be shown clearly in the graph in Figure 8.1.

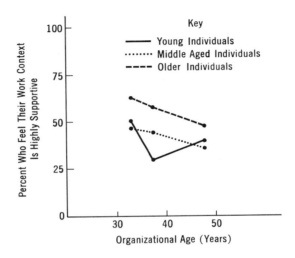

Source: Data from Table 8.6 above.

FIGURE 8.1 Percentage Distribution of a Job Satisfaction Measure by Age of Individuals and Their Organization Context for Workers in Departments of a Research and Development Organization

In these graphs, each of the dots indicates one of the combinations of individual age and group context age. There are nine such combinations here and, thus, nine dots. Each dot is placed at a point which corresponds to (a) the percentage of individuals who feel that the work context is supportive, and (b) the average age of the department within which they are located. The dots representing young individuals are connected and, separately, those dots for the middle-aged individuals and for the older individuals. There are three lines on the graph, one for each category of individual age and the lines reflect changes in the dependent variable, percentage feeling the context is supportive, across the differently aged departmental contexts. These lines converge or cross each other, which means that there is statistical interaction; the level of the dependent variable depends not only on the addition of a group effect to an individual age effect but depends on the specific combination of those two variables.

Figure 8.2 illustrates some of the other outcome possibilities one might find in two-level analysis of this sort. In Figure 8.2a, for example, the two lines

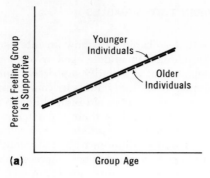

(a)

(a) *Group Effect Only.* Here there is a difference in the dependent variable for contexts of different kinds, but there is no difference within any of the contexts in terms of the other individual characteristic. If the lines were together as they are here, but parallel with the *X*-axis, there would be no group or individual difference in the dependent variable.

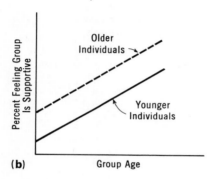

(b)

(b) *Separate Individual and Group Effects.* In this graph, the lines are parallel, sloped, and different. This indicates that there is a change in the dependent variable for different kinds of contexts and that the effect is the same on each kind of individual within these contexts. There is also an individual effect since the two lines are separated. Within each kind of context, there is an individual difference on the dependent variable. Note that the dotted line might be above or below the solid line. That is, the correlation of the group variable may differ in sign from the correlation of the individual-level variable.

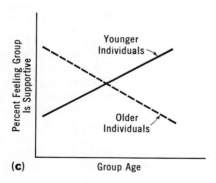

(c)

(c) *Interaction Effects.* Here the lines are different, both sloped, and they are not parallel. This indicates that the dependent variable depends upon the specific combination of individual and group level independent variables. It is not a simple case of adding together separate group and individual effects as in situation (b), above. Here, as the context examined is older, older individuals tend to decline on the dependent variable, but younger individuals tend to increase.

FIGURE 8.2 SOME POSSIBLE PATTERNS OF GROUP AND INDIVIDUAL EFFECTS [For a Discussion of Some of These Patterns, See General References, Riley (1963), and also Davis *et al.* (1961).]

BOX 8.2 STATISTICAL INTERACTION

If two variables, *A* and *B*, each explain some of the variation in a dependent variable, their combined explanatory power may be simply a sum of
their separate effects. That is, they each contribute a part to their combined effect on a dependent variable. They have an *additive effect.*

Contrasted with this additive effect are *interaction effects* in which
specific combinations of categories of two or more independent variables
(or independent and control variables) explain more of the variation in a
dependent variable than would be expected from a simple additive combination of their separate effects. The combination of certain categories of
individual age and group age, for example, seems to result in differences
in satisfaction beyond what would be expected from a sum of their separate effects.

Statistical interaction is an important kind of outcome of the relationship of two or more independent variables to a dependent variable, not
only because it helps determine the kind of analysis to use, but also because our theories often lead us to expect interesting and unusual effects
of particular combinations of values of two or more independent variables.

---

which represent the different categories of one of the independent variables are
identical. This means that there is no individual-level effect. The fact that the
lines have a slope indicates, however, that there is a group-level effect on the
dependent variable. Here the dependent variable within a given context for a
certain kind of people is measured in terms of percentages, although it could be
measured in terms of medians or means, etc., depending upon the kind of measurement or feature of interest.

In Figure 8.2b, there is an added effect due to individual-level differences
in the independent variable. Notice that the individual differences are the same
within the different categories of group context, and thus both the group and the
individual level variables make separate, additive contributions to the explanation (or prediction) of the dependent variable. To say it somewhat differently, the
individual-level difference occurs regardless of the particular group-level context
one is talking about (and vice versa). In Figure 8.2c, however, the level of the
individual-age effect on the dependent variable depends upon the group context
in important ways. Older individuals will have a higher level of the dependent
variable than younger individuals only if the group context happens to be
younger. The reverse is true in this example, where group contexts are older and
there is a type of middle-age group context for which there are no individual-level
differences. This is an example of statistical interaction, since the relationship
between two variables (independent and dependent) depends critically upon the
value of the other independent variable. In this case, since one of the variables
is group-level and the other is individual-level, the analysis permits us to draw
conclusions about group and about individual effects. Interaction could also occur,
of course, between variables both at the same level of analysis (*e.g.* both group-
level or both individual-level), and this was the case in the example of specification discussed earlier in this chapter.

8.2.6 Recapitulating Patterns of Elaboration

Some of the more frequent and interesting patterns of outcome are of the type referred to as *specification* or *statistical interaction* (Section 8.2.1), a condition in which the conditional tables differ substantially from each other. Patterns where there is an original association but the conditional associations are near zero are interpreted as evidence that a causal hypothesis is *spurious* (8.2.2a), that a *causal sequence* hypothesis is supported (8.2.3), or that there is *independent causation* (8.2.3a), depending upon the antecedent, intervening, or consequent theoretical ordering of a test factor. Finally, there is the pattern in which a *suppressor* variable (8.2.4) operates to mask out an original association, and this is discovered only after examining other conditional and total tables. The *Lazarsfeld accounting formula* (8.1.4a) is useful in organizing patterns of outcome when total and conditional associations are examined. In general, the procedure used is one of (a) examining lower-order tables first and higher-order tables later in an analytic sequence, and (b) controlling on other relevant variables in the examination of an *X-Y* relationship of interest. What is controlled and how depends critically upon the ideas brought to the research by the investigator.

8.3 THE AVERAGE PARTIAL TABLE

The lines of elaboration we have been discussing direct the investigator to examine (a) any difference there may be in the conditional tables, or (b) the overall change in degree of association in the conditionals. In situation (a), the only analysis procedure is elaboration (or some form of dummy-variable regression analysis, as discussed toward the end of the next chapter), and elaboration involves the examination of the different conditional tables. In situation (b), however, where we are merely interested in whether the association in the conditionals remained the same, decreased, or increased, there are some other types of statistical summary which could be carried out to simplify the analysis. Two of these procedures will be discussed in this section. One is *standardization* and the other is *partial correlation*. In both instances the result is a kind of "average" of the outcome in a set of conditionals. In the first instance an average partial table is the result, and in the second it is an average of the measures of association that might be computed on separate conditionals.

In either case, these further descriptions are used in the same way they were used earlier. One would compare the original association of two variables with the association after a test factor has been "partialled out" or controlled. If, for example, the test factor were antecedant variable, and if the partial association dropped to zero when the test factor was controlled, the conclusion would be as it was when individual conditional tables were examined — any causal hypothesis would then be a *spurious* interpretation of the relationship between the main independent and dependent variables. Let us discuss the idea of standardization first and then turn to partial correlation coefficients.

BOX 8.3 CONDITIONAL TABLES AND PARTIAL CORRELATION

One of the organizing themes in this book has been the search for ever more powerful summary statistics. This search led to the step from a univariate distribution to summary index numbers such as the mean and standard deviation. Again, at the point where several univariate distributions were being contrasted, we stepped up to an overall treatment of these separate distributions as columns in a bivariate table, and this led to the use of measures of strength and nature of association. In the first part of this chapter we began by looking at a basic table relating two interesting variables within categories of other control variables. Now, in this section, we are again looking for a more powerful summary procedure which will express in one table or in one number what we would otherwise get from a potentially large number of conditional tables.

Although terminology is not altogether consistent in statistics, we will here observe a distinction between the examination of *conditional* tables and their associated *conditional association* measures (the last section) as against *partial association* measures, which summarize a set of conditional relationships and express the part of the total association which exists after the effects of control variables have been statistically removed. It should be noted, however, that some texts refer to the examination of conditional tables as "partialling."

8.3.1 Standardization

Standardization is a procedure which statistically removes fluctuations in the data due to some control variable, thus permitting an investigator to examine and compare tables without this contaminating effect. Two procedures will be discussed, both of which are called "direct" standardization. The first procedure applies to figures, such as rates, which we may want to compare, and the second applies to whole tables. We will use the first to explain the idea of standardization. Computational procedures for the second procedure are presented in Diagram 8.2.

8.3.1a STANDARDIZING RATES

Suppose that we are interested in studying the rate at which women of different educational backgrounds produce children. Examining Census reports, we discover that among those women in the child-bearing ages (*i.e.* 15–49 years) there are 302 children under 5 years old per 1000 women who had 8 years of elementary school education, and that the rate increases to 393 per 1000 for women with 4 years of high school, and it drops again to 383 per 1000 for those with 4 or more years of college (U.S. Bur. Census, 1970). There appears to be a difference in number of children under 5 by education.

At this point we might be somewhat suspicious of our comparison because, after all, women in their 20's are more likely to have young children than women in their 40's. If there is a higher percentage of young women in the high-school-educated group, we would expect a higher rate. Some of the difference in rates may be due to differences in age distribution of elementary, high-school, and college trained women. The problem, then, is to create three rates which somehow take out the effects of any differences there may be in the distribution of age.

To do this, we will choose some standard age distribution as our **standard population.** The choice is arbitrary but the rates will be more interesting if the standard population is realistic. For this purpose we will use the actual overall age distribution of women in the U.S. in 1969. This distribution is as follows:

"STANDARD POPULATION" NUMBER OF WOMEN BY AGE BETWEEN AGES 15 AND 49, U.S., MARCH, 1969 DATA

Age of Woman	Number (in 1000's)
15 to 24	17,109
25 to 29	6,608
30 to 39	11,388
40 to 49	12,472
Total	47,577

Source: U.S. Bur. Census, 1970.

Now we need detailed "children-under-five" rate figures for women of different ages and for the three different education categories. These rates are given below.

NUMBER OF CHILDREN UNDER 5 YEARS OLD PER 1000 WOMEN, BY AGE OF WOMAN AND NUMBER OF YEARS OF SCHOOL COMPLETED, U.S., 1969

	Schooling Completed		
Age of Woman	Elementary	High school	College
15 to 24	251/1000	413/1000	110/1000
25 to 29	916/1000	879/1000	673/1000
30 to 39	456/1000	407/1000	572/1000
40 to 49	96/1000	76/1000	88/1000

Source: U.S. Bur. Census, 1970.

The standardization procedure involves multiplying each of the *rates by the number of women in the standard population who are in that age bracket.* This produces an "expected" number of children under 5 if there were as many women in that age group as there are in the standard population. The expected number of children under 5 can then be summed separately for each of the levels of schooling, divided by the number of women in the standard population, and expressed as a rate per 1000 women. Thus 17,109 (1000's) women aged 15 to 24 would be *expected* to have 4,294,359 children if they all had completed only 8 years of elementary school (*i.e.* multiply the rate, −251 from the table above for those in the 15–24 age bracket with elementary schooling – by the 17,109 women in that age group in the standard population). On the other hand, one would expect 7,066,017 children under 5 years of age ($413 \times 17,109 = 7,066,017$) if all of the women of this age in the standard population had a high-school education. Finally, one would expect fewer children under 5 if this same group had a college background ($110 \times 17,109 = 1,881,990$). These computations are shown below:

(a) Computation Using Rates for Women with Elementary School Education.

Age of Woman	Rate per 1000		Standard Population (1000's)		Expected Number
15–24	251	×	17,109	=	4,294,359
25–29	916	×	6,608	=	6,052,928
30–39	456	×	11,388	=	5,192,928
40–49	96	×	12,472	=	1,197,312
Totals			47,577		16,737,527

$$\text{Standardized Rate} = (1000)\frac{16,737,527}{47,577,000} = 352$$

(b) Computation Using Rates for Women with a High-School Education.

Age of Woman	Rate per 1000		Standard Population (1000's)		Expected Number
15–24	413	×	17,109	=	7,066,017
25–29	879	×	6,608	=	5,808,432
30–39	407	×	11,388	=	4,634,916
40–49	76	×	12,472	=	947,872
Totals			47,577		18,457,237

$$\text{Standardized Rate} = (1000)\frac{18,457,237}{47,577,000} = 388$$

(c) Computation Using Rates for Women with College Education.

Age of Woman	Rate per 1000		Standard Population (1000's)		Expected Number
15–24	110	×	17,109	=	1,881,990
25–29	673	×	6,608	=	4,447,184
30–39	572	×	11,388	=	6,513,936
40–49	88	×	12,472	=	1,097,536
Total			47,577		13,940,646

$$\text{Standardized Rate} = (1000)\frac{13,940,646}{47,577,000} = 293$$

As a result of applying the different rates to the same standard population, we can compute rates which can be *compared*: 352, 388, and 293 per 1000 women. The following table summarizes the rate of children-under-5-years-old per 1000 women aged 15 to 49 both before standardization on age and after standardization.

RATE OF CHILDREN UNDER 5 YEARS OLD PER 1000 WOMEN AGED 15 TO 49, U.S., 1969, BEFORE AND AFTER STANDARDIZATION ON AGE

Education Completed	Not Standardized	Standardized On Age
Elementary	302	352
High school	393	388
College	383	293

The age structure of the population upon which the rates are computed is the *same* for each education group, so the overall differences between age-standardized rates must be due to the different rates which apply to differently educated women. These are called age-standardized rates because the effect of age structure of the population is removed. There are a number of uses of this standardization procedure in demography in comparisons of death rates or birth rates or disease rates for populations of different makeup.

8.3.1b STANDARDIZED TABLES

The second application of standardization is called "test factor standardization" (*cf.* Rosenberg, 1963), and it too statistically removes the effect of control variables so that the relationship between independent and dependent variables can be examined without this source of contamination. This permits an investigator to compare an original total association of two variables and the same association where the effects of some test factor have been statistically removed. This would permit us to make some kind of judgment about what is happening to the strength of association in the conditionals in general. Test factor standardization is illustrated in Diagram 8.2.

To explain the logic behind standardization, consider the two conditionals from Table 8.3, above. They have been percentaged and reproduced in Diagram 8.2.

In these conditional tables there is no association between X and Y, although, when cell frequencies are added together, they produce a rather striking association ($\phi = .44$) in the total table. Looking at the differences between the total and conditional tables, we can see that the effect of the test factor has been to "rearrange" cases within each conditional table, and thus to rearrange the distribution of column and row totals, so that each cell frequency in a given conditional contributes a *differently weighted amount* to the total table. In the T-1 partial, for example, the "4" in the upper left cell contributes 17 percent of the 24 in that cell of the total table, while the "1" contributes only 2 percent to its combined-cell total, and the cell with 40 cases contributes 95 percent of the cases in its cell in the total table. This differential weighting of cells does not reflect the relative number of cases in the distribution in a column of the conditional table and, thus, it does not reflect the pattern in the conditionals.

To handle this differential weighting, we can take two steps. *First*, per-

DIAGRAM 8.2 Test Factor Standardization

Conditional Tables:

		T-1					T-2		
		X					X		
FREQUENCY		4	1	5		20	60	80	
	Y	40	10	50	Y	2	6	8	
		44	11	55		22	66	88	
PERCENTAGE		9%	9%	9%		91%	91%	91%	
		91	91	91		9	9	9	
		100	100	100		100	100	100	

		Total		
		X		
		24	61	85
	Y	42	16	58
		66	77	143
		36%	79%	59%
		64	21	41
		100	100	100

Weights:

T-1 conditional contains 55/143 = .385 of the total number of cases.
T-2 conditional contains 88/143 = .615 of the total number of cases.

$$\text{sum of weights} = 1.000$$

Computation:

T-1	9	9	9	each cell	3.5	3.5	3.5	
	91	91	91	→ multiplied →	35.0	35.0	35.0	
	100	100	100	by .385	38.5	38.5	38.5	summed, cell by
	(44)	(11)	(55)					cell, to form the
				each cell				standardized
T-2	91	91	91	→ multiplied →	56.0	56.0	56.0	table below
	9	9	9	by .615	5.5	5.5	5.5	
	100	100	100		61.5	61.5	61.5	
	(22)	(66)	(88)					

STANDARDIZED PERCENTAGE TABLE				STANDARDIZED FREQUENCY TABLE		
					X	
59.5	59.5	59.5		39	46	85
40.5	40.5	40.5	Y	27	31	58
100%	100%	100%		66	77	143
(66)	(77)	(143)				

Source: Data from Table 8.3.

DIAGRAM 8.2 *(Continued)*

Summary of Steps In Creating A Standardized Table.

1. Create conditional tables, controlling on desired test factors. The table may be of any size ($r \times c$).*
2. Properly percentage all conditional tables.
3. Select a weight to apply to all cells of a given conditional table. These weights might be the proportion of cases which are in a given conditional table, as in the example above. Weights should sum to 1.00 over all tables.
4. Multiply each cell percentage by the weighting factor, for each conditional table.
5. Sum these weighted percentages across all conditional tables, cell by cell. The resulting table is the standardized percentage table.
6. Using the marginal frequencies from the total table, convert the standardized table percentages back into frequency form.
7. Compute measures of association on the standardized frequency table for comparison with measures computed on the total table.
8. Compare total and standardized tables (and association measures) to assess the effect of the test factor/s.

*Note that the conditional tables must have some non-zero frequency in each category of the independent variable (*i.e.* the base of percentages) so that percentages in each category of the independent variable in the standardized table will total to 100 percent.

centage each conditional table so that the effect of different column (or row) totals is removed. If Y is the dependent variable, percentaging would be in the direction of the independent variable. In effect, this gives proper "rates" of appearance of the different values of Y within the separate categories of the independent and control variables. Then, all of the cells in a conditional table (*i.e.* all cells in one category of the control variable) are weighted equally (*i.e.* multiplied by the same weight) and the weighted percentages can then be summed over all conditional tables to create a standardized percentage table.

$$\Sigma(w_iP_i) = \text{standardized percentage for a cell}$$

where w is the weight and P is the cell percentage, summed over all of the conditional tables.

There is no mathematical reason for picking any particular set of weights. The important point is that whatever they are, they should be *uniform* within any one conditional table. There are some subsidiary reasons for selecting certain weights, however. If the sum of weights used in the different partial tables is equal to 1.00, then the resulting standardized table will be a percentaged table with column (row) totals equal to 100 percent. If weights total to more than 1.00 then column (row) totals in the standardized table will be larger than 100 and would have to be re-percentaged, following the usual procedures but being careful to percentage in the same direction that the conditionals were percentaged. It is also useful to select a weighting factor for a given conditional table that is equal to the proportion of all of the cases which fall in that category of the control variable. This, in effect, gives more weight to the conditional table which has the greater number of cases (and may, therefore, be more stable) and gives less weight to conditionals with very few cases (which may therefore be less stable). This is the procedure described in Diagram 8.2, although again, the important point is that weights within a partial not be changed from cell to cell. Computations for a 2×2 table are shown in Diagram 8.2, although test factor standardization is a technique which applies equally well to any sized table and any number of categories of control variables.

The standardized percentage table may be converted back to frequencies, using the total table marginals as the base of the corresponding 100-percents. Appropriate measures of strength of association could be computed on the standardized frequency table in the usual way, and the original total association could be compared with the association computed on the standardized table.

Standardization was used as an analysis technique by McAllister in a study of residential mobility among blacks and whites in the U.S. (McAllister *et al.*, 1971). The literature, they note, suggests that blacks move more often than whites and that blacks' mobility is more likely to be local. Using data from a national survey, the investigators examined moving behavior between 1966 and 1969 for blacks and whites. The data are given in Table 8.7. Gamma (G) equals −.20 meaning that whites were more likely to have stayed than is true of blacks. The comparison, as they point out, is not an appropriate one, however, because blacks are more likely to be renters, and renters of any ethnic status tend to move more frequently than owners. The standardized table in Table 8.7 controls for the effects of the owner-renter variable. You will notice that the association

TABLE 8.7 MOBILITY DIFFERENCES BETWEEN RACES: STANDARDIZED AND TOTAL

Total Association

Mobility Behavior	Ethnicity Black	White	Total
Stayed	48.7	58.6	56.9
Moved	51.3	41.4	43.1
	100.0	100.0	100.0
	(263)	(1226)	(1489)
	gamma $(G) = -.20$		

Total Association Standardized on Owner/Renters

Mobility Behavior	Ethnicity Black	White	Total
Stayed	58.4	55.9	56.3
Moved	41.6	44.1	43.7
	100.0	100.0	100.0
	(263)	(1226)	(1489)
	gamma $(G) = +.11$		

Source: McAllister *et al.,* 1971. Used by permission.

drops to a G of $+.11$, indicating that there are minor ethnic differences in moving behavior and, if anything, blacks tend to be the stayers.

Test factor standardization is useful whenever we are interested in what happens in a set of conditional tables in general. It does not permit us to examine *differences* between conditional tables (*i.e.* interaction effects).

8.3.2 Partial Correlation Coefficients

The third approach to an analysis of three or more variables to be discussed in this chapter, is the computation of some type of "average" over the measures of association for each of the conditional tables. These coefficients are called **partial correlation coefficients** and, like the standardized table, they are compared with the original total association to determine what happened in general to the strength of association when one or more test factors were introduced. Like the standardized table, partial correlation coefficients do not provide information about any pattern of *differences* between separate conditional tables over which they are computed. Two procedures for computing a partial correlation coefficient will be introduced here.

8.3.2a ORDINAL PARTIAL ASSOCIATION COEFFICIENTS

A relatively direct approach to the creation of ordinal partial association coefficients involves combining computations based on each conditional table into a single, "average" coefficient. For those ordinal measures of association which make use of counts of pairs (*i.e.* gamma, Somers' d_{yx}, etc.), the combination is accomplished by simply adding together the count of a certain type of pair computed on each of the conditional tables. Thus a total of concordant pairs (N_s) could be arrived at by adding up the N_s computations on each of the conditional tables. A similar summing could be made for other types of pairs, such as the discordant pairs (N_d), pairs tied on X but not on Y (T_x), pairs tied on Y but not on X (T_y), and pairs tied on both X and Y (T_{xy}). The appropriate totals would then be substituted into the formula for the ordinal coefficient one wants. For example, ΣN_s could be used instead of N_s, ΣN_d could be used instead of N_d, and so on.

The formula for *partial gamma* (G_p) then becomes this:

(8.1)

$$G_p = \frac{\Sigma N_s - \Sigma N_d}{\Sigma N_s + \Sigma N_d}$$

where G_p refers to "partial gamma" and the N_s and N_d sums are taken over the N_s and N_d components computed on each conditional table separately. This formulation of partial coefficients for ordinal measures would be appropriate for Somers' d_{yx} and other ordinal measures as well.

The creation of a partial G can be illustrated with data from an article by Ransford on "Skin Color, Life Chances, and Anti-White Attitudes" (1970), in which some 312 black males were interviewed shortly after a mid-60's race-riot in the Watts area of Los Angeles. His hypothesis was that skin color itself has an influence on the structure of opportunity, even when such variables as educational experience are taken into account. Table 8.8 presents the total and conditional associations of occupation and skin color, controlling for three categories of formal education.

The original, zero-order G was −.26, indicating that the lighter the skin color, the higher the occupational standing. The N_s and N_d counts are indicated in Table 8.8. N_s and N_d are also shown in Table 8.8 for each of the three conditional tables, where education is controlled. What is the effect of education controls? The partial G can be computed to answer this question by summing N_s and N_d counts over the three tables as follows:

$$\Sigma N_s = 412 + 754 + 833 = 1999$$
$$\Sigma N_d = 714 + 526 + 1695 = 2935$$

The partial G, then, is:

$$G_p = \frac{1999 - 2935}{1999 + 2935} = \frac{-936}{4934} = -.19$$

Comparing the original G of −.26 with the G_p of −.19 indicates that indeed the association does drop when education is taken into account. It is also clear, however, that the association does not drop to zero, thus partially supporting the author's initial expectation.

Again it should be pointed out that the partial G, like partial correlation coefficients, answers only the question of what happens in the conditional tables in general. Notice in Table 8.8 that there are interesting differences in the strength of association between the G coefficients computed on the separate tables. The G_p indicates the proportionate reduction in error in predicting rank on

TABLE 8.8 PERCENTAGE DISTRIBUTION OF OCCUPATIONAL LEVEL BY SKIN COLOR AND EDUCATION FOR BLACK MALES INTERVIEWED IN LOS ANGELES IN THE MID-1960's

	TOTAL			Less than H.S.			H.S. Grad.			Some College		
	Skin Color			Skin Color			Skin Color			Skin Color		
Occupation	Lt	Md	Dk	Lt	Md	Dk	Lt	Md	Dk	Lt	Md	Dk
	%	%	%	%	%	%	%	%	%	%	%	%
White Coll.	52	40	29	15	05	13	32	17	9	83	70	58
Blue Collar	39	48	50	69	70	45	50	67	76	17	26	36
Unemployed	9	12	21	15	24	42	18	15	14	0	4	6
	100	100	100%	100	100	100%	100	100	100%	100	100	100%
	(64)	(159)	(85)	(13)	(37)	(31)	(22)	(46)	(21)	(29)	(76)	(33)

EDUCATION

$N_s=6640$
$N_d=11239$
$G=-.26$

$N_s=412$
$N_d=714$
$G=-.27$

$N_s=754$
$N_d=526$
$G=-.18$

$N_s=833$
$N_d=1695$
$G=-.34$

Source: Based on rearranged data from Ronsford, 1970:171, Table 1.

one variable from rank on the other variable after the effects of education have been taken out.*

8.3.2b PARTIAL CORRELATION COEFFICIENT FOR INTERVAL VARIABLES

A frequently used partial correlation coefficient for interval-level variables is $r_{yx \cdot z}$ which is computed from Pearson's r (discussed in Chapter 7). Although r is symmetrical, subscripts are used to indicate which variables the correlation is between (the first two subscripts in front of the dot), and the variable(s) used as controls (those which are listed after the dot).

The partial correlation coefficient which statistically controls the effects of one control variable is called a **first-order partial correlation,** and it is computed from zero-order correlation coefficients as follows:

(8.2)
$$r_{yx \cdot t} = \frac{r_{yx} - (r_{yt})(r_{xt})}{\sqrt{(1-r_{xt}^2)(1-r_{yt}^2)}}$$

Higher-order partial correlation coefficients can be computed in a similar manner, using the next lower partial correlation coefficient in the general formula above. Thus, for two control variables, the second-order partial becomes:

(8.3)
$$r_{12 \cdot 34} = \frac{r_{12 \cdot 3} - (r_{14 \cdot 3})(r_{24 \cdot 3})}{\sqrt{(1-r_{14 \cdot 3}^2)(1-r_{24 \cdot 3}^2)}}$$

Higher-order partials may be formed in similar ways.

Like the total correlation, r, the partial correlation varies from -1.00 to

*A more precise statement of the meaning of gamma (G) is found in Section 7.3.2b. It is the proportionate reduction in error resulting, in this case, from using the "opposite-rank order" rule to predict the rank of pairs on one variable from a knowledge of the rank order on the other variable, rather than making a random guess of rank order (the minimum guessing rule), among pairs which are ranked differently on both variables (*i.e.* the $N_s + N_d$ pairs), after the effects of education have been taken into account. It is relevant to note that education was taken into account to the extent that three categories were used. Somewhat different results may occur if more or fewer categories of the control (and other variables, for that matter) are used.

+1.00. Its square expresses the proportion of the variation in Y (or X) explained by its linear association with the other variable, X (or Y), after the linear effects of the control variables have been taken into account (statistically removed).*

An example of the use of the partial correlation coefficient is provided by Lightfield (1971), who studied factors influencing the recognition of sociologists by their peers. His data are based upon responses of 200 university sociologists, and as independent variables he used (a) status of the department from which the rated person received his PhD., (b) the quality of his publications, and (c) his quantity of publications. The dependent variable was a peer-recognition score. In order to guide his analysis he presented an arrow diagram shown in Figure 8.3.

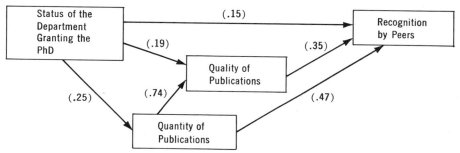

Source: Based on data from Lightfield, 1971.

FIGURE 8.3 DIAGRAM OF THE EXPECTED RELATIONSHIPS BETWEEN THREE INDEPENDENT VARIABLES AND PEER RECOGNITION OF SOCIOLOGISTS (Partial Correlation Coefficients Are Entered on the Diagram)

The numbers in brackets on the diagram are partial correlation coefficients, controlling on prior variables which influence the relationship between a given independent and dependent variable. Thus the .35 on the line between quality of publications and recognition by peers is the partial correlation of these two variables, with quantity of publications and status of the PhD. department controlled. The .47 between quantity and recognition is the first-order partial correlation controlling for department status, etc. From this set of partial correlation coefficients Lightfield is able to examine the strength of association of publication variables, without the "contamination" of the general linear effects of departmental status. The relationship between recognition and either of the publication variables is positive and relatively strong even when departmental status is taken into account.

These partial correlation coefficients can also be expressed in terms of the

*Another way to express the meaning of the partial correlation coefficient is in terms of a correlation between two sets of residuals. Think of two linear regression equations, $Y' = a_{yt} + b_{yt}T$ and $X' = a_{xt} + b_{xt}T$, where T is the control variable whose effects are to be partialled out, statistically, and X and Y are the main independent and dependent variables whose relationship is of interest. If T is related to X and to Y then the two regression equations will be able to improve the prediction of Y and X somewhat, but there will likely be some residual in both Y and X yet to be explained. That is, for many scores, there will be both a $Y - Y'$ and an $X - X'$ difference. The partial correlation coefficient is the Pearsonian correlation, r, between these two sets of residuals which remain after the linear effect of T has been statistically removed. After T has explained all it can in terms of a simple linear regression, the remaining correlation between X and Y is the partial correlation coefficient.

proportion of variance in one variable explained by its linear association with the other variable, by simply squaring the coefficient. Here, quality contributes about 12 percent to the explanation of recognition and quantity contributes 22 percent.

It should be recalled that the correlation coefficient r indicates how well a straight line explains the relationship between two variables. One of the reasons for a low correlation (or low partial correlation) may be that the relationships are not very close to linear, either in general, or within categories of test variables.

8.4 STATISTICAL CONSIDERATIONS IN RESEARCH DESIGN

Statistical procedures for controlling on test factors are closely related to more general issues of research design. Courses and texts in research methods deal with these issues, and while we will not pursue these topics here, we would like to reemphasize their importance. Experimental designs approach the problem of handling other relevant variables somewhat differently, often through the use of random assignment of cases to control and experimental groups and through manipulation of an independent variable. Some of the advantages and possibilities of this approach are discussed in a classic article by the sociologist Samuel Stouffer (1962:Ch. 15).

The explanation of a dependent variable usually leads an investigator to consider not only other measured independent variables, but also the representativeness of the dependent variable (avoiding, for example, stratification on a dependent variable), independence of observations, the amount of variation on dependent and independent variables, and a number of other possible explanations of outcomes (such as chance or history, etc.), which are nicely described by Campbell and Stanley (1963).

Since the dependent variable generally is critical to a study, investigators often spend extra effort on its measurement to assure themselves that they are measuring the kind of phenomenon they wish to measure. Sometimes this care takes the form of including several separate measures of the dependent variable so that parallel analyses can be conducted using the different measures. In fact, there are recommended styles of analysis which specifically call for research designed to include different measurements and different methods to get at the same research problem (Campbell and Fiske, 1969).

There is a very close relationship between research design and statistical analysis. This book is designed to introduce you to some of the possibilities and requirements of descriptive statistics for sociological research.

8.5 SUMMARY

In this chapter we have been primarily concerned with the problem of simultaneously handling more than two variables. Our general concern is with condi-

TABLE 8.8 PERCENTAGE DISTRIBUTION OF OCCUPATIONAL LEVEL BY SKIN COLOR AND EDUCATION FOR BLACK MALES INTERVIEWED IN LOS ANGELES IN THE MID-1960's

| | TOTAL | | | Less than H.S. | | | H.S. Grad. | | | Some College | | |
| | Skin Color | | | Skin Color | | | Skin Color | | | Skin Color | | |
Occupation	Lt	Md	Dk	Lt	Md	Dk	Lt	Md	Dk	Lt	Md	Dk
	%	%	%	%	%	%	%	%	%	%	%	%
White Coll.	52	40	29	15	05	13	32	17	9	83	70	58
Blue Collar	39	48	50	69	70	45	50	67	76	17	26	36
Unemployed	9	12	21	15	24	42	18	15	14	0	4	6
	100	100	100%	100	100	100%	100	100	100%	100	100	100%
	(64)	(159)	(85)	(13)	(37)	(31)	(22)	(46)	(21)	(29)	(76)	(33)

$$N_s = 6640$$
$$N_d = 11239$$
$$G = -.26$$

$$N_s = 412$$
$$N_d = 714$$
$$G = -.27$$

$$N_s = 754$$
$$N_d = 526$$
$$G = -.18$$

$$N_s = 833$$
$$N_d = 1695$$
$$G = -.34$$

urce: Based on rearranged data from Ransford, 1970:171, Table 1.

one variable from rank on the other variable after the effects of education have been taken out.*

8.3.2b PARTIAL CORRELATION COEFFICIENT FOR INTERVAL VARIABLES

A frequently used partial correlation coefficient for interval-level variables is $r_{yx \cdot z}$ which is computed from Pearson's r (discussed in Chapter 7). Although r is symmetrical, subscripts are used to indicate which variables the correlation is between (the first two subscripts in front of the dot), and the variable(s) used as controls (those which are listed after the dot).

The partial correlation coefficient which statistically controls the effects of one control variable is called a **first-order partial correlation,** and it is computed from zero-order correlation coefficients as follows:

(8.2)
$$r_{yx \cdot t} = \frac{r_{yx} - (r_{yt})(r_{xt})}{\sqrt{(1 - r_{xt}^2)(1 - r_{yt}^2)}}$$

Higher-order partial correlation coefficients can be computed in a similar manner, using the next lower partial correlation coefficient in the general formula above. Thus, for two control variables, the second-order partial becomes:

8.3)
$$r_{12 \cdot 34} = \frac{r_{12 \cdot 3} - (r_{14 \cdot 3})(r_{24 \cdot 3})}{\sqrt{(1 - r_{14 \cdot 3}^2)(1 - r_{24 \cdot 3}^2)}}$$

Higher-order partials may be formed in similar ways.

Like the total correlation, r, the partial correlation varies from -1.00 to

*A more precise statement of the meaning of gamma (G) is found in Section 7.3.2b. It is the proportionate reduction in error resulting, in this case, from using the "opposite-rank order" rule to predict the rank of pairs on one variable from a knowledge of the rank order on the other variable, rather than making a random guess of rank order (the minimum guessing rule), among pairs which are ranked differently on both variables (i.e. the $N_s + N_d$ pairs), after the effects of education have been taken into account. It is relevant to note that education was taken into account to the extent that three categories were used. Somewhat different results may occur if more or fewer categories of the control (and other variables, for that matter) are used.

independent causation
statistical interaction
structural analysis
contextual analysis
social system analysis

standardization
standardizing rates
standard population
standardized tables
partial correlation coefficients

QUESTIONS AND PROBLEMS

1. Using data from Table 8.8, create a standardized table and compare it with the original association of occupation and skin color. Discuss the advantages and disadvantages of using a test factor standardization rather than a partial association measure to test the investigator's ideas. It may help to look up the article.

2. Select a theoretical model which has been drawn out as an arrow diagram (such as that in the middle of Section 8.1.3 or in the data sets of a statistics workbook). Explain how one might use conditional tables, standardization, or partial correlation coefficients to test the model. What relationships would the model lead us to expect of data?

3. Does the high-school environment have an effect on student performance? Select some "environment" variable, such as social class of the high school, an individual characteristic such as IQ, and student performance, and then draw out a graph such as those shown in Figure 8.2 to illustrate (a) only an individual-level effect on performance, (b) only a group-level effect on performance, and (c) both group and individual effects. Carefully label each graph and describe what the graphs show. It might help to read further about this type of analysis in Riley (1963) and the example of contextual analysis discussed by McDill *et al,* (1967).

GENERAL REFERENCES

Blalock, Hubert M., Jr., *An Introduction to Social Research,* (Englewood Cliffs, N.J., Prentice-Hall), 1970.
    Chapter 4 on "Explanation and Theory" is especially relevant to this chapter.
Davis, James A., *Elementary Survey Analysis,* (Englewood Cliffs, N.J., Prentice Hall), 1971.
Davis, James A., Joe L. Spaeth, and Carolyn Huson, "A Technique for Analyzing The Effects of Group Composition," *American Sociological Review* 26, (April, 1961), p 215–225.
Hyman, Herbert, *Survey Design and Analysis,* (Glencoe, Ill., The Free Press), 1955.
Riley, Matilda White, *Sociological Research: A Case Approach* volume 1, (New York, Harcourt, Brace and World), 1963.
    See especially the commentary after Unit 12, pages 700–738, which discusses social system analysis, structural and contextual analysis.
Rosenberg, Morris, *The Logic of Survey Analysis,* (New York, Basic Books), 1968.

Stouffer, Samuel A., *Social Research To Test Ideas,* (New York, The Free Press of Glencoe), 1962.
>See especially the 15th chapter, "Some Observations on Study Design."

OTHER REFERENCES

Blalock, Hubert M., *Theory Construction: From Verbal to Mathematical Formulations,* (Englewood Cliffs, N.J., Prentice-Hall), 1969.

Campbell, Donald T., and Donald W. Fiske, "Convergent and Discriminant Validation by the Multitrait-Multimethod Matrix," *Psychological Bulletin* 56, (March, 1969), p 81–105.

Campbell, Donald T., and Julian C. Stanley, *Experimental and Quasi-Experimental Designs For Research,* (Chicago, Rand McNally), 1963.

Erbe, William, "Social Involvement and Political Activity: A Replication and Elaboration," *American Sociological Review,* 29 (April, 1964), p 198–215.

Lazarsfeld, Paul F., Bernard Berelson and Hazel Gaudet, *The People's Choice,* (New York, Columbia University Press), 1948.

Lazarsfeld, Paul F., and Morris Rosenberg (editors), *The Language of Social Research,* (Glencoe, Ill., The Free Press of Glencoe), 1955, 231.

Lightfield, E. Timothy, "Output and Recognition of Sociologists," *American Sociologist* 6, (May, 1971), p 128–133.

McAllister, Ronald, Edward Kaiser, and Edgar Butler, "Residential Mobility of Blacks and Whites: A National Longitudinal Survey," *American Journal of Sociology,* 77 (November, 1971), p 445–456.

McDill, Edward L., Edmund D. Meyers, and Leo C. Rigsby, "Institutional Effects on the Academic Behavior of High School Students," *Sociology of Education* 40, (Summer, 1967), p 181–199.

Merton, Robert K., *Social Theory and Social Structure,* Revised and Enlarged Edition, (Glencoe, Ill., The Free Press), 1957, Part I.

Messer, Mark, "The Possibility of an Age-Concentrated Environment Becoming a Normative System," *Gerontologist* 7 (December, 1967), p 247–251.

Ransford, H. Edward, "Skin Color, Life Chances, and Anti-White Attitudes," *Social Problems* 18, (Fall, 1970), p 164–179.

Reiss, Ira L., *The Social Context of Premarital Sexual Permissiveness,* (New York, Holt, Rinehart and Winston), 1967, p 59 and 61.

Reynolds, Paul Davidson, *A Primer in Theory Construction,* (New York, Bobbs-Merrill Company), 1971.

Rosenberg, Morris, "Test Factor Standardization As A Method of Interpretation," *Social Forces* 41, (October, 1962), p 53–61.

Stinchcombe, Arthur L., *Construction of Social Theories,* (New York, Harcourt, Brace and World), 1968.

Stouffer, Samuel A., *Social Research to Test Ideas,* (New York, The Free Press of Glencoe), 1962, Chapter 15 on "Some Observations on Study Design."

U.S. Bureau of the Census, "Population Characteristics," *Current Population Reports,* Series P-20, No. 205, Washington, D.C., 1970.

Zeisel, Hans, *Say It With Figures,* Revised Fourth Edition, (New York, Harper and Row), 1957, Chapter 10.

PATH ANALYSIS AND MULTIPLE REGRESSION

There are several analysis techniques used in sociology which fit under the general label of multiple regression analysis. They are appropriate where an investigator is interested in predicting or analyzing scores on one dependent variable by combining the predictive power of several independent variables by means of an equation which is called a **multiple regression equation.** How well this equation is able to predict scores on the dependent variable is indicated by the **multiple correlation coefficient,** R. In many ways this procedure is simply an extension of correlation and regression procedures we have discussed where only one independent variable is used to predict one dependent variable.

This chapter is an introduction to some of the multiple regression techniques you are likely to encounter in reading reports of sociological research. Topics we will discuss include multiple correlation and multiple regression, path analysis, the use of dummy variables, and stepwise multiple regression procedures. These are all quite easily understood at an interpretative-theoretical level, even though various computational alternatives and their derivation are details we will reserve for a separate course in regression analysis.*

*Clerical mathematics needed to compute some of the coefficients will generally be left to existing computer programs, as done by most investigators. Your instructor will explain how to use your computer and the programs that are available for multiple regression. These are generally quite easy to use in problems you may be assigned.

It is well to use some caution in accepting the output of "canned" computer programs which are not known to have been checked out by someone with sufficient statistical and mathematical insight to enable him to detect possible errors. Some checking procedures are provided in this chapter, but our focus will be on the theory necessary for an interpretative understanding of these techniques. With an adequate computer program you will be able to make use of the procedures yourself, An interesting commentary on the accuracy of some existing multiple regression programs is provided in Wampler (1970).

It is quite worthwhile and interesting to work through a more mathematical treatment of these topics in other books and courses. This would be especially helpful in interpreting results of more unusual applications of these techniques. See, for example, Draper and Smith (1966), in General References.

9.1 MULTIPLE REGRESSION AND MULTIPLE CORRELATION

9.1.1 Some Assumptions of Multiple Regression

Multiple regression techniques are among the more interesting and useful because they help handle the kind of complexity that begins to reflect theoretical notions sociologists have about the social world they are trying to explain. Even so, a number of simplifications are involved in multiple regression analysis, and these may mean that the regression model as described here simply is not appropriate or useful for many research problems. Figure 9.1 indicates other "multivariate" procedures which take into account more dependent variables, dichotomous dependent variables, underlying "factors" and the like.

One basic assumption of multiple regression analysis is that variables are related to the dependent variable in a simple *linear* fashion, and it is usually a good procedure to construct scatter diagrams to check this assumption. Sometimes simple transformations (such as a logarithmic transformation) can be

Number of Independent Variables To Be Used At One Time	Number of Dependent Variables To Be Used At One Time	
	One	Two or More
None	(A) Univariate descriptive statistics.	(B) Same as cell (A). Where several items measure the same variable, one might use: Index Forming Scaling Factor Analysis Smallest Space Analysis
One	(C) Bivariate statistical description: Tables— Measures of association— Correlation regression—	(D) Same as cells (B), (C), (E), or some combination. Treating dependent variables one at a time and/or in scales.
Two or More	(E) Partial tables— Standardization— Partial correlation coefficients— Multiple regression and correlation— Discriminate function analysis—	(F) Same as cells (B), (E), in combinations treating dependent variables as scales or individually. Canonical correlation.

FIGURE 9.1 Some Alternative Procedures for Statistical Description

used to uncover a linear relationship. Another assumption is that effects of variables can be *added* together to form a prediction of the dependent variable. "Statistical interaction" cannot be handled unless it is "scored" and included as a separate variable in the regression equation. Further, all of the variables included in the multiple regression equation should be interpretable as *interval-level* measures. Finally, there is an assumption of zero correlation between independent variables, so that the effects of each variable on the dependent variable, with others taken into account, can be reliably computed.

Some other assumptions are involved in specific applications of multiple regression (see Figure 9.2) and these will be discussed when introduced later in this chapter.†

Basic assumptions.
   1. Independent variables are related in a linear fashion with the dependent variable and among themselves.
   2. Effects of independent variables can be added together to yield a prediction of the dependent variable.
   3. Independent variables are not correlated.**
   4. All variables are interval-level variables.

Added assumptions if one is interested in running statistical tests of hypotheses about a population from random sample data.

   5. The dependent variable is normally distributed within categories of independent variables, singly and in combination.
   6. The variance in the dependent variable is equal across categories of the independent variables.

Added assumptions if multiple regression analysis is to be applied to testing causal models of the relationship between variables.

   7. The theoretical ordering of independent and dependent variables should be known and such that independent variables change first and dependent variables later.
   8. The set of independent and dependent variables should be inclusive of all (major) variables influencing the dependent variables. That is, it should be a closed system.
   9. Measures should have high (demonstrated) reliability and validity.
   10. Disturbance terms (error terms) should be uncorrelated with each other or with independent variables directly connected to the same variable.

**For a discussion of correlated independent variables, see Blalock, (1970).

FIGURE 9.2   The Assumptions of Multiple Regression Analysis

†Assumptions should be taken seriously and consequences of departures from one assumption upon the importance of other assumptions is the subject of debate and inquiry in the field. The interval-level measurement assumption, for example, can be handled in some cases for even nominal-level variables by using what are called "dummy variables." The "no-intercorrelation among independent variables" assumption is usually interpreted to mean "low intercorrelation" (low multicollinearity), but checking and caution are needed where there are small departures. It may also be the case that the theoretical idea of variables related in a simple, linear fashion is intrinsically interesting as a model (or first model) of some aspect of the social world. In this case, the results of a regression analysis would be interesting, even though all of the regression assumptions may not fit the world particularly well.

BOX 9.1 REVIEWING CORRELATION AND THE NATURE OF ASSOCIATION

At this point you may want to check back on the idea of *correlation* (Chapter 7) and particularly the *nature* of association and possibilities for linear and curvilinear association (end of Section 7.4.4). Sometimes some function of the scores (like logarithms) rather than the scores themselves will have a simple linear relationship with another variable and thus satisfy a presumption of the Pearson correlation coefficient and linear regression analysis. The transformation of scores to produce this effect is something that requires experience and usually involves double-checking through the use of scatter diagrams both before and after transformations.

9.1.2 One Independent Variable: A Review

In Chapter 7, "simple" (one independent and one dependent variable) linear regression equations were expressed in the following form where the *b*-value represents the slope or amount of change in the dependent variable for each unit change in the independent variable and a_{yx} represented the Y-intercept where the regression line crossed the Y-axis.

(9.1)
$$Y' = a_{yx} + b_{yx}X$$

If the scores for both the Y and X variables were expressed not as raw measures but as standard scores (z-scores), the regression equation could be expressed as follows.† Note that we are changing the notation slightly so that all variables including the dependent variable are referred to by a different subscript.**

(9.2)
$$z'_1 = b_1^* + b_{12}^* z_2$$

The b_1^* (*b*-star or beta-weight) coefficient in (9.2) corresponds to a_{yx} in equation (9.1) and in fact the two equations are identical, term for term, except for the notation and the use of z-scores rather than raw Y and X scores in (9.2).

Since the mean of a distribution of z-scores is zero, and since the regression "line" passes through $\overline{X}_1$, $\overline{X}_2$, then the value of b_1^* will always be zero, and the regression equation in (9.2) can be simplified to this:

---

†Recall that z-scores are simply the difference between a score and the mean of its distribution expressed in terms of the number of standard deviation units it is from the mean. The formula for z-scores is this: $z = (X_i - \overline{X})/s$. It is discussed in Section 5.4.7.
**Note on symbolism. Dependent variables are referred to in a number of different ways, for example, as: Y or X_0 or X_1 etc. To indicate that this is a predicted value, some texts use a prime (X') and some use a "hat" ($\hat{X}$). We will use subscripts starting at 1, generally, to refer to variables and explain in context whether each variable is to be treated as an independent or dependent variable. A predicted dependent variable will be indicated by a prime, X'_1. Weights in the regression equation will be written in two ways, b for weights in an equation which uses raw scores, and b^* (*b*-star) for weights in an equation where standard scores (z-scores) are used. Appropriate subscripts will also be added: the first indicating the dependent variable; the second indicating the independent variable (and other variables in the equation will be listed following a dot in the subscript). Some texts also introduce Greek letters where the population value (rather than sample value) is used. To simplify symbolism at this point, sample notation is used. Later on (in the field of inferential statistics), where the distinction between population and sample values is of concern, further symbolism may be introduced and explained.

(9.3)
$$z_1' = b_{12}^* z_2$$

It can be shown that in the case where there is only one independent variable, $b_{12}^* = r_{12}$. (Of course $r_{12} = r_{21}$ since r is a symmetrical measure of association.) Thus the regression equation in Formula (9.3) could be expressed (with one independent variable) as follows:

(9.4)
$$z_1' = r_{12} z_2$$

The correlation coefficient is simply the slope coefficient in a two-variable situation where standard scores are used. The correlation coefficient can be seen as a correlation between the score on the dependent variable *predicted* by using the regression equation and the *actual* score of the dependent variable. The closer the prediction comes to the actual score, the higher the degree of linear association and the closer r comes to plus or minus one.

The coefficient of determination (the square of the correlation coefficient), r_{12}^2, indicates the proportion of variation in one variable (for example the dependent variable) which is explained by its linear association with the other variable expressed in the right-hand side of the linear regression equation. Unexplained variation is expressed as $1 - r_{12}^2$ and is referred to as the **coefficient of non-determination.** In the two-variable situation, these interpretations also apply to b_{12}^*, b_{12}^{*2}, and $1 - b_{12}^{*2}$.

9.1.3 Two or More Independent Variables

When more than one independent variable is used to explain variation in a single dependent variable, the basic regression equation in (9.3) can be extended as in (9.5), below, to include terms which combine a beta-weight (b^*) coefficient and the z-score of k independent variables. Thus we have the **multiple regression equation:**

(9.5)
$$z_1' = b_{12 \cdot 34 \ldots k}^* z_2 + b_{13 \cdot 24 \ldots k}^* z_3 + b_{14 \cdot 23 \ldots k}^* z_4 + b_{1k \cdot 234 \ldots}^* z_k$$

Here the standard scores for each independent variable are weighted according to the contribution that variable makes to the overall predicted sum, z_1'. Each b^* value represents the relative amount of contribution of that variable, after contributions of the other variables included in the regression equation are taken into account. In that sense, the b^* values are like a partial correlation coefficient in "holding constant" or "correcting" for the contribution of other included variables. Often this controlling effect is indicated in the subscripts for the b^* coefficients, as illustrated in the three-variable regression equation, below. The dependent and independent variables to which the b^* value refers are written in front of the dot in the subscript, and the other variables included in the regression equation are listed after the dot. Those after the dot are "held constant," *i.e.* their contribution is partialled out. As usual, the first subscript is the dependent variable and the second is the independent variable for that particular b^* coefficient. Using two independent variables, Formula (9.5) becomes this:

(9.6)
$$z_1' = b_{12 \cdot 3}^* z_2 + b_{13 \cdot 2}^* z_3$$

Beta-weights (b^*) are computed in a way that minimizes the sum of squared deviations between predicted and actual scores on the dependent variable. This is called the **least-squares criterion.**

(9.7)
$$\Sigma(z_1 - z_1')^2 = \text{a minimum}$$

Using only two independent variables and substituting the right-hand side of equation (9.6) for z_1', the quantity to be minimized is this:

(9.8)
$$\Sigma(z_1 - b_{12\cdot3}^* z_2 - b_{13\cdot2}^* z_3)^2 = \text{a minimum}$$

This results in a maximum linear correlation between predicted and actual scores on the dependent variable.

To carry out the computations implied by the least squares criterion, a set of normal equations (*not* related to the idea of a normal curve in any way), predicting correlations between each variable and the dependent variable, are created and solved for unknown b^*s. For the three-variable problem, these normal equations would be as follows:

(9.9)
$$b_{12\cdot3}^* + r_{23}b_{13\cdot2}^* = r_{12}$$
$$r_{23}b_{12\cdot3}^* + b_{13\cdot2}^* = r_{13}$$

Note that solution for the b^*s is possible because there are as many equations as unknowns. The intercorrelation of variables can be computed directly from the data in the study being used in the multiple regression analysis. Thus, in a three-variable regression equation with two independent variables, the two normal equations in (9.9) could be solved for the two betas, $b_{12\cdot3}^*$ and $b_{13\cdot2}^*$.

Hand computation of the b^* coefficients is illustrated in such books as Walker and Lev (General References, 1953; Chapter 13, discusses the Doolittle method of solution). Usually b^* coefficients are computed by means of computer programs for multiple regression, where raw scores on all variables are transformed into standard scores as a first (often optional) step in the computer program. The beta coefficients can also be computed from a correlation matrix of the interrelationship between all pairs of variables to be included in the regression equation, but this procedure becomes tedious for more than one or two independent variables. Diagram 9.1 illustrates these procedures.

The b^* coefficients provide an investigator with a basis for comparing the relative contribution of one variable to a prediction of the dependent variable with the contribution of other variables in the equation. If $b_{12\cdot3}^*$ were larger than $b_{13\cdot2}^*$, then one would be able to conclude that a given amount of change in z_2 would result in more change in the dependent variable than the same amount of change in the z-score of variable z_3. z_2 is a more potent influence than z_3. If $b_{12\cdot3}^*$ is twice the size of $b_{13\cdot2}^*$, then a given change in z_2 has twice the effect of the same change in z_3. Variables with b^* coefficients which are very nearly zero have very little separate influence on the dependent variable, at least in the linear, additive way described by the multiple regression equation. We might, on this basis, argue that such variables could well be eliminated from the prediction equation, and the beta coefficients could be re-computed.

At this point we are only talking about the way changes in some variables are related to changes in other variables, and not about influence in a "cause-

DIAGRAM 9.1 Standardized Regression Coefficients

The problem: Compute the standardized regression weights (b^*) for the following 3-variable, multiple regression equation.[**]

(D1)
$$z_i' = b_{ij \cdot k}^* z_j + b_{ik \cdot j}^* z_k$$

Computation from correlations among the variables:

(D2)
$$b_{ij \cdot k}^* = \frac{r_{ij} - r_{ik} r_{jk}}{1 - r_{jk}^2}$$

where the subscript i refers to the dependent variable and j is the independent variable for which the regression-weight is being computed. Variable k is the third variable involved in the regression equation in (D1). Note that two such regression weights must be computed, the one given in (D2) and this:

$$b_{ik \cdot j}^* = \frac{r_{ik} - r_{ij} r_{jk}}{1 - r_{jk}^2}$$

Computation from unstandardized regression coefficients:

(D3)
$$b_{ij \cdot k}^* = b_{ij \cdot k} \frac{s_j}{s_i}$$

where i refers to the dependent variable and j to the independent variable for which the b^* coefficient is being computed. k is the third independent variable in the equation. s_j is the standard deviation on the independent variable. s_i is the standard deviation on the dependent variable. b_{ij} is the *un*standardized or *raw* score form of the regression coefficient.

In addition to (D3), one would have to compute this:

$$b_{ik \cdot j}^* = b_{ik \cdot j} \frac{s_k}{s_i}$$

Computation using standard computer programs:

Many universities have existing computer programs which will compute regression coefficients from information on each variable for each case. To compute standardized regression coefficients, select the control-card option which converts the raw score data into standard score form prior to computations. The transformation and regression computations generally occur in the same computer

---

[**]Note that these formulas can be extended easily to the situation where there are more independent variables, simply by adding subscripts to specify the specific betas of interest and adding terms to the standardized regression equation, one for each additional variable.

DIAGRAM 9.1 *(Continued)*

run. The computational technique used is likely to be one that makes use of matrix algebra. Although this topic is not discussed in this volume, it would provide one clear basis for expressing the relationship between correlations of the input data and standardized regression coefficients. If you are interested in this way of solving the problem of standardized coefficients you should see (in General References) the following: Walker and Lev (1953), Chapter 13; Draper and Smith (1966), Chapter 6.8; or Cooley and Lohnes (1962), Chapter 3.

Example

Duncan (Other References; 1961:124) presents data on a socioeconomic index for occupation groups (a social status measure), income level and educational level for the same occupational groups. The correlation matrix is as follows:

	X_1	X_2	X_3
X_1 Duncan"s SEI		.84	.85
X_2 Income Level			.72
X_3 Education Level			

Compute coefficients for this:

$$z_1' = b_{12 \cdot 3}^* z_2 + b_{13 \cdot 2}^* z_3$$

from formula (D2) above:

$$b_{12 \cdot 3}^* = \frac{r_{12} - r_{13} r_{23}}{1 - r_{23}^2}$$

$$= \frac{.84 - (.85)(.72)}{1 - (.72)^2}$$

$$= \frac{.84 - .61}{1 - .52} = \frac{.23}{.48} = .48$$

and

$$b_{13 \cdot 2}^* = \frac{r_{13} - r_{12} r_{23}}{1 - r_{23}^2} = \frac{.85 - (.84)(.72)}{1 - (.72)^2} = \frac{.85 - .60}{1 - .52} = \frac{.24}{.48} = .50$$

The equation would thus be written as follows, predicting the standard score of variable 1, Duncan's Socioeconomic Index from variable 2, income, and variable 3, education.

$$z_1' = .48z_2 + .50z_3$$

Income makes about the same contribution as education to the prediction of Duncan's SEI score.

effect" sense, although clearly, given other kinds of information, such as the theoretical ordering of the influence of variables, we might use evidence from a multiple regression equation in evaluating a theoretical cause-effect argument.

9.1.4   Regression Weights and Partial Correlation Coefficients

The standardized beta weight (b^*) and the partial correlation coefficient share some characteristics. They both reflect the effect of an independent variable on a dependent variable when the effects of other included independent variables are taken into account, statistically. The dependent variable scores to be predicted are adjusted by subtracting out predictions that would be made by linear regression equations that omit a given independent variable. Thus the b^* for a given independent variable is computed so that it best predicts (in the least squares sense) the adjusted scores for the dependent variable. The partial correlation coefficient expresses the relationship between such predicted scores and the adjusted scores on the dependent variable.

The two coefficients provide different information, since the b^* indicates the *amount of change in the dependent* variable which is associated with a unit change on the independent variable (when other independent variables are taken into account). As such it is an asymmetric measure. The partial correlation coefficient is a symmetric measure which indicates the closeness of relationship, overall, between a dependent and independent variable when scores of the dependent variable have been adjusted to take out the effect of variation in other independent variables implied by their linear relationship with the dependent variable. The partial correlation coefficient provides a measure of the accuracy of prediction and the beta coefficient provides a measure of the contribution of a variable to the prediction. By squaring the partial correlation coefficient, one can measure the proportion of the variation in the dependent variable that is explained by the direct contribution of an independent variable when effects of other included variables are taken into account. Both coefficients provide useful and somewhat different information.

9.1.5   Multiple Correlation

Multiple correlation ($R_{1 \cdot 23}$), like the simple product-moment correlation coefficient r_{yx}, is simply the correlation between the actual scores on the dependent variable, and the scores on the dependent variable predicted by use of the multiple regression equation. The beta weights (b*), in fact, are computed so that this correlation is as high as possible for a given set of data. The multiple correlation coefficient is symbolized by the capital letter, R, and it varies on a scale from 0 to +1.00. The smaller the coefficient the poorer the correlation, and the larger the coefficient, the stronger the correlation.

Like the coefficient r, the multiple correlation coefficient can be interpreted more usefully by squaring it. R^2 has an interpretation quite akin to r^2, namely, the proportion of the variation in the dependent variable which is explained by the regression equation.

$$R^2 = \frac{\text{Explained variation in } X_1}{\text{Total variation in } X_1}$$

(9.10)

$$R^2 = \frac{\Sigma(X_1' - \overline{X}_1)^2}{\Sigma(X_1 - \overline{X}_1)^2}$$

R^2 is called the coefficient of multiple determination. $1 - R^2$ is the proportion of variation in the dependent variable left unexplained by the multiple regression equation.

Diagram 9.2 explains the computation of the multiple correlation coefficient. If all of the intercorrelations of independent variables were zero, then the square of the multiple correlation coefficient would simply be the sum of squared correlations between each independent variable and the dependent variable as in Formula (9.11), below.

(9.11)

$$R^2_{1 \cdot 23} = r^2_{12} + r^2_{13}$$

If, as is usually the case, some independent variables are related to each other, the "overlap" in contribution to the explanation of the dependent variable would have to be taken into account and eliminated from (9.11) in order to arrive at R^2. This is done simply by adjusting each r by multiplying it times the related beta weight, b^*, as in (9.12).

(9.12)

$$R^2_{1 \cdot 23} = r_{12} b^*_{12 \cdot 3} + r_{13} b^*_{13 \cdot 2}$$

Both (9.11) and (9.12) could be extended to include more than two independent variables by simply adding additional terms.

It is apparent from (9.11) that R will be zero if all the correlations between dependent and independent variables are zero, and R cannot be less than the highest r relating any independent and dependent variable. R exceeds the highest r relating any independent and dependent variable by the largest amount when independent variables are independent of each other (*i.e.* have zero intercorrelations), since each variable contributes an added, separate amount to the prediction of the dependent variable.**

9.1.5a Corrected *R*. The multiple correlation coefficient based on a sample tends to be inflated compared with the multiple correlation coefficient computed on a larger sample or on the population values themselves. This "bias" in the direction of a higher R for sample data is due to the fact that the multiple regression equation is "tailored" to the sample data to produce the highest R possible. This operation takes advantage of any chance difference between the sample and population distribution of scores to find a higher R by "tailoring" the b^*s to the data. The computations, in a sense, pursue opportunities for finding the highest possible R rather than the lowest possible R or some intermediate value of R. This effect can be corrected as follows:

**Your attention should be called to another variation on the multiple correlation coefficient. It is a "multiple partial correlation coefficient," and it indicates the multiple correlation between a set of independent variables and a dependent variable when other independent variables are statistically controlled. Thus it is useful in examining the explanatory power of one set of independent variables on a dependent variable, controlling for effects of another set of independent variables. The multiple partial coefficient is introduced by Blalock, (1972), in General References, pages 458–459.

DIAGRAM 9.2   The Multiple Correlation Coefficient

The Problem:

Compute a measure of the proportion of the variation in a dependent variable which is explained by the linear combination of a set of independent variables, R^2 (the coefficient of multiple determination).

Computation of R^2 *from Correlation Coefficients and Standardized Regression Betas:*

(D1)
$$R^2_{1\cdot23} = r_{12}b^*_{12\cdot3} + r_{13}b^*_{13\cdot2}$$

where: variable 1 is the dependent variable and 2 and 3 are independent variables. Correlation coefficients are zero-order associations between the dependent and each independent variable.

Note that this can be extended for any number of independent variables by adding comparable terms to the right-hand side of (D1) and listing all independent variables in the subscript of R.

Computation of R^2 *from Zero-Order and Partial Correlation Coefficients; Illustrated for Three Variables:*

(D2)
$$R^2_{1\cdot23} = r^2_{12} + (1 - r^2_{12})r^2_{13\cdot2}$$

where variable 1 is the dependent variable.

Note that r^2_{12} is the proportion of variation in the dependent variable explained by the linear association with variable 2. $1 - r^2_{12}$ is the unexplained portion. Of this unexplained portion, variable 3 can explain an added amount symbolized by the partial correlation coefficient $r^2_{13\cdot2}$.

Computation of R^2 *from Zero-Order Correlation Coefficients; Illustrated for the Three-variable Case.*

(D3)
$$R^2_{1\cdot23} = \frac{r^2_{12} + r^2_{13} - 2r_{12}r_{13}r_{23}}{1 - r^2_{23}}$$

where variable 1 is the dependent variable.

Note, if the intercorrelation of the independent variables is zero, equation (D3) reduces to this:

$$R^2_{1\cdot23} = r^2_{12} + r^2_{13}$$

and this can be generalized to any number of independent variables.

Corrected R^2:

(D4)
$$R^2_c = 1 - \left(\frac{N-1}{N-k}\right)(1 - R^2)$$

where N is the sample size; k is the number of independent variables included in the multiple regression equation; R^2 is the uncorrected coefficient; R^2_c is the corrected coefficient.

DIAGRAM 9.2 *(Continued)*

This correction is for bias in R. It is computed on a sample which will be inflated from the R computed on a large sample, or the population, because of "tailoring" of the regression equation to sample data in a way that takes advantage of chance factors in finding a best equation resulting in the highest possible R for the data at hand. If variables are pre-selected, the bias is larger than this and not corrected by this formula.

Example:

In the data from Duncan where occupational social status scores (Duncan's SEI) are the dependent variable and income and education are independent variables, the following partial correlation and zero-order correlation coefficients are provided.

$$r_{12} = .84 \qquad r_{12 \cdot 3} = .61$$
$$r_{13} = .85 \qquad r_{13 \cdot 2} = .65$$
$$r_{23} = .72$$

From (D3), above:

$$R^2_{1 \cdot 23} = \frac{r^2_{12} + r^2_{13} - 2r_{12}r_{13}r_{23}}{1 - r^2_{23}}$$

$$= \frac{.84^2 + .85^2 - 2(.84)(.85)(.72)}{1 - (.72)^2}$$

$$= \frac{.706 + .723 - 2(.514)}{1.00 - .518}$$

$$R^2_{1 \cdot 23} = \frac{.400}{.482} = .83 = \begin{array}{l} \text{Coefficient of} \\ \text{Multiple Determination} \end{array}$$

$$R_{1 \cdot 23} = \sqrt{.83} = .91 = \begin{array}{l} \text{Multiple Correlation} \\ \text{Coefficient} \end{array}$$

Note that variable 2 explains $.84^2 = .706$ of the variation in variable 1 and leaves $(1 - .706)$ or .294 unexplained.

Of the .294 left unexplained by variable 2, variable 3 is able to explain an additional 42 percent (*i.e.* $.65^2$), or .423 of .294 is .124. Thus the two variables can explain a total of $.706 + .124$ or .83 of the variation in variable 1 by their linear association with variable 1.

Eighty-three percent of the variation in variable 1 is a rather high amount to explain. Perhaps by adding another carefully chosen variable, one could explain even more of the variation in variable 1.

Because of bias involved in taking advantage of sampling variability to find the highest possible R, a corrected R could be computed from Formula (D4). Duncan's sample size was 45 occupations. There were two independent variables.

$$R^2_{1 \cdot 23} = 1 - \frac{45 - 1}{45 - 2}(1 - .83) = 1 - (1.02)(.17) = 1 - .173 = .827 \text{ or } .83$$

DIAGRAM 9.2 *(Continued)*

Here, the sample size compared to the number of independent variables was sufficiently large to result in a negligible correction.

Alternative computation of R^2:

Using Formula (D1), the same R^2 could be obtained since the b^* values are available from computations in Diagram 9.1, as follows:

$$b^*_{12 \cdot 3} = .48 \qquad r_{12} = .84$$
$$b^*_{13 \cdot 2} = .50 \qquad r_{13} = .85$$

from (D1)

$$R^2_{1 \cdot 23} = r_{12} b^*_{12 \cdot 3} + r_{13} b^*_{13 \cdot 2}$$
$$R^2_{1 \cdot 23} = (.84)(.48) + (.85)(.50) = .403 + .425 = .828 \text{ or } .83$$
$$R_{1 \cdot 23} = .91$$

(9.13)
$$R_c^2 = 1 - \left(\frac{N-1}{N-k}\right)(1 - R^2)$$

where R^2 is the uncorrected coefficient; R_c^2 is the corrected coefficient; N is the sample size; k is the number of independent variables included in the multiple regression equation.

Generally, the investigator is interested in finding sets of independent variables which will provide the best prediction of the dependent variable, the highest value of R. If he preselects independent variables by looking for independent variables which are most highly correlated with the dependent variable in his sample data, and then introduces these into a multiple regression equation, the inflation of R is even greater than that eliminated by the correction in Formula (9.13) above. An R, re-computed on a larger sample or on the population would be less than that found by preselecting independent variables. For this reason, an investigator may want to replicate his study on other new data and use relatively large samples as the basis of computing multiple regression coefficients and R.

Notice in Formula (9.13) that when the sample size, N, and the number of independent variables, k, are equal, R^2 and R will always be equal to 1. This is because b^*s would be calculated to perfectly fit each individual score, and there would be no difference between predicted and observed scores. The numerator in Formula (9.10) would be equal to the denominator simply because of this, and R^2 would equal 1. To compute the multiple regression and multiple correlation coefficients, then, the number of cases must exceed the number of variables.

9.1.6 An Illustration

Koslin and a group of investigators at Princeton University studied a group of 29 eleven to thirteen year old boys at a boys camp in Canada (Koslin et al., 1968). In this study they developed a regression equation to predict the standing of a boy in a group, using several measures of the expectations group members had for each other's performance on several tasks. They argue that individuals within groups develop ways of evaluating the performance of their associates, and that expected performance is related to status in the group. Higher-status individuals are expected to perform better than lower-status individuals on tasks of central concern to the group regardless, of actual performance. If this is the case, then one should be able to predict status within a group by knowing whether an individual's performance is "over-rated" or "under-rated" when compared with his actual performance.

Four different tests were devised to measure over-under rating: (1) a rifle task, (2) a canoe task, (3) a sociometric "preference" test and (4) a height perception test. The rifle test, for example, involved having each boy in turn shoot four shots at a target while other group-members watched. The target disappeared immediately after a shot was fired and the boy who shot as well as others in the group was asked to record how close to the "bull's eye" the shot hit. The score on this task for each group member was the average "over" or "under" estimate of his shooting accuracy (compared with where the actual shot hit) as made by group members who watched him shoot. The canoe task involved group esti-mates of the time a boy took to go a given distance. The sociometric question-naire asked for teammate preferences, and the height test involved comparisons of an individual's height in relation to other individuals in the group. In each case, the test was conducted in an ambiguous situation (*i.e.*, participant mem-bers had no watches to measure time; people were too far apart to allow actual comparisons of height, etc.). The dependent variable, group status, was deter-mined by the investigators through careful observation of the boys over the course of the experiment. Data from the study are as follows:

TABLE 9.1 CORRELATION MATRIX FOR THE PREDICTOR AND CRITERION VARIABLES

	(2) Canoe test	(3) Socio-metric test	(4) Height Guess test	(5) Observed Social Status
1. Rifle test	.52	.58	.48	.67
2. Canoe test		.61	.65	.67
3. Sociometric			.66	.64
4. Height guessing				.51

The regression equation computed by Koslin using standardized beta weights was as follows:

(9.14)

$$z_5' = .37z_1 + .37z_2 + .25z_3 - .07z_4$$

where z_1 is the rifle test; z_2 is the canoe test; z_3 is the sociometric test; z_4 is the height guessing test; z_5 is the investigator's rating of individual social status in the group on the basis of careful observational data.

It is immediately evident that the rifle and canoe tests are equally good predictors of observed status, the sociometric test is somewhat poorer but still a positive contributor to the prediction of observational status independently of the other three variables. Only height-guessing makes a very minor contribu-tion to the prediction, and that contribution is a negative one. Thus their expec-tations were supported; over-under ratings on relevant tasks could be used to predict observed status and over-under ratings on irrelevant tasks contributed little in addition. Notice that this conclusion is not immediately apparent in Table 9.1 where zero-order correlation coefficients are all relatively high. In fact, from the b^* coefficients, one could say that a unit change in the rifle and canoe tests results in the same amount of change in observed status; but the sociome-tric test contributes only two-thirds as much as either of these variables (.25/.37 = .676). The impact of height is only 19 percent of that of the rifle or the canoe tests, and only 28 percent of the impact of sociometric choice.

Partial correlation coefficients provide somewhat different but consistent information. The partial correlation coefficient .42 in Table 9.2 is the correlation between the rifle test scores and observed status when effects of the canoe test, sociometric choice, and height-guessing were taken into account. The square of these coefficients provides a way of judging the proportion of the variation in the

TABLE 9.2 MULTIPLE CORRELATION USING OBSERVED SOCIAL STATUS AS THE CRITERION (DEPENDENT) VARIABLE

Predictor	$b*$	Partial r
1. Rifle test	.37	.42
2. Canoe test	.37	.39
3. Sociometric	.25	.26
4. Height guess	−.07	−.08
	Multiple R = .79	

Source: Koslin, 1968. Used by permission.

dependent variable accounted for by a given independent variable after other effects are taken into account. Thus the rifle test explained 18%, the canoe test 15%, the sociometric test 7%, and the height guessing test about one-half of one percent.

Overall, the multiple regression equation yielded a multiple correlation between predicted and observed social status scores of .79. Squaring this coefficient, it becomes evident that 62% of the variation in the dependent variable is accounted for by the multiple regression equation and 38% (the difference between 62% and 100%) is left unexplained. Since there were four independent variables and a sample size of only 29, a better estimate of a population multiple correlation coefficient would be R = .76, a corrected value computed from Formula (9.13).

9.2   PATH ANALYSIS: AN APPLICATION OF MULTIPLE REGRESSION TO PROBLEMS OF THEORY

9.2.1   Path Analysis

The use of standardized multiple regression equations in examining theoretical models is called **path analysis.** The objective is to compare a model of the direct and indirect relationships that are presumed to hold between several variables to observed data in a study, in order to examine the fit of the model to the data. If the fit is close, the model is retained and used or further tested. If the fit is not close, a new model may be devised, or, more likely, the old one will be modified to better fit the data and then be subjected to further tests on new data.

This is precisely the interest we have if we want to build theoretical explanations of social phenomena. Where the underlying assumptions of path analysis are reasonably met, it provides a very pertinent way to relate theory and data when many variables are to be handled simultaneously. Correlation analysis alone, although helpful, does not provide as useful a measure of the impact of variables directly and indirectly on others.

In addition to the basic assumptions of multiple regression, path analysis

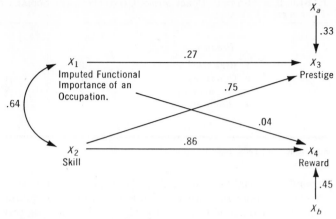

Source: Land, 1970. Used by permission.

FIGURE 9.3   Davis-Moore Model of Social Stratification

includes two others (see Figure 9.2). First, the variables included in a model must be known to fall in some specific theoretical order in their effect on individuals; the independent variables must fall in causal order *before* the dependent variable. This is important and not always obvious.** Secondly, the model must be treated as a closed system in the sense that all important variables are explicitly included in the model. To some extent one can assess the extent to which this is true in the process of conducting the path analysis itself. Finally, for the purposes of this presentation, it is assumed that the influence of one variable on another is a one-way influence, or, in other words, the model is *recursive*; there is no "feedback."

Path analysis models are generally illustrated, as in Figure 9.3, by means of one-headed arrows connecting some or all of the variables included in the model. Variables are distributed from left to right, depending upon their theoretical-ordering, with the first independent variables at the extreme left. Intercorrelations (zero-order) between variables not influenced by other variables in the model are given as numbers on curved, two-headed arrows. These are correlations between *exogenous* variables, those influenced only by variables prior to and outside the model. Exogenous variables provide a link between a model under consideration and outside variables.

Numbers entered on the direct paths reflect the amount of direct contribution of a given variable on another variable when effects of other related variables are taken into account. Path coefficients are symbolized by the letter *p*, with subscripts indicating the two variables it connects. It turns out that path coefficients are identical to the b^* coefficients in the standardized multiple regression equation discussed earlier, where the regression equation reflects the structure of the model one is testing. These are computed as described earlier,

---

**At this point you may wish to refer back to discussions in Chapter 8 on the ordering of variables and the use of diagrams to make explicit the relationships between variables implied by a theory.

from scores ultimately measured on a group of subjects. Thus the path model and the path coefficients provide a picture of the bit of the social world an investigator is interested in explaining, together with the coefficients describing the impact of independent variables. The impact is in terms of the amount of change in the dependent variable which is associated with a unit change in a given independent variable, over and above the contribution of other variables to the dependent variable.

The basic theorem of path analysis, and the way by which a specific structural model is reflected in the computation of **path coefficients** is as follows:

(9.15)
$$r_{ij} = \sum_k (p_{ik} r_{kj})$$

where: k includes each of the variables connected directly to the dependent variable i and prior to i in theoretical ordering shown in a path diagram. Let us develop these ideas in terms of a particular model and some actual data.

9.2.2 An Example of Path Analysis in Sociology

The Davis-Moore theory of social stratification argues that some type of social stratification will be found in every society because some types of duties must be performed for the society to continue as a functioning unit, and by some means individuals must be motivated to accept and perform these duties (see Land, 1970). The stratification system is one means of assuring the placement and motivation of individuals in the social structure. Rewards used in the process include income, leisure, and prestige. These are distributed among occupations, for example, in terms of (a) the importance of that occupation in the society, and (b) the scarcity of appropriately trained individuals needed for the occupation. Figure 9.3 describes this model, except that income and leisure are combined as "other rewards," distinguished from "prestige." Note that two other "variables" (X_a and X_b) are included to reflect variables external to the model and measurement errors that may influence the dependent variables.

Using X rather than z to stand for the *standard score* of a given variable (since this is the convention here), one could express the graphic model in terms of a "Path Model" as follows:

(9.16a)
$$X_3 = p_{31}X_1 + p_{32}X_2 + p_{3a}X_a$$

(9.16b)
$$X_4 = p_{41}X_1 + p_{42}X_2 + p_{4b}X_b$$

This is a "fully" recursive model, since all of the possible one-way arrows are drawn between the four explicit variables included in the model. These structural equations correspond to the multiple regression equations in (9.6), above, except for the addition of the residual variables X_a and X_b.† These equations can be rewritten in terms of path coefficients and zero-order correlation coefficients in a fashion parallel to that in Formula (9.9), remembering that path coefficients are standardized b^*s. In fact, in this example, one could use a computer program for a multiple regression equation with standardized data using X_1 and X_2 to

---

†The X_a and X_b terms are called residual variables or, sometimes, the "random shock" or "error" terms.

predict X_3, and X_1 and X_2 to predict X_4.** From the information provided all of the path coefficients would be readily available.

Using path coefficients and correlation coefficients, one could write a series of equations which would predict the correlation of independent and dependent variables. The basic theorem of path analysis (9.15), provides the model for constructing these path estimating equations.

(9.17a) $\qquad r_{31}=p_{31}r_{11}+p_{32}r_{21}$ (or, since $r_{11}=1.0$) $p_{31}+p_{32}r_{21}$

(9.17b) $\qquad r_{32}=p_{31}r_{12}+p_{32}r_{22}$ (or, since $r_{22}=1.0$) $p_{31}r_{12}+p_{32}$

(9.17c) $\qquad r_{41}=p_{41}r_{11}+p_{42}r_{21}$ (or, since $r_{11}=1.0$) $p_{41}+p_{42}r_{21}$

(9.17d) $\qquad r_{42}=p_{41}r_{12}+p_{42}r_{22}$ (or, since $r_{22}=1.0$) $p_{41}r_{12}+p_{42}$

Taking (9.17a) as an example and referring to the path diagram in Figure 9.2, notice that the correlation between variables 3 and 1 can be written in terms of the path between variables 3 and 1, *times* the correlation of variable 1 with itself (which is taken as 1.00, and so r_{11} and r_{22} could be dropped from these equations), *plus* the path from 3 to 2 and the correlation of variable 1 and 2. Here, k in the path theorem, Formula (9.15), has taken on two values, 1 and 2, reflecting the fact that variables 1 and 2 are directly connected and prior to variable 3. Four such equations are possible to predict each of the four correlations between independent and dependent variables. Since these four equations have only four unknown path coefficients, they can be solved for the path coefficients, and there are computer programs which carry out the calculations. All we need at this point is data from a study which measure variables included in the model. Land (1970) examines this model by using data gathered from 185 junior and senior highschool students in Nevada and Massachusetts in 1962, where they made judgments of the functional importance, skill, prestige and rewards of 24 occupations (Lopreato and Lewis, 1963).

The zero-order intercorrelation (r) of variables is as follows:

Variables	(2)	(3)	(4)
(1) Imputed functional importance of an occupation	.64	.75	.59
(2) Skill	—	.92	.89
(3) Prestige	—	—	.87
(4) Reward	—	—	—

From these data and the path estimating equations in (9.17), path coefficients can be computed for the model. A multiple correlation coefficient could be obtained for the regression equation predicting each dependent variable as illustrated in Diagram 9.2. Both path coefficients and the multiple correlation coefficients are generally provided by standard computer regression programs.

With computed coefficients shown in Figure 9.3, one can turn to the crux of the problem, the evaluation of the "fit" of the model to the data. "Goodness of

**A helpful discussion of path analysis and a program for computing path coefficients is provided by Nygreen (1971), in General References.

fit" of the model can be examined in a number of ways. Land (1970) cites three general approaches.

(a) One could examine the amount of *variation* in dependent variables which is *explained* by variables linked as specified in the model.

(b) One could examine the *size of path coefficients* to see whether they are large enough to warrant the inclusion of a variable or path in the model.

(c) One could evaluate the ability of the model to *predict correlation* coefficients which were not used in computation of the path coefficients themselves.

In each of these cases, an investigator usually contrasts the usefulness of his model in these three respects with alternative models, and this is the heart of explanatory progress in any science.

Taking the "goodness of fit" criteria one at a time, and applying them to the example, we see the following. The two multiple correlation coefficients, squared, provide an estimate of the proportion of variation in the dependent variable explained by the linear combination of specific independent variables. In this case:

$$
\begin{array}{ccc}
\textit{Explained} & & \textit{Unexplained} \\
R_{3 \cdot 12} = .94 & R^2_{3 \cdot 12} = .89 & 1 - R^2_{3 \cdot 12} = .11 \\
R_{4 \cdot 12} = .89 & R^2_{4 \cdot 12} = .80 & 1 - R^2_{4 \cdot 12} = .20
\end{array}
$$

Explaining eighty and eighty-nine percent of the variance in a dependent variable is quite high, although clearly not perfect. The model only leaves unexplained 11% of the variation in variable 3, and 20% in variable 4. In this respect the model is relatively satisfactory. The "unexplained" variation is due to variables or measurement error not included in the model and, for the sake of completeness, the square root of these $(1 - R^2)$ values are ascribed to the residual variables a and b, in Figure 9.3.

(9.18)
$$
\begin{array}{ll}
p_{3a} = \sqrt{1 - R^2_{3 \cdot 12}} & p_{3a} = .33 \\
p_{4b} = \sqrt{1 - R^2_{4 \cdot 12}} & p_{4b} = .45
\end{array}
$$

If these "residual" paths become large, then an investigator would begin to search for an alternative model which included other independent variables and/or he would examine his measurement process for measurement error.

In terms of the second criterion of goodness of fit, the model shows some weaknesses. Most of the path coefficients are moderately high except the path from variable 1 to 4. One might consider eliminating this path from the model for this reason and recompute path coefficients. The indirect effect of functional importance on rewards can be found by multiplying path coefficients (or correlation coefficients on curved lines in the model) times each other, along each route connecting the two variables of interest, and then by summing over all connecting paths. In this case $(.64)(.86) = .54$, which represents the indirect effect of variable 1 on variable 4. This is considerably stronger than the direct effect of 1 on 4.

Thirdly, one could examine the "fit" between observed correlation coeffi-

cients not previously used in formulas for calculating path coefficients and predictions of correlation coefficients which would be derived from the model. If the
fit is good, the model is supported; if not, some modification is perhaps needed.
In this instance, the correlation between variables 3 and 4 was not used to estimate path coefficients in equations shown in (9.17).

Since a correlation equals the sum of products of coefficients along all connecting paths, the model would lead to the following prediction of r_{34}

(9.19)
$$r'_{34} = p_{41}p_{31} + p_{41}r_{12}p_{32} + p_{42}r_{12}p_{31} + p_{42}p_{32}$$

or
$$
\begin{aligned}
(.04)(.27) &= .011 \\
(.04)(.64)(.75) &= .019 \\
(.86)(.64)(.27) &= .149 \\
(.86)(.75) &= \underline{.645} \\
r'_{34} &= .824
\end{aligned}
$$

This corresponds quite closely with the observed correlation of prestige and reward of .87.**

9.2.3 Testing an Alternative Model

Land goes on to contrast the goodness of fit of the Davis-Moore model with that
of the Parsonian model, postulating an added variable, *values,* an unmeasured,
underlying variable which is thought to account for the other four variables:
skill, importance, prestige, and reward. This model and the path estimation
equations are presented in Figure 9.4. Land concludes that neither the model
in Figure 9.3 nor the model in Figure 9.4 can be rejected on the basis of the goodness of fit criteria, but that the Parsonian model somewhat more consistently
fits these data. Other theoretical work suggests that the Davis-Moore theory of
social stratification would be a better representation in social systems where
there is *high* interdependence of work activities, and the Parsonian model would
be better under conditions of *low* interdependence—theoretical ideas that suggest
greater refinement and the possibility for further productive research.

Path analytic models may be extended to include more variables, as is
illustrated in Figure 9.5, in which Sewell et al. (1970) revised and extended
earlier work aimed at explaining the occupational attainment of Wisconsin high
school seniors. The data upon which path coefficients in this model are based are
from 4388 high school seniors first interviewed in 1957 and then re-interviewed
in 1964.

**What is "quite closely" and what is not depends to a large extent upon the investigator's experience
and judgment. Differences of .05 or .10 are likely to be considered small unless a meaningful alternative model is able to make closer predictions.

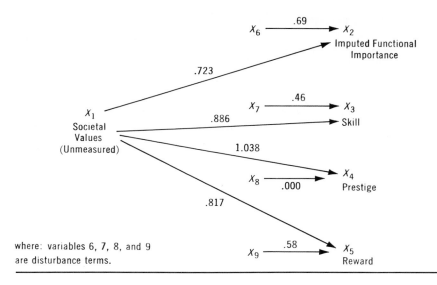

where: variables 6, 7, 8, and 9 are disturbance terms.

Path Model

$$X_2 = p_{21}X_1 + p_{26}X_6 \qquad X_4 = p_{41}X_1 + p_{48}X_8$$
$$X_3 = p_{31}X_1 + p_{37}X_7 \qquad X_5 = p_{51}X_1 + p_{59}X_9$$

Path Estimation Equations

$$r_{23} = p_{21}p_{31} \qquad\qquad p_{26} = \sqrt{1 - p_{21}^2}$$
$$r_{24} = p_{21}p_{41} \qquad\qquad p_{37} = \sqrt{1 - p_{31}^2}$$
$$r_{25} = p_{21}p_{51} \qquad\qquad p_{48} = \sqrt{1 - p_{41}^2}$$
$$r_{34} = p_{31}p_{41} \qquad\qquad p_{59} = \sqrt{1 - p_{51}^2}$$
$$r_{35} = p_{31}p_{51} \;{}^{**}$$
$$r_{45} = p_{41}p_{51} \;{}^{**}$$

Correlation Matrix (From Lopreato-Lewis matrix above, following Formula 9.17)

	(3)	(4)	(5)
2. Imputed Functional Importance	.64	.75	.59
3. Skill		.92	.89
4. Prestige			.87
5. Reward			

Goodness of Fit of Model in Figure 9.4

1. Predictability of dependent variables.
   Unexplained Variation in:
   Functional Importance   48%
   Skill   21%
   Rewards   25%
   Prestige   00%
2. Path coefficients large. The unmeasured, hypothetical variable, "values," is virtually identical to prestige.
3. Predicted $r_{35} = p_{31}p_{51} = (.886)(.817) = .72$ (Actual $r_{35} = .89$)
            $r_{45} = p_{41}p_{51} = (1.038)(.817) = .85$ (Actual $r_{45} = .87$)

**These equations, not needed to compute path coefficients, are used to check model's fit.

Source: Land, 1970. Used by permission.

FIGURE 9.4 PARSONIAN MODEL OF SOCIAL STRATIFICATION

Intercorrelation of Variables (Pearsonian *r*):

	Variables (2)	(3)	(4)	(5)	(6)	(7)	(8)
(1) 1964 Occupational Attainment	.618	.483	.463	.438	.384	.331	.363
(2) Education		.632	.696	.609	.535	.417	.486
(3) Level of Occupational Aspiration			.771	.565	.470	.366	.445
(4) Level of Educational Aspiration				.611	.459	.380	.418
(5) Influence of Significant Others					.473	.359	.438
(6) Academic Performance						.194	.589
(7) Socioeconomic Status							.288
(8) Mental Ability							

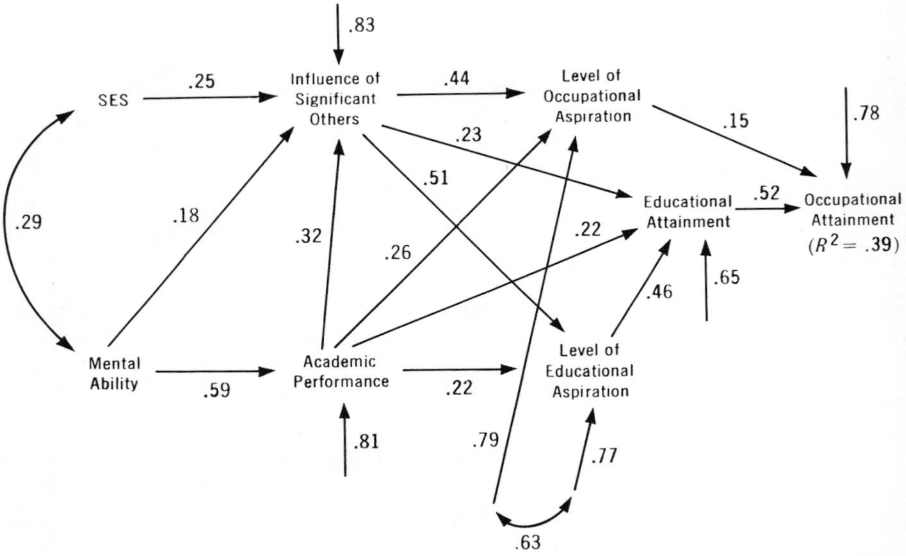

Source: Sewell et al., 1970. Used by permission.

FIGURE 9.5 The Sewell Model of Occupational Attainment

9.3 MULTIPLE REGRESSION USING UNSTANDARDIZED SCORES

Up to this point, we have been converting raw scores on each variable to *z*-scores before computing coefficients for a multiple regression equation. This transformation sets the mean of each variable equal to zero and the standard deviation equal to unity. Because of this transformation, we could legitimately compare beta weights (b^*) or path coefficients (p) to determine the relative contribution of each variable to the explanation of variation in a dependent variable. In this sense we could determine which of several independent variables is "most important."

Often, however, one is more interested in *predicting* the value of a dependent variable rather than analyzing a theoretic model or comparing the importance of independent variables. Using z-scores as data in a multiple regression equation yields a prediction of the z-score of the dependent variable, rather than a predicted raw score expressed in units such as miles or feet, pounds or ounces, number of births, or number of friendship choices, etc. The raw scores of variables used as independent variables in the prediction equation also have units of measurement, and it may be useful not to convert them to standard scores in making predictions. This means that the beta coefficients (b^*) would have to be altered somewhat to take account of the particular units of measurement used in the regression equation.

This type of situation would occur most frequently in an applied condition in which the multiple regression equation is used to make some actual prediction of the value of a dependent variable. Such predictions might then be used to guide actions such as turning on air-conditioners, adding more of some ingredient, hiring more truck drivers, building more schools, deciding on closer supervision of new parolees, or admitting a college applicant. Regression weights (b) for predicting height in inches, using age in years and weight in pounds, would be quite different from what they would be if the prediction were to be made in feet rather than inches, or if the weights were to be expressed in ounces rather than pounds.

Currently, much of the research in sociology is oriented toward testing general ideas about which variables are most important to include in a theory, rather than toward predicting actual score outcomes, although there is an indication that this situation may be changing. Voting studies, for example, predict the actual percentage vote for a given candidate. Population studies predict the actual birth rate or the size of a population, and those involved in controlling crime predict the likelihood that a new parolee will commit the same crime again (recidivate).

The following equation is written in a form appropriate for raw data. Notice that a constant term, $a_{1 \cdot 234}$, has been added to adjust for the location of scores on the dependent variable. This corresponds to the Y-intercept term in a simple regression equation discussed earlier in this book, $Y' = a_{yx} + b_{yx}X$. The regression coefficients are now written without an asterisk ($*$) to indicate that we are not using standard score input data, but rather, the raw scores themselves in their original measurement units.

(9.20)
$$X'_1 = a_{1 \cdot 234} + b_{12 \cdot 34}X_2 + b_{13 \cdot 24}X_3 + b_{14 \cdot 23}X_4$$

Again, the regression coefficients are *partial* regression weights, in the sense that they reflect the additional contribution of a variable beyond the contributions of other variables in the specific equation.

In order to change from a standardized beta weight (b^*) to an unstandardized one (b), the relative amount of variation in the dependent variable and independent variables must be taken into account. This is accomplished by multiplying the standardized beta by the *ratio* of the standard deviation of the dependent variable to the standard deviation of the specific independent variable to which the standardized beta weight refers. This is shown and illustrated in Diagram 9.3.

DIAGRAM 9.3 Converting to Unstandardized Regression Coefficients in a Four-Variable Equation†

The Problem

To convert from a standardized regression equation, as follows:

$$z_i' = b^*_{ij \cdot kl} z_j + b^*_{ik \cdot jl} z_k + b^*_{il \cdot jk} z_l$$

to an unstandardized regression equation as below:

$$X_i' = a_{i \cdot jkl} + b_{ij \cdot kl} X_j + b_{ik \cdot jl} X_k + b_{il \cdot jk} X_l$$

Converting Standardized into Unstandardized Beta Weights

(D1)
$$b_{ij \cdot kl} = b^*_{ij \cdot kl} \frac{s_i}{s_j}$$

where subscript i refers to the dependent variable, and j to the independent variable for which the beta is being computed. Variables k and l are two other independent variables in the multiple regression equation for four variables illustrated here.

    In this problem, two other beta-weights would have to be computed as follows:

$$b_{ik \cdot jl} = b^*_{ik \cdot jl} \frac{s_i}{s_k}$$

$$b_{il \cdot jk} = b^*_{il \cdot jk} \frac{s_i}{s_l}$$

Computing the Regression Constant, $a_{i \cdot jkl}$

(D2)
$$a_{i \cdot jkl} = \overline{X}_i - b_{ij \cdot kl} \overline{X}_j - b_{ik \cdot jl} \overline{X}_k - b_{il \cdot jk} \overline{X}_l$$

where i refers to the dependent variable, and other subscripts refer to the three independent variables in this example.

COMPUTING BETA WEIGHTS FOR A FOUR-VARIABLE REGRESSION EQUATION FROM BETA WEIGHTS FOR A THREE-VARIABLE REGRESSION EQUATION

(D3)
$$b_{ij \cdot kl} = \frac{b_{ij \cdot k} - b_{il \cdot k} b_{lj \cdot k}}{1 - b_{jl \cdot k} b_{lj \cdot k}}$$

Example

Hal H. Winsborough, in a study discussed by Duncan (1955:8), uses three variables which, in combination, serve to define population density in the 74 community areas of Chicago in 1940. In the study, the logarithms of each variable were taken, because this transformation resulted in the components being additive, an assumption of the regression model. The variables were these:

†Note that these formulae can be extended easily to the two or to the more-than-three variable cases by adding (or deleting) subscripts to specify the specific regression weights of interest and adding (or deleting) terms (one for each independent variable) from the regression equation.

DIAGRAM 9.3 *(Continued)*

X_1 = Density (*i.e.* population divided by land area).

X_2 = Household Density (*i.e.* population divided by the number of dwelling units in the area).

X_3 = Dwelling Unit Density (*i.e.* number of dwelling units divided by the number of structures such as apartments, hotels, single family dwellings, etc.)

X_4 = Structure Density (*i.e.* the number of structures divided by the land area).

Correlation Matrix

	(1)	(2)	(3)	(4)
(1)		−.419	.636	.923
(2)			−.625	−.315
(3)				.305

The standardized regression equation relating these variables was this:

$$z_1 = .132z_2 + .468z_3 + .821z_4$$

Standard deviations in this study were:

for variable $X_1 = .491$
for variable $X_2 = .065$
for variable $X_3 = .230$
for variable $X_4 = .403$

from formula (D1)

$$b_{12 \cdot 34} = b^*_{12 \cdot 34} \frac{s_1}{s_2}$$

$$= .132 \frac{.491}{.065} = .132(7.55) = .997$$

similarly,

$$b_{13 \cdot 24} = .468 \frac{.491}{.230} = .468(2.13) = .997$$

$$b_{14 \cdot 23} = .821 \frac{.491}{.403} = .821(1.22) = 1.00$$

The constant, $a_{1 \cdot 234}$ could be computed from (D2), above, if means of variables were available, simply by substituting these values below.

$$a_{1 \cdot 234} = \overline{X}_1 - b_{12 \cdot 34}\overline{X}_2 - b_{13 \cdot 24}\overline{X}_3 - b_{14 \cdot 23}\overline{X}_4$$

$$a_{1 \cdot 234} = \overline{X}_1 - .997\,(\overline{X}_2) - .997\,(\overline{X}_3) - 1.00\,(\overline{X}_4)$$

$$b_{12} = b_{12}^* \frac{s_1}{s_2}$$

where s_1 is the standard deviation of the dependent variable, and s_2 is that for the independent variable.

In general, the conversion can be expressed as follows for a four-variable problem:

$$b_{ij \cdot kl} = b_{ij \cdot kl}^* \frac{s_i}{s_j}$$

where the subscript i refers to the dependent variable, and subscript j to the specific independent variable in a regression equation with variables k and l.

The intercept coefficient can be computed as follows, again for the four-variable problem. These procedures can be generalized for more variables simply by including comparable terms for each of the variables.

(9.21)
$$a_{i \cdot jkl} = \overline{X}_i - b_{ij \cdot kl} \overline{X}_j - b_{ik \cdot jl} \overline{X}_k - b_{il \cdot jk} \overline{X}_l$$

Computation of these coefficients would usually be left to a checked-out multiple regression computer program, where raw scores are specified as input. It is helpful and highly desirable to be able to double check some of the computations and make simple conversions by hand, as illustrated in Diagram 9.3.

9.3.1   An Example of Multiple Regression Using Raw Scores

A very nice illustration of raw-score multiple regression procedures comes from the social stratification literature, where these procedures were applied to the problem of predicting an occupational prestige score which could then be used in further research involving a social class variable.

You have probably read about the NORC-North-Hatt scale of occupational prestige, since it is widely used in research, and it is frequently quoted in introductory books in social sciences. Cecil North and Paul K. Hatt directed a study by the National Opinion Research Center in March, 1947 in which some 2920 respondents were interviewed. Each respondent was asked to give his own "personal opinion of the general standing" of some 88 different occupations.

Responses on a five-point scale (excellent, good, average, somewhat below average, and poor) were summarized to create scores which could vary from 20 to 100 (actually ranging from 33 for shoe shiner to 96 for U.S. Supreme Court Justice), and these scores on 88 occupations are referred to as the North-Hatt scale.

Unfortunately for later investigators desiring to use these prestige scores for occupations in their own research, the 88 occupations did not cover the range of occupations that would come up in their data, so they were faced with the problem of guessing an approximate score, or of predicting missing scores by using some prediction formula based on other available information. Otis Dudley Duncan helped solve the problem by multiple regression techniques, using income and education as predictor variables (Duncan, 1961). Forty-five of the 88 North-Hatt occupations matched sufficiently well with one of the occupational categories of the inclusive Census classification of all jobs into 425 categories

(U.S. Bur. Census, 1960). For each of these categories, information was available on (a) the proportion of men in the occupation with 1949 incomes of $3,500 or more, and (b) the proportion of men in the occupation with four years of highschool or more formal education. These variables were then used to predict the percentage of respondents who judged an occupation to be of "excellent" or "good" standing in the North-Hatt data.** The regression equation developed on these 45 occupations is as follows:

$$X_1 = -6.0 + .59X_2 + .55X_3$$

where X_1 is the occupation score; X_2 is income; X_3 is education.

Using these weights in the multiple regression equation, Duncan could create social class scores for the rest of the 425 Census occupational categories for which income and education data were available in the Census publications. Truck drivers, for example, are in an occupation in which 21 percent of the males in 1950 had 1949 incomes of $3,500. or more, and 15 percent had graduated from highschool or had further education (both standardized for age).

Using the regression equation above, one could predict that the percentage of people who would rate that occupation as "excellent" or "good" would be 15 percent; this then becomes Duncan's Socioeconomic Index Score. The original NORC prestige rating was actually 13 percent, so the prediction missed the mark by only two percentage points. The coefficient of multiple determination, R^2, using the data on the 45 occupations, was .83; that is, for the 45 occupations, 83 percent of the variance in occupational prestige was accounted for, statistically, by this particular linear combination of indicators of income and education for these occupations.

Prior to using the multiple regression procedure, scatter plots of X_1 by X_2, X_2 by X_3, and X_1 by X_3 were inspected, and the relationships were found to be essentially linear. One could compute the regression weights and R^2 from the following information using formulas discussed earlier in this chapter.

$$r_{12} = .84 \qquad r_{12\cdot3} = .61$$
$$r_{13} = .85 \qquad r_{13\cdot2} = .65$$
$$r_{23} = .72$$

It is interesting to note that a correlation of .99 was found between prestige scores for the 90 occupations in the 1947 North-Hatt study and a 1963 replication reported by Hodge and others (1964). Regression analysis was also used in this study to examine shifts over the 16-year period. One of the findings was that there had been an upward shift of scores for blue-collar occupations as compared to professionals and white-collar workers.

9.4 DUMMY VARIABLE MULTIPLE REGRESSION

Sometimes it happens that an independent variable we would like to use in a multiple regression analysis is a nominal-level variable, rather than an inter-

**Because, overall, income and education are related in a curvilinear fashion with age—the young and old are low on both—these two variables were standardized on age, and the age-adjusted proportions were used in the multiple regression equation expressed here. Standardization is discussed in Chapter 8.

val-level as the model assumes. It is possible to include these variables in the analysis by creating what is called a "dummy variable." These are dichotomous variables indicating the presence (scored 1) or absence (scored 0) of a certain characteristic for each individual respondent.

If five categories for marital status were useful as an independent variable, one could represent the same information by four dummy variables as follows:

Marital Status	Dummy Variables
1 Currently married	1 Currently married (1 = Yes) (0 = No)
2 Never married	2 Never married (1 = Yes) (0 = No)
3 Widowed	3 Widowed (1 = Yes) (0 = No)
4 Separated	4 Separated (1 = Yes) (0 = No)
5 Divorced	

Using this scheme, if a person were widowed, rather than have a score of 3 on the marital status variable, he would have four scores, one on each of the four dummy variables: 0,0,1,0. That is, he is 0 on currently married, 0 on never married, 1 on widowed, and 0 on separated dummy variables. The "0,0,0,0" pattern would indicate a person who is *none* of the four explicitly mentioned marital statuses — so he would have to be "Divorced," the only other coded possibility. In general, it is conventional to create one dummy variable fewer than there are categories of the nominal-level variable we are interested in including.† These dummy variables are all included in the usual multiple regression analysis. If an individual has a score of zero on one of the dummy variables, then that regression weight and term in the regression becomes zero for him. Otherwise, the regression weight represents the value of that particular marital status — that is, the amount that is to be added in the regression equation to represent the value of being of some particular marital status. Dummy variables can be used as independent variables, whether one is expressing scores in standard-score form or raw-score form, and they can be used in path analysis problems as well. Dummy variables provide a useful way to "score" specific combinations of values of variables in order to handle expected statistical interaction in multiple regression equations where otherwise the model would assume an additive relationship among variables.

Duncan used dummy variables in predicting the percentage of respondents rating occupations as "excellent" or "good" as part of the study discussed in the previous section (Blau and Duncan, 1967). Instead of the education variable he used the dichotomy "white-collar" versus "manual workers." Since there were only two categories in this variable, only one dummy variable is needed, with $Z = 1$ if the occupation is white-collar and $Z = 0$ if the occupation is a manual occupation. Again using the data on 45 occupations from the North-Hatt study for which Census data on the independent variables was available, Duncan derived the following regression equation:

$$X_1' = 3.9 + .79X_2 + 19.8Z$$

$$R_{1 \cdot 2Z}^2 = .76$$

†For an explanation of dummy variables, see Suits (1957), in the General References.

This means that 19.8 points are added if the occupation is a type where $Z=1$, that is, "white-collar." If $Z=0$, then the 19.8 points would not be added, since 19.8 times 0 is 0.

The correlation between social class scores for occupations using the first formula and the dummy-variable formula above is .96. That is, education and the "white-collar/manual worker" variables produced very nearly the same ordering of scores.

9.5 STEPWISE REGRESSION PROCEDURES

If an investigator is interested in searching his data for the best set of predictor variables, he may utilize a procedure which is called stepwise multiple regression. Usually carried out with the help of a computer, the stepwise regression procedure examines a larger number of potential predictors, starting with a single independent variable which is the best predictor of the dependent variable. Then a further variable is added, and this added variable is one which explains as much of the remaining variation in the dependent variable as possible. Then the "next best" variable is added, and so forth, each time adding a term to the multiple regression equation. The purpose is to find a small set of independent variables which produce the highest R^2 possible. An investigator could drop variables out of the multiple regression equation whenever their addition would produce little increase in the coefficient of multiple determination, R^2.

It sometimes occurs that the most highly predictive set of variables is not the one "discovered" by starting with the "most predictive" variable in the procedure outlined above. Some computer programs solve this situation by examining essentially *all* of the possible combinations of different numbers of independent variables chosen from the original data set.** This procedure would permit an investigator to pick the "best" set of predictor variables, in the sense of explaining the maximum amount of variation in the dependent variable with a minimum number of linearly related independent variables.

Regardless of which of the approaches is used, stepwise regression analysis is a search procedure which capitalizes on any unusual predictive power in the data at hand. The results are, so to speak, "tailored" to the existing data, and because of this the regression equation may not be applicable to data beyond that included in the study. It is a helpful search procedure, but as in the case of results from any search, we would want to replicate the study to see if variables included are still the best predictors beyond the data on which they were derived.

9.5.1 An Example of Stepwise Multiple Regression

One example of the use of stepwise multiple regression procedures is in a study of factors predictive of the number of demonstrations among 104 selected,

---

**Some of these computational alternatives are presented in the early part of chapter 6 in Draper and Smith (1966) in General References.

state-supported, non-technical, non-specialized colleges and universities during 1964 and 1965 (Scott and El-Assal, 1969). Representatives of 69 of the 104 schools responded with a variety of information including size of school. It was hypothesized that "multiversities" (those more complex in terms of number of degrees granted, size of departments offering various degrees, the ratio of dormitory to non-dormitory students, professor-student ratio, etc.) ferment more student unrest than other types of schools.

A stepwise multiple regression analysis among size, complexity (the multiversity measure), quality, and community size was conducted, with the dependent variable being number of student demonstrations. The table below shows the multiple correlation coefficient and the coefficient of multiple determination, R^2, at each step as new variables were added to the multiple regression equation. It is evident that in these data, school size is the best predictor of incidence of student protest demonstrations. Other variables added little additional explanatory power to the regression equation.

STEPWISE MULTIPLE REGRESSION ANALYSIS, PREDICTING NUMBER OF STUDENT DEMONSTRATIONS AT SELECTED, STATE, NON-TECHNICAL, NON-SPECIALIZED COLLEGES AND UNIVERSITIES DURING 1964–5

Independent Variables	R	R^2
School Size	.580	.336
School Size & Complexity	.591	.349
School Size, Complexity & School Quality	.593	.352
School Size, Complexity, School Quality & Community Size	.594	.353

Source: Scott and El-Assal, 1969.

The authors note that the multiple regression model is not a very good fit, since some of the variables are not "interval level of measurement," and, in fact, statistical interaction may be expected, rather than additive relationships between variables. In spite of this, they argue, the multiple regression analysis helped pinpoint school size as a central variable in explaining the incidence of demonstrations.

9.6 CURVILINEAR ASSOCIATION IN MULTIVARIATE ANALYSIS

The basic assumption underlying the discussion of linear regression in this chapter is that variables are related in a simple straight-line fashion. This, of course, does not exhaust the possibilities and, in fact, a fair number of relationships in the field of sociology are either known to be or suspected to be curvilinear in nature. The relationship between income and age is an example. Where relationships do not come very close to the linear expectation, the multiple regression equation will not be a very good fit, will not explain very much of the variation in a dependent variable and, at worst, may be misleading to an investigator who is interested in the relative importance of variables for theory-construction purposes.

Figuring out exactly the most appropriate form of relationship for a given set of variables is beyond this introductory book, although two kinds of comments may help to provide a basis for further inquiry. First, it is an excellent practice to examine the *nature* of relationship between all pairs of variables in an analysis using either (a) a scatter plot of pairs of variables, or (b) a careful comparison of the Pearsonian Product-Moment Correlation coefficient r with eta (E), as discussed in Chapter 7. Computer programs are generally available which will print out scatter plots (or r's and E's). If the relationship is not linear between some of the variables, we might attempt a transformation of the data, such as the logarithmic transformation used by Winsborough (see Diagram 9.3). This may straighten the relationships and permit us to use the multiple regression procedures we have discussed. It may also be possible to standardize or "adjust" the raw data, to take account of curved patterns in the data, before the regression analysis is attempted. Duncan, for example, adjusted income and education scores for age differences prior to predicting social status scores. His regression equation included only education and income scores after these scores had the effects of age "standardized out," so to speak.

Secondly, we might attempt to deduce or compute an equation which describes the non-linear relationship between variables. Some computer programs are available which search data and fit a more complex equation.

9.7 SUMMARY

In this chapter we discussed the general topic of multiple regression and multiple correlation, in which interval-level variables are related in a linear, additive fashion. The problem is to explain as much as possible of the variation in a single dependent variable by the linear association of two or more independent variables. R^2, the coefficient of multiple determination, provides a measure of the proportion of the variation in the dependent variable which has been explained by the multiple regression equation.

One use of the multiple regression equation is based on the use of standard scores (z-scores) as the input data. Beta-weights (b^*), which result, can be used to compare the relative importance of independent variables used in the regression equation. With the aid of some notion of how variables are linked theoretically, we could use the procedure called "path analysis" to examine the fit between actual data and our theoretical model.

A second use of multiple regression analysis involves an interest in predicting the actual value, rather than standard score, of the dependent variable. Computation procedures for finding non-standardized regression weights (b) were discussed.

Finally, we discussed some of the procedures encountered when multiple regression analysis is used. *Dummy variables* help handle categorical independent variables or anticipated interaction patterns. *Stepwise multiple regression* is a procedure for selectively adding more variables to a regression equation in a search for a maximally predictive set of independent variables. While the multiple regression equations we have discussed assume a linear relationship between variables, it is possible to deal with curvilinear relationships by removing them, either through some type of transformation of the data prior to regression analysis, or through the use of more complex regression equations. Computer programs become exceedingly useful in handling the clerical complexity of multiple regression mathematics.

The multiple correlation coefficient, R, like the bivariate measure, r, expresses how well a regression equation permits one to predict scores on a dependent variable. Like r^2, the square of the multiple correlation coefficient, R^2, can be interpreted as the proportion of the variation in the dependent variable, which is explained by the use of the regression equation rather than merely the mean of the dependent variable.

CONCEPTS TO KNOW AND UNDERSTAND

multiple regression equation
assumptions of multiple regression
regression weights and partial correlation coefficients
standardized regression (beta) weight, $b*$
unstandardized regression weight, b
multiple correlation
coefficient of multiple determination, R^2
path analysis
corrected R
path coefficient
basic theorem of path analysis
path diagram
stepwise multiple regression
dummy variables

PROBLEMS AND QUESTIONS

1. Find an example of the use of multiple regression for either predictive or analytic purposes and describe its use for the problem the author describes. Are assumptions met? If not, what consequences may there be as far as you can tell? Is multiple regression the most appropriate technique for the problem? What alternatives might there be? Express clearly in your own words what it is that the multiple regression equation, the regression weights, and the multiple correlation coefficients mean.

2. Blau and Duncan (see Other References, 1967:170) present a correlation matrix showing the zero-order relationships between five variables, as follows:

Zero-order Correlations of Five Status Variables				
	(2)	(3)	(4)	(5)
(1) 1962 Occupational Status	.541	.596	.405	.322
(2) First job status		.538	.417	.332
(3) Education			.438	.453
(4) Father's Occupational Status				.516
(5) Father's Education				

Using the 1962 occupational status of the respondent as a dependent variable, create a path diagram showing the linkages between variables you would hypothesize to exist. Compare this with the Blau and Duncan model. Now, using information in this chapter about path analysis, create the equations needed to compute path coefficients for your model from the zero-order correlation matrix, above. If you have access to computational facilities, compute the path coefficients and appropriately label your path diagram. Again, compare these coefficients to those computed by Blau and Duncan. Finally, examine the model to reach a conclusion about how well the model fits the data. (Blau and Duncan's data are from a national survey of some 20,700 men aged 20 to 64 years old, gathered in 1962).

3. Explain the difference between standardized beta weights, unstandardized regression weights, partial correlation coefficients, and multiple correlation coefficients.

GENERAL REFERENCES

Blalock, Hubert M., Jr., *Social Statistics,* Second Edition, (New York, McGraw-Hill), 1972. See especially Chapter 19 and Section 20.4.

Cooley, William W., and Paul R. Lohnes, *Multivariate Procedures for the Behavioral Sciences,* (New York, John Wiley and Sons), 1962, Chapter 3.

Costner, Herbert L., editor, *Sociological Methodology, 1971,* (San Francisco, Jossey-Bass), 1971.
See especially Chapter 5 by George Bohrnstedt and T. Michael Carter for a discussion of "Robustness in Regression Analysis"; also Chapter 6 by Morgan Lyons, on "Techniques for Using Ordinal Measures in Regression and Path Analysis."

Draper, Norman R., and Harry Smith, *Applied Regression Analysis,* (New York, John Wiley and Sons), 1966.

Duncan, Otis Dudley, "Path Analysis: Sociological Examples," *American Journal of Sociology* 72, (July, 1966), p 1 – 16.

Land, Kenneth C., "Principles of Path Analysis," chapter 1 in Edgar F. Borgatta, editor, *Sociological Methodology, 1969,* (San Francisco, Jossey-Bass), 1969.

Nygreen, G. T., "Interactive Path Analysis," *American Sociologist* 6, (February, 1971), p 37 – 43.

Suits, Daniel, "The Use of Dummy Variables in Regression Equations," *Journal of the American Statistical Association* 52, (1957), p 548 – 551.

Walker, Helen M., and Joseph Lev, *Statistical Inference,* (New York, Holt, Rinehart and Winston), 1953.
See especially Chapter 13 on multiple regression and Chapter 17 on transformation of scales.

Wonnacott, Thomas H., and Ronald J. Wonnacott, *Introductory Statistics,* (New York, John Wiley and Sons), 1969, Chapters 13 and 14.

OTHER REFERENCES

Blalock, Hubert M., Jr., *An Introduction to Social Research,* (Englewood Cliffs, N.J., Prentice-Hall), 1970, p 73.

Blau, Peter M., and Otis Dudley Duncan, *The American Occupational Structure,* (New York, John Wiley and Sons), 1967, p 125.

Duncan, Otis Dudley, "A Socioeconomic Index for All Occupations," Chapter 6 in Albert J., Reiss, *Occupations and Social Status,* (New York, The Free Press of Glencoe), 1961, p 124.

Duncan, Otis Dudley, (See General References, 1966), p 8.

Hodge, Robert W., Paul M. Siegel, and Peter H. Rossi, "Occupational Prestige in the United States, 1925–1963," *American Journal of Sociology* 70, (November 1964), p 286–302.

Koslin, Bertram L., Robert N. Haarlow, Marvin Karlins, and Richard Pargamet, "Predicting Group Status from Members' Cognitions," *Sociometry* 31, (March, 1968), p 64–75.

Land, Kenneth C., "Path Models of Functional Theories of Social Stratification as Representations of Cultural Beliefs on Stratification," *Sociological Quarterly,* 11, (Fall, 1970), p 474–484.

Lopreato, J., and L. S. Lewis, "An Analysis of Variables In The Functional Theory of Stratification," *Sociological Quarterly* 4, (Fall, 1963), pp 301–310.

Scott, Joseph W., and Mohamed El-Assal, "Multiversity, University Size, University Quality, and Student Protest: An Empirical Study," *American Sociological Review* 34, (October, 1969), p 702–709.

Sewell, William H., Archibald O. Haller, and George W. Ohlendorf, "The Educational and Early Occupational Status Attainment Process: Replication and Revision," *American Sociological Review* 35, (December, 1970), p 1014–1027.

U.S. Bureau of the Census, *1960 Census of Population, Alphabetical Index of Occupations and Industries* (Revised edition), (Washington, D.C.), 1960.

Wampler, Roy H., "A Report on the Accuracy of Some Widely Used Least Squares Computer Programs," *Journal of the American Statistical Association* 65, (June, 1970), p 549–565.

SPACE ANALYSIS IN SOCIOLOGY

Space analysis refers to a collection of techniques which offer an interesting and useful perspective on multivariate problems in sociology. Although the basic ideas are old, their extensions and new applications open up some exciting analysis possibilities. This chapter is designed to explore a few of these techniques.

10.1 MULTIDIMENSIONAL SOCIOLOGICAL SPACE

In a nutshell, the basic theme of space analysis is simply an extension of the two-dimensional scatter diagram idea, discussed in Chapter 4, to an n-dimensional world defined by the investigator. In creating a scatter diagram, each case was represented by a dot placed in such a way that its score on two variables was simultaneously indicated. This was essentially a two-dimensional representation of the way several cases differ, and we could describe how closely cases were clustered in some respects and stretched out in other respects within this space. But individual cases may well differ in other ways, too; in fact, two dimensions may not adequately portray many of these other differences. Thus, we could measure

---

BOX 10.1 Scatter Diagrams

Scatter diagrams are discussed in Chapter 4 (Section 4.4.2) as a graphic technique. They are used in an explanation of the correlation and regression of interval-level variables in Chapter 7 (Section 7.4, for example).

an individual's "location" on a number of variables (or dimensions or "factors") of particular interest to us, which define a region of *sociological space*.

In a sense, we are locating individuals in a space which has as many dimensions as there are variables we choose to measure. If we measure two variables, we can draw this space on a sheet of paper; if we measure three variables, we can arrange to suspend "dots" in a box; if we measure four or more variables, our usual visual means of viewing space will not work, but the conceptual imagery still will. It is in this sense that we might think of locating individuals in a defined, multidimensional, sociological space. The problems confronting an investigator who wishes to think in these terms are two: (a) how to handle many variables simultaneously while describing and exploring this space, and, (b) how to use any insights gained to develop and test sociological theories.

The solution to the first problem requires techniques for expressing distances in a complex space, and techniques for simplifying that space. Consider a two-dimensional example; think back about the scatter diagrams drawn in Chapter 7, where we were concerned about the association of two interval variables. In a sense, we "simplified" this two-dimensional space by looking for (and sometimes finding in data) a straight line through the data (the regression line) along which the plotted dots most closely fell. In fact, if the correlation is near 1.0, a straight regression line will accurately characterize the location of the plotted data-points. We could then measure distances *between* dots quite accurately by measuring them along the regression line. In a sense, we could replace two yard-sticks (the X and Y axes) with a single yard-stick (the regression line). We might be able to reduce two dimensions to only one dimension if the correlation is quite high. Space analysts follow a similar line of reasoning. They ask, "Are there a smaller number of underlying dimensions which could be used to define the space; smaller than the number of variables that are measured in the first place?" If there are, then they can simplify the space and thus more easily describe and explore it, without losing the essential ability to characterize distances between cases which are measured. Techniques such as *cluster analysis, factor analysis* and *smallest-space analysis* are oriented toward finding a simpler space which adequately describes the distance between "dots" plotted in multidimensional space.

The second problem indicated above, that of interpreting the results in the context of developing theory, will be handled by citing several examples. To date, space analysis techniques have been used primarily in an exploratory and clarifying way, often to develop better *measurement scales* or to describe the way cases *cluster* or differ from each other.

The purpose of this chapter is to introduce you to the ideas of space analysis without venturing very far into any of the specific techniques, although references are given for those who wish to pursue the topics further. In virtually every instance, space analysis techniques are carried out with the help of computer programs rather than by hand. The frequency with which these techniques are being used in sociology suggests that readers and investigators will have to pursue these topics in statistics at greater length in the future. We will introduce cluster analysis and smallest space analysis, leaving factor analytic techniques (of the three mentioned earlier) for the student to pursue in the references cited later. Let us start with the example we introduced at the end of the correlation chapter (Chapter 7).

10.2 CLUSTER ANALYSIS

Why do people choose the jobs they do? Is it income or is it their values which make the difference, or both? Marsh and Stafford (1967) note that economists generally focus on income and ignore values, and sociologists generally make a similar error in reverse. These authors tried to take both into account in their study of 13 professional specialties. University-employed scientists and engineers with at least a B.A. degree earned less money in 1962 than those employed in industry. The reason for this kind of difference, it is thought, stems from the value to academics of various freedoms—from strict supervision, to pursue one's own ideas, etc.—which, where they are valued, are part of the "wages" of academic scientists and engineers. To test this idea Marsh and Stafford needed a measure of attitudes toward work to measure whether academic and industry groups differed in terms of "professional" and "acquisitive" attitudes.

They devised a set of thirteen questionnaire items to measure these two kinds of attitudes, and respondents were asked to indicate preferences for each item on a 4-point response scale. The items and their intercorrelations are shown in Table 10.1. This study was based on responses by 51,505 people in 13 professional specialties, although for their analysis Marsh and Stafford dealt only with males who had an M.A. or Ph.D. degree as of April, 1962, the interview date.

Two of the items were judged to be poor items and were dropped early in the analysis and are not shown in the correlation matrix for Table 10.1. Attitude toward work items were intercorrelated over all of the individuals in their sub-sample. The next step in preparation for their analysis was to confront this question: "To what extent do the patterns in the intercorrelation matrix suggest that there are indeed two different kinds of attitudes operating—professionalism and acquisitiveness—which are reflected in the way these workers answered the set of eleven items?" If each of the eleven items tap primarily one or the other of these two attitudes, then we should be able to discover two general clusters of items. Each cluster should include items which are more highly intercorrelated with each other in their own cluster than they are correlated with items outside that cluster. One cluster should include only "professionalism" items and the other cluster should contain only the "acquisitiveness" items.

The investigators discovered these clusterings of items by rearranging the rows and columns of the correlation matrix (as indicated by the re-ordering of question numbers shown in Table 10.1) so that more highly intercorrelated items form triangular "bunches" at different points along the diagonal. These bunches form because more highly correlated items are placed next to each other and thus their intercorrelations are nearer the diagonal. The triangles Marsh and Stafford drew in the correlation matrix in Table 10.1 illustrate the

TABLE 10.1 "Professional" and "Acquisitive" Work Attitudes among M.A. and Ph.D. Professionals in Universities and in Industry

Questionnaire Items:

Please indicate your preference for each of the listed work characteristics by circling one of the four answers provided.

	Strongly desire	Desire some- what	No prefer- ence	Do not desire
1. Opportunity to be original and creative.	1	2	3	4
*2. Opportunity to work with things.	1	2	3	4
3. Relative independence in doing my work.	1	2	3	4
4. A chance to exercise leadership.	1	2	3	4
5. A nice community or area in which to live.	1	2	3	4
*6. Opportunity to be helpful to others or useful to society.	1	2	3	4
7. Social standing and prestige in my community.	1	2	3	4
8. A chance to earn enough money to live comfortably.	1	2	3	4
9. Pleasant people to work with.	1	2	3	4
10. Freedom from pressures to conform in my personal life.	1	2	3	4
11. Opportunity to work with people.	1	2	3	4
12. Freedom to select areas of research.	1	2	3	4
13. Opportunity to work with ideas.	1	2	3	4

Correlation Matrix for Selected Attitudes Toward Work

Attitudes	1	3	10	12	13	11	9	4	5	7	8
1 Opportunity to be original and creative		.36	.29	.42	.49	.14	.25	.31	.24	.18	.27
3 Relative independence in doing my work			.31	.36	.36	.11	.26	.23	.25	.17	.21
10 Freedom from pressures to conform in my personal life				.35	.31	.26	.37	.17	.34	.23	.33
12 Freedom to select areas of research					.47	.12	.19	.18	.24	.20	.21
13 Opportunity to work with ideas						.29	.31	.29	.24	.24	.26
11 Opportunity to work with people							.43	.39	.35	.44	.27
9 Pleasant people to work with								.29	.45	.36	.39
4 A chance to exercise leadership									.26	.34	.31
5 A nice community or area in which to live										.45	.41
7 Social standing and prestige in my community											.36
8 A chance to earn enough money to live comfortably											

Source: Marsh and Stafford, 1967. Used by permission.
*Dropped because of inconsistent intercorrelations. Bad items.

result of this process of rearrangement of rows and columns. Coefficients in the triangles are, by and large, higher than correlations in the remaining part of the correlation matrix (the rectangular part, away from the diagonal, outside the triangles), which shows correlations between items that are in different clusters.

10.2.1 "Belongingness Coefficients" (*B*-coefficients)

We could come up with a measure of how much *different* our clusters are from the items *not* included in the cluster by means of a **coefficient of belonging,** called *B,* defined as follows (Fruchter, 1954: Ch. 2):

(10.1)

$$B = \frac{\text{Average of intercorrelation of items within the same cluster.}}{\text{Average of intercorrelation of pairs of items, where one item in each pair is from the cluster of interest.}}$$

The numerator expresses the intercorrelation of items within the same cluster; it indicates how closely they are interrelated among themselves. The denominator expresses the intercorrelation of items all of which are in the same cluster with all other items which are not in that cluster; it shows how well inside items correlate with outside items. One would expect the numerator to be larger than the denominator if the cluster is well chosen, reflecting higher intra-cluster correlations than correlations between cluster items and outside items. If $B = 1.00$, the cluster of items would be intercorrelated at about the same level that they are correlated with outside items, and we would conclude that this set of items is not a distinctive cluster. If B is greater than 1.00, the cluster items would indeed be more alike (in the sense of being intercorrelated more highly) internally than they are like other outside items. How big does B have to be before an investigator would conclude that he has identified a distinctive cluster? A suggestive cutoff point proposed by Holzinger is that the B-coefficient should be at least 1.30 or larger before we conclude that a cluster has been identified. That is, the average of "inside" coefficients should be about 1 1/3 times the average correlation with outside items.

In Table 10.1, for the "professionalism" item cluster $B_p = 1.58$ (the subscript on B is to indicate that this is for the "professionalism" cluster), and for the "acquisitive" cluster of items, $B_a = 1.56$. These "belongingness coefficients" (B-coefficients) can be computed for the "professionalism" cluster as shown in Diagram 10.1.

The result is above 1.30, the judgmental cutoff point mentioned earlier, so we would conclude that a cluster of items has been found. The same computational procedures shown in Diagram 10.1 would be used to compute the coefficient of belonging for the items in the acquisitive cluster. The numerator and denominator would be computed from Table 10.1 with the following result:

$$\overline{X}_a = \frac{5.50}{15} = .367$$

$$\overline{X}_o = \frac{7.08}{30} = .236$$

$$B_a = \frac{.367}{.236} = 1.56$$

Although visual inspection of a matrix with reordered columns and rows is one way to create or identify cluster patterns in a correlation matrix, the B-coefficient could be used in a somewhat different search process to *find* the "best" clustering of items in a matrix. One could start with the highest intercorrelation in a matrix and then compute a B-coefficient for that two-item "cluster." Then

DIAGRAM 10.1   Computing "Belongingness Coefficients" (B-coefficients) For the Marsh-Stafford Study)

Step 1: Sum the correlation coefficients for pairs of items which are both in the same cluster. The ten correlations in the upper triangle in Table 10.1 would be added together and that total is this:

$$\text{Sum} = 3.72$$

There are 10 unique intercorrelations between pairs of five items that were included in this cluster. This number can be computed as follows, where k is the number of items in a cluster:

$$\frac{k(k-1)}{2} = \text{number of unique correlations among } k \text{ items}$$

The arithmetic mean correlation, for the professionalism cluster, is this:

$$\overline{X}_p = \frac{3.72}{10} = .372$$

Step 2: Sum the correlation coefficients for all pairs of items where only one item in the pair is from the cluster of interest, for which the B coefficient is to be computed. These are all of the correlations between any one of the five items in the cluster and all other items. In Table 10.1 these are the correlations *outside* the two triangles (since each item is included in one of the triangles). For the "professionalism" items, the sum is this:

$$\text{Sum} = 7.08$$

There are 30 correlations making up this sum and this total number of correlations can be simply computed by the following formula:

$$k(n-k)$$

where n is the total number of items and k is the number within the cluster of interest.

The arithmetic mean correlation with *outside* items, then, is this:

$$\overline{X}_o = \frac{7.08}{30} = .236$$

Step 3: The Coefficient of Belonging to the professionalism cluster is the ratio of the two averages, above:

$$B_p = \frac{\overline{X}_p}{\overline{X}_o}$$

$$= \frac{.372}{.236} = 1.58$$

another item could be added to the cluster, making three items, and again a *B*-coefficient could be computed. Items could be added and thrown out of a cluster in an extensive (perhaps exhaustive) searching operation with *B*-coefficients computed on each trial cluster to see when the *B*-coefficient begins to dip sharply toward 1.0 with the addition of items. By examining the series of *B*-coefficients to see when the coefficient dips toward 1.0, it would often be possible to find an optimum set of items to form a cluster, one which has a relatively high *B* value but for which the *B* value drops fairly sharply with the addition of any other item or group of items. This cluster could be set aside and the highest remaining intercorrelation between items used as the "starter" for another search operation to find any additional clusters.

Except for very small sets of items, such a searching procedure would be done by a computer. There are a number of different cluster analysis programs, some of which use slightly different criteria for measuring the "differentness" of a cluster from surrounding "non-cluster" items in a matrix.*

10.2.2 Hierarchical Cluster Analysis

Figure 10.1 illustrates the use of a **hierarchical cluster analysis** program in analyzing the correlations in Table 10.1. Here the items are examined to see which items are most closely related to which, starting with a situation where *each item is a different cluster* (at the top of the figure), and proceeding down toward a situation where *all items are considered a part of the same group*. In between, the graphics of the print-out indicate points at which items are merged with others to form a larger group. The numbers at the top of the page are item numbers and the numbers at the left are distance measures. Here, these distance measures refer to the correlation coefficients in Table 10.1. At the top of Figure 10.1, for example, the X's indicate items which are most highly correlated. This approach also shows essentially two main clusters of items, which was the conclusion based on our earlier analysis.

In this analysis, item 10 is grouped with the other cluster because it has slightly higher intercorrelations with some items in that cluster than it had with items in its original cluster. Notice that this item also is correlated at a lower level with some items in the second (acquisitive) cluster. On this basis, Marsh and Stafford included it in the first cluster, as shown in Table 10.1. On the basis of Figure 10.1, we might arrive at a somewhat more refined set of "professionalism" items by taking only items 1, 12 and 13. Items 5, 7, 8, 9, and 11 appear to form a refinement of the "acquisitive" cluster. The two different clustering approaches may lead to greater insight into the scales and refinement in measurement. Hierarchical cluster analysis permits an investigator to select rather gross groupings or more tightly related groupings depending upon his research needs.

In the Marsh and Stafford example, test items were the focus of interest, and the closeness of items was expressed in terms of correlation coefficients, with pairs of items correlated across the *N* individuals responding to the ques-

*See, for relevant discussions, Cureton et al. (1970); Ward (1963); Hartigan (1967); Johnson (1967).

	QUESTION NUMBERS	
	0 1 0 1 1 0 1 0 0 0 0	
	3 2 1 3 0 4 1 9 5 7 8	
.49	. . XXX	
.47	. XXXXX	
.45	. XXXXX . . . XXXXX .	
.44	. XXXXX . . XXXXXX .	
.41	. XXXXX . . XXXXXXXXX	
.39	. XXXXX . XXXXXXXXXX	
.37	. XXXXX XXXXXXXXXXXX	
.36	XXXXXX XXXXXXXXXXXX	
.35	XXXXXXXXXXXXXXXXXXXX	

FIGURE 10.1 HIERARCHICAL CLUSTER ANALYSIS OF MEANING OF WORK ITEMS SHOWN IN TABLE 10.1

tionnaire. While this is a typical procedure, it is not the only approach, as we shall see. Marsh and Stafford used cluster analysis to see whether their eleven scale-items indeed measured somewhat different attitudinal clusters, and with the scale they were able to show that academic scientists and engineers do have higher scores on "professionalism" items and lower scores on "acquisitiveness" items than do their peers in industry. This use of cluster analysis helped clarify and support the use of a specific measurement scale.*

10.3 THE SIMILARITY/DISSIMILARITY MATRIX

As this chapter has already shown, we are interested in exploring the patterns in a matrix which contains numbers indicating closeness or distance between those "things" which are indicated by row and column labels. In Table 10.1 the column and row headings referred to *items* in a questionnaire. Each cell in the matrix indicated the "closeness" between a pair of items. By examining the matrix in terms of some cluster analysis technique, whatever it is that is indicated by row and column headings might be clustered.

10.3.1 Measures of Similarity or Dissimilarity

A correlation matrix may be thought of as a "similarity" matrix or "proximity" matrix because numbers vary with the "closeness" of relationship between pairs of items and the *bigger* numbers represent *greater* closeness. Where bigger numbers represent greater distance, the matrix is called a **"dissimilarity" matrix** or "distance" matrix and the measures included are called dissimilarities.

It is not of any great consequence whether similarities or dissimilarities

*For an interesting use of cluster analysis to derive typologies of cities, see Bruce and Witt (1971).

are used in a matrix of this sort, although it is important that one be clear about what the numbers represent. For example, we could express the same information in Table 10.1 in terms of dissimilarities by converting each Pearsonian r to the coefficient of nondetermination (discussed in the latter part of Chapter 7, Sections 7.5 and ff.).

$$\text{Coefficient of nondetermination} = 1 - r^2$$

Correlation coefficients are often used, however, so it is often the pattern in a correlation matrix which is the subject of space analysis examination. There are alternative measures of distance. To start with, any of the measures of association discussed in Chapter 6 or 7 would do quite nicely to express the closeness of pairs of items or cases that have been intercorrelated. Or other measures could be used. Blau and Duncan (1967:67–69), for example, used an average percentage difference to express distance between occupations.

Frequently, distance in Euclidian space will be computed from the following general formula, to express the straight-line distance between two points, i and j.*

$$d_{ij} = \sqrt{(X_i - X_j)^2 + (Y_i - Y_j)^2 + \cdots + (Z_i - Z_j)^2}$$

That is, the distance between i and j is the square root of the squared difference between their scores on each independent dimension, summed over all dimensions upon which the pair, i and j, are both measured. In two dimensions, this is the essence of the Pythagorean theorem from geometry, that the hypotenuse of a right triangle can be computed as the square root of the sum of the squares of the two sides of the triangle. Here, the *difference* between the scores of two cases on a variable is the "length" of a side.†

10.3.2 The *R*-matrix and the *Q*-matrix

If a correlation coefficient is used as the similarity measure, it is computed by correlating information about the different pairs of things there are to be compared. For example, if test items are to be compared in terms of closeness, then the correlation coefficient would correlate scores on *each pair of items* available from N individuals answering the items. This is an example of a simple use of correlation between scores discussed in Chapter 7 on bivariate correlation. This

---

*John Ross (1970: Ch. 17) briefly describes general distance measures and procedures for handling multidimensional data. The Minkowski distance measure, d_{xy} between x and y is this:

$$d_{xy} = \sum_{i=1}^{k} \left[(x_i - y_i)^r \right]^{1/r}$$

where i varies over the k number of different dimensions upon which objects x and y are measured. The value of r determines the kind of distance being measured. If $r = 1$, the distance is called "city block" distance. If $r = 2$, the distance is a straight line Euclidian distance between x and y, etc.

†An interesting use of this distance measure and triangles to represent distances among the concepts "middle-aged man," "old-man," and "myself," as expressed by a sample of 425 white males near retirement age, appears in Guptill (1969).

matrix of correlations between all pairs of items is called an **R-matrix**, and the methods for examining it are R-methods.

Another way the coefficients might be computed is over scores on the same set of variables for *pairs of objects* or cases. For example, if we are interested in differences between cities of various types, we might measure each of the cities on a number of different variables (*e.g.* size, percent unemployed, percent in white-collar occupations, median income, median years of education). Then we could correlate the same set of measures for each possible pair of cities. This results in a correlation matrix showing the correlation between pairs of cities, and such a matrix is sometimes called a **Q-matrix** because of this way of running correlation coefficients. Methods for examining such a matrix are called Q-methods.

The first way of computing distances correlates k items over N individuals (R-analysis), resulting in distances between the $k(k-1)/2$ unique pairs of *items*. The second way of computing distance measures (Q-analysis), correlates N individuals over k items upon which they have been scored, resulting in $N(N-1)/2$ distances between pairs of *individuals*. In the first case, the correlation coefficient (or other distance measure) represents similarity (distance) between *items,* and in the second case the correlation expresses the similarity (distance) between *individuals*. The same type of coefficient could be used in an R-matrix or in a Q-matrix. A cluster analysis of an R-matrix, such as the example cited earlier, provides an idea of the clustering of items. A cluster analysis of a Q-matrix provides insight into possible clustering of individuals.

10.4   SMALLEST SPACE ANALYSIS

While cluster analysis generally orients an investigator toward the possibility of clusters of items (or individuals) between which distances have been measured, clusters are not necessarily the only or the main pattern one might expect from a distance matrix. There may be a large amount of scatter between items, or few may be at all similar, or their differences may be structured, rather than in clusters, in some other type of pattern that has its own substantive meaning (such as the points on an equilateral triangle, in a circle, etc.). In fact, an investigator constructing a test may, on the basis of a cluster analysis, decide to select one or a few items from a cluster and include items from other clusters, thus specifically creating a test of items which do not cluster very much but instead measure quite different facets of some topic.

Smallest space analysis is a general approach to the examination of the patterning in a distance (proximity) matrix.* It is a non-metric approach which is focused upon the *rank order* of distance measures. Through smallest space

---

*Smallest Space Analysis has been developed mainly by Louis Guttman, although there are a number of other similar approaches used by W. S. Torgerson, R. N. Shepard, G. Young, J. B. Kruskal, etc. Introductory literature on smallest space analysis can be found in Ross (1970); Guttman (1966); Lingoes (1965); Lingoes (1968); Guttman (1968). Uses of smallest space analysis appear in Laumann and Guttman (1966); Krauss (1971); Robinson and Hefner (1968); Blau and Duncan (1967).

analysis, differences and similarities of items (or individuals) are displayed in such a way that a minimum number of dimensions in space are used to portray relatively accurately the rank order differences between distance measures in the original distance matrix. An illustration will make the procedure more evident.

Suppose we wished to investigate how people perceive the geography of the United States, and to do this we asked a person to estimate the distance between five major cities: New York, Los Angeles, Miami, Chicago, and New Orleans. Given five cities ($k=5$), we will have to get $5(5-1)/2 = 10$ estimates of distance. These estimates are shown in thousands of miles in the following distance matrix. Notice that the matrix is a distance matrix rather than a proximity matrix, because bigger numbers indicate greater distance.

ESTIMATE OF THE NUMBER OF THOUSANDS OF MILES BETWEEN U.S. CITIES MADE BY A MIDWESTERNER

	Cities			
	(1)	(2)	(3)	(4)	(5)
(1) New York		3.0	1.0	1.0	1.8
(2) Los Angeles			3.5	2.0	1.5
(3) Miami				1.8	1.0
(4) Chicago					1.0
(5) New Orleans					

Source: Robinson and Hefner, 1968.

Now, starting with an area such as the circle shown in Figure 10.2, we could pick out of the above matrix of distances the largest distance, and place these cities at the opposite edges of the circle. This was done in Figure 10.2, below. A map of the United States with the actual location of cities has been superimposed on the space diagram. The largest perceived distance (3.5) is between Los Angeles and Miami. Now, pinpointing New York, its dot has to be placed in a way which preserves the rank order of distances between it and Los Angeles and Miami. The midwesterner saw New York as being farther from Los Angeles than from Miami, so the dot could be tentatively placed in line with the Miami-Los Angeles distance, and closer to Miami.

So far the space map could look pretty much like a straight line — it could be one-dimensional rather than two-dimensional. Now let us add another city, New Orleans. Referring back to the distance matrix above, New Orleans is perceived to be closer to Miami than to New York and somewhat farther from Los Angeles than from Miami, but still closer to Los Angeles than to New York. There is no way we can preserve these rank orders and still have all four cities represented on a single line. At this point you may want to try out different configurations to see how many different places you can place the cities and still maintain the same rank order of distances in the space map that are in the distance matrix itself. Taking all of the distances into account, the placement of cities on Figure 10.2 can be achieved. This space map does maintain correspondence to the distance matrix — in terms of rank order of distances. This is essentially what smallest space analysis does. As you can see, the result is that it takes two di-

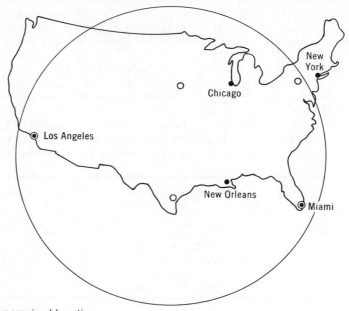

○ perceived location
• actual city location

Note: The greatest perceived distance (between Los Angeles and Miami) was made to correspond to the actual distance as one means of adjusting perceived and actual distances for comparison here.

FIGURE 10.2 ILLUSTRATION OF SMALLEST SPACE ANALYSIS PROCEDURES USING THE JUDGMENTS OF DISTANCE BETWEEN FIVE U.S. CITIES PROVIDED BY A MIDWESTERNER

mensions to hold the distances portrayed in the original matrix. It would be impossible to "force" these two dimensions down to one dimension without improperly representing some of the ranks among distances.

Computer programs are usually used to carry out a smallest space analysis, and these programs provide a "stress" measure which indicates how well the ranked distances are represented in one dimension, two dimensions, three dimensions, or more. In this example, the "meaning" of the up and down or left and right distances is relatively understandable because of the task set for the midwesterner who did the judging. Notice that that rater has the East offset westward, or relatively closer to the actual midwest locations. One last point should be made about this example. The one rating might have been the average rating of a group of midwesterners, and, it might be interesting to have contrasted these judgments with "westerners" and "easterners" or "southerners."

A similar procedure was used by Robinson and Hefner (1968) to study judgments of the similarity of seventeen nations. Their samples were (a)557 people from the Detroit area in 1964, and (b) 220 faculty members at the University of Michigan who were from various academic specialties. Each person

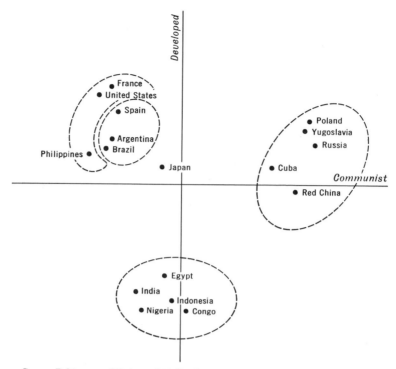

Source: Robinson and Hefner, 1968. Used by permission.

FIGURE 10.3 PERCEPTUAL MAPS OF THE WORLD — 1964 PUBLIC SAMPLE

was asked to indicate, for each country, three other countries which he would consider to be similar to it in any respect he wished to use.

The measure of difference they used was the percentage of people who judged one country to be like another. Since the larger numbers here indicated "closer" countries, the matrix of percentages in this case would be a proximity matrix. The matrix consisted of a comparison of all countries with each other in terms of these percentages. The smallest space analysis resulted in the two-dimensional configurations shown in Figures 10.3 and 10.4. The investigators concluded that a three-dimensional space was more appropriate, and their diagrams show dashed lines drawn around groups of countries which were seen as similar in the three-dimensional space solution. Figure 10.3 shows the space diagram for the Detroit *public* sample and Figure 10.4 shows the results for the *academic* sample.

The public perceptions of these seventeen countries appear to result in essentially three groupings — a pro-American group, an anti-American or Communist group, and a neutral group. They note that the third dimension helps make further distinctions within the pro-American group. Interestingly, Japan seems not to fall in any of the groups in the view of the public sample. The academic sample appears to have made more distinctions than the public sample

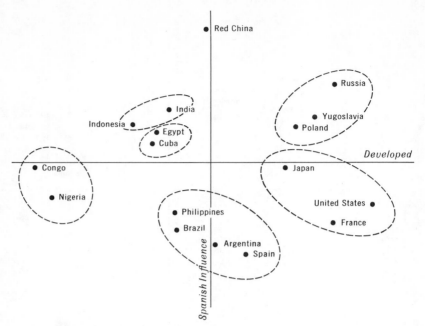

Source: Robinson and Hefner, 1968. Used by permission.

FIGURE 10.4 Perceptual Maps of the World—1964 Academic Sample

and, furthermore, somewhat different bases of discrimination appeared to be important. For academics similarity appears to have been judged in terms of development, and for the public sample it appears to be political ideology which governed judgments of similarity of nations. The investigators concluded that essentially the same types of differences are involved in both public and academic samples, and on the basis of a close examination of these space diagrams, they drew and labeled the axes shown in the two figures. In the case of the public sample, ignoring the third dimension, it appears that countries differ in terms of level of development and Communist-Capitalist ideology. For the academic sample, differences shown in the smallest space diagram appear to be level of development and extent of Spanish influence.

The important point is that the smallest space analysis has resulted in a presentation of the structure of the distance matrix. The presentation is one in which the attempt is to place countries so that the rank order of distances in the space analysis diagram corresponds to the rank order of distances in the original proximity matrix. In this instance it appeared to take a three-dimensional space to handle these rank differences relatively well.

A final illustration of smallest space analysis shown in Figure 10.5 makes use of the correlation matrix in Table 10.1, a proximity matrix which we had previously expected to yield two clusters of items concerning orientations toward work.

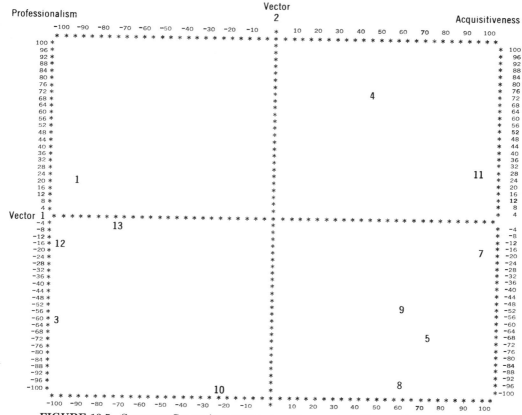

FIGURE 10.5 SMALLEST SPACE ANALYSIS OF THE CORRELATION MATRIX SHOWN IN TABLE 10.1*

10.5 FACTOR ANALYSIS

Factor analysis is a somewhat more specialized space analysis technique, differing from smallest space analysis not only in the level of measurement of data it uses (interval-level), but also in the way it approaches the problem of describing similarity and difference among scores on a series of different items. Factor analysis searches for a linear combination of variables, much like the multiple

*The Guttman-Lingoes "Stress" measure for this space diagram in two dimensions is .11 (for three dimensions it is .07 and for four dimensions it is .04). In general, the attempt is to minimize the stress measure and at the same time to limit the dimensionality to a small and meaningful number of dimensions. Stress measures of .10 or less are considered acceptable. In this instance, the main consequence of going to three dimensions is for item #8 to lift off the page upward and items #3, #9, and #11 to drop down in the third dimension below the plane of the page here.

regression equations (discussed in Chapter 9), such that as much of the variance in original scores as possible is explained. This is called a "factor" of the original matrix of scores, and generally more than one "factor" is needed to begin to explain the variance in the scores. There are a large number of different approaches to factor analysis, and we will leave the discussion of these to other references.* Factor analysis is used for a number of purposes, often related to the problem of sorting out different facets of some concept an investigator wishes to clarify.

10.6   SUMMARY

In this chapter we have only touched upon three approaches to space analysis. Each of the approaches focuses in somewhat different ways upon the distance or proximity between scores on k items measured on N things. This type of analysis permits an investigator to examine more complex contrasts between those things he is interested in studying, and because of this we would predict that these techniques will become more widely used for certain kinds of multivariate analysis in sociology. The purpose of this chapter is to alert you to these possibilities and provide some references you may wish to pursue.

CONCEPTS TO KNOW AND UNDERSTAND

sociological space	R-matrix
cluster analysis	Q-matrix
B-coefficients	smallest space analysis
hierarchical cluster analysis	factor analysis
similarity/dissimilarity matrices	

REFERENCES

Blalock, Hubert M., *Social Statistics,* (New York, McGraw-Hill), 1960, Chapter 21.

Blau, Peter M., and Otis Dudley Duncan, *The American Occupational Structure,* (New York, John Wiley and Sons) 1967, pp 67–75.

Bruce, Grady D., and Robert E. Witt, "Developing Empirically Derived City Typologies: An Application of Cluster Analysis," *Sociological Quarterly* 12, (Spring, 1971), p 238–246.

Cureton, E. E., L. W. Cureton, and R. C. Durfee, "A Method of Cluster Analysis," *Multivariate Behavioral Research* 5, (January, 1970), p 101–116.

Fruchter, Benjamin, *Introduction to Factor Analysis,* (Princeton, N.J., Van Nostrand), 1954. Chapter 2.

Guptill, Carleton S., "A Measure Of Age Identification," *Gerontologist,* 9 (Summer, 1969), p 96–102.

*Useful discussions of factor analysis appear in Rummel (1967); Kerlinger (1965: Ch. 36); Blalock (1960: Ch. 21); Nunnally (1967: Ch. 9).

Guttman, Louis, "The Non-metric Breakthrough for the Behavioral Sciences," *Proceedings of the Second National Conference on Data Processing* (Israel), 1966, p 495–510.

Guttman, Louis, "A General Non-metric Technique for Finding the Smallest Coordinate Space for a Configuration of Points," *Psychometrika,* 33 (December, 1968), p 469–506.

Hartigan, J. A., "Representation of Similarity Matrices by Trees," *Journal of the American Statistical Association,* 62 (December, 1967), p 1140–1158;

Johnson, Stephen C., "Hierarchical Clustering Schemes," *Psychometrika* 32 (September, 1967), p 241–254.

Kerlinger, Fred N., *Foundations of Behavioral Research,* (New York, Holt, Rinehart and Winston), 1965, Chapter 36.

Krauss, Wilma R., "Toward a Theory of Political Participation of Public Bureaucrats," *Administrative Science Quarterly,* (June, 1971), p 180–191.

Laumann, E. O., and Louis Guttman, "The Relative Associational Contiguity of Occupations in an Urban Setting," *American Sociological Review,* 31 (1966), p 169–178.

Lingoes, J. C., "An IBM 7090 Program for Guttman-Lingoes Smallest Space Analysis, I," *Behavioral Science,* 10 (1965), p 183–184.

Lingoes, James C., "The Multivariate Analysis of Qualitative Data," *Multivariate Behavioral Research,* (January, 1968), p 61–94.

Marsh, John F., Jr., and Frank P. Stafford, "The Effects of Values on Pecuniary Behavior, The Case of Academicians," *American Sociological Review,* 32 (October, 1967), p 740–754.

Nunnally, Jum C., *Psychometric Theory,* (New York, McGraw-Hill), 1967, Chapter 9.

Robinson, John P., and Robert Hefner, "Perceptual Maps of the World," *Public Opinion Quarterly* 32 (Summer, 1968), p 273–280.

Ross, John, "Multidimensional Scaling of Attitudes," Chapter 17 in Gene F. Summers (editor), *Attitude Measurement,* (Chicago, Rand McNally), 1970.

Rummel, R. J., "Understanding Factor Analysis," *Conflict Resolution,* 11 (December 1967), p 444–480.

Ward, J. H., "Hierarchical Grouping to Optimize an Objective Function," *Journal of the American Statistical Association* 59 (March, 1963), p 236–244.

SUMMARY AND CONCLUSIONS

THE PLACE OF DESCRIPTIVE ANALYSIS IN SOCIOLOGY

11.1 THEMES IN DESCRIPTIVE STATISTICS

We have covered most of the primary techniques sociologists use to describe their data statistically. Although sociologists are most often interested in multivariate description simply because their ideas usually involve more than two variables, we have seen that the differences among techniques unfold from a few basic themes. Starting with simple differentiation of a common collection of cases, we have moved into techniques for analyzing two or more groups on the basis of some characteristic that interests us.

11.1.1 Quality of Data

The first basic theme is that *the results of analysis depend heavily on the quality of data*. "Garbage-in-garbage-out" is a snide remark sometimes made about those who unthinkingly "computerize" data. As with any analytic process, no matter how impressive or compact the result, if the original data are biased or measurements invalid or unreliable, no amount of statistical summary will remove these defects. Investigators should force themselves to confront their original data and ask: Are these data worth *any* analysis? The answer should be a firm yes or no, and investigators should firmly accept the result of that binary (yes-no) decision.

11.1.2 The Defined Meaning of Scores

A related theme here has been that the *scores* an investigator examines have a *specific meaning* which has been defined from the start. Scores are always measurements from certain kinds of cases collected at specific points in time and place. Scores thus measure variables whose particular meanings have already been defined and limited in advance. Certain information about the state of a case, on the scale of a particular variable, is the meaning a score conveys. In the measurement process some essential elements may not be gathered, and thus some information may be lost. Exactly which components of the meaning of a score are most important to preserve depends upon the research project. Often it seems that measurement problems loom so large that other elements of the meaning of a score shrink beside them. We have emphasized level of measurement (nominal, ordinal, interval and ratio), scale continuity (continuous, discrete), and role in research (independent, control, intervening, dependent) as useful features of the meaning of scores. We have also devoted considerable space to discussing the different levels of units which may be examined—individual and group.

11.1.3 Identifying Relevant Data

The third basic theme is that it is positively useful to ignore or drop some data. In fact, we tended to divide data into two parts: the information the investigator wants and needs for a certain problem, and the other detail—perhaps equally sound in every other sense—which he does not want. The general objective of descriptive statistics is to provide tools which permit the investigator to distinguish basic research information from annoying or irrelevant detail. What is basic information, of course, stems directly from the research questions a sociologist is asking, and what is good information to one investigator may be irrelevant or annoying detail to another. Worse, the detail, if it is not carefully controlled and separated from interesting information, may often turn out to be a basic contamination which makes valid comparisons impossible. Many of the statistical techniques are of the sort which permit unwanted sources of variation to be controlled. It is probably painfully clear by now that no complete description of a set of scores is either possible or wise. There are just too many different descriptions that could be made for this to be a useful research strategy.

11.1.4 The Importance of Comparison

A fourth theme here is the central importance of comparison and contrast to research in general, and to the statistical techniques we have covered. Contrasts are made between an individual score and the group from which the score comes. The z-score or standard score was a statistical description which permitted us to make some of the valid comparisons here. Frequently contrasts are made between groups—either groups selected separately for comparison, or subgroups within one general sample. Means and standard deviations, percentages and rates, histograms and scattergrams, correlation coefficients and path coefficients—all were statistical means for making these contrasts. Finally and importantly, contrasts were made between the actual data on hand and models of the way the data might be or should be. Measures of association, to take one example, were often designed to contrast real data with some abstract model, such as a model of no association or a model of perfect association. In multivariate analysis, an investigator often graphically lays out relationships between variables which he expects on the basis of his theory. Elaboration, standardization, partial correlation, path analysis, and factor analysis are techniques which help describe the "fit" between actual data and model. This theme is so essential that one could summarize it by saying that *where there is no contrast to be made, there is no study to be done.* Carried further, where there is no variation between scores, no statistical analysis is meaningful.

11.1.5   The Usefulness of Ratios

A fifth theme has been the importance of the simple ratio as a means for handling and describing contrasts of interest. Virtually all of the statistical descriptions presented in this book are, at root, only ratios. The trick, of course, is to pick the numerator and denominator so that the measure is useful. Often the numerator is a measured sub-part of a whole represented in the denominator. *PRE* measures of association, for example, were ratios of predictive error. How much error might be made in predicting the dependent variable with only its distribution as information, and how much of this potential error can be reduced or eliminated if certain added information on an independent variable is available as a basis of prediction? Most of the association measures we discussed were simply contrasts between some of the different methods for making predictions.

11.1.6   Working with Variation

A sixth theme, mentioned earlier, is that statistics is designed to handle variation in scores—to describe in the presence of variation. Variation, however, comes from many sources, not all of which may be interesting or helpful to consider. Clearly, if there is no variation in the dependent variable, there is nothing to explain. Thus there are relatively few studies of the number of heads humans are born with. Given some variation, we can ask why, and introduce independent variables to help explain. There is also no progress to be made in explanation unless independent variables have some variation. If there were no variation in independent variables, then only one prediction would always be made for the dependent variable, which would hardly help account for differences in scores on the dependent variable. Investigators jealously guard and try to increase variation in the scores of dependent and explanatory variables. Other sources of variation are not desired and a segment of multivariate description dealt with ways to statistically remove unwanted sources of variation in data. For example, if an investigator wants to examine the relationship between ethnicity and moving, then variation in home ownership and rentership has to be removed by standardization or partial correlation coefficients or, perhaps, by elaboration techniques.

11.1.7 The Active Role of the Investigator

Finally, the most important theme of the book is that the investigator's ideas take command of the statistical description from start to finish. Without a research question there is no study, without a knowledge of what is information and what is contaminating detail the proper measures can not be selected, without knowing what is to be measured appropriate descriptions can not be made, and without some sound question or theory the contrasts most useful to answering the question can not be determined. The role of an investigator's ideas and expectations is very clearly seen at key points in his research: (a) in his choice of what is "relevant" as a control variable or independent variable; (b) in the decision to use standardization or partial correlation techniques rather than various forms of elaboration; (c) in setting up a path diagram and the resulting computations to evaluate it; (d) in the choice of measures of association which contrast observed data with specific models of "independence" or "perfect association." Thus, for example, the concern with multivariate descriptive statistics in sociology is a direct result of the way sociologists develop theory.

From start to finish, the organizing core of statistical analysis in sociology is the sociologist's ideas. This, in fact, is the primary reason for a statistics course in sociology or any discipline. The tools of inquiry must be closely woven into the fabric of the inquiry itself. Of course this is not to deny the value of the expert in tools or the tool designer as a separate specialist, any more than it is to disparage the role of computer operator or clerical mathematician or computer designer or professional interviewer. Within a field like sociology, however, the problem is organized around substantive inquiry and not around the formal completeness of systems of logical tautology. Naturally, the more refinements we develop in appropriate kinds of computers and math and formal statistics and data-gathering mechanics, the more efficiently sociologists can get on with the task of using these analytic tools to perform substantive analysis.

11.2 DESCRIPTIVE AND INFERENTIAL STATISTICS

In the beginning of this volume we talked about statistics and parameters. A **statistic** (defined in Chapter 1) is a description of a set of data which was defined by the investigator to be a **sample** from some population, and a **parameter** is a description of scores which the investigator had determined to be *all* of the relevant scores, that is, a total **population.**

This volume has been concerned only with the idea of *describing,* whether or not the scores were from samples or populations. To be sure, we did couch the description in what we take to be the typical situation of sociologists, namely describing samples, but eventually we are interested in the populations from which the samples are drawn.

For a number of reasons — expense, necessity, convenience — investigators with interests in parameters base their descriptions on carefully drawn samples from those populations rather than on a complete census or enumeration of the population.* The question immediately posed, of course, is how to leap from a description of one group (sample) to conclusions about a description of another group (population). The answer, which is partly developed in the field of inferential statistics, is that we know quite a bit about how certain kinds of samples (probability samples) behave. This permits us to develop expectations about the relationship between a description of a sample (a statistic) and a description of a population (a parameter). Furthermore, we are able to make statements about the accuracy of these expectations. We can describe and take account of "chance" variation in the samples we might draw from a population. The study of these chances and their role in supporting the logical ¹eap from statistics to parameters (or vice versa, for that matter) is the subject of inferential statistics.†

The relationship between statistics and parameters is, of course, central to a sociologist's interest in talking about his kinds of score populations. Inferential statistics, then, is equally central to a sociologist. But the inferential leap is always from one *description* of data to another, and the tools of description are thus equally central. Given the descriptive techniques in this volume, and using inferential statistics to evaluate chance variation in data, an investigator can answer his specific questions about general classes of phenomenan. Statistical description is basic to this pursuit.

---

*A classic example of a situation where sampling is a useful procedure would be in tests of the number of hours of life durability for light bulbs, where the test itself destroys the bulb, and therefore should not be applied to each bulb produced.
† See H. J. Loether and D. G. McTavish, *Inferential Statistics for Sociologists*.

APPENDIX
Statistical Tables

TABLE A Table of Areas under a Normal Curve*

THE USE OF TABLE A

The use of Table A requires that the raw score be transformed into a z-score and that the variable be normally distributed.

The values in Table A represent the proportion of area in the standard normal curve which has a mean of 0, a standard deviation of 1.00, and a total area also equal to 1.00.

Since the normal curve is symmetrical, it is sufficient to indicate only the areas corresponding to positive z-values. Negative z-values will have precisely the same proportions of area as their positive counterparts.

Column B represents the proportion of area between the mean and a given z.

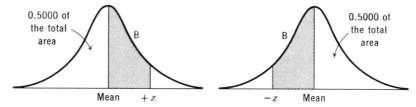

Column C represents the proportion of area beyond a given z.

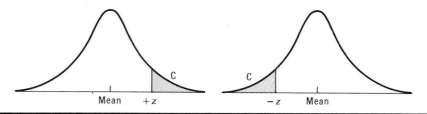

*Source: Table A, Richard P. Runyon and Audrey Haber, *Fundamentals of Behavioral Statistics*, Second Edition, Addison-Wesley Publishing Company, Reading, Massachusetts, 1971. Reprinted by permission.

TABLE A TABLE OF AREAS UNDER A NORMAL CURVE *(Continued)*

(A) z	(B) area between mean and z	(C) area beyond z	(A) z	(B) area between mean and z	(C) area beyond z	(A) z	(B) area between mean and z	(C) area beyond z
0.00	.0000	.5000	0.55	.2088	.2912	1.10	.3643	.1357
0.01	.0040	.4960	0.56	.2123	.2877	1.11	.3665	.1335
0.02	.0080	.4920	0.57	.2157	.2843	1.12	.3686	.1314
0.03	.0120	.4880	0.58	.2190	.2810	1.13	.3708	.1292
0.04	.0160	.4840	0.59	.2224	.2776	1.14	.3729	.1271
0.05	.0199	.4801	0.60	.2257	.2743	1.15	.3749	.1251
0.06	.0239	.4761	0.61	.2291	.2709	1.16	.3770	.1230
0.07	.0279	.4721	0.62	.2324	.2676	1.17	.3790	.1210
0.08	.0319	.4681	0.63	.2357	.2643	1.18	.3810	.1190
0.09	.0359	.4641	0.64	.2389	.2611	1.19	.3830	.1170
0.10	.0398	.4602	0.65	.2422	.2578	1.20	.3849	.1151
0.11	.0438	.4562	0.66	.2454	.2546	1.21	.3869	.1131
0.12	.0478	.4522	0.67	.2486	.2514	1.22	.3888	.1112
0.13	.0517	.4483	0.68	.2517	.2483	1.23	.3907	.1093
0.14	.0557	.4443	0.69	.2549	.2451	1.24	.3925	.1075
0.15	.0596	.4404	0.70	.2580	.2420	1.25	.3944	.1056
0.16	.0636	.4364	0.71	.2611	.2389	1.26	.3962	.1038
0.17	.0675	.4325	0.72	.2642	.2358	1.27	.3980	.1020
0.18	.0714	.4286	0.73	.2673	.2327	1.28	.3997	.1003
0.19	.0753	.4247	0.74	.2704	.2296	1.29	.4015	.0985
0.20	.0793	.4207	0.75	.2734	.2266	1.30	.4032	.0968
0.21	.0832	.4168	0.76	.2764	.2236	1.31	.4049	.0951
0.22	.0871	.4129	0.77	.2794	.2206	1.32	.4066	.0934
0.23	.0910	.4090	0.78	.2823	.2177	1.33	.4082	.0918
0.24	.0948	.4052	0.79	.2852	.2148	1.34	.4099	.0901
0.25	.0987	.4013	0.80	.2881	.2119	1.35	.4115	.0885
0.26	.1026	.3974	0.81	.2910	.2090	1.36	.4131	.0869
0.27	.1064	.3936	0.82	.2939	.2061	1.37	.4147	.0853
0.28	.1103	.3897	0.83	.2967	.2033	1.38	.4162	.0838
0.29	.1141	.3859	0.84	.2995	.2005	1.39	.4177	.0823
0.30	.1179	.3821	0.85	.3023	.1977	1.40	.4192	.0808
0.31	.1217	.3783	0.86	.3051	.1949	1.41	.4207	.0793
0.32	.1255	.3745	0.87	.3078	.1922	1.42	.4222	.0778
0.33	.1293	.3707	0.88	.3106	.1894	1.43	.4236	.0764
0.34	.1331	.3669	0.89	.3133	.1867	1.44	.4251	.0749
0.35	.1368	.3632	0.90	.3159	.1841	1.45	.4265	.0735
0.36	.1406	.3594	0.91	.3186	.1814	1.46	.4279	.0721
0.37	.1443	.3557	0.92	.3212	.1788	1.47	.4292	.0708
0.38	.1480	.3520	0.93	.3238	.1762	1.48	.4306	.0694
0.39	.1517	.3483	0.94	.3264	.1736	1.49	.4319	.0681
0.40	.1554	.3446	0.95	.3289	.1711	1.50	.4332	.0668
0.41	.1591	.3409	0.96	.3315	.1685	1.51	.4345	.0655
0.42	.1628	.3372	0.97	.3340	.1660	1.52	.4357	.0643
0.43	.1664	.3336	0.98	.3365	.1635	1.53	.4370	.0630
0.44	.1700	.3300	0.99	.3389	.1611	1.54	.4382	.0618
0.45	.1736	.3264	1.00	.3413	.1587	1.55	.4394	.0606
0.46	.1772	.3228	1.01	.3438	.1562	1.56	.4406	.0594
0.47	.1808	.3192	1.02	.3461	.1539	1.57	.4418	.0582
0.48	.1844	.3156	1.03	.3485	.1515	1.58	.4429	.0571
0.49	.1879	.3121	1.04	.3508	.1492	1.59	.4441	.0559
0.50	.1915	.3085	1.05	.3531	.1469	1.60	.4452	.0548
0.51	.1950	.3050	1.06	.3554	.1446	1.61	.4463	.0537
0.52	.1985	.3015	1.07	.3577	.1423	1.62	.4474	.0526
0.53	.2019	.2981	1.08	.3599	.1401	1.63	.4484	.0516
0.54	.2054	.2946	1.09	.3621	.1379	1.64	.4495	.0505

TABLE A TABLE OF AREAS UNDER A NORMAL CURVE *(Continued)*

(A) z	(B) area between mean and z	(C) area beyond z	(A) z	(B) area between mean and z	(C) area beyond z	(A) z	(B) area between mean and z	(C) area beyond z
1.65	.4505	.0495	2.22	.4868	.0132	2.79	.4974	.0026
1.66	.4515	.0485	2.23	.4871	.0129	2.80	.4974	.0026
1.67	.4525	.0475	2.24	.4875	.0125	2.81	.4975	.0025
1.68	.4535	.0465	2.25	.4878	.0122	2.82	.4976	.0024
1.69	.4545	.0455	2.26	.4881	.0119	2.83	.4977	.0023
1.70	.4554	.0446	2.27	.4884	.0116	2.84	.4977	.0023
1.71	.4564	.0436	2.28	.4887	.0113	2.85	.4978	.0022
1.72	.4573	.0427	2.29	.4890	.0110	2.86	.4979	.0021
1.73	.4582	.0418	2.30	.4893	.0107	2.87	.4979	.0021
1.74	.4591	.0409	2.31	.4896	.0104	2.88	.4980	.0020
1.75	.4599	.0401	2.32	.4898	.0102	2.89	.4981	.0019
1.76	.4608	.0392	2.33	.4901	.0099	2.90	.4981	.0019
1.77	.4616	.0384	2.34	.4904	.0096	2.91	.4982	.0018
1.78	.4625	.0375	2.35	.4906	.0094	2.92	.4982	.0018
1.79	.4633	.0367	2.36	.4909	.0091	2.93	.4983	.0017
1.80	.4641	.0359	2.37	.4911	.0089	2.94	.4984	.0016
1.81	.4649	.0351	2.38	.4913	.0087	2.95	.4984	.0016
1.82	.4656	.0344	2.39	.4916	.0084	2.96	.4985	.0015
1.83	.4664	.0336	2.40	.4918	.0082	2.97	.4985	.0015
1.84	.4671	.0329	2.41	.4920	.0080	2.98	.4986	.0014
1.85	.4678	.0322	2.42	.4922	.0078	2.99	.4986	.0014
1.86	.4686	.0314	2.43	.4925	.0075	3.00	.4987	.0013
1.87	.4693	.0307	2.44	.4927	.0073	3.01	.4987	.0013
1.88	.4699	.0301	2.45	.4929	.0071	3.02	.4987	.0013
1.89	.4706	.0294	2.46	.4931	.0069	3.03	.4988	.0012
1.90	.4713	.0287	2.47	.4932	.0068	3.04	.4988	.0012
1.91	.4719	.0281	2.48	.4934	.0066	3.05	.4989	.0011
1.92	.4726	.0274	2.49	.4936	.0064	3.06	.4989	.0011
1.93	.4732	.0268	2.50	.4938	.0062	3.07	.4989	.0011
1.94	.4738	.0262	2.51	.4940	.0060	3.08	.4990	.0010
1.95	.4744	.0256	2.52	.4941	.0059	3.09	.4990	.0010
1.96	.4750	.0250	2.53	.4943	.0057	3.10	.4990	.0010
1.97	.4756	.0244	2.54	.4945	.0055	3.11	.4991	.0009
1.98	.4761	.0239	2.55	.4946	.0054	3.12	.4991	.0009
1.99	.4767	.0233	2.56	.4948	.0052	3.13	.4991	.0009
2.00	.4772	.0228	2.57	.4949	.0051	3.14	.4992	.0008
2.01	.4778	.0222	2.58	.4951	.0049	3.15	.4992	.0008
2.02	.4783	.0217	2.59	.4952	.0048	3.16	.4992	.0008
2.03	.4788	.0212	2.60	.4953	.0047	3.17	.4992	.0008
2.04	.4793	.0207	2.61	.4955	.0045	3.18	.4993	.0007
2.05	.4798	.0202	2.62	.4956	.0044	3.19	.4993	.0007
2.06	.4803	.0197	2.63	.4957	.0043	3.20	.4993	.0007
2.07	.4808	.0192	2.64	.4959	.0041	3.21	.4993	.0007
2.08	.4812	.0188	2.65	.4960	.0040	3.22	.4994	.0006
2.09	.4817	.0183	2.66	.4961	.0039	3.23	.4994	.0006
2.10	.4821	.0179	2.67	.4962	.0038	3.24	.4994	.0006
2.11	.4826	.0174	2.68	.4963	.0037	3.25	.4994	.0006
2.12	.4830	.0170	2.69	.4964	.0036	3.30	.4995	.0005
2.13	.4834	.0166	2.70	.4965	.0035	3.35	.4996	.0004
2.14	.4838	.0162	2.71	.4966	.0034	3.40	.4997	.0003
2.15	.4842	.0158	2.72	.4967	.0033	3.45	.4997	.0003
2.16	.4846	.0154	2.73	.4968	.0032	3.50	.4998	.0002
2.17	.4850	.0150	2.74	.4969	.0031	3.60	.4998	.0002
2.18	.4854	.0146	2.75	.4970	.0030	3.70	.4999	.0001
2.19	.4857	.0143	2.76	.4971	.0029	3.80	.4999	.0001
2.20	.4861	.0139	2.77	.4972	.0028	3.90	.49995	.00005
2.21	.4864	.0136	2.78	.4973	.0027	4.00	.49997	.00003
						4.50	.4999966	.0000034
						5.00	.4999997	.0000003
						5.50	.4999999	.0000001

TABLE B TABLE OF SQUARES AND SQUARE ROOTS OF NUMBERS

k	$\sqrt{k}$	$\sqrt{10k}$	k^2	k	$\sqrt{k}$	$\sqrt{10k}$	k^2
1	1	3.16228	1	51	7.14143	22.5832	2601
2	1.41421	4.47214	4	52	7.2111	22.8035	2704
3	1.73205	5.47723	9	53	7.28011	23.0217	2809
4	2	6.32456	16	54	7.34847	23.2379	2916
5	2.23607	7.07107	25	55	7.4162	23.4521	3025
6	2.44949	7.74597	36	56	7.48331	23.6643	3136
7	2.64575	8.3666	49	57	7.54983	23.8747	3249
8	2.82843	8.94427	64	58	7.61577	24.0832	3364
9	3	9.48683	81	59	7.68115	24.2899	3481
10	3.16228	10	100	60	7.74597	24.4949	3600
11	3.31662	10.4881	121	61	7.81025	24.6982	3721
12	3.4641	10.9545	144	62	7.87401	24.8998	3844
13	3.60555	11.4018	169	63	7.93725	25.0998	3969
14	3.74166	11.8322	196	64	8	25.2982	4096
15	3.87298	12.2474	225	65	8.06226	25.4951	4225
16	4	12.6491	256	66	8.12404	25.6905	4356
17	4.12311	13.0384	289	67	8.18535	25.8844	4489
18	4.24264	13.4164	324	68	8.24621	26.0768	4624
19	4.3589	13.784	361	69	8.30662	26.2679	4761
20	4.47214	14.1421	400	70	8.3666	26.4575	4900
21	4.58258	14.4914	441	71	8.42615	26.6458	5041
22	4.69042	14.8324	484	72	8.48528	26.8328	5184
23	4.79583	15.1658	529	73	8.544	27.0185	5329
24	4.89898	15.4919	576	74	8.60233	27.2029	5476
25	5	15.8114	625	75	8.66025	27.3861	5625
26	5.09902	16.1245	676	76	8.7178	27.5681	5776
27	5.19615	16.4317	729	77	8.77496	27.7489	5929
28	5.2915	16.7332	784	78	8.83176	27.9285	6084
29	5.38516	17.0294	841	79	8.88819	28.1069	6241
30	5.47723	17.3205	900	80	8.94427	28.2843	6400
31	5.56776	17.6068	961	81	9	28.4605	6561
32	5.65685	17.8885	1024	82	9.05539	28.6356	6724
33	5.74456	18.1659	1089	83	9.11043	28.8097	6889
34	5.83095	18.4391	1156	84	9.16515	28.9828	7056
35	5.91608	18.7083	1225	85	9.21954	29.1548	7225
36	6	18.9737	1296	86	9.27362	29.3258	7396
37	6.08276	19.2354	1369	87	9.32738	29.4958	7569
38	6.16441	19.4936	1444	88	9.38083	29.6648	7744
39	6.245	19.7484	1521	89	9.43398	29.8329	7921
40	6.32456	20	1600	90	9.48683	30	8100
41	6.40312	20.2485	1681	91	9.53939	30.1662	8281
42	6.48074	20.4939	1764	92	9.59166	30.3315	8464
43	6.55744	20.7364	1849	93	9.64365	30.4959	8649
44	6.63325	20.9762	1936	94	9.69536	30.6594	8836
45	6.7082	21.2132	2025	95	9.74679	30.8221	9025
46	6.78233	21.4476	2116	96	9.79796	30.9839	9216
47	6.85565	21.6795	2209	97	9.84886	31.1448	9409
48	6.9282	21.9089	2304	98	9.89949	31.305	9604
49	7	22.1359	2401	99	9.94987	31.4643	9801
50	7.07107	22.3607	2500	100	10	31.6228	10000

TABLE B   *(continued)*

k	$\sqrt{k}$	$\sqrt{10k}$	k^2	k	$\sqrt{k}$	$\sqrt{10k}$	k^2
101	10.0499	31.7805	10201	151	12.2882	38.8587	22801
102	10.0995	31.9374	10404	152	12.3288	38.9872	23104
103	10.1489	32.0936	10609	153	12.3693	39.1152	23409
104	10.198	32.249	10816	154	12.4097	39.2428	23716
105	10.247	32.4037	11025	155	12.4499	39.37	24025
106	10.2956	32.5576	11236	156	12.49	39.4968	24336
107	10.3441	32.7109	11449	157	12.53	39.6232	24649
108	10.3923	32.8634	11664	158	12.5698	39.7492	24964
109	10.4403	33.0151	11881	159	12.6095	39.8748	25281
110	10.4881	33.1662	12100	160	12.6491	40	25600
111	10.5357	33.3167	12321	161	12.6886	40.1248	25921
112	10.583	33.4664	12544	162	12.7279	40.2492	26244
113	10.6301	33.6155	12769	163	12.7671	40.3733	26569
114	10.6771	33.7639	12996	164	12.8062	40.4969	26896
115	10.7238	33.9116	13225	165	12.8452	40.6202	27225
116	10.7703	34.0588	13456	166	12.8841	40.7431	27556
117	10.8167	34.2053	13689	167	12.9228	40.8656	27889
118	10.8628	34.3511	13924	168	12.9615	40.9878	28224
119	10.9087	34.4964	14161	169	13	41.1096	28561
120	10.9545	34.641	14400	170	13.0384	41.2311	28900
121	11	34.7851	14641	171	13.0767	41.3521	29241
122	11.0454	34.9285	14884	172	13.1149	41.4729	29584
123	11.0905	35.0714	15129	173	13.1529	41.5933	29929
124	11.1355	35.2136	15376	174	13.1909	41.7133	30276
125	11.1803	35.3553	15625	175	13.2288	41.833	30625
126	11.225	35.4965	15876	176	13.2665	41.9524	30976
127	11.2694	35.6371	16129	177	13.3041	42.0714	31329
128	11.3137	35.7771	16384	178	13.3417	42.19	31684
129	11.3578	35.9166	16641	179	13.3791	42.3084	32041
130	11.4018	36.0555	16900	180	13.4164	42.4264	32400
131	11.4455	36.1939	17161	181	13.4536	42.5441	32761
132	11.4891	36.3318	17424	182	13.4907	42.6615	33124
133	11.5326	36.4692	17689	183	13.5277	42.7785	33489
134	11.5758	36.606	17956	184	13.5647	42.8952	33856
135	11.619	36.7423	18225	185	13.6015	43.0116	34225
136	11.6619	36.8782	18496	186	13.6382	43.1277	34596
137	11.7047	37.0135	18769	187	13.6748	43.2435	34969
138	11.7473	37.1484	19044	188	13.7113	43.359	35344
139	11.7898	37.2827	19321	189	13.7477	43.4741	35721
140	11.8322	37.4166	19600	190	13.784	43.589	36100
141	11.8743	37.55	19881	191	13.8203	43.7035	36481
142	11.9164	37.6829	20164	192	13.8564	43.8178	36864
143	11.9583	37.8153	20449	193	13.8924	43.9318	37249
144	12	37.9473	20736	194	13.9284	44.0454	37636
145	12.0416	38.0789	21025	195	13.9642	44.1588	38025
146	12.083	38.2099	21316	196	14	44.2719	38416
147	12.1244	38.3406	21609	197	14.0357	44.3847	38809
148	12.1655	38.4708	21904	198	14.0712	44.4972	39204
149	12.2066	38.6005	22201	199	14.1067	44.6094	39601
150	12.2474	38.7298	22500	200	14.1421	44.7214	40000

TABLE B *(continued)*

k	$\sqrt{k}$	$\sqrt{10k}$	k^2	k	$\sqrt{k}$	$\sqrt{10k}$	k^2
201	14.1774	44.833	40401	251	15.843	50.0999	63001
202	14.2127	44.9444	40804	252	15.8745	50.1996	63504
203	14.2478	45.0555	41209	253	15.906	50.2991	64009
204	14.2829	45.1664	41616	254	15.9374	50.3984	64516
205	14.3178	45.2769	42025	255	15.9687	50.4975	65025
206	14.3527	45.3872	42436	256	16	50.5964	65536
207	14.3875	45.4973	42849	257	16.0312	50.6952	66049
208	14.4222	45.607	43264	258	16.0624	50.7937	66564
209	14.4568	45.7165	43681	259	16.0935	50.892	67081
210	14.4914	45.8258	44100	260	16.1245	50.9902	67600
211	14.5258	45.9347	44521	261	16.1555	51.0882	68121
212	14.5602	46.0435	44944	262	16.1864	51.1859	68644
213	14.5945	46.1519	45369	263	16.2173	51.2835	69169
214	14.6287	46.2601	45796	264	16.2481	51.3809	69696
215	14.6629	46.3681	46225	265	16.2788	51.4782	70225
216	14.6969	46.4758	46656	266	16.3095	51.5752	70756
217	14.7309	46.5833	47089	267	16.3401	51.672	71289
218	14.7648	46.6905	47524	268	16.3707	51.7687	71824
219	14.7986	46.7974	47961	269	16.4012	51.8652	72361
220	14.8324	46.9042	48400	270	16.4317	51.9615	72900
221	14.8661	47.0106	48841	271	16.4621	52.0577	73441
222	14.8997	47.1169	49284	272	16.4924	52.1536	73984
223	14.9332	47.2229	49729	273	16.5227	52.2494	74529
224	14.9666	47.3286	50176	274	16.5529	52.345	75076
225	15	47.4342	50625	275	16.5831	52.4404	75625
226	15.0333	47.5395	51076	276	16.6132	52.5357	76176
227	15.0665	47.6445	51529	277	16.6433	52.6308	76729
228	15.0997	47.7493	51984	278	16.6733	52.7257	77284
229	15.1327	47.8539	52441	279	16.7033	52.8205	77841
230	15.1658	47.9583	52900	280	16.7332	52.915	78400
231	15.1987	48.0625	53361	281	16.7631	53.0094	78961
232	15.2315	48.1664	53824	282	16.7929	53.1037	79524
233	15.2643	48.2701	54289	283	16.8226	53.1977	80089
234	15.2971	48.3735	54756	284	16.8523	53.2917	80656
235	15.3297	48.4768	55225	285	16.8819	53.3854	81225
236	15.3623	48.5798	55696	286	16.9115	53.479	81796
237	15.3948	48.6826	56169	287	16.9411	53.5724	82369
238	15.4272	48.7852	56644	288	16.9706	53.6656	82944
239	15.4596	48.8876	57121	289	17	53.7587	83521
240	15.4919	48.9898	57600	290	17.0294	53.8516	84100
241	15.5242	49.0918	58081	291	17.0587	53.9444	84681
242	15.5563	49.1935	58564	292	17.088	54.037	85264
243	15.5885	49.295	59049	293	17.1172	54.1295	85849
244	15.6205	49.3964	59536	294	17.1464	54.2218	86436
245	15.6525	49.4975	60025	295	17.1756	54.3139	87025
246	15.6844	49.5984	60516	296	17.2047	54.4059	87616
247	15.7162	49.6991	61009	297	17.2337	54.4977	88209
248	15.748	49.7996	61504	298	17.2627	54.5894	88804
249	15.7797	49.8999	62001	299	17.2916	54.6809	89401
250	15.8114	50	62500	300	17.3205	54.7723	90000

NAME INDEX

A

Adams, Stuart, 143, 152–153
Anderson, Theodore R., 208
Artis, Jay W., 32
Asimov, Isaac, 70

B

Bales, Robert P., 29
Berelson, Bernard, 305
Berry, Brian J. L., 96
Biller, Robert, 286–287
Blalock, Hubert M., Jr., 13, 262, 271, 304, 308, 356
Blau, Peter M., 334, 349, 350
Bohrnstedt, George, 339
Bonjean, Charles M., 28, 29
Brotman, Herman B., 67
Bruce, Grady D., 348
Burke, Cletus J., 20
Butler, Edgar, 297–298
Byrnes, Mary E., 113

C

Campbell, Donald T., 29, 302
Carter, Michael T., 339
Chapin, Stuart, Jr., 95, 98, 99
Chase, Helen C., 113
Chiricos, Theodore G., 62
Cloud, Jonathan, 119–123
Coleman, James S., 3–6, 40, 109–110, 255, 263
Cooley, William W., 313
Coombs, Clyde, 18
Costner, Herbert L., 32, 213, 262–263, 339
Cureton, E. E., 347
Cureton, L. W., 347

D

Datta, Lois Ellin, 67
Davis, James A., 181, 274, 288, 304
Davis, Vernon, 156–157
Descartes, Rene, 70
Donnelly, Thomas G., 95, 98, 99

Draper, Norman R., 313, 335
Duncan, Otis Dudley, 32, 313, 317,
    332–333, 334, 337, 349, 350
Durfee, R. C., 347

E

El-Assal, Mohamed, 336
Elder, Glen H., Jr., 27–28
Erbe, William, 272
Erskine, Hazel, 38, 105, 181

F

Ferdinand, Theodore N., 63
Ferriss, Abbot L., 81
Festinger, Leon, 18
Fischer, Claude S., 171–174
Fiske, Donald W., 302
Foner, Anne, 71, 83, 86
Freeman, Linton C., 212, 263
Fruchter, Benjamin, 344
Furstenberg, Frank F., Jr., 223–227

G

Gaudet, Hazel, 305
Goodman, Leo, 228
Gove, Walter R., 262
Gray, Louis N., 159
Guptill, Carleton S., 349
Guttman, Louis, 350

H

Haarlow, Robert N., 319–321
Hagood, Margaret J., 13, 66, 163
Haller, Archibald, 326, 328

Hamblin, Robert L., 18, 32
Hammond, Kenneth R., 166, 232
Hammond, Phillip E., 66
Harris, Chester W., 114
Hartigan, J. A., 347
Haug, Marie R., 236, 237
Hawkes, Roland K., 156
Hefner, Robert, 350, 351, 352–354
Hill, Richard, 28, 29
Hodge, Robert W., 333
Hoiberg, Eric O., 95–97, 100
Householder, James E., 166, 232
Huff, Darrell, 50
Hunter, Albert, 209–212
Huson, Carolyn, 304
Hyman, Herbert, 304

J

Jacobs, Ann M., 181
Jacobson, Paul H., 83
Johnson, Stephen C., 347
Jones, Bryan D., 18

K

Kaiser, Edward, 297–298
Karlins, Marvin, 319–321
Karth, Joseph, 38
Katz, Daniel, 18
Kaufman, Herbert, 91–92
Kendall, Maurice G., 156, 228
Kerlinger, Fred N., 356, 357
Kim, Jae-On, 205, 213
Kolko, Gabriel, 38
Koslin, Bertram L., 319–321
Krauss, Wilma R., 350
Kruskal, J. B., 228, 350

L

Labovitz, Sanford, 20
Land, Kenneth C., 322, 323, 324–327

Laumann, E. O., 350
Lazarsfeld, Paul F., 272, 279, 305
Leik, Robert K., 262
Leu, Joseph, 313
Lewis, L. S., 340
Lightfield, E. Timothy, 301
Lingoes, J. C., 350
Linn, Erwin L., 156–157
Lohues, Paul R., 313
Lopreato, J., 340

M

McAllister, Ronald, 297–298
McDill, Edward L., 285
McLemore, S. Dale, 28, 29
Maris, Ronald W., 93–94
Marsh, John F., 251–252, 343–348
Marsha, Robert M., 26
Martin, David J., 159
Mayer, Lawrence S., 20
Mauldin, W. Parker, 83–84
Mendelsohn, Harold, 38
Merton, Robert K., 273, 305
Messer, Mark, 265–266, 273, 275
Meyers, Edmund D., 285
Mueller, John H., 32, 155, 263

N

Neal, Arthur G., 13–15, 27
Newman, James R., 166
Nunnally, Jum C., 356, 357
Nygreen, G. T., 324

O

Ohlendorf, George W., 326, 328

P

Pargamet, Richard, 319–321
Petersen, William, 56, 90

Population Reference Bureau, 38, 84
Price, Daniel O., 13, 66, 163
Price, James L., 33

R

Ransford, H. Edward, 299–300
Reiss, Ira L., 128–129, 283–284
Reynolds, Paul Davidson, 271
Rigsby, Leo C., 285
Riley, Matilda White, 39, 70, 71, 83,
    86, 208, 259, 272, 284, 285, 288
Roberts, Harry V., 139
Robinson, John P., 350, 351, 352–354
Robinson, Richard, 15, 33
Robinson, W. S., 263
Rosenberg, Morris, 208, 272, 279–281,
    294, 304
Ross, John, 349, 350
Rossi, Alice, 231
Rossi, Peter H., 333
Rummel, R. J., 356, 357
Rushing, William A., 156–157

S

Schmid, Calvin F., 70
Schuessler, Karl F., 32, 155, 263
Schwartz, Richard D., 29
Schweitzer, Donald G., 20
Scott, Joseph W., 336
Sechrest, Lee, 29
Seeman, Melvin, 13–15, 27
Seidman, David, 91–92
Sewell, William H., 183, 326, 328
Shah, Vimal P., 183
Shaw, Marvin E., 29
Shepard, R. N., 350
Shorter, Richard, 18
Siegel, Paul M., 333
Smith, Harry, 313, 335
Somers, Robert H., 228
Spaeth, Joe L., 304

Stafford, Frank P., 251–252, 343–348
Stanley, Julian C., 302
Stevens, S. S., 15
Stinchcombe, Arthur L., 271
Stouffer, Samuel A., 39, 40, 302
Suits, Daniel, 334
Sussman, Marvin B., 236, 237
Sykes, Richard, 29

T

Torgerson, W. S., 350
Treitel, Ralph, 190

V

VanAtta, Loche, 13
Vargo, Louis G., 20
Vaughn, Graham M., 119–123

W

Waldo, Gordon P., 62
Walker, Helen M., 313
Wallis, Allen W., 139
Wampler, Roy H., 340
Ward, J. H., 347
Webb, Eugene J., 29
Weiss, Robert S., 208
Weiss, Shirley F., 95, 98, 99
Weitzman, Murray S., 80
Winsborough, Hal H., 337
Witt, Robert E., 348
Wonnacott, Ronald J., 340
Wonnacott, Thomas H., 340
Wray, Joe D., 114–115
Wright, Jack M., 29

Y

Yoels, William C., 231
Young, G., 350

Z

Zeisel, Hans, 64, 208, 272

SUBJECT INDEX

A

Abscissa, 70
Absolute deviation, average, 150–151
Accounting formula, Lazarsfeld, 274–275, 277
Accumulation, low to high scores, 55
Acquiescence bias, 120
Activity theory, 270
Adolescent ideals, 109–110
Age homogeneity, 270
Age specific fertility rate, 62
Analysis:
  contextual, 285–290
  level of, 284–289
  structural, 285
  unit of, 5
Antecedent test factor, 271
Area under a curve, 153–154
Arithmetic mean, 132–134, 138
Array, 44–45
Arrow diagram, 27–28, 271, 272, 322
Aspirations, college, 182–185
Assimilation, 209–212
Association, 185
  analysis of conditional, 273
  conditional, 266

degree (strength) of, 189, 191–192
direction of, 189–192
  negative, 189
  positive, 189
existence of, 186–191
four features of, 190–192
measures of, developing:
  less restrictive model, 200
  model of no association, 187–189
  normed measures, 192–202
  perfect association, 193
  sufficient or necessary conditions for, 200–201
nature of association:
  curvilinear, 190, 246, 336–337
  linear, 190
  monotonic, 191
  nature and strength uses, 255
relationship of partials and total, 273–274
Association measures:
application of, 190–192
asymmetric, 204–205
characteristics of, 256–257
cautions in interpretation of, 258–260
developing (see Association, developing measures of)
interpretation of, 255–258

Association measure (Cont.)
margin-free, 195
selecting, 252–258
symmetric, 204–205
of two interval variables: 232–251
eta, 251, 284
Pearson's r, 233, 243–246, 251
of two nominal variables: 214–221
delta-based measures, 195–197
epsilon, 178, 187, 204
lambda, 214–218
tau-y, 219–221
of two ordinal variables: 221–232
gamma, 228–229
Somer's d_{yx}, 229
Spearman's rho, 230–232
tau-a, 228
tau-b, 229–230
tau-c, 230
Asymmetry, 253–254
Attitude scales, balanced, 122
Attributes, 25
Average, 132–134
moving, 141–142
Average absolute deviation, 150–151
Average partial table, 290–302
Averages, weighted, 152
Axes, 70

B

Bar chart, 73, 86–89
Basic relationships of two variables
268
Belonging, coefficients of, 344–347
computing, 346
Beta weights, 310–311
Bimodal, 123
Birth cohort, 70
Birth rates:
crude, 61
world, 87
Bivariate distributions, 171–174
how to create, 175–176
of percentage, 174
Boundaries, class, 48

C

Career patterns of women dentists,
156–157
Cartesian coordinates, 70
Categorical data, 25
Categories:
of no opinion, 47, 180–181
of non-response, 47, 180
Causal hypothesis, 275–278
Causal sequence of influence, 279–281
Causation, independent, 281
Causation and association, 258–259
Cause, 276
definition of, 259
Cell, 176
Cell frequency, 47
computing expected, 188
Central tendency, 122
measures of, 135–138
selecting a measure of, 139–140
Chebyshev's Theorem (inequality), 154
Children, number desired, 83
Children under 5 per woman, 291–294
Cities, distance between, 351–352
Class, 46
boundaries, 48
grouping scores into classes, 22–26
midpoint, 23, 48–49
width, 48
Cluster analysis, 343–348
hierarchical, 347–348
stepwise, 345–347
Coefficient of:
belonging, 344
contingency (C), 196
multiple determination (R^2), 315
nondetermination (K), 245, 349
Cohort, 70
marriage, 81–82
College enrollment by race, 192
Comparison:
basic operations, 42–64
of correlation coefficients, 211
group-group, 39
group-individual, 40
illustrations, 38
importance of, 359–360
individual-group, 159
kinds of, 39–42
logic of, 37

Comparison (Cont.)
  making valid, 65
  outcome-standard, 40–41
  of partial and total association, 273–274
  of regression weights and partial correlation, 314
  of standardized and unstandardized rates, 294
Computer plots, 95
Concept, 14–15
Consequent test factor, 271
Conservation scale, 119–120
Contextual analysis (C), 285–290
Contingency coefficient (C), 196
Continuity, scale, and levels of measurement, 25
Control variable, 267
Coordinate system, 70
  Cartesian, 70
  semi-log, 110
  triangular, 102
Correlation:
  multiple, 307–321
  partial, 298–300, 301
    first order, 300
    second order, 300
Correlation coefficient, 4, 232
  comparison of, 211
Correlation matrix, 344
Correlation ratio, 248–251
Correlations, built-in, 260
Cramer's V, 197
Crime cleared by arrest, 89
Crime rate, 63
Cumulative distributions, 55–56
Curve, area under, 153–154
Curves, smoothing, 141–143
Curvilinear nature of association, 192, 336
  test for, 251

D

D, Index of dispersion, 147, 155–157
d_{yx}, Somer's, 229
Data, 15
  identifying relevant, 359
  quality, 358

Davis-Moore Stratification Theory, 322–323, 326
Death rates, 62
  world, 87
Decile, 56, 145
Degree of freedom, 197
Delta (Δ), 74, 188
Dependency ratio, 57
Dependent variable, 173
Descriptive statistics, 361–362
  themes in, 358–361
Designs, longitudinal, 272
Detail:
  avoiding irrelevant, 271
  dropping, 122–123
  selective loss of information, 45
Determination, coefficient of, 310
Diagram:
  arrow, 272
  path, 272
Dichotomy, 20
Disability (severity of) and education, 190–192
Disengagement theory, 265, 270
Dispersion, 143
Dissimilarity matrix, 348–350
Distance matrix, 348–349
Distance measures, 349
  average per cent of difference, 349
  Euclidian distance, 349
  Minkowski distance measures, 349
Distributions, 47–56
  bivariate, 171–174
  conditional, 174
  conditional complex, 182–185
  creating, 52–54
  cumulative, 55–56
  features of, 121–122
  form, 125
  grouped, 48
  location of, 125–143
  percentage, 54–56
  univariate, 119–123
Division of labor, 156–157
Divorces by marriage cohorts, 81–82
Dummy variables, 333–334

E

Earners in families, 248–250

Earnings and age, 1967, 191
Ecological fallacy, 95, 259–260
Educational opportunity, 3
Effects:
  direct, 325
  indirect, 325
Elaboration, 264–266
  patterns of, 275–290
  strategies of, 282
Elderly and total population increases,
  101–102
Electoral activity and social class, 205
Epsilon, 178, 187, 204
Error term in multiple regression, 323
Errors, 202–204
  grouping, bivariate, 202–204
  grouping, univariate, 49–50
  rounding, 54
Eta (E_{yx}), 234–251
  interpretation of, 251
Exogenous variables, 322
Expected frequency in a table, 187
Exploratory research, 271
Expressed limits, 48

F

Factor analysis, 355–356
Fertility ratio, 62
Form of a distribution, 122, 159–164
  bell-shaped, 124
  defined, 123
  J-shaped, 124
  other descriptions of, 164
  rectangular distribution, 124
  U-shaped, 124
Fractile, 56, 145
Frequency:
  expected, in a table, 187
  observed, in a table, 187
Frequency distribution, 47
  rules for creating, 50–54

G

Gamma (G), 228–229

Geometric mean, 139, 247
Goodman and Kruskal's tau-y, 219–221
Graphic analysis, use of, 70
Graphing:
  basic techniques, 70–86
  cautions in constructing graphs, 78
  distortions in, 83–86
  how to construct, 74–78
Grouped data, computations using, 51
Grouped distribution, 48
Grouping error:
  bivariate, 202–204
  univariate, 49–50
Grouping scores into classes, 46–47
Guttman scaling, 128–129
Guttman-Lingoes stress measure, 355
Guttmans coefficient of predictability
  (λ_{yx}), 214

H

Harmonic mean, 139
Hierarchical cluster analysis, 347–348
Histogram, 72–73
  how to construct, 74–75
Hollerith cards (computer punch
  cards), 44

I

Impairment by age, 218
Income distribution, U.S., 130–132
Income and ethnicity, 180
Independence, statistical, 189
Independent causation, 281
Index of dispersion (D), 155–157
Index of integration, 80
Index numbers, 97, 121
Index of qualitative variation, 155
Indicator, 15
Inductive statistics, 6
Infant mortality trend, 113
Inferential statistics, 361–362
Inmates, by state, 41–43, 51, 60
Interaction coding, 29

Interaction, statistical, 275, 285, 289
Interquartile range, 144–145, 149–150
Interval variables, 17
Interval width, 48
Intervening opportunity, 40–41
Intervening variable, 271
Investigator role, 361
Isolines, 95–96
Isopleth, 97

K

Kendall's Tau-a, 228
Kendall's Tau-b, 229–230
Kendall's Tau-c, 230
Kurtosis, 124, 148
  beta-two measure, 148, 161
    leptokurtic, 124
    mesokurtic, 124, 162
    platykurtic, 124

L

Lambda (λ_{yx}), 214–218
  interpretation, 217
Land development index, 95
Lazarsfeld accounting formula,
    274–275, 277
Least-squares criterion, 239–240, 311
Leptokurtic, 124
Level of analysis:
  group, 285
  individual, 284
Limits:
  expressed, 48
  real, 48
Line graph, 82–83
  how to construct, 77
Linear relationship, 237
Location of a distribution, 122
Logarithm:
  anti-logarithm, 112
  characteristics, 112
  mantissa, 112
  use in statistics, 112

Logic of comparison, 37
Longitudinal design, 272
"Loop-back" box, 5
Lorenz curve, 164

M

Maps, statistical, 92–97
Marginals of a table, 177
Marital dissolution by death, 83
Marital status and household type,
    214–216
Marriage cohort, 81–82
Marriage mobility, 27–28
Matrix, correlation, 251–252
Mean:
  arithmetic, 132–134
  geometric, 139, 247
  harmonic, 139
  weighted, 139
Mean deviations, 160
Mean square contingency (C), 196
Measurement, 14–28
  to last whole unit, 24–26, 48
  levels of, 15–21
  to nearest whole unit, 22–23, 48
  problems of, 29
  questioning and, 29
  in sociology, 28–30
Measurement categories:
  establishing, 16
  exhaustive set of, 16
  mutually exclusive set of, 16
  precision of, 16
Measurement, level of, 253–255
  interval, 17
  nominal, 16
  ordinal, 17
  ratio, 17
Measurement schemes, properties
    of, 16
Measures, unobtrusive, 29
Median, 56, 127–132, 134–138
  of a grouped distribution, 127
Mesokurtic, 124, 162
MIDCARS (interaction recording), 29
Midpoint of a class, 23, 48, 49
Migration, 102
Mobility, residential, 297–298
  reasons for, 55

Mobility orientation, 223–227
Mode, 126–127, 135
Model:
  Davis-Moore stratification,
    322-323, 326
  independence (no association),
    187–189
  Parsonian stratification, 326–327
  path, 323
  perfect association, 193
Modes, number of, 123
Moment system, 160–162
  first moment, 160
  fourth moment, 148, 160
  second moment, 147, 160
  third moment, 147, 160
Morale, conditional tables of, 268–269
Morale and interaction, 264–266
Morality ratio, 114–115
Moving average, 141–142
Multicolinearity, 308
Multimodal, 124
Multiple correlation (R), 307–321
  computation of, 316–318
  corrected (R_c), 315
Multiple partial correlation, 315
Multiple regression, 307–321
  assumptions, 307–309
  dummy variable, 333–335
  standard score form, 310
  stepwise, 335–336
  unstandardized score form, 328–333

N

Nations, similarity of, 352–354
Nature of association, 190–192
No opinion category, 47, 180, 181
Nominal variables, 16
Nondetermination, coefficient of, (K),
  245, 349
Non-response category, 47, 180, 181
Normal curve:
  area under, 162–164
  equation, 162
  ordinates for, 163
  standard normal distribution,
    162–164
Normal equations, 311
Normed measures of association, 193
North-Hatt prestige scale, 143,
  332–333, 334–335

O

Observation, statistical, 5, 14
Observed frequency in a table, 187
Occupational attainment, 326–328
Occupational origins of physicians,
  143, 152–153
Occupational prestige, 26, 332–333
Ogives, 80–82
  how to construct, 76
Ordinal partial association
  coefficients, 298–300
Ordinal variables, 17
Ordinate, 70, 163
Organization of scores, 44–46
Organizational age context, 285–289
Organizational hierarchies, 92
Organizational membership, 27
Origin in a graph, 70

P

Pairs, types of, 222
  concordant, 222
  discordant, 222
  tied pairs, 222
Panel study, 272
Parameter, 7, 361
Partial correlation coefficients, 298–302
Partial correlation compared to
  regression coefficients, 314
Partial gamma, 299
Partial table, average, 290–302
Partialling, 266
Participant observation, 29
Path analysis, 321–328
  assumptions, 322
  basic theorem of, 323
Path coefficients, 323
Path diagram, 272, 322
Path estimating equations, 324
Path model, 323
  evaluation of fit, 325
Pearson product-moment correlation
  coefficient (r), 233, 244–246, 251
  computation procedures, 243
Percentage change, 63–64

Percentage distribution, 54–56
  bivariate, 174
  rules for percentaging, 177
Percentages, base of, 55
Percentile, 56
  computation, 58–59
  decile, 56, 145
  fiftieth percentile (median), 56
  fractile, 145
  quartile, 56, 145, 150
Permissive attitudes and social
    class, 283–284
Persons per household, 73
Phi coefficient (ϕ), 196, 199
Physician visits, place of, 88
Pictograph, 86
Pie chart, 91
Platykurtic, 124
Political participation, 272
Polygon, 79–80
  how to construct, 75–76
Population, 5
Population, black, in Chicago, 96
Population change, 141–142
Population pyramid, 89–91
Population, world growth of, 93
Positive relationship, 185
Powerlessness, 13, 27
PRE measures, 214
Prediction, 212–214, 329
Proportionate reduction in error
    (PRE), 214
  measures, 212–214
  interpretation, 198
Proportions, 54
Proximity matrix, 348
Pseudo-random numbers, 124
Punch cards (hollerith cards), 44
Pyramid, population, 89–91

Q

Q-analysis, 350
Q-matrix, 349–350
Quadrants, 70
Quality of data, 358
Quartile, 56, 145
  first, 150

  second (median), 56, 127–132,
    134–138
  third, 150

R

r, Pearson's product moment
    correlation, 233, 244–246, 251
  computation, 243
R-analysis, 350
R-matrix, 349–350
Random shock term (error term), 323
Range, 144, 149
Rate of change, 111
  percent change, 63–64
Rates, 61
  age specific fertility, 62
  cautions in interpreting, 63
  comparison of standardized and
    unstandardized, 294
  crime, 63
  death, 62
  retention, 62
  standardized, 291–294
  suicide, 62
Ratio, 43
  dependency, 57
  fertility, 62
  mortality, 114–115
  sex, 56–57
Ratio variables, 17
Ratios for comparison, 56–61
  time based, 61–64
    rate, 61
    percent change, 63–64
  usefulness of, 360
Reactive measures, 29
Real limits, 23, 48
Recognition, peer, 301
Record data, 30
Recursive model, path analysis, 323
Reference system, coordinate
    system, 70
Regression:
  computation, 241–242
  constant term (a_{yx}), 329
  equations, 233–244

Regression (Cont.)
  multiple, 307–321
  simple, standardized, linear, 309
  standardized form, 310, 311
  unstandardized form, 237, 329
Regression line, 235
  best fitting, 238–239
Relationship between variables,
    basic, 268
Reliability, 14, 30
Research design, 302
Retention rate, 62
rho, Spearman's (r_s), 230–232
Rounding errors, 54
Rounding off, 23–24

S

Sample, statistical, 6, 361
  consequences for percentaging,
    179–180
  stratified, 179
Scale continuity, 21–22
Scales, 29
Scatter diagram, 97–102, 235, 341
  how to construct, 103
School enrollment by age, 79
Scores, 4–5, 15
  meaning of, 358–359
Semi-logarithmic chart, 106–108,
    110–115
  coordinates, 110
Sex ratio, 56–57
  change in, 69–70
Sexual permissiveness scale, 128–129
Significant digits, 23–24
  rounding off, 23–24
Similarity matrix, 348–350
Simulation, 95
Skewness, 124
  Beta-1 measures of skewness,
    147, 161
  negative (left), 124
  other measures of skewness, 160
  positive (right), 161, 124
Slope, regression, 235
Smallest space analysis (SSA),
    350–355
Social class, 236–237
  predictions, 319–321
  scores, scatter diagram, 236

Social system analysis, 284–289
Sociology departments, ranking,
    231–232
Somers' d_{yx}, 229
Space analysis, 341–343
  cluster analysis, 343–348
  factor analysis, 355–356
  hierarchical cluster analysis, 347–348
  smallest space analysis (SSA),
    350–355
Space dimensionality:
  reduction, 342
  2 to n dimensionality, 342
Spearman's rho (r_s), 230–232
Specification, 265–266, 275
Spurious interpretation, 277
  testing for, 276–278
Standard deviation, 146, 151–155
  interpretation of, 153–154
Standard error of estimate, 239
Standard population, 292
Standard scores (z-scores), 153,
    159, 162
Standard score form of correlation
    and regression, 246–247
Standardization, 291–298
  direct, 291–294
  test factor, 295–296
Standardized regression equation, 247
  computing coefficients for, 312–313
Standardizing rates, 291–294
  computation for, 293
Statistic, 7
Statistical independence, 189
Statistical interaction, 275, 285, 289
Statistical maps, 92–97
Statistical model, 95
Statistical observation, 5
Statistics, 6
  appropriate data for, 18–21
  descriptive, 6, 7
  field of, 6, 7
  history of, 7
  how to study, 9–10
  inferential (inductive), 6
  in sociology, 8
Stepwise multiple regression, 335–336
Stratification, 332
  Davis-Moore model, 322–323, 326
  Duncan socio-economic index, 332
  Parsonian model, 326–327
Stress measure, Guttman's, 352, 355

Structural analysis, 285
Structural equations, 323
Student demonstrations, 336
Suicide rate, 62, 92–94
Sum of squares, 146
Suppressor variables, 281–284
Symbol usage, 46
Symmetry:
    association measures of, 253–254
    of a distribution, 124

T

Table:
    basic table of interest, 182, 267
    conditional, 266–267
    first order, 267
    how to set up, 174–185
    layout of, 175–177
    partial, 266
    percentaged, 177–182, 183
    possible total and conditional, 270
    second order, 267
    standardized, 294
    third order, 267
    total, 266–270
    zero order, 266–267
Tally, 47
Tau-a, Kendall's, 228
Tau-b, Kendall's, 229–230
Tau-c, Kendall's, 230
Tau-y, Goodman and Kruskal's,
    219–221
Tchebycheff's inequality
    (see Chebyshev's Theorem)
Test factor standardization, 295–296
Test factors, 275
    antecedent, consequent, 271
Test variable, 267
    notation, 272
Theoretical order of variables, 271
    establishing, 272
Theory, role of, 270–273
Time order of variables, 271
Tolerance, 171–174
Trend line, 82, 111
Trends, 114
Triangular coordinates, 102

Triangular plot, 102
    how constructed, 104–105
Tschruprow's T coefficient, 197

U

Unimodal, 123
Unit of analysis, 5
Unit of measurement, 22–23, 47
Univariate distribution, 119–123
    three features of, 123
Universe, 5
    conceptual, 5
Unobtrusive measures, 29
Unstandardized regression
    coefficients, 330–331

V

Valid comparisons, making, 65
Validity, 14, 30
Variability measures, selecting,
    157–158
Variable, 4, 14, 25
    continuous, 21
    control, 267
    dependent, 26
    dichotomous, 274, 334
    discrete, 22
    dummy, 333–334
    establishing order of, 272
    exogenous, 322
    independent, 27
    interval, 17
    intervening, 27–28, 271
    nominal, 16
    ordinal, 17
    ratio, 17
    role in research, 26–28
    suppressor, 281–284
    test, 267
Variance, 146, 151–155
    of the estimate, 239
    normed measures of, 159
    and standard deviation,
        interpretation, 153–154

Variation, 122, 143–159
  explained, 244
  total, 244
  unexplained, 244
  working with, 360
Variation and form measures,
      computation, 144–148
Variation ratio, 158–159
Vote intention, 180–181, 279–281

W

Weighted mean, 139
Women, roles of, 180–181
Women dentists, 156–157

Work, attitude toward, 251–252,
      343–347
Work context, 285–289

Y

Y-intercept, 237
  computing intercept constant, 243
Yule's Q, 201–202, 229

Z

z-score, 153, 159, 162, 246–247
z standard deviations, 153–154